Race, Culture, and the Intellectuals, 1940–1970

Race, Culture, and the Intellectuals, 1940–1970

Richard H. King

Woodrow Wilson Center Press
Washington, D.C.

The Johns Hopkins University Press
Baltimore and London

EDITORIAL OFFICES
Woodrow Wilson Center Press
One Woodrow Wilson Plaza
1300 Pennsylvania Avenue, N.W.
Washington, D.C. 20004-3027
Telephone 202-691-4029
www.wilsoncenter.org

ORDER FROM
The Johns Hopkins University Press
Hampden Station
P.O. Box 50370
Baltimore, Maryland 21211
Telephone 1-800-537-5487
www.press.jhu.edu/books

Parts of chapters 1 and 5 have appeared as "The Ambiguities of Enlightenment: Gunnar Myrdal and African American Culture," in *Transatlantic Encounters: Multiculturalism, National Identity and the Uses of the Past,* edited by Guenter H. Lenz and Peter J. Ling (Amsterdam: VU University Press, 2000), 167–83. Reprinted with permission.

An earlier version of chapter 6 appeared as "Domination and Fabrication: Rethinking Stanley Elkins's *Slavery,*" in *Slavery and Abolition* 22, no. 2 (2001): 1–28 at http://www.tandf.co.uk/journals. Reprinted with permission.

Parts of chapter 8 appear as "Richard Wright: From the South to Africa—and Beyond," *Look Away! The U.S. South in New World Studies,* edited by Jon Smith and Deborah Cohn. Durham, NC: Duke University Press, 2004. Reprinted with permission.

Library of Congress Cataloging-in-Publication Data

King, Richard H.
   Race, culture, and the intellectuals, 1940–1970 / Richard H. King.
      p. cm.
   Includes index.
   ISBN 0-8018-8065-3 (hardcover : alk. paper) — ISBN 0-8018-8066-1 (pbk. : alk. paper)
    1. Racism—United States—History—20th century. 2. United States—Race relations. 3. Antisemitism—United States—History—20th century. 4. United States—Ethnic relations. 5. African American intellectuals—Political activity—History—20th century. 6. Intellectuals—United States—Political activity—History—20th century. I. Title.
   E185.61.K557 2004
   305.8´009´04—dc22

2004005897

Contents

Acknowledgments

At a distance of over a half century from the Holocaust and from the first real confrontation of the West with the racism endemic to its modern history, it is easy to sound glib about what thinkers in that early couple of decades after the war failed to understand about anti-Semitism, or color-coded racism, or both together. It must have been incredibly difficult, emotionally and intellectually, to think through those wrenching matters "without banisters" as Hannah Arendt once said of the experience of thinking without guidelines or precedents.

The first acknowledgment I offer takes the form of an appreciation of several of the thinkers I have written about here. Four figures in particular seemed to me to stand out for their intellectual and moral courage. Gunnar Myrdal is a much more complex thinker than he is often given credit for being. He is usually treated as a naïve son of the Enlightenment, who bought into the myth of America; but that is a seriously one-sided misreading of his analysis of American race relations. I was moved by Richard Wright and the sense of lonely embattlement that his work suggests. I have come to a greater appreciation of Wright's moral courage, and, as a result, I am no longer particularly taken with the criticisms that James Baldwin and Ralph Ellison leveled against him. I was continually fascinated by the intellectual and moral trajectory of C. L. R. James's life and his refusal to become bitter at the neglect (and the persecution) he suffered for most of his life. Finally, as always, Hannah Arendt's independence of mind is impressive, even, I am tempted to say, when she was close to being "wrong." These four figures are striking examples of the way that a willingness to think independently about matters of the deepest moral and political seriousness is as important as thinking "correctly" about them. We need, of course, to get things right *and* to think independently; there's no guarantee, as Isaiah Berlin once noted, that the truth will be interesting. But an independent thinker, besides offering certain truths, provides a moral and intellectual example of *how* rather than just *what* to think. Free thought in particular needs to be treasured on the topics of race and culture, where there is a considerable amount of nonsense written.

Because I have been at work on this book for over a decade, there are many people to thank and much institutional support to acknowledge. During this period, I was fortunate enough to have two years free and clear of regular academic duties. One of those years (1997–98) was spent in the stimulating environment of the Woodrow Wilson International Center for Scholars in Washington, D.C. Among the office staff of the Center I would like particularly to thank Lindsay Collins and Susan Nugent for their constant good cheer and willingness to help. Ann Sheffield helped make the Center a lively place to be; Mike Lacey was exemplary in the way he could bring alive the intellectual history of public service and public policy; and George Liston Seay's invitation to talk on his weekly PRI radio show "Dialogue" was one of the most enjoyable experiences of that year. Zed David in the Wilson Center library was always helpful, even though the cramped quarters in the Smithsonian Castle made things difficult.

During my year at the Center, many of my fellow "fellows" provided valuable advice and friendship, but I thank Bill McClay, Gary Marx, Marshall Brown, and Ernst Falzeder in particular for their help and friendship. Though I spoke some with African philosopher Paulin Hountondji during the year, I am ashamed to say I did not realize his eminence until later, when I read his trenchant critique of the negritude movement. I was also significantly aided by my research assistant, Joel Revill. Not only was Joel diligent about getting books for me from the Library of Congress; he was of immense help in sorting out the various issues with which I was dealing, besides later reading and commenting on a couple of the chapters of the manuscript. Finally I owe a particular debt of gratitude to Jim Reston for helping me to get to the Wilson Center in the first place and for providing good company and good cheer in what was once my hometown.

I would also like to thank E. Ethelbert Miller of the African American Resource Center at Howard University for talking at length with me about the Black Arts movement of the 1960s and 1970s and supplying me with copies of some of the fugitive magazines and journals devoted to that movement. I also want to thank another old friend, Priscilla Ramsey of Howard University, for reading early versions of several chapters. In addition, the Moorland-Spingarn Center at Howard provided access to the

E. Franklin Frazier papers, while the Library of Congress made available both the Hannah Arendt papers and the newly opened Ralph Ellison papers, under the able supervision of John F. Callahan.

The second "special" institution to which I am indebted is the Robert Penn Warren Center for the Humanities at Vanderbilt University in Nashville, where I was the visiting Fellow in 2001–2002. The Center seminar group that year focused on "Memory, Identity and Political Action," and from that group Larry Griffin and Lou Outlaw read one of the chapters of my work in progress. Under the extremely able direction of Mona Frederick, the Warren Center is responsible for much of the intellectual excitement at Vanderbilt, in part by bringing a steady stream of visiting speakers and programs to campus. My office in the Center was a perfect place to work. I also spent the next academic year 2002–2003 at Vanderbilt as visiting professor in the history department. During that time, I gave a version of one chapter to the history department "work in progress" seminar. Matt Ramsey, Helmut Smith, and Bill Caferro were particularly important in helping me to clarify my argument, while Jane Landers, Dennis Dickerson, and Devin Fergus later commented insightfully on part of the manuscript dealing with C. L. R. James. Other members of the department—Don Doyle, Marjorie Spruill, Jim Epstein, Richard Blackett, and Sam McSeveney—made me feel particularly welcome and became good friends as well as colleagues. I also enjoyed conversations with George Graham of the political science department and thank him for inviting me to teach in his summer seminar for graduate students, a truly enjoyable experience. Two graduate students in history—Peter Kuryla and Steven Miller—were very good intellectual company and represent a certain hope that intellectual history is not yet dead. I should mention that the academic year 2002–2003 was shadowed by the untimely and wrenching deaths of two of my colleagues in history—Simon Collier and Shafali Lal. I was very much impressed by the way the history department responded with care and compassion to these tragic events. Under the leadership of Marshall Eakin and aided by the office staff of Brenda Hummel and Vicki Swinehart, the department showed that it was a community of scholars and friends and not just a collection of individuals pursuing their separate professional destinies.

A third institution also deserves special thanks—the C. L. R. James Institute in New York. Director Jim Murray and Ralph Dumain were unfailingly generous in responding to my emails about James and his world—I was after all a perfect stranger to them. It is a source of deep sadness to all those who have had any association with the Institute that just as Jim Murray's efforts to obtain more recognition for the Institute and find an academic home for the James archives were coming to fruition, he died unexpectedly in the summer of 2003. One can only hope that the C. L. R. James Institute will continue to flourish and find the kind of intellectual, moral, and financial support it deserves. It would be a fitting tribute to Jim Murray's memory.

I should also mention colleagues at my home institution, the University of Nottingham, and in Britain generally. In an academic culture of technocratic rationalization and hyper-assessment, the School of American and Canadian Studies has managed to remain something of an oasis. Colleagues such as Dave Murray and Peter Ling in particular read chapters along the way; and friends such as Pete Messent, Douglas Tallack, Judie Newman, Sharon Monteith, and Graham Taylor provided aid and comfort at various times. In the early stages of the project I was supervising Yvette Hutchinson's Ph.D. thesis on the Black Arts movement and I learned much from her in the process. Matt Connell and Tim Youngs of Nottingham Trent University read earlier versions of the chapter on the Frankfurt School and provided valuable criticism, while Dan Stone of Royal Holloway College also read an earlier version of the Arendt chapter.

Though it is easy to forget, delivering papers to strangers at "other" institutions is one of the most important ways of learning from one's mistakes, since mistakes there will always be. Over a decade, I have read parts of my manuscript in progress at the universities of: DeMontfort, Warwick, Lancaster (an especially profitable experience), Liverpool Hope, and Manchester in Britain. In my two separate stays in America, groups at the universities of Wyoming, Delaware, Southern Mississippi, Tennessee (Chattanooga), Maryland (College Park and Baltimore County), Dartmouth, and Wheelock College in Boston heard versions of various chapters. On two occasions I delivered papers to the Southern Intellectual History Circle (SIHC), once at Chapel Hill, N.C., in 1998 and then at the University of South Florida in St. Petersburg in 2000. The brainchild of Michael O'Brien, the SIHC has been a particularly important intellectual organization in a time when the meetings of professional academic organizations are so large that they no longer seem a particularly useful place for academic interchange. Colleagues at its meetings such as Ray Arsenault, Charles Joyner, David Chappell, and Anne Goodwyn Jones have been the source of intellectual stimulation and personal friendship, as have people as far flung (and near) as Noel Polk and Richard Godden, Richard Gray and Ted Ownby, John David Smith and Berndt Ostendorff, Deborah Cohn and Jon Smith, Helen Taylor, Paul Jenner and Martin Halliwell. Larry Friedman helped tremendously by reading several chapters very quickly when time was of the essence.

Two hardy souls read through earlier versions of my manuscript in its entirety: Walter Jackson and Steve Whitfield. I owe them a lot for their patience and help in whipping into shape what seemed an unusually ornery manuscript. I would also like to express deep gratitude to Joe Brinley of the Woodrow Wilson Center Press not only for his early interest in my manuscript but also his lasting commitment to it. Working with Yamile Kahn and the editing staff at the Wilson Center Press has been a real pleasure.

My wife Charlotte has also read the manuscript and was a huge help in that respect. However, that is the least of what I want to thank her for after our quarter century together.

Richard H. King
Nottingham–Washington–Nashville–Nottingham

Race, Culture, and the Intellectuals, 1940–1970

Introduction

All in all, race is the modern West's worst idea.[1] Despite the modest, medical benefits that may have followed from thinking in terms of race and the remarkable cultural achievements of the racially oppressed, it is hard to think of any idea that has had more destructive consequences. Millions of men, women, and children have been brutalized, enslaved, and exterminated in its name. *Race, Culture, and the Intellectuals, 1940–1970* deals with race as a concept or a symbolic construct rather than as a "natural kind" or biological entity. Thus, I am not interested in judging empirical claims about alleged racial differences or in arguing for or against the use of the term "race," however defined.[2] I take it to be uncontroversial that race and racism are new historical phenomena, if by "new" we mean since the late fifteenth century. Put another way, assigning fixed biological traits to a human grouping is neither a permanent historical phenomenon nor is racism a fancier name for "xenophobia" or the fear of the "other." Interestingly, race was, according to George Fredrickson, "originally articulated in the idioms of religion more than in those of natural science"[3] in fifteenth-century Spain. Nevertheless, it was under the aegis of both the pre- and post-Darwinian biological sciences of the nineteenth century, underpinned by an Enlightenment commitment to a materialist-naturalistic worldview and combined with the Romantic emphasis on group spirit or mentality (*Geist*), that race and racism had such a massive impact over the last two centuries.[4]

Something like a consensus also exists on the demise of race as a valid scientific idea, particularly in the English-speaking world. Several recent studies fix on the years between 1920 and 1945 as the period in which race, racial difference, and racial hierarchy were largely discredited among intellectual and scientific elites.[5] What has not yet been undertaken, however,

1

is the intellectual history of the explanations for why and how people become racists. What does becoming or being racist "do" for an individual
or group? And why do those who have been the object of racism sometimes proceed to embrace race-thinking? Again, why does thinking in
terms of race remain such a compelling, even appealing, notion? It is only
since the 1930s that such a question could be posed. Up to that time, the
dominant understanding was that racial prejudice was a natural phenomenon that no more needed explanation than did eating or sleeping. At best,
prejudice might be scrutinized for its situational rationality and restricted
to certain types of expressions. All that had changed by the mid-1940s
when the destructive implications of organizing a state around racist assumptions and the contradictions between supposed American commitment to equality and the existence of legal racial segregation became clear.

Universalism to Particularism

The first part of my general thesis is that, in the wake of World War II, a
universalist vision in which the different races were understood to be
equal in natural capacities and legal-political rights became a consensus
position among intellectual and scientific elites in the West.[6] This vision
found expression in the founding documents of the United Nations, especially the Declaration of Human Rights, the 1948 Convention on the
Prevention and Punishment of the Crime of Genocide and the UNESCO
Statement on Race in 1950, which began as follows: "Scientists have
reached general agreement that mankind is one; that all men belong to the
same species, *Homo Sapiens*."[7] Indeed, although the challenge to racism
and prejudice originated among elites, public opinion polling in the United
States showed a gradual, if all too slow, decline in anti-Semitism and
white racism in the decades after 1945.

Nor was this universalist vision confined to official documents of the
UN. In international law, the new category of "crimes against humanity"
was introduced at the Nuremberg Trials. Although generally serving as a
catchall for acts falling outside the established categories of "war crimes"
and "crimes against peace," it also implied that certain sorts of actions
constituted a threat to the very idea of humanity. The French jurist at
Nuremberg, François de Menthon, spoke of it as a "crime against human
status," and Hannah Arendt later equated crimes against humanity with
crimes against "human diversity."[8] Most importantly, the idea of a category of actions that might be called "crimes against humanity" suggested

that humanity was not merely a biological but also a normative category referring to beings, to whom a special moral value was attached. By extension, genocide, which was defined in article 2 of the 1948 Convention as the "intent to destroy, in whole or in part, a national, ethical, racial or religious group," was also a crime against humanity. Generally, in light of the various new charters, declarations, and conventions, it became increasingly difficult to see how European colonialism in Africa, Asia, and parts of the Western Hemisphere, and/or forms of differential citizenship/nationality such as racial segregation in the United States, the caste system in India, and apartheid in South Africa could stand up to moral or legal-political scrutiny.

Furthermore, the universalist hope was that racial (and cultural) differences would fade in light of the assumption that all races enjoyed equal capabilities and aspirations. Even when appreciated or celebrated, cultural differences were not considered intrinsic to individual or human identity. That is, particularistic (i.e., group) identities had no deep ontological or philosophical anthropological status. From this it tended to follow that social/cultural assimilation and legal-political integration of ethnic and racial minorities were of prime value; internationally, it was assumed that non-Western nations would and should embrace the same sort of political, social, economic, and cultural institutions that had transformed life in the West, that is, capitalist modernization. Specifically, the ideal legal-political order was to be a morally and legally homogeneous space, in which there were neither "over- nor under-privileged" citizens, as Hannah Arendt once put it.

Specific examples from post–World War II American life illustrate the predominance of the universalist ethos. Although not addressing the issue of race as such, William Faulkner's Nobel Prize Address of 1950 registered a protest against the threat of nuclear destruction by invoking a universalist, if stoic, vision of human existence: "I decline to accept the end of man. . . . I believe that man will not merely endure: he will prevail." Less bleak was Edward Steichen's "Family of Man" exhibition of photographs and an accompanying text. Three years in the making and seen by over 9 million people in thirty-eight countries between 1955 and 1962, the vision informing the exhibition forcefully conveyed this universalist spirit. As Steichen noted in explaining his conception of the exhibition, which was funded not by the UN but by the U.S. Information Agency:

We can't overlook the differences, but unless we arrange these pictures so that they stress the alikeness—the similarity—we have lost out. We

are not as alike in everything as we are in such direct things as birth
and death. But there is also love. That is the same all over the world. . . .
This is the one thing that we have really learned the importance of.[9]

As historian Eric Sandeen has summed it up: "[I]ncreasingly, the message
of the photographs became one of human sameness and emotional unity."[10]
Clearly, the "family of man" was *e pluribus unum* writ large, a kind of
universalism without national borders.

There were other, more questionable ways that cultural, racial, and religious differences were downplayed or denied in postwar America. When
the stage version of *The Diary of Anne Frank* opened in 1955, its specific
Jewish provenance was considerably de-emphasized. As Garson Kanin,
the director of the play and himself Jewish, explained: "The fact that in
this play the symbols of persecution and oppression are Jews is incidental
and Anne, in stating the argument so, reduces her magnificent stature."[11]
African American writers such as James Baldwin and Ralph Ellison were
often praised for writing as "human beings who just happen to be Negroes"
and were themselves uncomfortable when their color rather than talent
was emphasized. Later in the 1960s, social critic Harold Cruse noted a
typical enlightened white reaction to Lorraine Hansberry's *A Raisin in the
Sun* (1959), a play about the Youngers, a black family that is trying to escape the inner-city ghetto and purchase a home in the (white) suburbs:
"We really didn't think of it as a Negro play at all. . . . [T]hat Younger
family was just like us."[12] Clearly, the comment was offered in praise of
Hansberry's popular drama. Indeed, to many white viewers, the Youngers
seemed, in the words historian Kenneth Stampp applied to the antebellum
slave population in his work of the mid-1950s, *The Peculiar Institution*
(1956), like "white men [sic] with black skin."[13]

Much of postwar American life was marked by a quest for a general
consensus on values and behavior and a commitment to a national version
of universality. The currency of the term "Judaeo-Christian" in the postwar world reflected the (disgracefully) belated attempt to extend the protection of the Christian tradition to its parent religion, Judaism, and assumed that there was a spiritual consensus linking them. Sociologist Will
Herberg claimed that divisive ethnicity had largely disappeared in America,
leaving only benign religious differences, such as Protestant–Catholic–
Jew, underpinned by common allegiance to a "democratic creed." Clearly
Herberg's "democratic creed" was a close cousin of the "American Creed,"
to which Swedish sociologist Gunnar Myrdal claimed most Americans

pledged allegiance. All of these notions anticipated Robert Bellah's valedictory celebration of what he called the American "civil religion" in an
essay of that name in 1967, and reflected what Daniel Bell famously
referred to as the "end of ideology" mood of postwar American political
culture.[14]

Nor was the civil rights movement an exception to the universalizing
tendency in postwar culture and politics, for its core ideology emphasized
rights as individual rather than group possessions. At the time, most
thought that the *Brown v. Board of Education* decision of 1954 affirmed
a "color-blind" Constitution, while the dominant image/ideal of the civil
rights movement until the mid-1960s was "black and white together." In
his "I Have a Dream" speech of August 1963, Martin Luther King Jr.
touched all the racial and religious bases, as though echoing Herberg,
when he imagined the day when "black men and white men, Jews and
Gentiles, Protestants and Catholics, will be able to join hands. . . ." Indeed,
earlier that year King had powerfully evoked his ideal of a society in
which African Americans would be judged "by the content of their character and not by the color of their skins."[15] From the universalist perspective, the civil rights movement was not a black movement working for
group rights and aimed at developing African American consciousness,
but a movement of black and white people dedicated to helping the former win their individual rights as American citizens.

Finally, it is important to be clear on what remains compelling about
the universalist vision, even though from our vantage point it can seem
naive at best and hypocritical at worst. First, the history of the West in the
first half of the twentieth century seemed to demonstrate the disastrous effects of emphasizing and then politicizing racial and cultural differences.
Second, members of oppressed and excluded groups, as well as their supporters in the majority population, needed the moral and intellectual lever-
age of universalism to make their arguments for equality of worth and of
rights effective. To emphasize group differences made it easier for majority opponents of equality to justify treatment of minorities as unequals,
since the slippage between being different and being unequal was almost
impossible to avoid. Third, explicit racial or ethnic designations often
seemed to be a way of damning with faint praise. It *was* infuriating for a
black writer or a Jewish playwright to have his or her achievement always
linked with color or religion. Finally, a kind of a collective avoidance
made confrontation with the historical and moral enormity of the Final
Solution difficult until the 1960s; but it was still clear to many that what

had happened to European Jewry could be traced back to racist policies implemented on a mass scale. It was not that the "facts" of the Holocaust were hidden. The figure of "6 million," or variations thereon, was already used just after the War.[16] But though the centrality of the Holocaust to Jewish history and the centrality of the Jews to the Nazi exterminationist vision had not come fully into focus, what had happened during the war in Europe ultimately could be traced back to the racialization of anti-Semitism and the National Socialist vision of a racially pure society.[17] Again, most people assumed that the best way to avoid a repetition of the racist genocide was to focus on what people shared rather than what divided them.[18]

Not surprisingly, the universalist claim that the differences in capabilities between races are no greater than differences within a single race and that differences in physical appearance indicate little or nothing about genetic capabilities had other implications for the study of race and racial prejudice. For instance, it was generally assumed that all forms of prejudice were essentially the same in origins, dynamics, and impact. The title of Gordon W. Allport's influential *The Nature of Prejudice* (1951) tells the whole story.[19] Moreover, the primary focus in the universalist paradigm fell upon the perpetrators rather than the victims of racism or anti-Semitism. As Myrdal famously put it, the American dilemma is "the white man's problem."[20] Still, the effects of racism on victims were by no means simple to remedy and could not be rectified in the way that a vitamin deficiency or even poverty could be. Particularly in the postwar atmosphere of what Philip Rieff has called "the triumph of the therapeutic," it was assumed that those who had been the objects of prejudice and discrimination were psychologically scarred. By extension, although the universalist paradigm rejected inherent differences in racial capacity, the culture of a marginalized group might be inferior for all practical purposes to the dominant culture, although that cultural inferiority or pathology could eventually be undone. Similarly, it was assumed that eventually "primitive" cultures or "backward" peoples could be brought up to the standard of the dominant culture through the modernization process. Indeed, to modernize was to throw off or leave behind the old group, that is, racial or ethnic, traits and to become assimilated into the modern world.

In retrospect, at least, there was something a bit disingenuous about the postwar universalist consensus, however valuable an achievement it was at the time. Recent studies of race and ethnicity from World War II to the mid-1960s have noted several peculiar characteristics of "race-thinking."

First, the racialization of differences among various European peoples was also no longer acceptable. They "became" ethnics, as it were. What Matthew Frye Jacobson refers to as "nonblack nonwhites," became "Caucasians," a promotion up the race/ethnicity ladder. The effect, however, was that so-called European ethnics "effectively disappeared from public discussion of race, power, and social policy" until the late 1960s.[21] Moreover, although differences among the three "major" races were considered negligible, Asian Americans pretty much disappeared from view. At the same time, the overwhelming focus fell on the relationship between blacks and whites. Nor was it entirely clear why the concept of race continued to be used at all, if the differences among the so-called races were genetically so trivial. Still, even though inherent racial differences were considered negligible, race consciousness proliferated.[22] Race was dead; long live awareness of race.

Much of this intense focus on black-white relations was understandable, since African Americans had suffered systematic, long-term, and violent oppression to a much greater extent than other ethnic and racial groups. Although European ethnics and Asian Americans had historically suffered social and cultural prejudice, and occasionally political exclusion, by the postwar period they no longer were second-class citizens in political and legal terms. In addition, the South, where the Jim Crow system was still extant and under siege until the mid-1960s, lacked a significant European ethnic population. Ironically, the black power movement of the late 1960s helped reinforce the sense of Caucasian solidarity by reference to all white people as "honkeys." In fact, only since the 1920s had black Americans been fully consolidated into one people.[23] By that time not only the U.S. Census but African Americans themselves, no matter how light-skinned they were, considered themselves Negroes (later blacks or African Americans), even though black colleges, for instance, discriminated in admissions on the basis of skin color up to the mid-1960s.

The postwar fate of American Jews is also important to note, since they were the European ethnic group that historically had been most often picked out for special, that is, negative, treatment and were most often compared with African Americans. On the one hand, postwar America saw Jews increasingly accepted in social and cultural terms as Caucasians. Their general economic and educational success meant that Jews were never subject to the same sort of prejudice and discrimination as African Americans. Yet the fact that Jews had their own religion, sacred texts and rituals, and history, along with the creation of the state of Israel in 1948 and, most importantly, the nagging awareness of the Holocaust, meant that Jewish Americans never quite disappeared into the general white population. Overall, the universalist consensus was built on a certain amount of denial: white ethnics were not quite white; blacks were not equal; and Jews were in some ways neither and both.

Nor should the Cold War context of all this be forgotten.[24] To mention only one contradiction generated by international political considerations after 1945: at home the U.S. government initiated actions to desegregate certain important institutions (such as the armed forces) and filed an amicus curiae brief for the plaintiffs in the *Brown v. Board of Education* case of 1954. Yet abroad, the United States was in the process of shouldering the colonial burdens, particularly in the Middle East and Asia, that the British and French were shedding. Where the United States had been a bulwark of democracy in Europe against totalitarianism of the left and the right, in the Third World, the United States was an upholder of the status quo and supporter, for good measure, of the apartheid regime in South Africa.

All this leads to the second part of my thesis: by the 1960s in the United States, universalism was increasingly challenged by cultural particularism. Even as the universalist consensus was emerging, there were powerful counter-currents at work. The most resolute universalist vision needed grounding in specific political and legal institutions and cultural values. American values, it was claimed, were universalist ones, but they were instantiated in the racial, cultural, and social diversity of America as a "nation of nations."[25] In fact, there were two sorts of particularist visions at work in postwar intellectual history. One represented a continuation of the racist ideologies that peaked in strength around World War I but had declined in intellectual respectability by 1945. In this conception, cultural differences were attributed to actual racial differences among various peoples. But the other form of cultural particularism *within* the universalist paradigm rejected racial differences as an explanation for group differences, but, at the same time, insisted that it was important to preserve them. German-Jewish refugees such as Theodor Adorno and Max Horkheimer, along with Hannah Arendt, feared the power of American mass society and culture to bleach out the disparate and different. Adorno and Horkheimer traced this homogenizing tendency to an "anger against all that is different,"[26] while Arendt assumed human plurality as an ontological fact of human existence. Moreover, Arendt claimed that the massive collapse of European traditions and institutions and the rise of totalitarian regimes after World War I revealed that declarations of universal human rights had been useless in protecting national minorities and state-less people.[27] Thus, particularist identities and cultural differences needed to be protected by an actual political order, although Arendt, like most other cultural particularists, was opposed to any polity founded on ethnic rather than universal principles.

Symptomatic of the gradual shift of emphasis from a universalist to a particularist perspective was the trial of Adolf Eichmann in Jerusalem in 1961 where the main charge was that Eichmann had committed genocide, that is, "crimes against the Jewish people." Arendt, who covered the trial for *The New Yorker* and later published her dispatches as *Eichmann in Jerusalem* (1963), captured the legal and moral ambivalence involved in this shift from universalism to particularism when she wrote:

> Insofar as the victims were Jews, it was right and proper that a Jewish court should sit in judgment; but insofar as the crime was a crime against humanity, it needed an international tribunal to do justice to it.[28]

Overall, the 1964 Auschwitz Trials in Frankfurt (1963–65), Rolf Hochhuth's play *The Deputy* (1963), and films such as *Judgment at Nuremberg* (1961) and *The Pawnbroker* (1965) served notice that the long-delayed public discussion of the Holocaust was beginning to take place in Israel, Europe, and the United States, and that the universalist consensus was under severe pressure. Indeed, the overall effect of the 1967 Six-Day War was to re-introduce into Western Jewry an ethnic consciousness that took pride in Jewishness and in the accomplishments of the state of Israel.[29]

Other developments signaled a heightened racial and ethnic consciousness in the United States in the 1960s. By the end of the decade, the country was full of "unmeltable ethnics,"[30] a matter of considerable irony since much of the revived ethnic consciousness drew on the newly emergent black consciousness as its model. Before his assassination in February 1965, Malcolm X had preached black pride, black self-sufficiency, and contempt for "white devils" and "Uncle Toms." Cultivation of racial or ethnic consciousness rather than color-blind universalism seemed increasingly more compelling. At the time, sociologist Nathan Glazer recognized that the color-blind world of individual rights was more a noble illusion than a social reality. Wrote Glazer in *Commentary*:

> The Negro now demands entry into a world, a society that does not exist, except in ideology. In that world there is only one community,

and in that world, heritage, ethnicity, religion, race are only incidental and accidental personal characteristics.[31]

The implication was that Myrdal's American Creed no longer fit the social or cultural reality of America, if it ever had. Faced with this realization, African American intellectuals and political activists increasingly agreed with the point that W. E. B. Du Bois, who died in 1963, had spent his whole life making: the group was more important than the individual, and race was a necessary destiny rather than a contingent burden. By the end of the decade, the overlapping emergence of black consciousness, black arts, and black power movements testified to a new level of political and cultural self-awareness among America's black population. After 1965, "Negroes" became "blacks" and black became "beautiful."

Nor was this cultural and intellectual sea change an exclusively American or Western European matter. The Bandung Conference in Indonesia in 1955 served notice that the universalist visions of both liberal democracy and Marxism–Leninism had lost their appeal to the non-aligned nations of the Third World. Covering the conference as an observer, Richard Wright was struck by the power of race and religion, the one-time preserves of colonialists and reactionaries, to inspire movements of political and cultural independence outside of Europe.[32] Where English-speaking intellectuals of the black diaspora generally pursued the goal of political independence for African nations, French-speaking intellectuals such as Leopold Sedar Senghor of Senegal and Aimé Césaire of Martinique forged an ideology of negritude that emphasized black values and traditions. Césaire attacked the "pseudohumanism" of the West, while describing negritude as "really a resistance to the politics of assimilation." He also rejected the idea that citizens of Martinique or Africans were merely "Frenchmen with black skin."[33] Frantz Fanon later echoed his one-time teacher's scorn for Western humanism when he urged from the killing fields of Algeria:

Leave this Europe where they are never done talking of Man, yet murder men everywhere they find them, at the corner of every one of their own streets, in all the corners of the globe.[34]

Although Senghor ultimately considered negritude to be a complement rather than an alternative to Western universalism, in the context of the 1940s and 1950s it represented a powerful counter-statement against the universalism of the West. Overall, post-1945 cultural particularism called into question the desirability of a homogeneous and unitary universal culture by emphasizing the need to nurture cultural differences and to insist on cultural as well as political self-determination. Cultural autonomy might refer either to the retrieval of a culture from the past (lost during cultural assimilation or through colonial mis-education) or the forging of a new revolutionary culture in the struggle against the European oppressor. From the Third World and black American perspective, the universalist vision seemed like another example of white Western hypocrisy. It was used to bolster the idea of the West's cultural superiority, yet was never taken seriously enough to protect its internal minorities or its colonial subjects.

I have, of course, sharpened the contrast between universalism and particularism in order to provide a framework within which to understand the quite complex developments in thinking about racism and culture between, roughly, 1940 and the early 1970s in the trans-Atlantic world. In fact, this binary opposition between universalism and particularism reflects a tension in Western thought tracing back as far as the Enlightenment ideals of cosmopolitan universalism and natural rights, on the one hand, and the Romantic emphasis upon the organic community, the nation or people, on the other. Both universalism and particularism in their pure form are conceptually incoherent and self-refuting. Universalism claims that the values it espouses and the epistemological framework it establishes transcend cultural boundaries and have general validity. Yet, such claims have obviously arisen in a particular time, place, and culture, that is, the modern West. Thus, the objections to universalism are both logical and historical: it is a thin disguise for Western values and interests. On the other hand, the particularist claim that all cultural values are rooted in specific historical and cultural situations is asserted as though it was meant to apply in every situation. Thus, cultural particularism heads in one direction toward some form of racial or cultural essentialism; in another, it is a disguised form of universalism. Because both positions undermine themselves when conceptualized in reified terms, they are more analytically useful when expressed as tendencies rather than as fixed, mutually exclusive positions both within the West generally and within individual thinkers and movements. Clearly, as already hinted at, one can combine a belief in universal human equality with a strong belief in the aesthetic, moral, and even ontological importance of a particularist cultural identity. To summarize: when scientific racism was discredited and then replaced

by a universalist view of humanity, the focus shifted from race to culture
as a way of explaining group differences. But that in turn opened the way
for the emergence of an ideology of cultural particularism in which culture was not just an explanatory principle but also a normative ideal. Thus,
we have the emergence of an ideology of culture that challenged the very
universalism that had generated it.

Description and Explanation

As intellectual history, *Race, Culture, and the Intellectuals, 1940–1970*
focuses primarily on thinkers, movements, and traditions of thought rather
than on the institutional or social contexts within which those arguments
emerged. Yet, I have tried to have each of the positions that I describe and
analyze carry its own context with it. Overall, I have chosen to concentrate on the development of arguments, since that is—or should be—what
intellectual historians can do best, rather than reducing these ideas and arguments to functions, largely, of individual or group interests. In this
sense, my approach might be described as old-fashioned, even "severe"
intellectual history. In the process of analyzing the arguments about race,
racism, and culture, I have tried to construct a map or a network of the
ideological positions and intellectual influences in the period under
scrutiny. One thing that has surprised me is the remarkable overlap between thinkers who normally would not be yoked together. For instance,
although Hannah Arendt had not, as far as I know, read C. L. R. James's
work, James thought highly, but not uncritically, of Arendt's *Origins of
Totalitarianism* (1951). Independently, both of them latched onto the 1956
Hungarian uprising as a historically portentous event that bore witness to
the survival of democratic impulses against the stifling effects of totalitarian rule. In *The Authoritarian Personality* (1950), Theodor Adorno
et al. exerted considerable influence on psychologist Kenneth Clark and
his concern with the effects of racial prejudice on black children that
played such an important role in the arguments against segregation in the
Brown v. Board of Education case of 1954.

I have also tried to view this intellectual network from both a comparative and a transnational perspective, to stress both the differences and the
commonalities among its members. There was plenty of ideological disagreement among the intellectuals from Europe, Africa, the West Indies,
and North America who joined the post–World War II argument about
race, racism, and culture, not to mention their disparate backgrounds as far

as race, ethnicity, religion, education, and language were concerned. Yet Paul Gilroy's idea of the "black Atlantic" as a common culture is also central to my book, as is the idea that there is a trans-Atlantic intellectual tradition.[35] What links the various thinkers here are not the answers they offer but the common questions concerning race, racism, and culture they ask.

Specifically, as *Race, Culture, and the Intellectuals, 1940–1970* proceeds, I will be exploring common themes and concerns, including the relationship between anti-Semitism and white racism; the relative importance of caste, class, and race (and the possibilities of a black Marxism); the effects of modernization on traditional cultures; the existence of cultures of accommodation and cultures of resistance; the politics of culture generally; and the increasingly problematic status of Western humanism. Anglophone and Francophone (black) diasporic intellectuals were trained in quite different traditions and the resulting differences in tone, method, and ideology were often quite striking. Yet both groups worked with (in) a common "problematic" having to do with the end of Western colonialism, the rediscovery of older cultures, and/or the construction of new ones, and the appropriate attitude to assume toward the Western tradition generally. Their intellectual and conceptual tools were generally taken from that tradition, while the particular way they articulated their concerns derived from the sensibility shaped by their own cultural experience. Here, for instance, one thinks of the way Ralph Ellison and Albert Murray combined the aesthetics of the European modernism with the "down-home" tradition of the blues. Overall, the intellectual history of the race/racism/culture "problem" I am exploring takes place at the intersection of the North American–Caribbean history of black-white relations and the Jewish-Christian conflict at the heart of Western culture. Again, like Gilroy's *The Black Atlantic*, my focus falls upon the Atlantic basin constituted by the West Indies (or Antilles in French nomenclature), North America, Western Europe (especially Britain, France and, to an extent, Germany), and West Africa. The relationship of this black trans-Atlantic to the Iberian and the South African Atlantics remains unexplored here.

Where my intellectual debts are in all this is difficult to reconstruct. One crucial thing was living and teaching in Britain. From "there/here," things take on some interestingly different aspects. Several books from the late 1980s and first half of the 1990s stimulated my own thoughts. Despite all the controversy surrounding it, I found Martin Bernal's *Black Athena* (1987) extremely interesting, less because of his controversial thesis concerning the Egyptian influence on classical Greek thought than for his discussion of the pervasive racism and anti-Semitism that permeated classical studies and archaeology in the European academic world of the nineteenth and early twentieth centuries. Besides Gilroy's *Black Atlantic*, which I have already acknowledged, Robert J. C. Young's *White Mythologies* (1990) set me thinking with his claim that only postwar Francophone philosophers and intellectuals such as Césaire and Sartre made the connection between European fascism and Western imperialism. By and large, Young is correct, but he is wrong in the particular case of Hannah Arendt's *Origins of Totalitarianism*, where Arendt argues for the very strong connection of the repressive techniques and racist ideology developed in the service of imperialism with racist totalitarianism as it developed in Europe. Edward Said's *Culture and Imperialism* (1993) called attention to what should have been obvious but was not—that the high culture of the European novel was permeated by the influence of the imperial and colonial experience. Finally, Daryl M. Scott's *Contempt and Pity* (1997) helped clarify my thinking on the history of the idea of damage as applied to African American institutions and culture. There are undoubtedly other works that I might mention, but to these, at least, I want to acknowledge my particular indebtedness.[36]

Arrangement of Chapters

As an author, nothing seems stranger than to sum up the argument of a book in an introduction and then immediately to send readers off to bury themselves in the longer version. Yet operas have overtures in which main themes and motifs are adumbrated and so, I suppose, should a book. *Race, Culture, and the Intellectuals, 1940–1970* is not constructed as a chronological narrative, although it unfolds in roughly chronological sequence. I do not think that intellectual history is very interesting when done in narrative form. The relationship among arguments and between arguments and contexts tends to take precedence over the arguments themselves. Rather, my study is composed of a series of overlapping probes of thinkers and their arguments within, as already discussed, the historical shift from universalism to particularism between 1940 and the early 1970s.

Part I, "Analyzing Racism and Anti-Semitism," examines four separate postwar traditions of explaining racism and anti-Semitism within the post-1945 universalist paradigm. For this I have chosen to focus primarily on efforts (although others make their appearance in the chapters) that had an extra-academic audience and impact: that of Gunnar Myrdal, Jean-Paul

Sartre, Theodor Adorno with Max Horkheimer, and Hannah Arendt. Each study approaches race, racism and/or anti-Semitism, and culture from a different perspective: sociological, phenomenological, psychoanalytical, and historical, respectively. The funding for Myrdal's *An American Dilemma* (1944) and also for *The Authoritarian Personality* (1950), a joint effort between Adorno and a team of psychologists and psychiatrists, came largely from philanthropic foundations. Both studies were intended to shape the formulation of public policy and practical approaches to dealing with racism and prejudice in U.S. society after World War II. Both studies also had considerable immediate impact, which then faded fairly precipitously in the 1960s. Although Sartre's *Anti-Semite and Jew* (1946) had some impact on intellectual elites and educated reading publics in France and the United States, its most important effect was on the efforts of Francophone colonial intellectuals such as Frantz Fanon and Albert Memmi to analyze colonial domination by emphasizing what we would now call the "constructed" nature of colonial identity. Arendt's *The Origins of Totalitarianism* (1951) was extremely influential in the political debate about totalitarianism in the postwar era. More to the point here, however, her discussions of racism, imperialism, and anti-Semitism proposed a radical thesis about how those traditions of thought and action "crystallized" (one of her favorite tropes) to create the conditions for the triumph of National Socialist ideology within Germany and over much of Europe.

In Part II, "Modernization and Dominated Cultures," the focus shifts. If race was discredited as an explanation for group differences, and racism was condemned rather than accepted as inevitable, the question became: what *did* explain those differences? The answer was "culture." Specifically, Part II is concerned with the impact of modernization on two great minority cultures of the West—the African American and European Jewish cultures. More controversially, Part II looks at how both of these two subcultures had to respond to modernization—both to its promise as a transition to a more "rational" way of life and to it as nightmare process involving the enslavement and/or extermination of millions of human beings. Chapter 5 analyzes the efforts of four thinkers—Myrdal, E. Franklin Frazier, Richard Wright, and James Baldwin—to assess the impact of modernization on predominantly rural African American culture. In each case, though with different emphases, these figures saw African American culture as inadequate to the tasks with which modernity confronted it. This inadequacy was often conceptualized in terms of a "damage" or "pathology." In Chapter 6, I revisit Stanley Elkins's controversial *Slavery* (1959), which raised the explosive question of why there had been so few slave revolts in North America (and by extension, so few inmate revolts in the Nazi concentration camps). Elkins answered by comparing North American slavery to what had gone on in the capture and transportation of millions of Europeans to Nazi concentration camps. In both cases, Elkins claimed that a new acquiescent modal personality and a new "culture" of accommodation formed under the culture of "unopposed capitalism" were designed to minimize resistance. Chapter 7 examines the efforts of three thinkers—political scientist Raul Hilberg, psychoanalyst Bruno Bettelheim, and especially Hannah Arendt—to answer the analogous question for European Jewry: why had European Jews apparently demonstrated such relatively little resistance to the Nazis? Hilberg and Bettelheim, in particular, located the explanation for the lack of resistance in the traditional Jewish culture of Europe. In some of her earlier writings, Arendt had voiced similar sentiments, but her *Eichmann in Jerusalem* (1963) blamed the Jewish leadership for failing to provide sufficient opposition to the Final Solution. She, like Elkins, contended that modernization itself had created an extreme situation in which individual and group resistance to the destruction of one's culture and one's existence seemed futile. And she, like Elkins, thought it better to confront this fact rather than to pretend it did not exist and/or to stress what resistance there was.

Part III, "The Triumph of Cultural Particularism," shifts the focus to the contrary view that diasporic cultures were sites of cultural and political resistance and creativity. Rather than accommodation and passivity, by the end of the 1960s, celebration of particular racial/ethnic cultures seemed to have carried the day. Chapter 8 focuses on two important transitional intellectuals, Richard Wright and C. L. R. James. Writing in the 1940s and 1950s, both men stood ambivalently between the Western intellectual traditions that had shaped them *and* the new diasporic cultures that celebrated blackness and the African heritage. Yet both were militant advocates of political independence for black people in the Caribbean and in Africa. In Chapter 9, I trace the development of negritude, an ideology formulated primarily by Francophone writers and intellectuals in the 1940s and 1950s, and its rejection in the name of national political and cultural liberation by Frantz Fanon by the late 1950s. Where Wright and James were strong supporters of political independence for colonial peoples, negritude intellectuals stressed the cultural autonomy of people of African descent, while sidestepping the question of Third World political freedom.

This was one of Fanon's strongest reasons for rejecting negritude, although he also insisted that traditional Western culture was no longer a viable option.

Finally, Chapter 10 examines three different positions among African American intellectuals of the 1960s that privileged black culture over the mainstream white culture or elevated black culture to a co-equal status— Harold Cruse's black cultural nationalism, the black arts/aesthetic movements headed up by poet Amiri Baraka, and Ralph Ellison's and Albert Murray's incorporation of the Negro American cultural experience into the American democratic culture. While neither Cruse nor Murray-Ellison was influenced by negritude or by concerns with their African origins, the black arts/aesthetic movement was influenced by and echoed the negritude movement and sought to engage with the black diasporic culture outside the United States. One point to carry away from Part III is the lack of a determinant link between cultural vision and political ideology among these black intellectuals of the late 1960s.

But, all of this cleared the ground for the contemporary world of identity politics, multiculturalism, challenges to cultural canons and hierarchies, and cultural relativism. We cannot understand our own world unless we grasp the epic intellectual task accomplished by the intellectuals and thinkers we shall be examining: the undermining of racism in the name of universalism and the triumph of culture as the key concept in contemporary thought. The deletion of race from the discourse of, and about, "otherness" has been a distinct gain. Whether its replacement by culture is what we need is another matter.

Part I
Analyzing Racism and Anti-Semitism

1

Race, Caste, and Class: Myrdal, Cox, and Du Bois

The problem of the Twentieth Century is the problem of the color line.

W. E. B. Du Bois

Who was thinking of the Black Worker in 1935? Maybe ten people.

C. L. R. James

"White people today simply do not have a bad conscience over the fact that Negroes were brought here into slavery a long time ago," observed Gunnar Myrdal in 1964.[1] Although delivered in passing, Myrdal's pronouncement all but repudiated the central thesis of his massive *An American Dilemma* (1944) published exactly two decades earlier, which claimed that Americans were committed to something he called the "American Creed" and that the "American Dilemma" arose from the conflict between a general commitment to equality (and a certain type of freedom) and particularistic beliefs in racial inequality.

During the interwar years, a kind of epic sociology made up of large-scale, ambitious investigations of American life reached its peak. Helen and Robert Lynd's *Middletown* (1929) and *Middletown Revisited* (1937) were prime examples. Specifically, there were several studies focusing on the sociology of the South, or aspects of the region. Sometimes that focus fell on white farmers or mill hands or sharecroppers, but there were also numerous studies of black farmers and sharecroppers, and their families. Emanating from Yale and Chicago, Fisk and the University of North Carolina, funded by those institutions or by large philanthropic foundations, and written by men and women of both races, such studies provided the building blocks for President Roosevelt's 1938 *Report on the Economic*

21

Conditions of the South, which offered the memorable, and damning, description of the South as the "Nation's No. 1 economic problem."

Within this context, Myrdal's pathbreaking study of American race relations was perhaps the crowning achievement of progressive sociology on an epic scale. Incorporating the work alluded to above, *An American Dilemma* quickly established the frame of reference within which academic and policy elites addressed racial matters in post–World War II America up into the 1960s. It was, of course, cited by Chief Justice Earl Warren speaking for the Court in the *Brown v. Board of Education* (1954) decision outlawing school segregation and exerted considerable influence on *To Secure These Rights* (1947), the report of President Truman's Civil Rights Commission. Clearly, in the Cold War struggle for the loyalties of Third World peoples, the United States could ill afford to be saddled with the moral and political burdens of American-style apartheid.[2] But by the mid-1960s, the liberal consensus based on the work of Myrdal and his associates had begun to unravel.

With its publication, Myrdal's *An American Dilemma* also joined a distinguished set of works by foreign observers such as Alexis de Tocqueville, James Bryce, and Max Weber who had commented on salient aspects of the American experiment. More contemporaneously, *An American Dilemma* belonged with Theodor Adorno and Max Horkheimer, *The Dialectic of Enlightenment* (1944, 1947), Adorno et al., *The Authoritarian Personality* (1950), Jean-Paul Sartre, *Anti-Semite and Jew* (1946), and Hannah Arendt, *The Origins of Totalitarianism* (1951), as major theoretical efforts to understand the disfiguring presence of racism and anti-Semitism in the West. There was one major difference, however. Where the continuing viability of humanism and the Enlightenment was problematic in the works of the above thinkers, Myrdal's work largely avoided such historical or philosophical self-scrutiny. Although Myrdal was, as discussed in Chapter 4, well aware of certain blind spots in the Enlightenment perspective, he would have thought it bizarre to indict the Enlightenment or modern humanism as part of the problem rather than seeing them as ways of resolving the American dilemma.

An American Dilemma was, then, clearly a defense of the Enlightenment tradition of social analysis and prescription. It assumed that rationality was a necessary ingredient in any proposal for social reform and, more generally, that enlightenment was the means toward freedom and equality for all. The question that Myrdal's intellectual biographer, Walter Jackson, has identified as crucial in Myrdal's intellectually formative years captures the nature of his lifelong commitments: "How could one recover the heritage of the Enlightenment and subject the irrational in human behavior to scientific analysis so as to plan for a more rational future?"[3] Whether in Sweden or the United States (or later in studying Asian economic development), Myrdal maintained a general faith in rational reform and controlled modernization, grounded, as Timothy Tilton has noted, in the general Enlightenment assumption that "social goods are largely compatible."[4]

No work addressing a topic as explosive as American race relations could have escaped criticism at the time. White Southern racial conservatives (rightly) charged Myrdal with dismissing the validity of white supremacy; and Mississippi Senator James Eastland (wrongly) charged Myrdal in 1958 with being a "Socialist who had served the Communist cause."[5] Moderate white Southern academics, the dean of southern regional sociology Howard W. Odum among them, were afraid that Myrdal's candor endangered what progress had already been achieved in the South. Not surprisingly, Myrdal's Marxist critics such as Herbert Aptheker, Doxey Wilkinson, and Oliver C. Cox attacked him for not being a Marxist, while more recent critics of Myrdal from the left have charged that he offered an account of a "future status quo."[6] Historian Numan Bartley has claimed that *An American Dilemma* shifted the center of gravity of postwar political liberalism from social and economic reform to a moralistic obsession with dismantling segregation and attacking white racism. From Bartley's perspective, the decline of the Democratic Party and the rise of the politics of white resentment in the South and the North in the 1960s were the all-but-inevitable outcome of this shift in the nature of postwar liberalism.[7]

Though I will return to some of these points later, I want now to offer a closer analysis of the intellectual and political-cultural context in which Myrdal's project was formulated and then focus on the concepts central to his analysis. The overall thrust of my argument will be that Myrdal's position was much more complex and defensible than his critics allowed and stood up quite well to direct and indirect challenges from Oliver C. Cox on the issue of race and caste versus class and W. E. B. Du Bois on race as the best way to ground group identity.

The Interwar Years

The intellectual and political context in which Myrdal was chosen director of the Carnegie Corporation–funded project in 1938 is crucial to understanding *An American Dilemma*. Between the two world wars, the

Anglophone academic world witnessed a far-reaching paradigm shift in the study of race. In anthropology, biology, psychology, and sociology, the assumption of fixed racial differences came under withering intellectual scrutiny, even before the full horrors of Hitler's racial state came to light. By the end of World War II, a consensus firmly opposed to racial differences grounded in biology emerged among intellectual and academic elites. Overall, the preoccupation with allegedly objective traits of the separate races gave way to a concern with the subjective attitudes one group projected onto, or allegedly found in, another. This meant that "prejudice" and "racism," not "race" came much more to the fore in the study of race relations.[8]

In the same period, liberal politics underwent a subtle but important reorientation that was in some ways at odds with the social scientific reassessment of racial differences. As Gary Gerstle has put it:

> a new liberalism that emphasized the "economic" and neglected the "cultural" was the choice of influential liberal thinkers to put their embattled creed on a more secure foundation.[9]

While race and particularly ethnicity were openly debated in the Progressive Era, and while post-1945 liberalism elevated racial equality to prominence, New Deal liberalism stressed social and economic concerns, but neglected or avoided racial and ethnic matters. By 1936, most black Americans, where they could vote, had joined the ranks of the Democratic Party, but on the terms set by the white political class and electorate generally. In his work, Myrdal referred explicitly to the disparity between the intellectual elite's hostility to scientific racism and the white majority's continued adherence to racist assumptions and practices. This disparity helps explain the reluctance of politicians (of both races) to mount a fundamental challenge to white supremacy or to pass federal antilynching legislation. In times of economic crisis, questions of racial discrimination or ethnic difference seemed of less than compelling importance. One telling symptom of the neglect of race and ethnicity in the Depression era was evident in the Farm Security Administration–sponsored photography of the 1930s, which depicts poverty largely as a white phenomenon.

Myrdal's own intellectual formation placed him somewhat at odds with several of the general assumptions of American social and political science. For instance, his commitment to social democracy distanced him radically from William Graham Sumner's idea that "folkways" trumped "stateways." It also led him to challenge the leading sociologist of

American race relations, Robert Parks, who rejected the idea of state intervention in the four-stage process of racial and ethnic assimilation (competition, conflict, accommodation, and assimilation). Finally, Myrdal side-stepped the gradualism of Chapel Hill regionalists by supporting an interventionist policy to undermine the Jim Crow South. Myrdal also enlisted a whole cadre of (often younger) black and white students of African American life in the Carnegie project. The result was a general perspective at odds with the dominant consensus and one that helped Myrdal and company avoid much of the traditional wisdom of American race relations.

In other respects, Myrdal felt right at home in the United States. Myrdal's Swedish "third way," or social democratic approach, comported well with the idea of the strong state that was central to Roosevelt's New Deal, although President Roosevelt broke no lances for racial justice during the Depression. If white American academics and politicians were too timid to translate the New Deal interventionist impulses into race-sensitive policies, the Swedish economist was not. Little in Myrdal's background or in *An American Dilemma* suggested that racial tolerance and moral suasion alone were enough to resolve the nation's racial dilemma, later interpretations of Myrdal's intentions to the contrary notwithstanding. Thus, the Carnegie project that Myrdal presided over as an enlightened despot (one of Myrdal's most trusted associates, Ralph Bunche, once half-jokingly referred to him as a "Swedish Simon Legree") placed a social democratic spin on American liberal-progressive social and political thought. Although Myrdal had been influenced by John Dewey's thought, he (Myrdal) did not share Dewey's commitment to democratic participation as a counterbalance to the social engineering mentality of liberal social science elites.[10] It was not that Myrdal was an organization man per se, but he was convinced that the main route to effective reform of U.S. race relations ran through the established institutions of government and philanthropy. As a commissioned employee of the Carnegie Corporation, he was a determined reformer, but no radical destabilizer.

Most importantly, Myrdal shared the newly emerging interwar consensus about race and culture.[11] He believed that the definition of the Negro was "social" not "biological," a more economical way of saying that race is a social construct and not a natural kind: "[D]ifferences in behavior are to be explained largely in terms of social and cultural factors" (vol. 1, pp. 115, 149). Nor did the terms "white" and "black" match the empirical evidence or experience of most people, since at least 70 percent of so-called black Americans were of mixed race. For Myrdal, the great error lay not in admitting that real differences existed in culture, behavior, or achievement between the two races, but in "inferring that observed differences were innate and a part of nature" (vol. 1, p. 148).

This latter point was a tricky one. For, although the biological bases for white supremacy had been discredited, a new consensus on the issue of cultural difference had emerged by the 1940s: at least for the present, Negro American culture was seen by most social scientists as distinctly inferior to the dominant white American culture. Sociologists, as James McKee has summed it up, had "discarded the idea that black people were biologically inferior, but despite the arguments of anthropologists, they retained an image of them as culturally inferior."[12] Along with this, however, the new consensus held that the antiblack prejudice was not the expression of natural impulses; rather, it was learned and thus could be changed. Where prejudice against others was once seen as natural, prejudice was now something to be explained and then eradicated. This transformation in the way prejudice was conceptualized was as important a development as the re-description of race as a cultural rather than a natural phenomenon. Overall, on such issues, Myrdal marched in step with the new consensus, although he spoke with more urgency for active intervention to combat white prejudice. While not a revolutionary, Myrdal was no gradualist who believed that time was a natural emollient, healing all ills.

The American Creed

According to Myrdal, the "American Creed" provided the moral foundation of American culture and institutions and could be summed up as "a belief in equality and in the rights to liberty" (vol. 1, p. 8). He duly acknowledged the influences of the Judaeo–Christian tradition and the legal and political traditions of Britain, but located the chief sources of the Creed in "the great tradition of the Enlightenment and the American Revolution." As numerous commentators have noted, the last word of the two-volume study was "Enlightenment" (vol. 2, p. 1024).[13] Interestingly, when Myrdal returned to Sweden once World War II had broken out, he became even more convinced of the importance of the American Creed. From that distance, Americans seemed quite clear about what they were fighting to preserve. It was this wartime experience, claims Walter Jackson, more than any theoretical commitment to the causal priority of ideas over social and economic forces that led Myrdal to emphasize the importance of the Creed in both creating and resolving the American dilemma.

Indeed, that the Creed creates, but also helps resolve, the dilemma indicates its complex and protean nature. First, the Creed is a historical entity that provides the basis for the shared consensus among "ordinary Americans" of both races (vol. 1, p. lxxi). In this sense, it could be studied as a social fact. But the Creed is also obviously a normative standard for Americans, guiding and judging their thinking in racial matters. In this sense, it anticipates, though in more secular terms, what Robert Bellah later referred to as the American "civil religion." In another sense, Myrdal deploys the Creed as an analytical tool that supplies the standards by which to judge and predict (white) American performance in race relations. Discrimination is wrong, not because tolerance is an eternal value or equality a metaphysical right inscribed in the nature of things, but because "equality of opportunity" is a value the American people have pledged themselves to observe. Very shrewdly, Myrdal took Americans at their collective word rather than applying foreign standards or ideologies to judge them. Finally, Myrdal uses the Creed in a performative sense. If, in the (William) Jamesian sense, truth "happens" to an idea, an appeal to the Creed should itself help bring it into being.

It is not correct, strictly speaking, to couch the moral dilemma of white Americans as a conflict between "theory" and "practice," or "ideas" and "actions." Rather, Myrdal posited a conflict between two kinds of beliefs. Specifically, in opposition to the American Creed based on universalist notions stand the specific, particularistic values and ideologies that contradict it. Myrdal was thinking here primarily of the ideology of racial and caste superiority so endemic among Southern whites but also included

> personal and local interests; economic, social and sexual jealousies; considerations of community prestige and conformity; group prejudice against particular persons or types of people; and all sorts of miscellaneous wants, impulses, and habits. (vol. 1, p. lxxi)

Although white and black Americans share the Creed, the conflict between particularist racist beliefs and the general Creed is primarily "the white man's problem" (vol. 1, p. lxxi). Overall, then, Myrdal's work reinforced one of the most prominent traits of postwar racial liberalism—the suspicion of local and regional institutions, beliefs, and traditions. Myrdal also usually presented the dilemma as a conflict between the white South and the rest of the country, as a conflict *between* blocs of whites rather than as one *within* individuals. In the early 1940s, roughly 75 percent of

African Americans lived in the South, so directing his attention toward the South was not without justification, although there was postwar northern white opposition to desegregation of white neighborhoods.[14] By the 1960s, when around 50 percent of the nation's black population lived south of the Mason-Dixon line, the Southern focus of Myrdal's work would seem increasingly misplaced, thus perhaps contributing to the growing sense that *An American Dilemma* had lost its cogency.

Perhaps overoptimistically, Myrdal resisted the notion that white prejudice was inevitable or ineradicable. Indeed, the American "dilemma" arises from the fact that "people also want to be rational" (vol. 1, p. lxxiii). Rationality and morality are all but synonymous in *An American Dilemma*, since each entails the formal requirement to harmonize specific with general beliefs and, substantively, they assume the equality of all people. Just as clearly, one motivation driving Myrdal's analysis was the desire to undermine the power of the specific creeds: "The gradual destruction of the popular theory behind race prejudice is the most important of all social trends in the field of interracial race relations" (vol. 2, p. 1003). In keeping both with the hothouse atmosphere of wartime optimism and his Enlightenment-based assumptions, Myrdal also proposed "an educational offensive against racial intolerance," something that had "never seriously been attempted in America" (vol. 1, pp. 48–49).[15] Sociology in Myrdal's hands was thus a kind of moral pedagogy, an example of the Enlightenment on the offensive. At the same time, Myrdal's emphasis on the American Creed reintroduced commitment to universal moral principles and rights talk into a liberalism that had become wary of both abstract ideals and the appeal to rights, whether natural or otherwise.

But, Myrdal proposed more than popular education as a solution to the nation's massive problem. By suggesting a more comprehensive and complex "vicious circle of cumulative causation," he significantly extended the descriptive, explanatory, and normative reach of the American Creed. Putting clear water between himself and the Marxists, Myrdal's analytic model of causation denied that there was one single type of solution to America's racial agonies, although he did state clearly that "[d]iscrimination against Negroes is thus rooted in this tradition of economic exploitation" (vol. 1, pp. 207–8).[16] Specifically, Myrdal explains his model of change in the following manner:

A primary change, induced or unplanned, affecting anyone of three bundles of interdependent causative factors—(1) the economic level;

(2) standards of intelligence, ambition, health, education, decency, manners, and morals; and (3) discrimination by whites—will bring changes in the other two and, through mutual interaction, move the whole system along in one direction or the other. No single factor, therefore, is the "final cause" in a theoretical sense. (vol. 1, p. 208)

The key to reversing the spiral downward, that is, breaking the vicious circle/cycle, lay in introducing a positive change in any one of the three areas. Thus, along with presenting a complex, multifactorial model, Myrdal also assumed that outside intervention might be necessary.

Overall, then, Myrdal's analysis was hardly as naive as has sometimes been suggested. It makes no sense to criticize *An American Dilemma* for its optimism, since it was just the point of his study to arrive at analytical descriptions to serve as the basis for public policy prescriptions. Optimism comes with the generic and institutional territory and was not simply a function of Myrdal's personality or his ideological preferences. But Myrdal did perhaps simplify his analysis when he couched the tension between racial equality and racism in Manichean regional terms (North vs. South) rather than in intranational or even intrapsychic terms. Had Myrdal devoted more of his analysis to the psychic conflict within individuals, his work might have taken on some of the dense complexity Du Bois achieved when he posited a "double consciousness" at the heart of the African American experience. In short, Myrdal came close, but failed to develop, a notion of white double consciousness. Racist beliefs are irrational because they conflict with the Creed, the touchstone of rationality and morality.[17] Nor is Myrdal's claim that white Americans want to be "rational" as naive as it sounds. Rationality is clearly more than a capacity; it is an achievement, involving the overcoming of "particularistic" beliefs in the light of the general commitment to equality. Again, the Creed is a collective, performative utterance, a way of bringing itself into being.

Still, some readers of Myrdal's work were skeptical of his emphasis on the psychological and moral conflict experienced by white Americans. Sociologist E. Franklin Frazier praised Myrdal for his emphasis on the moral dimension of the problem, but wondered whether it was "on the conscience of white people to the extent implied in his statement." Although Frazier failed to elaborate on the types who might be more or less sensitive to the dilemma, he did suggest that there was a moral threshold beyond which the Creed might go into operation: "It is when the Negro emerges as a human being and a part of the moral order that discrimination against him is on the conscience of the white man."[18] In other words, Myrdal should have explicitly identified the threshold at which whites began to accept the fact that blacks were fully human. Another observer wondered at the time whether the white dilemma was a moral dilemma, since to call something a moral dilemma implies a conscious conflict among values rather than a conflict between conscious and unconscious values or impulses. Conversely, if unconsciously held beliefs are at issue, then it is not proper to hold an individual or group responsible. This is perhaps what Ralph Ellison was implying when he scored Myrdal for having sidestepped

> the problem of the irrational. . . where Marx cries out for Freud and Freud cries out for Marx. . . and which has taken the form of the Negro problem.[19]

It may also be appropriate to call Myrdal's position a "consensus" view of American history; but it was an embattled, problematic consensus to be achieved in the future rather than already an existing fact. No doubt Myrdal felt that racist beliefs were departures from the American Creed; and this clearly conflicts with more recent students of race in the United States who stress that American national identity has historically implied the centrality of "whiteness" and the denigration of African Americans and people of color. But Myrdal never claimed that racist beliefs are foreign to white Americans or at least to white Southerners; otherwise, there would have been no dilemma. Nor, as I have tried to suggest, is the Creed quite so central to Myrdal's analysis as it seemed, since it is superseded in certain respects by the principle of "cumulative causation" that posits *three* equally crucial factors at work. Any one, or a combination of all three, had to be addressed in order to resolve the dilemma.

The American Creed is, as Myrdal admitted, "less specified and articulated in the economic field than, for instance, in regard to civil rights." Historically, "equality of opportunity" has perennially collided with the belief in " 'liberty' to run one's business as one pleases" (vol. 1, p. 209). For instance, a strong belief in free market principles has nothing to do with racist beliefs or a defense of the caste system per se. But it could, and did, reinforce the racial status quo. Myrdal's optimism led him to believe that a greater commitment to economic equality was gaining ground. But resolving the tension between equality and liberty by calling for "equality of opportunity" was a sleight of hand rather than a genuine solution on Myrdal's part. Past oppression could not be ignored in creating opportunities in the present. This helps explain why, in 1964, Myrdal still thought that equality of opportunity was the key to resolving America's racial problems: "I am convinced that this demand for discrimination in reverse, i.e., to the advantage of Negroes, is misdirected."[20] According to Myrdal, it made little economic sense to target black Americans alone; in addition, preferential treatment would further alienate African Americans from the white population. "What the Negroes want," he asserted confidently, "is to have equal opportunities."[21]

Myrdal, Cox, and the Problem of Caste

With the possible exception of regionalism, it is hard to think of a concept that disappeared as suddenly as "caste" did from the vocabulary of postwar American sociology.[22] Although Myrdal put America's *racial* dilemma on the political and intellectual map, the term he preferred to race was "caste," a concept brought into currency in the 1930s by W. Lloyd Warner and perhaps best known through John Dollard's *Caste and Class in a Southern Town* (1937). Myrdal justified his choice of caste in the following manner. "Race" is a pseudo-biological concept and therefore better abandoned, while "class" refers to a social category that can be escaped in ways that American Negroes find impossible in their situation in the South, particularly. Finally, "minority group," he notes, generally refers to European ethnic groups who are only temporarily objects of prejudice and discrimination. The difference between caste and class derives from "the relatively large difference in freedom of movement between groups" (vol. 2, pp. 667–69, 693). Thus, for Myrdal, caste is the "extreme case of absolutely rigid class," and bears a certain resemblance to the caste system in India where the term is "applied without controversy" (vol. 2, pp. 675, 668). Myrdal was also out for bigger game when he added a slap at Marxism: "The Marxian conception of 'class struggle'. . . is in all Western countries a superficial and erroneous notion." In the South, the "concept of 'caste struggle,' on the other hand, is much more realistic." Finally, the ideology of racism provides a defense of "the color line," which has "the function of upholding the caste system itself, keeping the 'Negro' in his place" and serving to "preserve inequality for its own sake" (vol. 2, pp. 676–77, 592). Overall, though race is the ideological concept that holds together the entire caste system, caste rather than race is the crucial causal category in Myrdal's analysis.

Not surprisingly, Marxists began attacking *An American Dilemma* before the ink was dry, if not before. First in line was Herbert Aptheker, who charged that Myrdal had mistakenly applied the term "dilemma" to the racial situation facing America. According to Webster, a dilemma was "a situation involving choice. . . between equally unsatisfactory alternatives." But that, asserted Aptheker "is incorrect and absolutely vicious,"[23] since it implies that the America's racial situation is "a moral question" rather than a "socio-economic" or "material" one. In theoretical terms, it is a "question of idealism and materialism." Although there was in fact a choice in the matter, no dilemma existed for "believers in democracy and full rights for all people."[24]

Besides the obvious contradiction involved in railing against a moral approach to American racism, but then calling for democracy and full rights for African Americans rather than merely for economic justice, Aptheker's polemics bordered on the libelous. In his article in *New Masses* in 1946, he all but equated the way Myrdal, Richard Wright (who left the Communist Party in 1941), and Horace Cayton and St. Clair Drake, co-authors of *Black Metropolis*, had attacked materialism with the positions of Southern conservatives such as Allen Tate, Donald Davidson, and David Cohn—as well as Mississippi racist demagogues, Theodore Bilbo and John E. Rankin! Indeed, Aptheker also implied that Myrdal's anti-materialist and pro-moral point of view was not a surprise coming from an official of the Swedish government, whose country had remained neutral during the war. Finally, according to Aptheker, intellectuals such as Myrdal "tend to decry the morality of the masses" and, along with Wright, "slander the people," when they point to black inferiority in areas of education and health. For Aptheker, the masses, black or white, were not really affected by oppression: "The basic integrity of the masses will be untouched."[25]

Leaving aside the crude nature of his polemics, Aptheker's analysis confuses strategies for solving social problems with metaphysical debates about idealism and materialism. His assumptions that there was an obvious connection between metaphysics and social policy and that to focus on the psychological and sexual dimensions of racial conflict was racist substituted name-calling for analysis. In raising these issues, Aptheker ironically neglected the economic dimensions of Myrdal's argument. Aptheker's unstated objection to Myrdal's position was, of course, that Myrdal did not call for the replacement of capitalism with socialism and of bourgeois liberalism with proletarian democracy. The polemical, even hysterical, nature of Aptheker's attack also distracted from the valid point he had to make: that Myrdal underplayed the historical resistance of African Americans to slavery.

Far more impressive and cogent were the criticisms of the Trinidad-born sociologist Oliver Cox (1901–1974). Cox's fundamental argument with Myrdal concerns the most appropriate concept to describe racial/social stratification in America and what might be the political and economic solutions for America's racial problems. Cox himself was something of a maverick among sociologists because of his independent Marxism/black radicalism. While sociologist Charles Johnson had become president of Fisk University in Nashville and E. Franklin Frazier was well established at Howard University and president of the American Sociological Association in the late 1940s, Cox lacked the political or institutional connections enjoyed by such insiders. After earning his Ph.D. at the University of Chicago, he taught at predominantly black and obscure colleges such as Wiley College in Texas, Tuskegee Institute in Alabama, and Lincoln in Jefferson City, Missouri. An ideological maverick, he has been compared to Thorstein Veblen and C. Wright Mills.[26] The strength of Cox's work lay in the broadly comparative perspective he brought to an analysis of Myrdal's work. Although his independence from foundation funding and refusal of political respectability did not automatically make Cox's work unassailable, it did perhaps make his critique of Myrdal more acute than most of the criticism of Myrdal, then or since.

Cox's critique of Myrdal appeared as part of his *Caste, Class and Race* in 1948, though much of it had already been published in separate articles soon after the publication of *An American Dilemma*. On several major issues, Cox and Myrdal were in broad agreement. They agreed that race was a social not a biological phenomenon and thus was the province of the sociologist (and possibly the historian) rather than of the anthropologist or geneticist. Second, both believed that slavery and racial consciousness were capitalist in origins: "The interest behind racial antagonism is an exploitative interest. . . . characteristic of capitalist society." To this emphasis upon the social and economic etiology of race, Cox also added a historical dimension by repeatedly insisting that the importance of race is a distinctly modern phenomenon: "racial antagonism . . . had its rise only in modern times."[27] Finally, Myrdal and Cox shared the view that the cultural and institutional situation of Negro Americans was a dire one. Like Myrdal, Cox focused on the economic and social conditions of black American life, and he also spoke openly of America's

relatively illiterate, criminal, diseased, base, poor, and prostituted colored people. . . . This state of degradation tends to characterize the cultural life of the Negroes and to make it distinct from that of whites. . . . They [white Americans] seek, through myriad and powerful devices, to make the colored person, as a human being, ashamed of his very existence. (p. 367)

American Negroes were "[a] people without a culture peculiar to itself, but having only a truncated pattern of the general culture within which it lives. . . ." (p. 569). If anything, Cox was more, rather than less, skeptical than Myrdal about the viability of African American culture and institutions.

But Cox hammered away relentlessly at Myrdal's analysis of, and pre-scriptions for, the American racial situation. In particular, he attacked Myrdal's choice of caste as the most appropriate term to describe the sta-tus of black Americans in Southern society. The thrust of Cox's charges, based on a comparative analysis of caste in India and the racial caste sys-tem in the U.S. South, was that caste has almost nothing to do with race or skin color in its Indian setting: "The early Indo-Aryans could no more have thought in modern terms of race prejudice than they could have in-vented the airplane" (p. 91). Second, while caste society in India was en-tirely structured around a hierarchical system of castes, there was nothing approaching that situation in the South. In the latter, only one oppressed caste exists, while the rest of the region's population is classified accord-ing to a variety of criteria and functions, such as class and status, citizen-ship, profession and education, and ethnicity and color.

Finally, Cox's most interesting point was that, in a pure caste society, low-caste membership is not experienced as oppression since it is taken to be a metaphysical as well as social fact. Nor, by extension, did exclusion from the higher-caste privileges give rise to individual or group patholo-gies: "While a slave society is based upon some form of coercion, the caste system is maintained by consensus" (p. 20). Cox sums up his posi-tion in the following manner:

Castes in India constitute a natural system in one society, while Negroes and whites in the South tend to constitute status systems, i.e. two social-class systems in two societies that are in opposition. (p. 502)

In a genuine caste society, the inferior caste is an integral part of a larger society, but in the American South, black people "never appear as an in-tegral part of the society," which is itself a "temporary" and "hybrid" so-ciety (pp. 503–4). In the South, the black caste is exploited, discriminated against, and made to feel unwanted, however economically necessary it may actually be.

Moreover, although Myrdal wanted to avoid race/color as the key signifier of the socially weakest group in the South, all that the members of the Negro caste share, notes Cox, is their color and some other gross physical characteristics. As Myrdal himself admitted, members of the Negro caste are not members of it because "they are poor and ill-educated. . . ."[28] It is not something they have earned their way into or failed to "test" out of. Indeed, poverty or lack of education is the result, not the cause, of belonging to the Negro caste. Overall, Cox focused on the way that Myrdal used the concept of caste to escape the overly biological category of race, but then defined membership in the caste exclusively in terms of race/color. The result was an analysis that was needlessly complex, even counterintuitive.

Like most critics of the caste approach, Cox insisted that the concept of caste implied that the lines between the two races were so rigid that it was difficult to imagine how the system could be changed. Indeed, the logic of his position led him to jettison not only caste but also race and to elevate "class" to the central place in his analysis. Against Myrdal, Cox insisted that racial consciousness and the conflict generated by that consciousness were functions of the class struggle within capitalism: "[R]acial antagonism is part and parcel of this class struggle, because it developed within the capitalist system as one of its fundamental traits" (p. xxx).

If this is the case, then one "identifies the Negro problem in the United States with the problem of all workers regardless of color."[29] In the terms later used by black Marxists, Cox identified slaves, along with black sharecroppers and small farmers after slavery, as a racialized class, whose oppression is a function of the capitalist system and whose interests ultimately coincide with those of white workers.

But Cox's position was not without its problems. That racial antagonism and the ideology of racism originate with capitalism does not mean that they remain dependent on that system for their existence. That is, racism and racial conflict have historically taken on lives of their own in the United States and may have overridden conscious economic and social interests, particularly from the white side. This also means that it is highly problematic to assume with Cox (and Aptheker) that, if the race problem is primarily a moral question, it must naturally be resolved by moral means alone. Put another way, it is just the point of Myrdal's principle of cumulative causation that, even if the origins of the caste system are economic, the ways to attack it are not only economic, but also cultural and moral. Conversely, even if they were moral or cultural in origins, economic disparities would still have to be addressed. Here the Marxists backed themselves needlessly into a corner by denying that there was a moral-psychological dimension to the American dilemma or to its resolution.

Nor does the fact that both black and white workers, or blacks and whites of any description, are exploited as part of the capitalist system mean that they are exploited in the same ways, have identical interests, and are thus potential, if not actual, allies. (That this is not true of men and women in capitalist society suggests that it is probably not true of whites and African Americans either.) In the postwar American South, it was no ideological mystification to suggest that white and black workers had different interests and different degrees of self-consciousness. Cox's failure to see this, along with such statements as, "There will be no more 'crackers' or 'niggers' after a socialist revolution because the social necessity for these types will have been removed" (p. 537), points to the absence of a plausible historical psychology in Cox's thought. As a result, his analysis can hardly accommodate the idea that social groups are held together not just by economic and political interests but also by historical memories of shared experiences.

All that said, Cox does make some effective points in his critique of Myrdal's principle of cumulative causation. Suppose, he speculates, that there is a rise in Negro standards but that "Negroes increase their interest in white women" as part of the improvement. The white Southern reaction, especially, would not be hard to imagine. This suggests to Cox that "both race prejudice and Negro standards are consistently dependent variables. They are both produced by the calculated economic interests of the Southern oligarchy." Indeed, claims Cox, it is absurd to imagine that "the ruling class in the South will permit a free, objective discussion of race relations in its schools or public" (pp. 530–31). Cox's point here was that rising Negro standards of whatever sort might heighten, not reduce, white racial animosity, contrary to Myrdal's three-factor model. Overall, Cox assumed that the economic interests of a particular class were primary determinants of cultural, social, and political developments rather than being independent of, or co-equal with, them.

Finally, the thrust of Cox's political analysis was both overly pessimistic and too optimistic. In hindsight, he failed to imagine a situation in which the so-called white planter oligarchy would no longer need racial discrimination or prejudice to maintain its control and, more importantly, would lose its controlling grip on the Southern economy and also on race relations. Although it is a tremendously complicated story, something like that did happen after 1948 when Cox published *Caste, Class and Race*. Thus, much of his analysis came to seem off the point. Yet, he was correct that Myrdal urged black Southerners to look to the white upper middle-class, rather than to the white working class, for protection and aid. Predictably, Cox criticized Myrdal's emphasis on the antagonism between poor whites and Negroes and for refusing to highlight the powerful economic interests of the white "ruling class" that keep black Southerners in their place (pp. 521–23). Clearly, "racial antagonism is in fact political-class antagonism" and "race prejudice is initiated and maintained by labor exploiters" (p. 536). Again, Cox's theory dictates that the black and white working class should be natural allies.

The problem with Cox's political-class analysis, deriving not only from orthodox Marxism but also echoing the late 1930s Popular Front call for a white–black workers alliance, was its excessive optimism. There was, to be sure, a good deal of interracial cooperation in union struggles in the North and South during and shortly after the war. And there were a few elected politicians such as Alabama's Jim Folsom and Louisiana's Earl Long who forged fairly effective interracial, electoral coalitions for a time in the South after the War. But eventually they foundered on, among other things, the politics of Jim Crow, particularly after 1954. Indeed, much of the evidence suggests that white and black workers could cooperate on the shop floor for higher wages and better working conditions, but that when it became a matter of discarding Jim Crow rules inside or outside the factory gates, or encouraging black political power, white workers and their leaders lost their enthusiasm. Indeed, one cannot help feeling that black Southerners were much more in touch with regional reality than radical analysts such as Cox (or a socialist such as Bunche once had been) when they recognized that they were unlikely to garner much sympathy from the white working class. But on one important point, Cox was correct: Myrdal's public policy prescriptions hardly threatened the economic power of those who controlled the region.

Race and Class: The Twilight Years of W. E. B. Du Bois

If Myrdal was a social democrat and Cox a radical of the Popular Front variety, W. E. B. Du Bois (1868–1963) was much more ideologically elusive. In his early sixties when the 1930s began, Du Bois developed three distinct ideological positions over the next decade or so—a rejection of the biological conception of race; a class analysis of modern history, expressed most forcefully in *Black Reconstruction* (1935); and advocacy of a black communalism, which sounded at times not unlike his old adversaries Marcus Garvey and Booker T. Washington. Yet, these three developments in Du Bois's thinking were not entirely compatible. Was he an elitist or a democrat? A scholar or activist? A late Victorian or a proto-modernist? A black nationalist or a black Marxist? To understand Du Bois's often contradictory thinking is to understand much about the intellectual history of race in pre–Cold War America period and to catch Du Bois in the last great creative decade of his life.[30]

On the subject of race, Du Bois was in many respects the antithesis of Myrdal. While Myrdal firmly rejected a biological explanation of group difference and generally sought to undermine racial thinking, Du Bois found it very difficult to give up the concept of race. Du Bois has been called an "anti-race race man," someone who firmly rejected racial essentialism and adopted a "cosmopolitan" stance. Yet if any single African American thinker can be said to have been an "organic intellectual," whose every waking thought and action was devoted to the improvement of his people's welfare, it was Du Bois.[31] Both men thought it wrong to judge individuals or groups primarily by racial criteria; yet Du Bois spent much of his life championing the cause of colonized and oppressed peoples of the African diaspora and of the Third World, while Myrdal remained a leading spokesman for the social democratic–liberal vision of economic and social modernization largely along Western lines.

Both men were committed to broadening the reach of democracy, yet as the 1930s progressed, Du Bois was more concerned with social and economic power than with political or civil rights. Indeed, Adolph Reed has suggested that Du Bois's embrace of Marxism in the 1930s was not incompatible with, but a continuation of, his belief in the benevolent power of elites (e.g., the Talented Tenth) to guide the political and cultural development of the masses.[32] Both men were convinced of the inseparability of scholarship and political engagement, the search for truth, and the quest for justice. Yet, Du Bois's intellectual genealogy traced back less to Enlightenment universalism than to Hegel, Herder, and German Romantic social thought. Unusually for American thinkers of the twentieth, though not of the nineteenth, century, Du Bois found his intellectual sustenance in Germany more than he did in France or England. Nor did this have to do with the centrality of racial and cultural consciousness in German thought. Social policy in Wilhelminian Germany was perhaps the most progressive of its time. Moreover, Du Bois's stay in Germany as a doctoral student was the first time he was not made to feel hyperconscious about his color. Despite the greater strength of the liberal tradition in Britain and the republican tradition in France, racism seems to have been no more endemic in Germany in the late nineteenth and early twentieth centuries than it was in the former two cultures.[33]

Myrdal and Du Bois were never close personally, in part because the latter was nearly three decades the Swede's senior. In fact, the decision by the Carnegie Corporation to engage Myrdal to direct a study of U.S. race relations was complexly linked to Du Bois's failure to obtain funding for an *Encyclopaedia of the Negro*.[34] It had been Du Bois's dream since at least 1909 to undertake such an ambitious, even visionary, project; and it was Kwame Nkrumah's promise to help Du Bois realize this dream that persuaded the ninety-one-year-old to move to Ghana in 1961 where he died two years later. Although there is no ironclad evidence that the Carnegie Corporation saw matters in either/or terms, Carnegie wanted its study conducted in an "objective and dispassionate way," and some feared that a project under Du Bois's direction would not meet that standard. An absolutely final rejection of his project had not come yet in November 1938 when the two men met for the first time. "[S]crupulously gracious" to Myrdal, Du Bois, David Levering Lewis adds, was "impressed in equal parts by Myrdal's energetic brilliance and his unprejudiced ignorance of the Negro."[35]

Du Bois reviewed *An American Dilemma* favorably, albeit a bit perfunctorily, when it appeared in 1944. He praised its comprehensive coverage and willingness to take on such a daunting topic. He also gave favorable mention to Myrdal's refusal to appease the white South, his rejection of a narrow social scientism, and the way he took into account "emotions, thoughts, opinions and ideals." Du Bois also noted Myrdal's emphasis on the moral dimension of the problem, his refusal to attribute causal weight to racial differences, and his rejection of "the Marxian dogma of economic effort as ever dominant motive."[36] Still, it is hard not to wonder how Du Bois really felt about Myrdal's militant anti-Marxism and, even more so, about *An American Dilemma*'s treatment of African American culture and institutions as weak and inadequate.

When W. E. B. Du Bois subtitled *Dusk of Dawn* (1940), "An essay toward an autobiography of a race concept," he clearly signaled the importance that race played in his own self-identity. As he wrote in the introductory "Apology" to the volume,

> I seem to see a way of elucidating the inner meaning and significance
> of that race problem by explaining it in terms of the one human life that
> I know best.[37]

If ever there was a claim for representative status and a willing acceptance of the role of "race man," surely this was it. Yet not only in *Dusk of Dawn* but also in most of his writings, including his oft-cited "Conservation of Races" (1897), Du Bois emphasized the confusion surrounding the concept of race. As he wrote in an unpublished article of 1935 on "Miscegenation," a race is "not a clearly defined and scientifically measured group." What are now called races "are in no case pure races" and thus nothing definite can be said about inherent racial capacities.[38] Moreover, Du Bois felt that the concept of race had never been dealt with objectively, but was always placed in the service of political and economic interests. Like Cox and Myrdal, he located the emergence of racism at a specific historical juncture: "Undoubtedly, color prejudice in the modern world is the child of the American slave trade and the Cotton Kingdom."[39] The criteria for establishing the reality of race and the capabilities of each race have, as he suggested in *Dusk of Dawn*, continually shifted. By the 1930s, race was, for Du Bois, largely a political and social rather than scientific phenomenon. Even in "The Conservation of Races," when his commitment to the reality of race was at its height and he was pondering the meaning of difference among racial groups, he writes that though

> there are differences. . . which have silently but definitely separated
> men into groups. . . . At all times, however, they have divided human
> beings into races, which, while they perhaps transcend scientific defin-
> ition, nevertheless, are clearly defined to the eye of the Historian and
> the Sociologist.[40]

One way of reading this passage is as an expression of Du Bois's environmentalist view of race. Race is a historical rather than biological reality.

And yet, Du Bois could never quite shake himself loose from the concept of race and obviously did not want to. As Tommy Lott has observed, although Du Bois acknowledged that there were considerable difficulties with the concept of race, he typically resorted to it at every level of analysis, ranging from the personal to the world-historical,[41] even after he had largely abandoned his early definition of race as:

> a vast family of human beings, generally of common blood and language, always of common history, traditions and impulses, who are both voluntarily and involuntarily striving together for the accomplishment of certain more or less vividly conceived ideals of life.[42]

This oft-cited passage contains all the elements of Du Bois's idea of race as it unfolded throughout his life. The nineteenth-century doctrine of race as "common blood" is there, but the environmentalist notion of race as "common history, traditions and impulses" assumes a co-equal position. Indeed, it is hard to know whether Du Bois should be praised for the complexity of his conception of race or criticized for his equivocation on the topic and his refusal to give it up.[43]

Still one unduly neglected element may provide a different perspective on Du Bois's idea of race. The last sentence cited above identifies a characteristic of race that transcends the biological in the Darwinian sense and the historical in the positivist sense—namely, each race has a purpose, a telos, a meaning, which it seeks to realize in history. This is related to Du Bois's oft-expressed view that "the history of the world is the history, not of individuals, but of groups, not of nations, but of races."[44] Specifically, each historical race, of which Du Bois identifies eight early on in his writings and then later two or three, is

> striving, each in its own way, to develop for civilization its particular message, its particular ideal, which shall help to guide the world nearer and nearer that perfection of human life for which we all long. . .[45]

From this perspective, which combines a liberal-progressive philosophy of history with romantic racialism, Du Bois's point is that the historical time for people of African descent to make their contribution has arrived. They are to be led not by Africans but African Americans, themselves under the direction of a race elite, the Talented Tenth or New Negro, who, in turn, will find spiritual and intellectual guidance from the ultimate race man, W. E. B. Du Bois himself. Whether race is essentially biological or is based on shared tradition and experiences was less important to Du Bois than that it functioned as an identity, that is, as a source of individual and group definition. Overall, race was a foundational, transhistorical concept, although never primarily a biological one, for Du Bois.

Thus, race served two functions for Du Bois. It was the anchor of individual and group identity and also the mediating term between the individual and the universal. What class was for Marx, so race was for Du Bois. In each case, the mediating term (abstractly put) or historically privileged group (concretely put) lifts the isolated individual out of him/herself and makes the universal concrete. Not until "the ideal of human brotherhood has become a practical possibility" should "race identity" be abandoned.[46] Striving for social and political equality was not a way of assimilating into the dominant society, but of insisting that the dominant society recognize the rights of the minority race, so that it could fulfill its historical unique mission.

With this metahistorical framework in mind, the various meanings Du Bois imparted to the race concept come more clearly into view. In *Dusk of Dawn*, we see Du Bois analyzing race as *family lineage*, according to which he chooses his personal identity as a person of African descent, even though he also had Dutch, French, and Indian ancestors. This undoubtedly provides the basis of one of Du Bois's tropes—race as (like a) family—although it is a family that Du Bois, a mulatto, can choose. Second, in *Dusk of Dawn*, Du Bois discusses race as a largely discredited natural scientific *concept*, though it is still for him the potential object of study by the historian, political scientist, sociologist, and psychologist. Finally, race emerges by 1940 as an *experience*, which provides an anchor for individual and group *identity*. In summary, race is the name given to the historical, political, and social conditions of possibility for naming and experiencing one's self as the member of a group. It is grounded in a historical (as opposed to biological or metaphysical) ontology, but one with possible biological components.

Specifically, it is race as identity that proves central for Du Bois from the 1930s to the end of his life. Du Bois uses race as identity in three different ways. The first, race as a special historical version of class, would be shaped by Du Bois's immersion in Marxism beginning in the early 1930s. Its most cogent expression was in his most pioneering work, *Black Reconstruction* (1935). In general, Du Bois did not develop this "black Marxism" theoretically, but let it emerge in the historical narrative of the fate of African American slaves in the Civil War and then as freed people during Reconstruction. According to Du Bois, slavery was central to modern history because it was central to the history of Western capitalism. Slavery in the Western Hemisphere had been just as central to the development of capitalism as had the industrialization of Europe based on the labor of "free" workers, a claim that has recently re-emerged with new intellectual force in Paul Gilroy's *The Black Atlantic* (1993). Thus, in the

Western Hemisphere and particularly in North America what emerged was a racialized class struggle.[47]

It is important, for example, to note the language of *Black Reconstruction*. In chapter 1, Du Bois continually refers to slaves as "workers" and to slavery as an "industrial system."[48] Later, Du Bois claims, undoubtedly with Haiti in mind, what *Black Reconstruction* had only implied: "The slave revolts were the beginnings of the revolutionary struggle for the uplift of the laboring masses in the modern world."[49] But, contrary to the Bunche-Cox position, the likelihood that white and black workers could unite in one universal class was extremely slim. After the early, almost plaintive question of 1913—"Can the objects of Socialism be achieved as long as the Negro is neglected?"—Du Bois asserts in "Marxism and the Negro Problem" (1933) that "colored labor has no common ground with white labor" and thus black people are exploited by "white capitalists and equally from the white proletariat."[50] This was the great disappointing lesson of Reconstruction, one comparable to the failure of the proletariats of Europe to join forces rather than fighting for their individual nations in World War I. Neither industrial workers and middling-level white farmers in the North nor poor white and yeoman white farmers in the South proved reliable allies for the former slaves in their first days of freedom.

Race as identity was also exemplified in Du Bois's concern with the group life of black Americans. Insisting that he was not capitulating to conservative Bookerite self-development or radical Garveyite separatism, Du Bois broke with the National Association for the Advancement of Colored People (NAACP) and liberal opinion generally by calling for Negro Americans to develop their own institutions, such as schools and hospitals, to meet the concrete needs of African Americans until the advent of universal brotherhood—which is to say, for a very long time. This was a way to "put reason and power beneath this segregation" that had been forced on African Americans.[51] Du Bois justified his position in two ways. First, he admits that it was a "perfectly obvious fact" that circa 1940 "by practical present measurement Negroes today are inferior to whites" and "occupy a low cultural status. . ." (pp. 174, 179). In order to progress as a people, African Americans themselves needed to develop self-reliance. This obviously provides one answer as to why Du Bois was silent on Myrdal's controversial characterization of Negro American life as "pathological." He clearly agreed with much of Myrdal's analysis of black institutional weakness and admitted that health, education, and family strength among black Americans were low.

The second justification echoes his analysis of class relations in *Black Reconstruction* but brought into the present: "The split between white and black workers was greater than that between white workers and capitalists" (p. 205), a fact ignored by the Communist Party as well as by the labor movement, as they tried to attract black workers in the Depression decade. Rather than simply cultivating black proletarian consciousness, Du Bois also wants to encourage the emergence of a black capitalist bourgeoisie. Thus, he necessarily downplays the importance of the class struggle within the African American population in his black communitarian phase. In addition, Du Bois redefines black Americans as essentially consumers rather than producers and maintains that "[i]n the future organization of industry the consumer as against the producer is going to become the key man" (p. 208). This remarkable insight in the midst of the Depression was a prophetic foreshadowing of the civil rights movement's approach to African Americans as consumers—boycotters, marchers, sitters-in—rather than producers on the farm and in the factory. The whole "producerist" orientation of Marxism was soft-pedaled in his vision of race as defined by a national community of people of African descent. Du Bois the black Marxist gave way to Du Bois the protonationalist.

The final expression of racial identity in Du Bois's thought was the articulation of a pan-African consciousness, which rested on the conviction that people of color of the African diaspora have "a common history; have suffered a common disaster and have one long memory" (p. 117). After World War II in particular, Du Bois increasingly emphasized the conflict between European colonialism and the colonized Third World. In this emerging transnational consciousness, race—white versus black, brown and yellow—served as a concept defining the emerging global class conflict with the colored Third World played off against the "Free World" and the "Soviet Bloc." In common with race as group consciousness at home, race in the form of pan-African solidarity emphasized unity rather than divisions among colonized peoples of color.

Du Bois was fully aware that such a unity was historically quite tenuous. For instance, he admitted that his own "African" consciousness, up to 1923 when he first visited Africa, was largely an intellectual one. To be sure he remembered a song sung to him by his great-grandmother, which he later realized came from Africa. But that was all. Like Richard Wright in *Black Power* (1955), Du Bois recognized the rhythms of his childhood when he first heard Africans singing. But unlike Wright, he trusted his intuition that there was some commonality of feeling rather than doubting the feeling as Wright did. He also recognized that "color and hair" were markers of shared experiences, but whether "they stand for real and more subtle differences[,]. . . I do not know nor does science know today" (p. 117). In answer, then, to Countee Cullen's question "What is Africa to me?" Du Bois moved from the deeply personal to the broadly political level, without spending much time analyzing the psychological or cultural effects of colonialism upon the indigenous population of Africa.

Although the spirit of the Bandung Conference in 1955 dictated neutrality vis-à-vis the two great powers, Du Bois increasingly sailed under the colors of the Soviet Union, having understandably grown bitter with U.S. authorities for denying him a passport until 1957 and for attempting to try him for failing to register as an agent of a foreign government. His favorable comments on Stalin, the Soviet Union, and its Eastern European empire indicated at best self-deception and at worst mendacity, and they tarnished a lifetime of lustrous achievement.[52] He was sure, for instance, that the people of Eastern Europe were better off under Soviet control. In contrast with C. L. R. James, who celebrated the Hungarian Revolution in 1956 as a blow for freedom, Du Bois wrote: "I was glad that the Soviet Union intervened" to stifle the Hungarian Revolt in 1956, which was led by "pushing businessmen and artisans."[53] His reactions to the Soviet Union of the 1950s can only be described as embarrassing. "Secret dread? I sense none. . . if this is all a mirage, it is a perfect one. They believe it as I used to believe in the Spring Town Meeting in my village."[54] Du Bois's pronouncements can be explained as those of an old and embittered man. But there had always been a gullible streak in Du Bois, linked quite often with an attraction to strong leaders and authoritarian regimes that could mobilize their nations. For instance, after leaving Germany in 1936, he traveled on to Japan and became a blatant apologist for Japanese aggression against, and occupation of, China.[55] Even at that, Du Bois was more enamored with the Soviet Union in general than he was with its specific form of socialism as such. He did not call for the establishment of a Soviet-style economy when Kwame Nkrumah became head of state of the newly independent Ghana. Rather, he called for "Pan-African socialism"[56] and the establishment of welfare states in Africa.

Colonialism and the Final Solution

Du Bois's attitude toward Jews and Nazi Germany was unusually sensitive for his times. Although, as Lewis has observed, he was "essentially a brown skinned New England gentile," Lewis also adds, after surveying

Du Bois's record of pronouncements on the rise of Nazi Germany through to the emergence of the truth of the Holocaust, that he displayed "none of the Jewish antipathies so pervasive among such prominent contemporaries of his as Mencken, Dreiser, Lippmann, himself Jewish, and even Eleanor Roosevelt."[57] To be sure, Du Bois occasionally engaged in score keeping of the sort that complained that white Americans cared more about Nazi persecution of German Jews than they did about the oppression of black Americans in the South. Such a reaction was understandable coming from African Americans because it was, in large part, true. He also unfavorably contrasted Southern "lynch law" with the more systematic and legal approach Nazi Germany took to oppression of the Jews throughout the 1930s. On his visit to Germany in 1936, he was treated in a proper, even friendly, fashion. Du Bois was also guilty at times of "positing the moral equivalency" between Nazi Germany and the United States and Great Britain. He even once speculated, records Lewis, that "Nazi-Japanese cooperation" might well lead to, in Du Bois's words, "increased freedom and autonomy for the darker world, despite all theoretic race ideology."[58] Nevertheless, along with Langston Hughes, Du Bois was one of the few black or white public figures who "carefully followed and deeply cared about what was happening to European Jewry."[59]

While Du Bois expressed his opinions quite frequently on these matters, his thinking on the subject of racism grew less systematic as he grew older, if it ever had been. Du Bois wanted American Jews to be as concerned with the plight of African Americans as African Americans such as himself were about the plight of Jews in Germany, as concerned with "the fight for free Africa" as Negro Americans should be "to support the fight for a free Israel."[60] In this respect, he felt that the two peoples were natural political and moral allies. Like many others during and after the war, Du Bois believed that anti-Semitism and white racism shared "common origins in ethnocentric scapegoating and aggression." "[I]t springs," he wrote in 1943, "from the same cause; and what is happening to Jews may happen to us in the future."[61] Much later in his posthumously published *Autobiography*, Du Bois extracted a cautionary example for African Americans from the recent tragedy of European Jewry. This was, as we shall see, something that became increasingly common in the 1960s:

We must not make the error of the German Jews. They assumed that if the German nation received some of them as intellectual and social equals, the whole group would be safe.[62]

Finally, Du Bois underlined the link between European colonialism and Nazi oppression of Jews and other minorities. It is of special interest here, since it is a parallel that has been all but forgotten in the mainstream literature on the Holocaust. Indeed, early postwar analyses of Nazi totalitarianism, with the exception of Hannah Arendt in *Origins of Totalitarianism* (1951), comprehensively neglected such comparisons. But during and after the war, it was a quite commonplace comparison, particularly among intellectuals of the African diaspora such as Martinique's Aimé Césaire.[63] Du Bois was convinced that there was a crucial connection between what had happened to the Jews between 1933 and 1945 in Europe and what had happened to native peoples under European colonialism. His historical argument as of 1947 ran something like the following. Slavery, the slave trade, and colonialism in general had "degrade[ed] the position of labor and the respect for humanity as such" and had given rise to "the theory of 'race'. . . ."[64] This led to the "contradictions in European civilization and the illogic in modern thought" and even "the collapse of human culture."[65] Believing that the history of the modern West was the history of modern racism, Du Bois then drew the conclusion that:

> There was no Nazi atrocity—concentration camps, wholesale maiming and murder, defilement of women or ghastly blasphemy of childhood—which the Christian civilization of Europe had not long been practicing against colored folks in all parts of the world in the name of and for the defense of a Superior Race born to rule the world.[66]

Although one can quarrel with details of Du Bois's statement here, it clearly anticipates Arendt's thesis that what Europeans learned in ruling their colonies "blew back" into Europe and helped degrade the political thought, culture, and practice of Europe. Her thesis is not so much that European colonialism "caused" or led directly to the concentration camp universe, but that it helped prepare the way, psychologically and morally, for a world where "everything is possible." Du Bois's overall contribution was to make more complex the understanding of the importance of race and color in the twentieth century. By widening the field of concern from the United States to Europe and, then, to Africa and beyond, Du Bois's work suggested that the American dilemma was also a European and a global one.

In summary, where Myrdal and Cox joined in the social science consensus that rejected racially grounded explanations for group differences and supported interracial political cooperation of various sorts, Du Bois remained more committed to the group identity-confirming power of the race idea, though he never abandoned the goal of achieving equal political and legal rights and rejected any understanding of race that emphasized its biological dimension. But he also was willing to call for black political initiatives aside from the possibility of garnering white support.

Specifically, Myrdal saw the function of ideas of race and racism as ideological covers for the interests of the dominant white population rather than having any truth value of their own. White racist thinking was rational to the degree that it reinforced white caste power and interests but irrational in the universal terms set by the American Creed to which Americans allegedly gave their support. For Cox, neither the concept of race nor caste did anything to illuminate the economic and class interests underlying American race relations. To that degree, those who used race and caste as analytical tools were themselves obscuring social and economic reality and in particular, like Myrdal, neglected the possibilities of a political alliance between the white and black working class. Du Bois, on the contrary, contended that race was a rational concept insofar as it referred to a social group that shared certain experiences, beliefs, and traditions. In the case of African Americans, race was a way of reminding themselves who they were—people of African descent—and what their group interests were. Still, beyond all the differences among these three thinkers on matters of race, caste, and class, the universalist idea of racial equality was clearly a shared assumption.

2

Jean-Paul Sartre and the
Creation of the Jew

If one is attacked as a Jew, one must defend oneself as a Jew. Not as German, not as a world-citizen, not as upholder of the Rights of Man or whatever.

Hannah Arendt

To pass is to sin against authenticity, and "authenticity" is among the founding lies of the modern age.

Henry Louis Gates, Jr.

Jean-Paul Sartre (1905–1980) had a gift for identifying the crucial moral issues of his time, even if he never actually developed an ethics and even if the positions he took on some of those issues were wrongheaded. As Jews, Theodor Adorno, Max Horkheimer, and Hannah Arendt were in some sense "required" to confront the "Jewish Question"; and, as an African American, W. E. B. Du Bois felt compelled to devote his life to dealing with the "color line." Gunnar Myrdal headed up a research team to analyze America's race problem but had no experience as a victim or as a victimizer. But Sartre *chose* to engage with the Jewish question in *Réflexions sur la Question Juive* (1946), which was translated into English as *Anti-Semite and Jew* in 1948.[1] While the necessity of serious engagement with the question of anti-Semitism now seems obvious, it was by no means obvious at the time. In fact, many people in France felt that it was precisely the wrong time to raise such a contentious issue. In terms used by philosopher Thomas Nagel, the *knowledge* of what (later) came to be called the Holocaust existed, but its *acknowledgment* was highly problematic. Because Sartre chose to confront the Jewish question, he earned the deep gratitude of many French Jews at the time.[2]

49

Yet, like Adorno and Horkheimer in *Dialectic of Enlightenment* (1944, 1947), Sartre only mentioned the extermination of the Jews once, when he refers to "the gas chambers at Lublin" (p. 71), itself a mistaken reference to Maidenek. More recently, Enzo Traverso has asserted that what is "most striking" about Sartre's long essay is "his almost total silence about Auschwitz."[3] This is surely too harsh, but it does point to the silence about the entire topic that had already begun to descend in 1946. Silence, avoidance, and denial were particularly prevalent in France where, since the Dreyfus case, the political place of Jews qua Jews had rarely been publicly debated. Underpinning this evasion was the republican belief that the "facts" of race and ethnicity were politically irrelevant, indeed inimical, to the rights or responsibilities of French citizenship. The "twin pillars" of "Frenchness," Naomi Schor has written, were, and are, "universalism and assimilation."[4] Not only did French republicanism refuse to grant race and ethnicity (or religion) special legal or constitutional status, organizing French Jews politically to protect their interests was frowned upon. Nor was this a condition that French Jews had protested against with any great frequency. As Hannah Arendt noted in her analysis of the Dreyfus affair, French Jews failed to see that the issues in that case were primarily political matters: "justice, liberty and civic virtue."[5] But this is not to say that French Jews stayed out of politics. Many Jews were politically liberal, even radical—but rarely did they organize or act politically as Jews. As Pierre Vidal-Naquet has observed, most French Jews up to 1945 fit Sartre's category of the "inauthentic Jew," including Vidal-Naquet himself.[6]

Sartre was anything but an experienced player in radical political circles in the crisis-ridden 1930s. Himself the product of a distinguished, bourgeois family, and a recipient of the best education France could offer, via the lycée system and the L'École Normale Supérieure, his training had been literary and philosophical rather than political, historical, or sociological. Intellectually precocious and often very generous, there was also something of the spoiled child about him. His prewar political impulses are probably best characterized as anarchist and antibourgeois, if the latter can said to be a specific political position at all, since, historically, bourgeois baiting appealed both to segments of the fascist right and to the socialist left. But if the crass observation that someone "had a good war" was ever applicable, it was applicable to Sartre. Involved enough in the French Resistance to be significantly shaped by the experience and to earn the requisite credentials for having been so, he had also spent some time in a German POW camp. Like Arendt, he was politicized by the rise of fascism in the 1930s, the war, and the resistance; but his prewar writings reveal little concern with Jewish matters. (Needless to say, during the war publication of his views on such matters would have been extremely risky.) He published his massive philosophical treatise, *Being and Nothingness* in 1943, but was better known as a dramatist and for his novel *Nausea* (1938). He emerged from the war as one of the moral leaders on the French intellectual left and was among those who initially sought to forge a political third way between the two armed camps of the emerging Cold War. Politically, he was attracted by the tradition of worker and citizens councils; and, as we shall see, protopolitical concepts such as "choice" and "action" were central to his philosophical vision. As with Arendt, Sartre's lack of a conventional leftist background may have allowed him to acknowledge anti-Semitism as an important phenomenon in its own right rather than dismissing it as superstructural in origins and secondary in importance, as many leftists did before, during, and after the war. As we shall see, however, Sartre was certainly not averse to proposing a Marxist answer to the Jewish question, even as early as *Anti-Semite and Jew*.

In what follows, I would like to reconstruct the basic theoretical assumptions underpinning Sartre's approach to the Jewish question, offer a critique of his position, and finally look at the reception of Sartre's thinking on anti-Semitism among certain American Jewish intellectuals. As already suggested, *Anti-Semite and Jew* was enormously important in filling an intellectual and moral gap in the immediate postwar years, even if several of its major shortcomings were apparent right from the start. Generally, Sartre's analysis of, and solution to, the Jewish question well illustrated the contrary pulls of universalism and particularism in early postwar thinking on race and ethnicity. Sartre's work also raised the question of whether anti-Semitism was unique among, or similar to, other forms of ethnic and racial essentialism. In addition, like all analyses of prejudice that emphasize its subjective origins in the individual, Sartre's *Anti-Semite and Jew* had trouble explaining how prejudice at an individual level can lead to group or mass racialized essentialism, much less a state commitment to something like the Final Solution.

Intellectual Origins

Anti-Semite and Jew initiated Sartre's engagement with concrete moral and political problems. Seen in retrospect, it represented his first attempt to develop an ethics to complement, and mediate, the ontology of the self and the theory of revolutionary practice developed in *Being and Nothingness* (1943) and in the *Critique of Dialectical Reason* (1960), respectively. Included in the "applied" part of his *oeuvre* are his analysis of negritude in the 1948 essay, "Black Orpheus," along with the various articles and prefaces he wrote in response to the Third World decolonization and independence movements in the 1950s and early 1960s. He explored these concerns more systematically in *Cahiers pour une morale* (1983), which was translated into English as *Notebooks for an Ethics* in 1992.[7] Overall, Sartre was one of the few postwar thinkers on either side of the Atlantic to attempt to theorize racism and anti-Semitism separately *and* together. Perhaps because his efforts are less rigorous philosophically than his more systematic work, Sartre's interpreters still very much neglect his work on those social and political topics.

When *Anti-Semite and Jew* appeared, Sartre's Marxism was as yet underdeveloped and his knowledge of Freudian psychoanalysis was uneven. Thus, the most important source of *Anti-Semite and Jew* is *Being and Nothingness*, Sartre's re-working of the German tradition of phenomenology initiated by Edmund Husserl and its successor, *Existenzphilosophie*, as developed by Martin Heidegger and Karl Jaspers. In rough terms, the phenomenological method represents an attempt to grasp the "lived experience" (*Erlebnis*) of an individual or a group. It claims to describe rather than to judge or explain that experience, though the language of description is not necessarily offered in the terms the person or group in question would understand. It is not difficult to understand how such an approach might appeal to Sartre, the novelist and dramatist with little or no training in social or political theory. Second, a phenomenological approach is not interested in how and why someone becomes an anti-Semite; nor would it be concerned with the history of anti-Semitism. Third, the phenomenological method lends itself to the construction of rather static typologies, rather than stressing the fluidity of the past, present, or future development of individuals or groups. This characteristic stands in a certain tense relationship with Sartre's emphasis on the self as never coincident with itself, as always transcending its present situation, but always threatening to fall back into a position of fixity and security.

Specifically, Sartre was attracted by the phenomenological claim to return to, as Heidegger put it, "the things themselves" rather than to impose a theoretical framework upon reality. *Existenzphilosophie* rejects the notion that there is a fixed human nature or essence and, by extension, also refuses to see the individual self or group identity as pre-formed or permanent. The ego is worldly not transcendental; it emerges in and through experience, particularly the paradigmatic experience of being observed or objectified by the "other." Thus, freedom in Sartre's work is always at risk from the "other." In today's language, Sartre offers a constructivist rather than essentialist account of the self. In addition, Sartre was drawn to Heidegger's concepts of "inauthenticity" and "authenticity." Though Heidegger insisted that such terms were purely descriptive and had no normative significance, they do in fact take on a quasi-ethical charge in Sartre's work.[8] "Inauthenticity" refers to the individual's refusal to take responsibility for his own freedom within a specific set of social and historical circumstances, what Sartre calls a "situation." Finally, Sartre posits a dualistic model of subjectivity organized around self and the "other." In *Being and Nothingness*, Sartre's central task was to work out how the subject as freedom (*pour-soi*/being-for-itself) can maintain that freedom. The central concern of his later thought, culminating with *Critique of Dialectical Reason*, was how to move from a defensive sense of "me" or "us" as formed in reaction to the "other" in the situation of basic scarcity, to the concept of a collective "we" that can act together based on choices.

But if the self or subject is essentially free, that is, never coincident with itself, then why does it have such a difficult time choosing or asserting this freedom? For Sartre, there are two ways of answering this question. First, as mentioned, the self originates as the object of the "other's" "gaze" or scrutiny. In less abstract terms, other people (the "other") try to deny my freedom even as—and just because—they assert their own. As the famous line from his play *No Exit* says it, "Hell is other people." Although such a bleak view of interpersonal relationships obviously illuminates various forms of social, economic, racial, and ethnic domination, this view also reflects Sartre's judgment about the very nature of social interaction. The conflict with the "other" is built into reality, however defined. Thus, beneath Sartre's dialectic of self-formation, there is a stubborn Cartesian dualism: the individual ego does constant battle but never arrives at a reconciliation with the "other." The other answer to the freedom question is a more disturbing one: we find it easier to live an inauthentic existence. By handing our self over to the "other," we are relieved of the necessity to choose ourselves, including our courses of action, and thus no longer have to take responsibility for ourselves or for others.

In the early postwar years, Sartre suggested a way out of these impasses. In his essay, "Existentialism Is a Humanism" (1946), Sartre asserted his now familiar dictum that "existence precedes essence,"[9] a shorthand way of asserting that we create ourselves through our choices rather than acquiring a self with fixed traits and permanent characteristics. But in taking responsibility for ourselves, we implicitly choose this same possibility of choice for others. In choosing for himself, the individual "chooses for all men," and therefore, "I build the universal in choosing myself."[10] Finally, Sartre rejects the term "humanism" if it means "a theory which takes man as an end and a higher value." For Sartre, humans cannot be ends in themselves, since they are always "in the making." But existential humanism, a kind of subjective Kantianism, sees the subject as always in the process of transcending itself. There is "no law-maker other than himself."[11] This was as close as Sartre came to sketching in the ethical—and implicitly political—implications of his doctrine of radical freedom. Overall, it was a position that assumed what it set out to show—that in choosing ourselves and hence our freedom, we also affirm that as a possibility, and a necessity, for others.

Escape from Freedom

The most compelling part of *Anti-Semite and Jew* is Sartre's portrait of the anti-Semite, which also might be called "the portrait of the anti-humanist." "Anti-Semitism is a free and total choice of oneself" (p. 17),[12] but that choice denies freedom to the Jew. The anti-Semite is one who "hates" and considers himself "massive and impenetrable" (pp. 18–19). "He chooses," claims Sartre, "the irremediable out of fear of being free; he chooses mediocrity out of fear of being alone" (pp. 28–29). Thus, the anti-Semite refuses to believe that either he or the Jew can, or should, change. In choosing unfreedom for the Jew, the anti-Semite paradoxically chooses unfreedom for himself. By inverting what Sartre posits as the necessary relationship in "Existentialism Is a Humanism," the anti-Semite emerges as the quintessential anti-humanist. Moreover, the anti-Semite's whole existence is bound up in that choice. His distaste for Jews is independent of experience and thus hardly corrigible through education or programs of enlightenment. As Sartre sees it,

> no external factor can induce anti-Semitism in the anti-Semite. Anti-Semitism is a free and total choice of oneself, a comprehensive attitude that one adopts not only toward Jews but also toward men in general, history and society; it is at one and the same time a passion and a conception of the world (p. 17).

Put another way, anti-Semitism is not just one set of opinions among others but is a way of life, according to Sartre. Finally, the anti-Semite adopts a paranoid stance toward the world and toward others. As a worldview, anti-Semitism is a species of "Manicheaism" (p. 41), in which "history and society" are the battleground between good and evil.

Sartre's most basic but also most contentious idea about the anti-Semite follows from the above: the anti-Semite creates rather than discovers the Jew. The Jew is objectionable not because of the way he acts; rather, the way he acts is objectionable because he is a Jew. But, the anti-Semite is torn between two contradictory attitudes. Though he "finds the existence of the Jew absolutely necessary," he also "wishes, what he prepares, is the death of the Jew" (pp. 28, 49). Put another way, "the anti-Semite is in the unhappy position of having a vital need for the very enemy he wishes to destroy" (p. 28). Analogous to the relationship between slaveholder and the slave, the anti-Semite can't live with the Jew but also can't live without him.

How then should the Jew react to the obdurate anti-Semite? Here Sartre deploys the twin notions of authenticity and inauthenticity. In *Anti-Semite and Jew*, Sartre sums up authenticity as follows:

> Authenticity, it is almost needless to say, consists in having a true and lucid consciousness of the situation, in assuming the responsibilities and risks that it involves, in accepting it in pride or humiliation, sometimes in horror and hate. (p. 90)

Conversely, inauthenticity is the refusal to acknowledge one's freedom and/or to acknowledge one's situation. It is a form of self-deception not just about this or that particular matter but, analogous to anti-Semitism, about a whole way of life and about oneself.

Before analyzing the variety of Jewish reactions to anti-Semitism, Sartre takes up the mediating figure of the sympathetic non-Jewish "democrat." According to Sartre, the democrat, though firmly opposed to anti-Semitism, also manifests an inauthentic attitude toward the Jew insofar as he denies the political or moral relevance of the "fact" that someone is a Jew (or a member of any particular group or persuasion). Rather, the Jew like everyone else is a human being in general, who has certain rights by virtue of being human. (In light of Sartre's conclusion to *Anti-Semite and Jew*, the democrat is a "premature" universalist.) Unusually harsh on the democrat, perhaps because his own position skirts very closely to the democrat's position, Sartre links him with the anti-Semite in the following way:

> [T]here may not be so much difference between the anti-Semite and the democrat. The former wishes to destroy him [the Jew] as a man and leave nothing in him but the Jew, the pariah, the untouchable; the latter wishes to destroy him as a Jew and leave nothing in him but the man, the abstract and universal subject of the rights of man and the rights of the citizen. (p. 57)

Thus, the democrat denies that being a Jew has anything intrinsic to do with a Jew's existence, no more, that is, than a style of haircut or consumer preference or membership in a club. It is an accident, a contingency, a private fact in a public world.

Indeed, the only difference between the democrat and the inauthentic Jew is that the latter denies his own situation rather than someone else's. In denying himself as a Jew, he also overestimates his freedom to define himself as he pleases and thus he also denies his own "situatedness." The inauthentic Jew denies that to be Jewish means anything very particular *or* he tries to become the opposite of what the anti-Semite casts him as. More generally,

> [w]hat stamps the inauthentic Jew is precisely this perpetual oscillation between pride and a sense of inferiority, between the voluntary and passionate negation of the traits of his race and the mystic and carnal participation in the Jewish reality. (p. 107)

The inauthentic Jew thus allows himself be defined by the anti-Semite, whether the characteristics he assumes are the opposite of those imposed by the anti-Semite or he denies that Jews have any common characteristics.

But if the inauthentic Jew is controlled, even as he denies that control, the authentic Jew is free, even as he acknowledges that he is a Jew as the anti-Semite charges—but not in the way that the anti-Semite claims:

> Jewish authenticity consists in choosing oneself *as Jew*—That is, in realizing one's Jewish condition. The authentic Jew abandons the myth of the universal man; he knows himself and wills himself into history as a historic and damned creature. (p. 136)

Importantly, it is not *what* the authentic Jew becomes in choosing himself as a Jew that is crucial. Generous or stingy, ambitious or tricky, intellectual or materialistic, an intellectual or an entrepreneur, the point is that he chooses to take responsibility for himself:

> The moment he ceases to be passive, he takes away all power and virulence from anti-Semitism. . . . *[T]he authentic Jew makes himself a Jew*. . . . At one stroke the Jew, like any authentic man, escapes description. (p. 137)

Thus, through the triple movement—of choosing, making, and acting—the authentic Jew turns the tables on the anti-Semite.

Up to this point in *Anti-Semite and Jew*, Sartre had not discussed the social and political dimensions of anti-Semitism, but he concludes with those aspects of the problem. Penultimately, Sartre rejects Jewish assimilation or democratic humanism, that is, universalism, and opts instead for what he calls a "concrete liberalism." Jews, among others, have rights, not because of

> the possession of a problematical and abstract "human nature," but their active participation in the life of the society. . . . But they have these rights *as* Jews, Negroes, or Arabs—that is, as concrete persons. (p. 146)

Sartre then, however, proceeds to reverse himself. First, he suggests that if the idea of concrete rights were recognized freely by the dominant society, it might "make possible. . . that assimilation to which some would like to drive him [the Jew] by force" (p. 147). By implication, assimilation is a positive goal. More importantly, he springs a new understanding of anti-Semitism on the reader when he suggests that anti-Semitism is actually a class-linked phenomenon: "it is a mythical, bourgeois representation of the class struggle, and . . . could not exist in a classless society" where "members felt mutual bonds of solidarity" (pp. 149–50). Finally, Sartre proposes that, like the worker who works for the ultimate disappearance of classes but remains militantly class-conscious in the short run, the authentic Jew "renounces *for himself* an assimilation that is today impossible" (p. 150). Clearly, however, Sartre looks to the disappearance not only of anti-Semitism and the anti-Semite but also of Jews themselves when true socialism replaces capitalism. Sartre's solution to a quintessentially bourgeois problem is a Marxist one.

Critique

Any critique of *Anti-Semite and Jew* must acknowledge the power of Sartre's analysis, despite the fact that his "evidence" was drawn primarily from his own experience of prewar anti-Semitism in France and his own acquaintance with assimilated Jews rather than from any deep knowledge of European anti-Semitism. Although his phenomenological approach was often convincing in its identification of the structures of experience of the anti-Semite, it also was overly rigid and thus failed to encompass the varieties of anti-Semites/ism. Though rich in suggestive power, Sartre's typology easily became a stereo-typology.

On the positive side, Sartre's short work echoed several prominent themes developed by his postwar contemporaries who dealt with race and anti-Semitism in a theoretical way. For instance, Sartre's evocation of the anti-Semites' "fear of being free" (p. 27) clearly echoes Erich Fromm's "escape from freedom" thesis as central to the appeal of Nazism in particular and totalitarian movements in general. Gunnar Myrdal's central thesis in *An American Dilemma* (1944)—that America's racial dilemma is essentially a "white man's" problem—anticipates Sartre's claim that "anti-Semitism is not a Jewish problem; it is our problem" (p. 152). Theodor Adorno would later acknowledge in *The Authoritarian Personality* that Sartre's analysis of the "character" of the anti-Semite, particularly his paranoia and fragile ego, closely paralleled the results arrived at by the psychoanalytic social psychology informing that study,[13] even though Sartre rejected the psychoanalytic idea of the unconscious and explanations of adult behavior from childhood experience. With Hannah Arendt, once a student of Heidegger, whose presence looms largest in Sartre's *Being and Nothingness*, comparisons are both apposite and tricky. Both thinkers emphasize the need for Jews to develop a more active way of being in the world, a view closely linked with the general notion that freedom and action are defining features of the human condition. Most obviously, Sartre's idea of the "inauthentic Jew" closely resembles Arendt's idea of the "parvenu," the Jew who yearns to assimilate into the dominant gentile society.[14] Moreover, Sartre's insistence that the anti-Semite is all but immune to learning from experience anticipates Arendt's insistence in *Origins of Totalitarianism* (1951) that totalitarian ideologies construct their own realities and thereby resist empirical disproof. On the other hand, Arendt's shifting perspective on the nature of evil in *Eichmann in Jerusalem* (1963) emphasizes the radical split between Eichmann's private persona as a householder, good father, and devoted husband, and the monstrous effects of his actions as a Nazi bureaucrat. For Sartre, such a split between private and public personae in the anti-Semite is simply not credible. In *Anti-Semite and Jew*, Sartre responds to the question: "What if he [the anti-Semite] is like that only with regard to the Jews?" with "I reply that that is impossible" (p. 21). That said, Sartre's idea of the essential "mediocrity" of anti-Semites resembles what Arendt famously (or notoriously) referred to as "the banality of evil."

There are other issues where Sartre's analysis can be challenged, and especially his core thesis that "The Jew is one whom other men consider a Jew" (p. 69). How did Sartre arrive at what seems so patently wrong-headed a view? First, Sartre had contact mainly with assimilated Jews and the Nazi occupation of France may have created, as it were, a Jewish question in his own mind for the first time. Furthermore, wartime Nazi occupation would have further suppressed what remained of public Jewish traditions and practices. Thus, "creation" of the Jew by the anti-Semite refers to the images and stereotypes, falsehoods and half-truths foisted upon the Jews by the institutionalized anti-Semitism of the war years. Such a negative social construction might well have been internalized by some Jews and thus re-created them as stereotypically "Jewish."

Put another way, Sartre's mistaken ontology of the Jew can be traced to his own general ignorance of Judaism as a tradition of beliefs and rituals, sacred texts, and institutions. In *Anti-Semite and Jew*, Sartre rejects the idea that Jews are a biological race or that biology plays any significant role in their identity: "Thus we can neither deduce the moral from the physical nor postulate a psycho-physiological parallel" (p. 62). But Sartre also refuses to grant that French Jews actually see themselves as a religious faith or community: "The Jews who surround us today have only a ceremonial and polite contact with their religion" (p. 65). Over time, the Jewish community "has been deprived bit by bit" of both "*national*" and "*religious*" characteristics and is thus only "an abstract historical community," abstract because it has a "memory of nothing but a long martyrdom, that is, of a long passivity" (pp. 66–67). Generally, Sartre's dismissal of several thousand years of shared Jewish experience, and memory of that experience, as irrelevant to Jewish self-consciousness arises in turn from his quasi-Hegelian assumption that history belongs to those who act in and through the nation. Sartre, noted Harold Rosenberg, adopted the "nationalist sense of civic rebellions and wars."[15] No doubt, the modern age had seen a waning of Judaism as a religious position, something that was perhaps particularly pronounced in France. But Sartre's dismissal of Jewish history and tradition only confirms Ferenc Feher's judgment that "History is totally nonexistent in Sartre."[16] Still, as Robert Bernasconi reminds us, Sartre's formulation was, at the time, a powerful riposte to the common assumption that the Jewish "character" (or tradition) was the source of the problem and that "the Jewish problem" was something that Jews themselves rather than gentiles had to solve.[17]

A different sense in which Sartre's construction thesis has a certain plausibility is reflected in Arendt's lines prefacing this chapter: "If one is attacked as a Jew, one must defend oneself as a Jew."[18] Being "called out" as a Jew suddenly creates, as it were, one's Jewishness. Once this happens, that identity neither can, nor should be, denied to others or to oneself. In fact, Arendt's assertion—and her own life between the late 1920s and the late 1930s—clearly exemplified what it meant to be an "authentic Jew," her term for which was "conscious pariah." Yet, Arendt explicitly rejected Sartre's formulation in a 1968 statement:

> This, incidentally, is not to say that Jewish self-consciousness was ever a creation of anti-Semitism. . . a myth that has become somewhat fashionable in intellectual circles after Sartre's "existentialist" interpretation of *the* Jew as someone who is regarded and defined as a Jew by others.[19]

Overall, however brave Sartre's publication of *Anti-Semite and Jew* was, it was severely limited in its validity.[20]

Furthermore, if the Jew is a creation of the anti-Semite, it is also difficult to understand Sartre's argument about (in)authenticity. Just what is it that Sartre's authentic Jew chooses except marginal status and solidarity with other Jews, a sense of "us" as reactive not initiatory? How does the authentic Jew escape affirming the specific traits that the anti-Semite attributes to the Jew? Should he care, since no creed, ideology or institutional allegiance seems to be at stake? Indeed, Harold Rosenberg suggested at the time that if we, contra Sartre, attribute to Jews an identity and a history, "it is possible for him to be any kind of man. . . and still be a Jew. The Jew exists but there are no Jewish traits."[21] More complexly, Feher suggests that the postwar fate of the Jew (or "Jews" if we speak from a historical/sociological rather than phenomenological perspective) was not a matter of being swallowed up by *or* remaining completely separate from the dominant society. Rather, writes Feher, after 1945 there were at least four options available: (1) a "rational and contractual assimilation" in which Jews enter into a reciprocal agreement with the dominant society to learn the majority language and the like but do not necessarily give up all their cultural/ethnic characteristics; (2) "Zionist emigration" involving the establishment of a national homeland in Palestine; (3) "ethnic separation within a confederative system," that is, enclave multiculturalism; or (4) the stance of the "dissimilant" or "cosmopolitan intellectual."[22] When placed next to such a complex analysis of the historical situation of the Jews, Sartre's analysis seems a bit glib.

Still, one could salvage something of Sartre's central thesis by suggesting that it best fits the "cosmopolitan intellectual" category, what Isaac Deutscher called the "non-Jewish Jew," Rosenberg the "abstract intellectual," and Arendt the "conscious pariah." The authentic Jew was, as Rosenberg noted, a Jewish version of Sartre himself. Secular, post-Holocaust Jewish intellectuals, men and women of heightened historical awareness, found themselves choosing (or having chosen) to be Jews for reasons of moral solidarity rather than religious commitment. There was no content to their Jewishness or to their Judaism, except the personal memory of having once belonged to a Jewish community or having recovered the memory of their forbears in Eastern Europe and Russia.

Other aspects of *Anti-Semite and Jew* need closer examination. For instance, Sartre claims that the anti-Semite is attracted to, and indeed is, a "mediocrity." But he later quotes from the work of Louis-Ferdinand Celine, an anti-Semite and a moral monster, but also a genius. (One might also make the same point about Ezra Pound or Richard Wagner, men of genius who were also anti-Semites.) Sartre's untenable claim must have arisen from wishful thinking, but it was made considerably easier by his model of the subject, which has no place for anything like the Freudian unconscious or for unconscious defense mechanisms. Without them, Sartre has no way to account for how an individual might compartmentalize parts of his psyche and thus render them inaccessible to one another. Rather, for Sartre, all thought and behavior derive from conscious choice. Mediocre or hateful thoughts and actions can only emerge from mediocre or hateful people. In refusing to allow the individual to "escape" responsibility for his/her unconscious choices, Sartre impoverishes his own account of human thought and behavior.[23]

Another striking claim by Sartre—that the anti-Semite wants the "death" of Jews—also presents a problem. The problem is not a matter of empirical evidence, since Sartre knew about the massive extermination of much of European Jewry. It is rather, as we have seen, that much of Sartre's discussion also stresses the anti-Semite's need for the presence of the Jews. But we know that the Nazis gradually but decisively ceased wanting recognition or labor from the Jews; they simply wanted to expunge them from the earth. Jews had become, in Arendt's terms, "superfluous." Or, if we historicize Sartre's claim that the anti-Semite wants the death of the Jew, there is little evidence to support the claim that anti-Semitism anywhere in Europe was *primarily* exterminatory—as opposed to discriminatory or exclusionary—in its intention.[24] If this is the case, then what prevents the anti-Semite from carrying through on his wish for the death of the Jew, except his own desire to keep the Jew around to have someone to oppress? Finally, all this is a way of questioning whether Sartre's analysis of the mentality of the anti-Semite helps us understand how mass extermination happened.

Although Sartre implicitly understood the secular nature of the new anti-Semitism, also one of Arendt's major points, his phenomenological approach made it almost impossible to identify the institutional/industrial prerequisites for mass extermination that far transcended the causes or effects of traditional social anti-Semitism or even the periodic group violence of the pogrom. Anti-Semitism as a worldview, Sartre's prime interest, was not a sufficient condition for understanding or explaining the Holocaust.

Regarding the tension between universalism and particularism in Sartre's thought, two issues need discussion. As mentioned, Sartre attacks the democrat for his knee-jerk, *bien-pensant* universalism, which assumes that racial and ethnic identities are hindrances to full personal development and to the achievement of a society of equals. Yet what is wrong for the democrat is quite acceptable for the socialist. In the final analysis, Sartre himself seems to consider the dissolution of ethnic and racial identities as desirable for full human development under socialism. For Sartre, anti-Semitism is a bourgeois rather than a working class phenomenon, and thus a product of capitalism. By definition, the abolition of capitalism will mean the disappearance of all sorts of differences, beginning with class consciousness and including ethnic, racial, and religious consciousness.

Ultimately, a deep hostility to difference lurks somewhere in Sartre's political unconscious.[25] The claim that the disappearance of capitalism entails the disappearance of prejudice is true by definition but untrue historically. That is, if anti-Semitism does not disappear under socialist circumstances, it means that those circumstances are not authentically socialist—yet. Aside from its other problems, this ahistorical view assumes that historical memory can be abolished at will. Furthermore, while for liberalism natural rights represent the universal in human history, for

Marxism, the working class is *both* a particular historical formation with a specific historical identity *and* the carrier of the universal within history. In rejecting bourgeois assumptions, Sartre also denies that there is a definite human nature or that individual identity can be fixed. But in rejecting these things, Sartre also rejects the view that there can be "rights of man" or "inalienable rights." Yet, Sartre sneaks universalism in the back door after having kicked it out the front door, which is to say, he rejects a bourgeois democratic universalism but envisions a socialist universalism.[26]

Nor is it clear whether Sartre's phenomenology of anti-Semitism is applicable to all types of prejudice. Is the anti-Semite a particular example of a universal type of prejudiced person, at least in the West? Sartre's emphasis upon the unstable nature of identity would seem to suggest that there are many kinds of racisms and anti-Semitisms, and several different origins of prejudice as a total worldview, making generalizations across cultural divides extremely risky. Yet, he also writes as though the preconditions for creating the Jew as evil are constants, even universal. The anti-Semite, says Sartre, "is a man who is afraid" of almost everything "except the Jews." And "the Jew only serves him as a pretext; elsewhere his counterpart will make use of the Negro or the man of yellow skin." Anti-Semitism, in short, "is a fear of the human condition" (p. 54). Certainly the implication is that whoever suffers from the fear of freedom will likely "create a Jew" of some sort or another.[27]

Postwar American Intellectuals and Judaism

Sartre's *Anti-Semite and Jew* had considerable trans-Atlantic impact on the predominantly Jewish, postwar New York intellectual elite. An early excerpt from what became *Anti-Semite and Jew* was published in *Partisan Review* in 1946, while most of the rest of the book was published in three installments in the American Jewish Committee's house organ, *Commentary*, in 1948. This is not to say that the New York intellectuals were uncritical admirers of Sartre's analysis. But the fact that several of them tried to formulate a critique of it indicates its considerable impact. Perhaps the most intellectually acute of those responses came from Harold Rosenberg, whose essay "Does the Jew Exist?" was published in *Commentary* in January 1949 and from which I have already cited several points. Significantly, Rosenberg identified most of the serious problems with Sartre's essay, but also prefaced his critique with praise for Sartre's piece as "an act of generosity, feeling, courage and good sense" in a postwar France that shied away from discussing the topic of anti-Semitism.[28] Philosopher Sidney Hook also weighed in with a long review of *Anti-Semite and Jew* in *Partisan Review* later that same year. While criticizing its "vulgar and sentimental kind of orthodox Marxism," and noting the essentializing tendency of Sartre's analysis, Hook also praised it as a "brilliant psychoanalysis of the marginal Jew and the fanatical anti-Semite."[29] Readers who know the work of Rosenberg and Hook will recognize that this was high praise indeed coming from them.

Along with these direct responses to Sartre's text, interest among Jewish intellectuals in their Jewish roots grew apace in post-1945 America. Irving Howe later referred to this sea change in attitude as a departure from "the sterilities of their earlier 'internationalist' position'" as political radicals, usually of the Trotskyist persuasion, in the 1930s. In his memoirs, Howe joined Hook in characterizing Sartre's cast of character types as "bloodless, timeless essences," but also approved the French thinker's efforts to move the "entire discussion [of anti-Semitism] to a theoretical level." Howe also identified Rosenberg's 1949 essay on Sartre as "a turning point" in his (Howe's) re-assessment of his own Jewishness.[30] It was less Sartre's analysis than Rosenberg's identification of its weaknesses—that, especially, Sartre "has cut the Jews off from their past"[31]—that Howe remembered as crucial in transforming his own thinking. He was later instrumental in focusing critical attention on the vanishing Yiddish culture of Eastern Europe, particularly in raising I. B. Singer's fiction to general literary prominence, and also wrote a history of the American Jewish experience, *World of Our Fathers*.[32]

One other figure among the New York intellectuals illustrates the point about the postwar emergence of Jewish self-consciousness among New York intellectuals. In his *On Native Grounds* (1942), Alfred Kazin mentioned only one American writer, Ludwig Lewisohn, for whom Jewishness was an important literary "fact." Yet Kazin's next book, *Walker in the City* (1951), is a memoir of growing up in Brownsville of Russian Jewish parents. It traces with passion, and no little pain, the process of breaking with, but then retrieving in memory, his own Russian Jewish roots. In Kazin's later memoirs, *Starting Out in the Thirties* (1965) and *New York Jew* (1978), the Jewish dimension of his intellectual and personal trajectory is, if not quite so central, still crucial. I know of no evidence that Kazin was influenced by Sartre's essay, but his re-discovery of his Jewish roots in the postwar world reveals the climate within which Sartre's essay had considerable impact.

If Rosenberg, Hook, Howe, and Kazin illuminate the ways Sartre's text directly influenced, indirectly stimulated, or ran parallel to contemporary developments in the Jewish self-consciousness of certain American intellectuals, another, less visible New York intellectual, Anatole Broyard (1920–1990), wrote a fascinating—and neglected—piece in 1950 that mapped Sartre's analysis of the situation of the Jew onto that of African Americans.[33] Broyard spent the bulk of his *Commentary* essay, "Portrait of the Inauthentic Negro," identifying types of black inauthenticity, including "minstrelization" (roughly Uncle Tom-ing) and "romanticization" (acting out positive white fantasies of exoticism and eroticism), the acceptance of white stereotypes (as in the "bad nigger"), the cultivation of an image of brutishness and its opposite, the cultivation of a kind of effeminate prissiness. In some ways, Broyard's essay now reads like a preemptive strike against the notion of the "White Negro" that Mailer proposed in the 1957 essay of the same name. There Mailer imagines a type of white man, the hipster, who imitates blacks, who themselves are thought to be sexually freer and existentially closer to the "edge" than middle-class whites. In Broyard's terms, however, Mailer's hipster is doubly inauthentic —he is a white man imitating a black man, who is himself imitating the white man's stereotype of a black man.

As it happened, Broyard had already published a short piece, "A Portrait of the Hipster," in *Partisan Review* in 1948. There he describes the hipster in terms quite different from Mailer's later effort. He stresses not the hipster's proximity to the sources of rage and violence, but his detachment through language and the wish to "abstract himself in action" by means of "tea," that is, marijuana.[34] Broyard also suggests an interesting, if schematic, framework for tracing the development from blues to jazz to bebop along with the evolution of hipsterdom. As "the hipster's seven types of ambiguity," bebop, asserts Broyard, "seemed to consist, to a great extent, in evading tension."[35] But it is striking that Broyard never mentions, much less explores, race in this essay, though the world of black music and style is, of course, everywhere implied. Then, *after* the "Inauthentic Negro" piece, Broyard had another go at tracking the evolution of a black style from the "get hot" mode of the swing era through the transition phase of bebop in which the Negro is "lost between two cultures" to the dead end of "cool." While alcohol fueled the expressiveness of hot jazz, and "tea" (marijuana) was the drug of choice in the bebop era, it was heroin, says Broyard, that dominates the cool period: "the cool Negro suggests the stunned Negro of slavery. The irony is that coolness is self-enslavement."[36] In general, Broyard's point was that the growing self-consciousness of African American "hip" culture involved a progressive involution and detachment from the self or the larger society. Though fascinating in some of its parts, his analysis proved to be strikingly wrong about the changes in consciousness among black Americans, hip or not, by the mid-1960s, and the impact of black culture on the larger white culture.

But the "Portrait of the Inauthentic Negro" was a quite different matter. Broyard's comparison of Sartre's inauthentic Jew with the inauthentic Negro is always interesting and sometimes compelling. Broyard makes clear that the inauthentic black (or inauthentic Jew) may either totally deny the traits associated with his own group or he may display them in exaggerated form. The crucial thing is that real or imagined white/gentile attitudes create the situation to which the inauthentic Negro/Jew must react. But Broyard seems to misunderstand Sartre's notion of authenticity when he defines it as a "stubborn adherence to one's essential self" (p. 57), since Sartre explicitly rejects the idea of an essential self in his ontology. Still, Broyard's misreading of Sartre does point to a problem with Sartre's own position, since, as we have seen, it is difficult to see what the notion of authenticity might mean if there is no essential self, to which one tries to conform his/her values and actions.[37] For Sartre, authenticity is a matter of choosing one's freedom rather than adherence to one's essential self.

Broyard also elaborates on Sartre's essay on two other points. First, he suggests that because the Negro is usually unable to "conceal his identity," he must develop a wider range of strategies of accommodation and resistance than the Jew. Second, Broyard also emphasizes that, in contrast with Jews, Negroes lack cultural traditions or resources to fall back on: "Unlike the authentic Jew, he has no cultural residue to which he can secretly return, or by which he can at least negatively orient himself" (p. 63). This claim is doubly difficult to deal with. First, Broyard misreads Sartre's own analysis of the Jew, since Sartre sees the Jew, as already discussed, as a figure without identity or history. Second, the view of black American culture as nonexistent or derivative was to be challenged increasingly by the early to mid-1960s. In the early postwar context, Broyard's assertion that the great need of Negro Americans lay in developing a "group identity" beyond the "only common bond" of "*not being* anything else" (p. 63) fitted quite clearly into the tradition of Gunnar Myrdal, Richard Wright, and E. Franklin Frazier that characterized Negro American culture as inadequate to the tasks facing black Americans. This view was later challenged by Ralph Ellison, Albert Murray, and Harold Cruse, who were vocal in their rejection of this "damage" view of black life. Still, Broyard did stress the importance of the development of group consciousness among Negro Americans. Finally, however, Broyard's analysis suggests that Sartre's thesis about the constructed nature of the Jew might more plausibly be applied to the construction of the Negro. As Lewis Gordon has observed, it is "blatantly false" that the anti-Semite creates the Jew, but "it is not clear that blacks existed before anti-black racism."[38]

There is a final twist on how we should interpret Broyard's essays—and his own life. Once we learn from Henry Louis Gates Jr.'s essay of the mid-1990s that Broyard was himself of mixed blood and thus "black," a fact known to some of his friends but not revealed in his article or in his memoirs, (in)authenticity must be seen not only as the theme of these early postwar pieces, but also of his life.[39] When we learn that Broyard only began his life as a white man upon returning from military service, it becomes hard to (re-)read his work without a distinct uneasiness. In his memoir, *When Kafka Was the Rage,* he briefly describes his role as captain of a stevedore battalion engaged in cleaning up dockside areas in Yokohama just after the end of World War II. But he never even hints that it was a black unit. By moving from Brooklyn to Greenwich Village where he opened a bookstore just after the war, he made his break with the black world of his parents and "became" white. This move itself echoed, though with distorted reverberations, Kazin's move from his provincial Jewish Brooklyn roots to cosmopolitan Manhattan as a fundamental break with the past and as an attempt at re- or self-invention.

To return to his "Inauthentic Negro," Broyard opens by telling of seeing a black entertainer grotesquely represent the sufferings endured under racial oppression to his audience. He describes the entertainer's performance as a parodic version of that experience, an elaborate con game establishing complicity with his audience.

It wasn't a song about discrimination as I had so naively supposed—its actual theme was the *double entendre* between singer and audience, a kind of cultish collusion by which both denied the words. (p. 56)

But once we know what we know, Broyard's essay must be read as a duplication of the entertainer's bad faith. Both engage in a form of racial camping, of putting everything in inverted commas, of revealing and concealing at the same time. To whom is Broyard speaking and for whom?

To what extent was his essay a self-critique for the benefit of those who knew his own racial biography? How are we to understand his critique of Negro American culture and what difference does it make that the article appeared in *Commentary* rather than in a black-oriented journal such as *Freedomways?*

Finally, a fictional character named Coleman Silk turns up in Philip Roth's novel, *The Human Stain* (2000). Silk, a classics professor at a small New England college, is a black man who has been passing for white (and Jewish); but he is fired from his position for politically incorrect speech that insults two black students. Interestingly, a few pages into "A Portrait of the Inauthentic Negro," Broyard refers to the fact that black skin "strikes terror into every heart" and he adds, "This stain doggedly endures." Yet Broyard seems to reverse himself when he says "answering it [the problem of blackness] is so easy as to seem absurd," since thousands of Negroes "are accepted as whites merely because of light complexion." (p. 58). His racial "identity," that is, his refusal of a black identity and his becoming white, are hinted at by the words that conclude his posthumous memoirs: "There's a sociology concealed in the book, just as a body is concealed in its clothes."[40]

Though Broyard, both as an individual and as an analyst, presents a fascinating example of the uses to which *Anti-Semite and Jew* was put among American intellectuals, Sartre's short text would exert its most important influence not among Western Jewry or on the postwar academic study of racial prejudice, but among Third World, Francophone intellectuals. Sartre's basic thesis—that the anti-Semite creates the Jew—was accepted by thinkers such as Frantz Fanon and the Tunisian Jewish novelist and social thinker, Albert Memmi, and rephrased to claim that the colonizer creates the colonized. Once the idea that the self is constructed by the (hostile) "other" is accepted, the biological and cultural essentialism of the colonial powers in the Third World could hardly stand up to scrutiny. If the colonized was a construct, s/he could be de- and re-constructed. Thus, there was also a radical political position lurking in Sartre's phenomenological account of the origins of the subject and its relationship to the "other."

Despite its considerable influence in shaping early postwar conceptions of anti-Semitism, particularly in intellectual circles, Sartre's essay has not worn well as an analysis of French and/or European anti-Semitism or as a key to understanding the Holocaust, and certainly not as a description of what it means to be a Jew. That said, Sartre did attempt the imaginative leap into the mind of the anti-Semite so as to understand the worldview held by the self saturated by anti-Semitic prejudice. In addition, Sartre's was one of the first critiques from the left of what he called democratic, but we would call "liberal," universalism, even if he himself fell back into the position at the end of his piece. The problem with universalism, from Sartre's perspective, was not its refusal of freedom but the way that historical and social situatedness, specific forms of human belonging, were ignored in understanding what it meant to be human. Thus, we might say that the anti-Semite denies the humanity of the Jew and of himself, while the universalist fails to see that to be human one must be somewhere and something as well.

What follows in the next chapter—a psychoanalytically informed description of anti-Semitism and authoritarianism in general—represents an attempt to capture what is essential to the character structure of the person who is obsessed by power and the dialectic of power between self and "other," but expressed in another idiom than Sartre's.

3

The Europeanization of American Prejudice: Adorno and Horkheimer

Because they invented the concept of kosher meat, they are persecuted as swine.

Theodor Adorno and Max Horkheimer

In their effort to rescue the classical Enlightenment from the naiveté determined by its epoch and develop it further dialectically, the authors [of The Dialectic of Enlightenment*] let themselves be carried away and made horrendous claims that, taken literally, could serve as an alibi for the worst kind of obscurantism.*

Jean Amery

For Theodor W. Adorno and Max Horkheimer, anti-Semitism, a specific example of "[t]he anger against all that is different," was clearly the product of modernity.[1] The degree to which the hostility to difference was a uniquely German phenomenon, marking out an intellectual-cultural *Sonderweg*, was, however, an issue about which members of the Frankfurt Institute for Social Research were much less clear. But they tended to agree with Franz Neumann that "the German people are the least anti-Semitic of all." Indeed, according to Martin Jay, Neumann felt that German anti-Semitism was "imposed from above and lacked popular support."[2] Even though, beginning with the founding of the Reich, German Jewish organizations often joined with liberal and socialist allies to work against anti-Semitic political movements, hardly anyone, Gentile or Jew, assimilationist or Zionist, was prepared for what happened when the Nazis took over.[3] Still, it would be a mistake to see German anti-Semitism as a phenomenon that was only peddled by political demagogues, *lumpen*

70

intellectuals, and sour aristocrats. Rather, it pervaded the highest levels of cultural and intellectual life in Germany. As Albert Lindemann has suggested, a crucial function of anti-Semitism was as an *Integrationsideologie* (ideology of integration) to create a factitious unity in a rapidly splintering, modernizing society and this desire for "wholeness" affected mandarins and masses alike.[4]

In what follows I want to trace the Frankfurt School efforts to come to grips with anti-Semitism in the 1930s and early 1940s. Then, I will analyze the similarities and differences between the two major efforts to do so emanating from the Frankfurt School—"Elements of Anti-Semitism" in *Dialectic of Enlightenment* (1944, 1947) and Theodor Adorno's contribution to *The Authoritarian Personality* (1950). Overall I will be concerned with assessing the strengths and weaknesses of a culturally and socially attuned psychoanalytic approach to prejudice, particularly its effort to formulate a general theory of prejudice and its failure to be sufficiently sensitive to the aspects of both the American and the Enlightenment traditions that opposed, rather than fed, modern racism and anti-Semitism. The *Authoritarian Personality* was perhaps the most sophisticated psychoanalytic interpretation of prejudice and the sources of authoritarianism; yet it was also the beginning of the end of that tradition.

The Frankfurt School: From Germany to the United States

The members of the Frankfurt School for Social Research were almost all Jewish, but, with the exceptions of Erich Fromm and Walter Benjamin, they betrayed little or no interest in religious matters and came late to any serious engagement with anti-Semitism. Two contradictory reactions marked their reactions to the recrudescence of anti-Semitism in the 1930s. As already mentioned, like most German Jewish intellectuals, they initially found it hard to believe that anti-Semitism could become the driving force in German politics or society. This view derived in part from the generational psychology that identified becoming modern with abandoning mainstream Jewishness and/or the secular liberalism of their parents: what did anti-Semitism have to do with them? In the 1930s, Adorno dropped his Jewish father's name Wiesengrund because there were too many Jewish–sounding names among the Frankfurt School members already.[5] Overall, drawing attention to their Jewishness initially seemed unimportant and, then, gradually it seemed dangerous.

As Rolf Wiggershaus has observed of the Frankfurt School members circa 1933,

> none were [sic] politically active. . . . For all of them the awareness of the problem of anti-Semitism seemed to have lost its relevance in view of their intellectual activities, which were directed against capitalism.[6]

Since the primary concern of the Frankfurt School was with developing a critical theory of society and culture under monopoly capitalism, the Marxist attitude toward anti-Semitism is important to understand. Overall, the great blind spot in Marxism, beginning with Marx himself, was its failure to acknowledge the causal force of racial, ethnic, religious, and national consciousness. Moreover, liberal notions of equality, rights, and citizenship were dismissed as "bourgeois" concerns, at best strategically necessary but rarely considered as important in their own right. Thus, it was difficult to mount a theoretical defense of those civil and political rights that Jews already possessed. Even to social democrats, social and economic issues were of prime importance. It was members of the working class, not the Jews or other minorities, who were most in need of attention.[7] In sum, the Frankfurt School thinkers assumed that monopoly capitalism was the most important force shaping the modern world. The rest was relatively secondary in importance.

Indeed, for many Marxists, liberalism, totalitarianism, and anti-Semitism were somehow linked by their common origins in capitalism. Max Horkheimer began "The Jews of Europe" (1939), the first Institute piece explicitly concerned with the fate of the Jews, as follows:

> The new anti-Semitism is the emissary of the totalitarian order, which has developed from the liberal one. One must go back to consider the tendencies within capitalism.[8]

There are several theoretical slippages in this passage, but the easy move from liberalism to totalitarianism is the most glaring one, a textbook example of the *post hoc, ergo propter hoc* fallacy. Typically, however, the Frankfurt critical theorists would double back to quietly recognize the *historical* differences among these ideologies, especially the commitment of liberalism to individuality and autonomy. Just as crucial in the passage is the link that Horkheimer establishes between capitalism and fascism: "But whoever is not willing to talk about capitalism should also keep quiet about fascism. . . . Fascism is that truth of modern society which has been realized by the theory from the beginning."[9] Less apparent, but nevertheless also implied, is the view that liberalism is somehow complicit with anti-Semitism, since it masks the class contradictions of existing society, thus allowing anti-Semitism to isolate and then persecute the Jews.[10] But, once Adorno and Horkheimer began considering anti-Semitism in *The Dialectic of Enlightenment*, they tended to emphasize not its economic function or the way in which it masked class conflict, but how it might be understood anthropologically and psychologically.[11] Monopoly capitalism was of such self-evident causal importance that it, ironically, contributed little to their analysis of anti-Semitism. Martin Jay's verdict on these matters is essentially correct: "[I]t would . . . be an error to argue that these economic analyses were really integrated into the heart of Critical Theory."[12]

Besides Adorno and Horkheimer, three other members of the Frankfurt School addressed the relationship between anti-Semitism and Nazi totalitarianism. Herbert Marcuse's *Reason and Revolution* (1941) sought to rescue Hegel from the Nazis and *völkisch* (racial populist) nationalists; indeed, his book was a riposte to Karl Popper's attack on Hegel in *The Open Society* (1945) before the fact. Although he hardly spoke directly of anti-Semitism, Marcuse did sharply distinguish the Hegelian *Rechtsstaat* (the state under the rule of law) from the National Socialist emphasis upon the *Volkheit* (the people's community) and the Party. "This community," he writes, "is neither the union of free individuals, nor the rational whole of the Hegelian state, but the 'natural' entity of race." But Marcuse did emphasize the way that Nazi racial ideology "divert[ed] attention from the social and economic basis of totalitarianism," an analysis that echoes Horkheimer's even less fortunate formulation in his "The Jews and Europe": "The pogroms are aimed politically more at the spectators than the Jews."[13] While Marcuse's defense of Hegel and the tradition of German philosophy was convincing as far as it went, his analysis also illustrated the standard Frankfurt position that anti-Semitism was best understood as a relatively conscious, instrumental construct intended to obscure real intentions. Such an instrumental view of anti-Semitism made it easy to move from effects to intentions, to assume that if anti-Semitism diverted attention from class conflict, then such was the conscious—and only—intention behind its deployment.

Erich Fromm's link with the Frankfurt School was severed in 1939; nevertheless, his *Escape from Freedom* (1941) belongs to the early intellectual history of the Institute of Social Research. In fact, in *The*

Authoritarian Personality, Adorno referred quite respectfully to Fromm's work despite his earlier break with the Frankfurt group. Surprisingly, in light of Fromm's personal links with Judaism, his analysis in *Escape from Freedom* (1941) of the appeal of National Socialism to the "authoritarian character," a figure marked by the "simultaneous presence of sadistic and masochistic drives" and the "need for a symbolic relationship that overcomes this aloneness," paid little attention to anti-Semitism as such. Like Marcuse and Franz Neumann, Fromm viewed "racial and political minorities" as "objects of sadism upon which the masses are fed," thus implying the manipulation/scapegoat theory of mass anti-Semitism. Indeed, when Fromm identifies the objects of this politicized sadism, he lists, without rank ordering, Jews, communists, and the French. Thus, Jews appear as only one of several enemies, each of whom the Nazis seem to regard in much the same way.[14]

Much of the failure to grasp the unique role of anti-Semitism in Nazi ideology derived from the fact that the works just mentioned, as well as Franz Neumann's *Behemoth* (1942, 1944), were completed before the Nazi extermination policy had been set in motion. Of all of these analyses, Neumann's was the most ambivalent regarding the centrality of anti-Semitism to the Nazi ideology. On the one hand, Neumann intended his large study to be an economic analysis of National Socialism, an ideology that represented a return to "imperialist expansion" in which "industry and party have identical aims." Neumann not only rejects the analysis of National Socialism as a form of "state capitalism," he also declines the view of Emil Lederer—one which anticipated Hannah Arendt's in *Origins of Totalitarianism*—that German society is now "composed of a ruling party and the amorphous masses," that is, that Germany had become a classless society marked by spontaneous racism and "leadership adoration." Rather, according to Neumann, by destroying all autonomous institutions and by adopting the "ideology of the community and the leadership principle," National Socialism "has not eliminated class relations; on the contrary, it has deepened and solidified the antagonisms." Finally, Neumann accepts an instrumentalist understanding of anti-Semitism by identifying the "so-called non-rational concepts, blood, community, folk" as "devices for hiding the real constellation of power and for manipulating the masses."[15] The contrast that Neumann draws between "so-called" and "real" tells the whole story.

Yet as part of this impressive, if orthodox, Marxian analysis, Neumann took the anti-Semitic ideology very seriously. In the chapter titled "The

Racial People, The Source of Charisma," Neumann comes close to undermining the instrumentalist theory of anti-Semitism when he claims that it is "not merely . . . a device for persecution" but also "a genuine philosophy of life pervading the whole National Socialist outlook." More presciently, he suggests that "[a]nti-Semitism in present-day Germany is more than a mere device to be discarded when it has fulfilled its aims" and "National Socialism is the first anti-Semitic movement to advocate the complete destruction of Jews" in the name of "blood purification."[16] At the end of the chapter, he writes that the racial ideology functions as a "substitute for the class struggle" and a way of justifying "eastern expansion," and that it represents a "rejection of Christianity." Yet he also insists that because anti-Semitism functions as a substitute for the class struggle, the Nazis would "never allow a complete extermination."[17] Neumann's was a kind of prophecy by denial. Overall, his last point became a way of differentiating among the early analyses of Nazi anti-Semitism. The Marxist view, though not it alone, was that anti-Semitism entailed a conscious policy of scapegoating that diverted attention from social and economic exploitation and provided compensation to non-Jews who were also exploited. In this view, the Nazis were fundamentally cynics but with something approaching rational political goals. On the other hand, Neumann's sometime emphasis on the principled nature of Nazi anti-Semitism, signaled by his mention of extermination, suggested that something far more ominous than cynical self-interest might be at issue.

Studies in Prejudice, 1941–1950: The Origins

The Institute's most important, and best-known, work on anti-Semitism was pursued by Horkheimer, its director and keeper of the purse, and Adorno. Adorno had arrived in America in 1938 after several years at Oxford, punctuated by travel back and forth to Germany. For him, the work on anti-Semitism represented a sea change in the central concerns of the Institute: "Everything that we used to see from the point of view of the proletariat has been concentrated with frightful force upon the Jews."[18] In the meantime, Horkheimer obtained financial support from the American Jewish Committee to sponsor a study of prejudice that was to begin in 1941. What became *The Dialectic of Enlightenment* was printed privately in 1944 as *Philosophical Fragments*. Stimulated particularly by the late Walter Benjamin's thoughts on the relationship of culture and barbarism, its concluding forty-page chapter, "Elements of Anti-Semitism: The Limits of Enlightenment," was largely Adorno's work, although Horkheimer added a seventh section to the 1947 edition. Because *Dialectic of Enlightenment* did not appear in English until 1972, it is tempting to omit it in the discussion of the Frankfurt School's developing analysis of anti-Semitism.[19] Yet, *The Dialectic of Enlightenment* was a critique of *The Authoritarian Personality* before the fact; the latter work had been identified by project director Horkheimer as part of a pedagogic effort to dispel the effects of prejudice, a thoroughly Enlightenment-inspired aspiration.[20] "Elements of Anti-Semitism" provides a bridge between the theoretical and empirical dimensions of the Frankfurt School's work and between the European and American orientations toward anti-Semitism and prejudice.

Work began on what became *The Authoritarian Personality*, a book that Adorno co-authored and Horkheimer "produced," in 1943. The grant from the American Jewish Committee was renewed in 1944, with most of the questionnaire data gathered between January 1945 and June 1946. *The Authoritarian Personality* can thus be seen as an effort to flesh out the armchair theorizing of "Elements of Anti-Semitism" with empirical evidence. As Martin Jay notes, "Elements of Anti-Semitism" was concerned much more than *The Authoritarian Personality* with establishing the "objective" as opposed to the "subjective" determinants of anti-Semitism and of fascism generally.[21] Moreover, while *The Dialectic of Enlightenment* focused on anti-Semitism in one culture (Germany), *The Authoritarian Personality* sought to develop a single measure of prejudice in keeping with its Enlightenment, universalizing tendencies.[22]

Overall, *The Dialectic of Enlightenment* and *The Authoritarian Personality* vacillate between two views of anti-Semitism. In one view, anti-Semitism is essentially a process of scapegoating and projection onto Jews of unmanageable impulses harbored by the prejudiced person or group. The other view is that historically Jews have developed certain distinctive traits and beliefs that elicit opposition and persecution.[23] The *Dialectic of Enlightenment* focuses on the deep structures and tendencies of German and Western anti-Semitism that are linked fairly closely with traditional Jewish stereotypes, yet even in *Dialectic of Enlightenment*, Adorno and Horkheimer speak of "the victims" (of prejudice) as "interchangeable according to circumstances" (p. 171)[24] and identify "[t]he anger against all that is different" (p. 207) as the source of prejudice, irrespective of whether those who are different are Jews or Blacks or Asians. As the title indicates, *The Authoritarian Personality* regards prejudice as the projection of ambivalent impulses about authority onto the object of prejudice and constructs a generalized model of the "authoritarian personality" without really discussing the differences among types of prejudice. Thus, it tends toward the projection theory, while *Dialectic of Enlightenment* emphasizes the "Jewishness" of Jews and the way that it attracts anti-Semitic aggression.

There is an ambiguity to the term "enlightenment" itself in *The Dialectic of Enlightenment*. At times, it seems to refer to a trans-historical impulse that can be traced back to the very beginning of human attempts to comprehend the world. In this respect, enlightenment impulses clearly antedate modernity. As the authors state at the start: "myth is already enlightenment; and enlightenment reverts to mythology" (p. xvi). Yet they more often refer to "the Enlightenment" as the specific intellectual and cultural movement of the eighteenth century: as, for instance: "The program of the Enlightenment was the disenchantment of the world; the dissolution of myths and the substitution of knowledge for fancy" (p. 3). Or later:

> Ultimately, the Enlightenment consumed not just the symbols, but their successors, universal concepts, and spared no remnant of metaphysics apart from the abstract fear of the collective from which it arose. (p. 23)

This suggests that enlightenment in general resembles what Max Weber identified as the "rationalization of the world," a process that comes to full fruition in the Enlightenment in the West in the eighteenth century.

The "dialectic" in the title comes from the authors' view of modern history as a story of descent as well as ascent. Progress through the rational domination of nature has, they claim, generated its own opposite—the loss of control of human affairs and release of untold destructiveness. It is not that history is a Manichean struggle between two counterpoised principles (e.g., culture and barbarism, Eros and Thanatos, enlightenment and terror, or the rational and irrational); nor even that history has somehow departed from the course of reason and needs to be brought back on course. Rather, instrumental rationality, embodied in processes such as calculability and utility, formalization and instrumentalization, interchangeability and abstraction, remains the problem. And yet there are ambiguities even here. Adorno and Horkheimer admit in their introduction that "social freedom is inseparable from enlightened thought" (p. xiii), thus indicating that their critique of Enlightenment rationality is informed by a normative notion of critical rationality.[25]

Reading "Elements of Anti-Semitism" presents some severe challenges. The authors divide the chapter into seven sections that together make a kind of collage or "constellation" of theoretical probes. The temptation, however, to straighten out the argument by paraphrasing it deprives "Elements" (or any of the other parts of the book) of the power generated by the multifaceted, almost cubistic, construction of the text. The reading effect is one of circling the theme in question, while the analysis, when it does come, deploys any number of theoretical discourses (Marxist, psychoanalytic, epistemological, and philosophical-anthropological). Irony, sarcasm, and a mordant sense of play characterize these rhetorical pyrotechnics. At one point, the authors note that "[b]ecause they [Jews] invented the concept of kosher meat, they are persecuted as swine" (p. 186). Section VII begins, "But there are no more anti-Semites" (p. 200), a statement whose obvious irony is intended to provoke, since the data gathered at the same time for what became *The Authoritarian Personality* was showing that anti-Semitism was certainly alive and well. Yet, with their claim, Horkheimer and Adorno underline the larger truth that the near-extermination of European Jewry has meant that anti-Semitism is no longer a respectable public position; nor is it even very common since most European Jews had perished. Such a claim, coming as it does in the section added for the 1947 publication, alerts the reader to their central thesis: not anti-Semitism as such, but "ticket-thinking," the automatic and stereotypical approach to social and political reality in which "everything which stands for difference in society is threatened" is the ultimate danger (p. 202).

Overall, "Elements" offers an epistemology/cultural depth psychology of anti-Semitism. Sections I to III offer a relatively familiar exposition of Jews as a race and religion, of anti-Semitism as a "diversion" and "luxury for the masses" and as the "concealment of domination in production" for the bourgeoisie. The bourgeois rejection of Jews is a form of "self-hatred, the bad conscience of the parasite." Adorno and Horkheimer also note that the Jews are "scapegoats" because of their vulnerable and visible position in the "circulation sector" (finance, trade, and commerce) rather than in the productive sector. As "intermediaries," they have been a "thorn in the side of craftsmen and peasants," and thus aroused enmity better directed at those who hold real power. But with the fusion of "great concentrations of capital" and "the apparatus of the state," Jews are no longer needed, since the "sphere of circulation in which they occupied their positions of economic power is shrinking" (pp. 170–76). There is nothing startling in this general line of argument, which was echoed by Arendt in *Origins of Totalitarianism.*

Sections IV to VI probe the deep structures of anti-Semitism. The authors suggest, first, that anti-Semitism can be seen as an essentially religious phenomenon only if one remembers that the religious conflict between Christianity and Judaism has historically been energized by collective Oedipal impulses: "The adherents of the religion of the Father are hated by those who support the religion of the Son—hated by those who know better" (p. 179). Section V approaches the topic from a quasi-anthropological point of view.[26] Anti-Semites sense that Jews embody an impulse to maintain continuity with the archaic and primordial, what the authors call the "mimetic." The fascist devotion to rituals, formal ceremonies, and atavistic symbols testifies both to the appeal of the mimetic and to a desire to destroy it as insufficiently civilized and modern. For the fascist, "the mere existence of the other is provocative" (p. 183). Though "[t]hey cannot stand the Jews," they "imitate them" (p. 183). Echoing Plato on the inferior status of art, Adorno and Horkheimer contend that fascism is a "mimesis of a mimesis" (p. 185), that is, a ritualization and mythologization of those impulses seeking to maintain primordial bonds with reality. It is ersatz traditionalism in the service of the destruction of genuine tradition. The Nazi emphasis on "youth," "paganism," and the body celebrates the natural, yet ends by destroying it. As Horkheimer and Adorno express it in one of their most suggestive observations, "Fascism is also totalitarian in that it seeks to make the rebellion of suppressed nature against domination directly useful to domination" (p. 185).

Though Adorno and Horkheimer emphasize the way that Jews embody ritualized, archaic, and mythical thinking in "Elements of Anti-Semitism," they also recognize the Jewish role in "the victory of society over nature" and that Jews "have avoided the reversion to mythology which symbolism allows" (p. 186). From this point of view, a more familiar one in the later historiography of anti-Semitism, Jews are hated for the way they destroy the false mimesis of mythological and anthropomorphic thinking, through the invention of conscience and their important role in the secularization of the world, central to which are the subject/object and human/natural oppositions. In this respect, they are the carriers of modernity, whose basic impulse, according to Anson Rabinbach, is the "prohibition of the image and its displacement into the abstract system and the need to differentiate self from nature." While enlightenment blocks such regress, it is fascism that is regressive in seeking to "restore an archaic world of inauthenticity."[27]

One implication of the mimesis thesis is that Jewish–Christian conflict is so deeply embedded in the cultural ontology of the West that it seems fated to outlast its religious provenance. Adorno and Horkheimer suggest that anti-Semitism is so enduring because it is both a revolt against Christianity and a revolt in the name of Christianity against the corrosive effects of secularism and materialism. In this respect, Adorno and Horkheimer help explain the fascist, and Nazi, combination of the archaic and the modern, the symbolic and the rational, the primitive and the technological, the primordial and the up-to-date.

To explain how mimesis and its rejection are put into play, Adorno and Horkheimer suggest that the mind engages the world by balancing perception and conception, receptivity and activity. Alluding both to Kant and gestalt psychology, they suggest that projection, the imposition of a frame or order upon perception, is normally accompanied by the self-correcting capacity of reflection: "[R]eflection, the life of reason, takes place as conscious projection" (p. 189). The problem arises, however, when projection fails to be corrected by reflection. The result is then "false projection," which allows them to explain anti-Semitism as "the counterpart of true mimesis. . . . Mimesis imitates the environment, but false projection makes the environment like itself" (p. 187). False mimesis is a form of collective narcissism.

What makes anti-Semitism "morbid" is precisely the false projection at its core. The anti-Semitic personality is a paranoid. For him or her, domination, the result of false projection, is an end in itself: "[H]e makes everything in his image" (p. 190). In the Führer's "proverbial gaze . . . the subject is extinguished" (p. 191). Another name for false projection is stereotypical thinking, which is immune to change or nuance. The result is the "paranoiac insistence on rationality, the poor infinity of unchanging judgement" (p. 194). The individual is saved from the mental illness, this would suggest, by participating in its "socialized" form: "[T]he members are afraid of believing in their own delusion on their own" and "the normal member of society dispels his own paranoia by participating in the collective form" (p. 197). Generally, under modern conditions, the individual, "deadened by the culture industry" (p. 198), finds it increasingly difficult to think against the dominant reality. In such a situation, "[t]hought becomes restricted to the acquisition of isolated facts" (p. 197) and individual conscience is overridden by stereotypical judgments.

Finally, in Section VII, added in 1947, the authors suggest that this mind-set has become institutionalized as the norm. The dominant logic behind social reality is rational domination, the product of enlightenment thinking and embodied in advanced capitalism. It "behaves towards things as a dictator toward men" (p. 9) and "stereotypes replace individual categories" (p. 201). In this situation, the mechanisms and images that generate anti-Semitism and fascism generate a more general mentality in which "[f]ascist leaders could just as easily replace the anti-Semitic plank in their platform by some other" (p. 207). Even for progressives, the "ticket" mentality is pervasive:

> The anger against all that is different is teleologically inherent in the mentality, and, as the dominated subjects' resentment of natural domination, is ready to attack the natural minority—even when the social minority is threatened first. (p. 207)

As mentioned, one tension running throughout "Elements" is between anti-Semitism as a specific historical-cultural phenomenon and anti-Semitism as a manifestation of "the anger against all that is different." On Adorno and Horkheimer's account, European anti-Semitism can only be understood in terms of the Oedipal dynamics driving the religious conflict between Judaism and Christianity and/or the deep ambivalence toward the archaic or natural, that is, the mimetic, all of which is somehow released in the emergence of the modern. Yet surely hostility to difference does not always depend on these precise psycho-cultural mechanisms. White racism is not the product of the same psychological or cultural dynamic as European anti-Semitism. Though, for example, there are Oedipal dimensions at work in both forms of prejudice, Jews are generally identified with patriarchal and blacks with infantile impulses. And if we accept the analysis in the first six sections of "Elements," then it is difficult to see how Adorno and Horkheimer can replace Jews as the object of stereotypical thinking with other ethnic or racial minorities as they suggest at the end of Section Seven. As Zygmunt Bauman has suggested, there is no automatic connection between generalized fear of the other or "heterophobia" and anti-Semitism.[28]

One might also suggest that European anti-Semitism had less to do with Enlightenment reason than that it did with other, less consciously held, irrational impulses. The goal of Nazi anti-Semitism was racial purity. Although obviously facilitated by technological rationality, from scientific theories of racial superiority to the bureaucratic facilitation of extermination, the exterminationist impulse of the Nazis was, on Adorno's and

Horkheimer's own account, driven by unconscious, archaic impulses. Because such impulses were put into the service of domination does not necessarily mean that they were of the same nature as Enlightenment attempts to control nature. Finally, the attempt to create a master race and to carry out genocidal purification can scarcely be understood in terms of the desire to make everything the *same*. It is much more that Nazi genocide was an attempt to abolish certain categories of human being altogether. Needless to say, there is an enormous difference between homogenization of social reality and extermination, unless extermination is the means of homogenization.

Although written after the war, "Elements of Anti-Semitism" contains only one reference to "the extermination camps" (p. 206) and that by way of suggesting that the "special character by reason of which the victims were killed" (p. 206) no longer seems to matter. Ultimately Horkheimer's and Adorno's analysis rejoins Neumann's when they speak of prejudice and even extermination as economically rational:

> The administration of totalitarian states, which seeks to eliminate sections of the nation that have lost their contemporary relevance, merely implements economic verdicts issued long ago. (p. 206)

To be sure, this hints that perhaps eradication might be economically irrational; but the motive is still economic and hence "rational."

The *Authoritarian Personality* (1950) was intended as a "new approach to an old topic."[29] As such it displayed the same high ambition as did Myrdal's *An American Dilemma* (1944).[30] Funded by the American Jewish Committee, *The Authoritarian Personality* was the outgrowth of several years of group collaboration between Adorno and the Berkeley Public Opinion Study Group composed of a team primarily of psychologists and psychoanalysts. Over the course of the study, interviews, tests, and questionnaires involving some 2,099 people, including 700 college students, were conducted. From the total, 80 people were chosen for lengthier interviews and testing. Although there was a certain amount of diversity, "almost all," notes Martin Jay, "were white, native-born gentile, middle-class Americans."[31] Besides sidestepping the question of whether African Americans or Jewish Americans shared the prejudices and prejudiced personality of other Americans, the study also failed to include, as Adorno himself observed, representative samples of people from strong religious subcultures, such as the Bible Belt or heavily Catholic areas of the

Northeast.[32] And, as one critic observed, by taking a largely middle-class sampling, it was very difficult to measure the extent to which education levels and class membership influenced the intensity of prejudice.[33]

The research team constructed a set of scales that they refined in the process of conducting interviews. The scales were the AS (anti-Semitism), E (ethnocentrism), PEC (political-economic conservatism, i.e., ideological), and the best-known F (fascism) scale (F-Scale), all of which grew out of the original plan to measure anti-Semitic attitudes among Americans. The team developed a set of nonspecific questions that never mentioned specific groups or attitudes toward them and this was what led to the famous F-Scale. Overall, anti-Semitism was assumed to be the paradigm case of prejudice in *The Authoritarian Personality*,[34] although, strictly speaking, what the F-Scale measured was more than anti-Semitism. One of the co-authors, Daniel Levinson, did suggest that "anti-Semitism, while it is essentially a facet of a broader ethnocentric pattern, may nevertheless have certain independent determinants of its own" (p. 123), while, in his section, Adorno focused on some of the specific psychological determinants of anti-Semitism and on the characteristics of the authoritarian personality. Still, as already suggested, little was made of the differences between anti-Semitism and other sorts of prejudice. Writing in 1954, Richard Christie guessed rightly that the title of the volume had been an afterthought (it was originally to be called *The Fascist Character*), since "fascist," "antidemocratic," and "authoritarian" are all used as rough equivalents within the text, while "authoritarian personality" hardly occurs at all.[35] Adorno later wrote warmly of the nonpedantic, playful spirit suffusing the group, which allowed them to see how "without expressly asking about anti-Semitic and other fascistic opinions, one could indirectly determine such tendencies."[36] The F-Scale was thus designed to measure an underlying predisposition toward such general traits as conventional ways of thinking, submissiveness, aggressiveness, difficulty in sympathetically identifying with others, superstition, stereotypy and projective thinking, attraction to power, toughness, and destructiveness, a tendency toward cynicism, and difficulties with sexual matters (p. 228). These characteristics combined under certain conditions to constitute the character structure of the authoritarian personality.

Overall, Adorno's work on the project not only represented the closest the Frankfurt School came to entering into full intellectual cooperation with American academics; it also lent his theoretical orientation a certain specificity. The ultimate point, according to Adorno, was not that the psychological (or subjective) was the seat of prejudice, but that objective circumstances/systems maintained their hold on individuals by being internalized. Otherwise, as he notes, "invoking the supremacy of the system becomes a substitute for insights into the concrete relationship between the system and its components."[37] Although Adorno was committed in general to the priority of the objective, that is, of the social structure, the great preponderance of attention in *The Authoritarian Personality* fell on the subjective or psychological sphere. As Nathan Glazer noted at the time, the study "does not . . . demonstrate the relations of this type to larger structures of the society" such as family or class.[38] Still, Adorno, according to Martin Jay, never abandoned the priority of the theoretical to the empirical. It is a theoretical assumption, for instance, that an understanding of the "total personality," specifically the "psychodynamic processes" of the individual, will explain prejudiced beliefs and behavior.[39] Locating the sources of the authoritarian personality in the largely unconscious character structures implied that merely exposing one group to another did not automatically decrease prejudice since "experience itself is predetermined by stereotype." The logic of Adorno's position points up the need to "reconstitute the capacity for having experiences" (p. 617), that is, the application of individual therapy or possibly social therapy of some sort. Thus, the primacy of the psychological *within* the study had implications for the practical measures implied by the analysis.

The complex interaction between social and psychological, objective and subjective meant that Adorno and his colleagues were difficult targets for their critics. Still, some important hits were made. Herbert Hyman and Paul Sheatsley's thorough methodological critique of the volume hammered away at the "disregard for the influence of formal education" and overemphasis on "personality differences." They also noted that the lack of strong correlation between scores on the PEC-Scale and on the F-Scale suggested that ideological factors were more crucial in the formation of opinions than *The Authoritarian Personality* allowed.[40] Edward Shils offered two important points for consideration. He underscored the study's neglect of the "extent and importance" of "adaptiveness to institutional roles," since most of the emphasis fell upon the primacy of "personality traits" in determining beliefs and behavior. Shils's point about role adaptation was extremely important, since it questioned the all-determining power of individual psychology, whether conscious or unconscious, in determining behavior. As Zygmunt Bauman has asserted much more recently, what we should learn from the Holocaust is not the importance of character structures but of power structures in determining behavior.[41] Like many other critics, Shils also objected to the loaded ideological nature of many of the questions. It was all but impossible for the notion of left-wing authoritarianism to be formulated in the terms set forth by the study. But generally Adorno and company managed to have it both ways: they could agree in principle with the importance of "objective" factors (economic and social structures, institutional roles, ideologies, education), but then remind critics that the purpose of the study was to measure the psychodynamic component of prejudice. Indeed, one co-author, Else Frenkel-Brunswik, suggested that in a relatively stable social situation (such as that in postwar America), a focus on the psychological etiology of authoritarian attitudes was justified (pp. 228–29).

Another aspect of the problem with linking the subjective and objective concerns how individual prejudice is augmented or diminished by group pressures. The study contained no analyses of political or social movements, mob actions, or even the shaping of public opinion in a democratic political order. Lynching, America's own contribution to racialized crowd psychology, was hardly touched on. While the weakness of Freud's *Massenpsychologie* (mass psychology) was its focus on dramatic crowd behavior, the authors of *The Authoritarian Personality* largely ignored such phenomena and thereby implied a static, reified link between individual and group psychology.

The dominant language of analysis in *The Authoritarian Personality* was drawn from the relatively new idiom of psychoanalytic "ego psychology."[42] Based on Freud's later structural model of the psyche, ego psychology built on Anna Freud's path-breaking work on defense mechanisms and the writings of Heinz Hartmann, Ernst Kris, and Erik Erikson. Emerging after the Second World War as the dominant theoretical perspective within the American psychoanalytic movement, it represented a shift away from the traditional psychoanalytic emphasis on the unconscious and drives. A sample of this new perspective is evident in Daniel Levinson's words: "[E]go weakness would seem to be a concomitant of conventionalism and authoritarianism," both of which are related to the subject's "overemphasis upon the ego and its supposed strength." Else Frenkel-Brunswik makes the same point when she notes that for high scorers (i.e., highly prejudiced people), "what is not acceptable to the ego tends . . . to become externalized, thus rendering the ego narrow and constricted" (pp. 234, 440). Though Adorno was less inclined than the others to use the idiom of ego psychology, he later attributed much of the success of the co-authors to

> our common theoretical orientation toward Freud. The four of us were agreed in neither tying ourselves inflexibly to Freud nor in diluting him after the manner of the psychological revisionists.[43]

This is an important point to pursue, since Adorno and Horkheimer, like Herbert Marcuse later, resisted Erich Fromm's revisionist psychoanalytic approach, which deprived psychoanalytic theory of a critical vantage point from which to mount a critique of society. Yet in formulating the ego as a conflict-free sphere, ego psychology also tended to de-emphasize the unconscious and the libidinal, that which escaped the constraints of social convention and adaptation. Put another way, ego psychology seemed to re-instate a normative notion of the ego much akin to the (liberal) idea of individual autonomy. In offering no instinctual resources for the self to resist society, ego psychology was left with no way to maintain the tension between self and society and thus adjustment, that is, conformity, could too easily become a therapeutic virtue.[44]

Yet ego psychology also contributed a certain subtlety to the findings in *The Authoritarian Personality* where emphasis falls on the ambivalence of high scorers toward authority rather than identification with it. This ambivalence indicates, claims Adorno, unresolved Oedipal conflicts that tend toward a "sadomasochistic resolution" (p. 759).[45] In general, the authoritarian type shows a low tolerance for ambiguity, desires to be seen as tough, and resists sympathy. Despite the general critique of revisionism developed later by Herbert Marcuse (and the attacks on ego psychology from Jacques Lacan in France), the ego psychological orientation of *The Authoritarian Personality* made the important point that what most people see as a strong ego is in reality weak and fragile, and represents inadequately integrated feelings of aggression and desire. On the other hand, the genuinely strong ego responds flexibly to external reality rather than imposing a rigid framework on it, as illustrated by Adorno's notion of "false projection." The healthy ego does not deal with threatening internal impulses by repressing them or projecting them onto the outside world. As Adorno characterizes what he calls the "Genuine Liberal" (one of the few times he has kind words for liberalism),

> [He] has a strong sense of personal autonomy and independence.... His ego is quite developed but not libidinized—he is rarely "narcissis-

tic." At the same time he is willing to admit id tendencies, and to take the consequence—as is the case with Freud's "erotic type" (p. 781).[46]

Generally, Adorno's 180-page section, "Qualitative Studies of Ideology," is rich in aperçus, and its formulations are less gnomic than those in *The Dialectic of Enlightenment*. His main assignment was to discuss the "objective" factors that the rest of the study largely ignored. At the same time, he offers a subtle defense of the subjective approach by contending that "anti-Semitic prejudice has little to do with the qualities of those against whom it is directed," although he also acknowledges that specifically Jewish traits may play a role in anti-Semitism. This reflects what he calls the "functional character of anti-Semitism" (pp. 607–8), and echoes the discussion in *The Dialectic of Enlightenment* of the way that the anti-Semite's projections fail to be corrected reflectively. In orthodox psychoanalytic language, there is a failure of reality testing in anti-Semitism. But Adorno speaks little about mimesis or of deep-seated, cultural/institutional Oedipal conflicts between Judaism and Christianity. He writes rather of "the underlying anti-Semitism of our cultural climate" and suggests that, as the German case showed, "extreme anti-Semitic statements" may work effectively as an "antidote for the superego and may stimulate imitation even in cases where the individual's 'own' reactions would be less violent." Finally, Adorno mentions the crucial "gap between stereotypy on the one hand and real experiences and the still accepted standards of democracy on the other, [which] leads to a conflict situation" (pp. 607–8). Echoing something like Myrdal's concept of the "American dilemma," Adorno concludes that "the anti-Semite's conflict is between the current, culturally 'approved' stereotypes of prejudice and the officially prevailing standards of democracy and human equality (p. 629)."[47] This is one of the few places that Adorno acknowledges the political cultural context within which he is writing.

Overall Adorno never really differentiates between German and American anti-Semitism. By implication, just as individual consciences were *gleichgeschaltet* (neutralized) in Germany, so could they be in America. It is in the area of comparative work that Adorno's lack of knowledge of America and the Frankfurt tendency to underestimate German anti-Semitism became most evident. As Rolf Wiggershaus has acutely observed, Myrdal took several trips around the South and talked with people of both races and various classes, while Adorno did no fieldwork at all. His conclusions were based solely on data drawn from questionnaires, tests, and interviews.[48] Indeed, another weakness in *The Authoritarian Personality* was the failure of Adorno and his associates to construct something like a D-Scale (democratic values), which is precisely what Myrdal and his colleagues did in developing the "American Creed." If the objective dimension were as important as Adorno certainly believed it to be, then *The Authoritarian Personality* should have acknowledged more clearly that American political culture offered what the German political culture did not: a democratic-liberal tradition that helped counteract the very real anti-Semitism and white racism in America.[49] Far from generating authoritarian and prejudiced modes of thought, a capitalist economy, along with a political culture of liberal individualism, could help undermine the culture of anti-Semitism historically associated with anticapitalist and antimodernizing tendencies. Besides their ignorance of American political culture, Adorno et al. neglected this political dimension because, as psychoanalytically oriented researchers and/or as quasi-Marxists, they did not consider the political realm in general or political values specifically to operate independently of the economic system.

On the other hand, Adorno's answer to one of the crucial questions regarding anti-Semitism—*cui bono*? (who benefits)—was more sophisticated than earlier Frankfurt responses had been. He acknowledges that, in the short run, anti-Semitism might be economically rational, as when an individual or community stands to gain from confiscation of Jewish (or, as he added, Japanese) property. But his overall emphasis in *The Authoritarian Personality* falls upon the psychological benefits accruing to the anti-Semite. From this point of view, anti-Semitism is best understood as a way of dealing with "alienation" from modern "supra-individual laws" and "social processes" through stereotyping and personalization. The Jew, who is "not defined by a profession or by his role in social life, but by his human existence as such" (pp. 618–19) becomes a likely, though not inevitable, target. Indeed, the "less anti-Jewish imagery is related to actual experience and the more it is kept 'pure,' as it were, from contamination by reality" (p. 619), the more dangerous it becomes. Overall, anti-Semitism specifically and authoritarian thinking in general are "means of pseudo-orientation in an estranged world" (p. 622). Though the overall system might link anti-Semitism and economic benefit, this did not imply that individual anti-Semites were necessarily motivated by conscious economic reasons.

Generally, Adorno's analysis of anti-Semitism in *The Authoritarian Personality* was more convincing than that of *The Dialectic of Enlightenment*.

Though Adorno is not consistent on the point, he seems to suggest that Jews are picked out because they are different, but not in any fixed or predictable way. Even more suggestive is his observation that the less the image of the Jew has to do with experience, the more potent the effects of that image. While *The Authoritarian Personality* all but drops the earlier analysis of anti-Semitism in terms of deep structural patterns, it gains another kind of complexity by evoking the alienating, mystifying dimensions of modernity, though without much specificity. In generally defining the Jew as having no fixed definition except as different, Adorno's picture of the authoritarian personality closely resembles Jean-Paul Sartre's phenomenological "portrait of the anti-Semite," a point that Adorno himself duly acknowledges. Thus, *The Authoritarian Personality* assumes that anti-Semitism and the authoritarian mentality arise from the specific conditions of modernity.[50]

One of Adorno's most interesting contributions was his typology of high (and low) scorers, of whom he identifies six types.[51] One kind of high scorer manifests a "surface resentment" and is prone to scapegoating, while the more conventionally prejudiced person integrates prejudice into his or her personality. More interesting, are the four other types. The "Authoritarian type" displays a "sadomasochistic" pattern of cringing obedience upward and an imposition of cruelty downward, while the "Rebel," far from obedient, is unable to acknowledge any sort of authority and recalls the "rebel without a cause" so much discussed in postwar American analyses of juvenile delinquency. Then there is the "Crank" who inhabits a "spurious inner world" and adopts a paranoiac stance toward reality.

But most interesting, considering the controversy aroused by Hannah Arendt's later analysis of Adolf Eichmann, is Adorno's description of the "Manipulative" type, which he suggests is "potentially the most dangerous one" (p. 767). Adorno mentions Heinrich Himmler as an example of this type who displays a lack of "intensity of his object cathexis" and "a certain emptiness and shallowness." Such types "do not even hate the Jews; they 'cope' with them by administrative measures without any personal contacts with the victims" (p. 768). With this description, we are not a million miles away from Eichmann and the "banality of evil."[52] Adorno's typological categories also imply that the "authoritarian personality" is not defined by a unified, constant configuration of traits, but by tendencies that combine in different proportions. Neither the Nazi movement nor any other movement can be characterized in terms of one of these types: the first three types might become the foot soldiers of an authoritarian or totalitarian movement; Rebels are potentially those who do the movement's dirty work; the Cranks might become the ideologists; and the Manipulators are the bureaucrat-managers and organizers of massive discrimination against—or eradication of—the target group.

Finally, the authors of *The Authoritarian Personality* failed to find any significant correlation between high scorers on the F-Scale and clinical psychotics. Indeed, the point of stressing that high scorers lacked integrated personalities was that the specific characteristics associated with high scorers are isolated affective fragments waiting to be crystallized in otherwise normally functioning individuals by an ideology or a political movement (both of which were of course relatively neglected in the study) in times of historical turmoil. Based on the long-standing Frankfurt School concern with the fragile modern ego, one incapable of autonomy and in thrall to ideologies of domination, Adorno located the most destructive manifestation of the modern self in modernity's authoritarian movements.

Overview and Assessment

There are several large areas where the Frankfurt School's psychoanalytically oriented analysis seems particularly vulnerable. First, Adorno and his research partners moved back and forth from the objective to the subjective, from the social to the psychological, from the theoretical to the empirical, without ever paying attention to the *historical*. As already noted, Adorno and his co-workers seem innocent of American history and culture, not to mention their failure to differentiate German anti-Semitism from American anti-Semitism. This is not to say that attention to the concrete details of historical and political phenomena is a panacea. The facts never simply "speak" for themselves. But to pay attention to the historical in this context strongly suggests the need for a comparative dimension to the study. Why, in a period when social anti-Semitism was pervasive in America, were Jews not rounded up or at least rounded upon, except in a few cases such as Father Coughlin's movement in the 1930s? And if Germany was less anti-Semitic than, say, France to the west or Poland to the east, how did the Holocaust happen under German auspices? Franz Neumann's *Behemoth* was so impressive because it sought to reconstruct the intellectual history of German anti-Semitism and *Völkisch* thinking, something that Horkheimer and Adorno never attempted in either of their works on anti-Semitism. And it is striking how neither "Elements of Anti-Semitism" nor *The Authoritarian Personality* took the trouble to offer an intellectual history of the various subdiscourses of anti-Semitism—the religious, the cultural, and especially the racial/biological—at work in German and/or Western thought and culture.

A striking example of this lack of attention to anti-Semitic ideology is the way that Adorno and company downplay the identification of post-emancipation Jewry with the spirit of the Enlightenment rationality and modernity. In fact, it is easy to miss the conceptual dilemma that the "dialectic of Enlightenment" thesis landed them in. If instrumental rationality strengthened the potential for domination, then Jews, insofar as they were identified with the spirit of modern rationality, were complicit in the emergence of a society of domination. But to explicitly assert that would have been a case of blaming the victim. Nor did secular Jews such as Adorno and Horkheimer—or Sartre and, to a degree, Arendt—offer any reason why Jews should preserve their differences. Nothing in their thinking suggested that Jews could have done anything but what Marx suggested: throw off both their religion and their stereotypical role as capitalists and become assimilated. That is, they were no more able to justify the existence of difference—as opposed to recognizing it—than anyone else.

The Institute's deep ambivalence toward (the) Enlightenment and modernity caused them problems in another area. In certain respects, the Frankfurt critique belonged to the Romantic or "expressivist" tradition of protest against the Enlightenment.[53] This Romantic critique of modernity is compatible with the Frankfurt emphasis on the preservation of difference rather than aiming for a universalized homogeneity of interchangeable parts and pleasures. But the Frankfurt understanding of the Enlightenment neglected the ideas of natural and civil rights central to that tradition. Instead, the Frankfurt emphasis fell on the Enlightenment as an all-encompassing process of "making the same" through domination, as expressed in modern capitalism (and it should be said, socialism). From their point of view, to make claims about universality of rights implied the desire to dominate and to eradicate those differences that resist the rationalization of the world. They never saw that the point of rights was not to eradicate but to protect difference.

Here, critical theory's crucial assumption about modernity—that the modern self was fragile—must have played a crucial role as well. Because modern society so dominated the individual, it was obviously difficult for quasi-Marxists Adorno and Horkheimer to give much credence to the "liberal," individualist language of rights. Moreover, as Axel Honneth has pointed out, the two dominant orientations of modern Western radical thought—social utopianism and natural law thinking—are divergent in their goals. The former, to which the Frankfurt School clearly belongs, emphasizes the achievement of happiness or satisfaction, however defined; the latter stresses the importance of recognition of dignity and respect. The former is a response to deprivation; the latter a response to degradation. With Honneth's analysis in mind, it is no wonder that the Frankfurt School was so unable or unwilling to adopt "rights talk" with its emphasis upon respect and dignity, though that would have been the most convincing way to defend, and even encourage, difference.[54]

Finally, the Frankfurt theorists forgot that, without the legal and political recognition of equal dignity and worth, preserving differences and particularities could lead to the justification of hierarchies. This was one destination of the Herderian idea that every people possesses a *Geist* (spirit) or *Seele* (soul) unique to it. In a German political culture, where the Enlightenment tradition of natural rights had never been robust, the idea of identifiable group differences offered relatively little resistance to the development, first, of cultural/racial essentialism and, then, of racial/cultural hierarchies. Similar intellectual and social developments were also strong in the mid-nineteenth to early twentieth century United States and Great Britain, although usually more closely tied to Darwinian than to Romantic organicist modes of thought. But resources existed within these political cultures to resist the total racializing of social and political life.

It is difficult to gauge the intellectual impact of the Frankfurt-inspired, American Jewish Committee–funded studies in prejudice. The reception of *The Authoritarian Personality* was generally enthusiastic; and, already in 1954, it had "inspired such a tremendous volume of research."[55] Even its sternest critics were impressed by its massive ambition and methodological sophistication. But there were dissenters. Sociologist David Riesman noted that *The Authoritarian Personality* came twenty years too late; and, it might be added, was (arguably) carried out in the wrong country and about the wrong sort of prejudice at that.[56] Indeed, what blocked the sustained influence of *The Authoritarian Personality* and its use of psychoanalytic theory was the emergence of the "race" problem as a major concern not only in the United States but also in the Third World just as the book was appearing. *The Authoritarian Personality* was not the wave of the future but the last of the great left-wing attempts, initiated by Wilhelm Reich in 1930s Germany and continued in America, to explain how the Nazis had come to power.

Yet one crossover from the Studies in Prejudice project to the postwar study of American race relations is apparent in the influential work of psychologist Kenneth Clark, who, along with his wife, Mamie Clark, studied the effects of white racism on black children and who was cited in the 1954 *Brown v. Board of Education* decision. In 1950, Clark used *The Authoritarian Personality* in a report to a White House Conference on Children to raise questions about the wider implications for "American democracy and freedom" of the existence of large numbers of prejudiced white people. Though Clark was reluctant to make any definitive judgment, he clearly believed that "prejudice and discrimination work very much to the disadvantage of the personality development of most minority-group members in one way or the other." In other words, the problem was not with the children but with a society in which highly prejudiced persons could voice and act on their deeply held, as well as conventional, racial beliefs. As John P. Jackson has noted, *The Authoritarian Personality*, along with Myrdal's *An American Dilemma*, were the two great influences on Clark's work.[57]

One other work of lesser scope but also part of the Studies in Prejudice project did address the other substantive issue that Adorno et al. neglected—the relationship between anti-Semitism and white racism. That was Bruno Bettelheim and Morris Janowitz's *The Dynamics of Prejudice* (1950). Based on work with 150 World War II veterans in Chicago, the study asked: "What are the factors essentially associated with anti-Semitism and are these factors also associated with anti-Negro attitudes?" They concluded that in Germany a whole list of negative traits had been attributed to Jews, but in America those traits had been split between Jews and blacks. Specifically, the negative traits associated with Jews had to do with superego tendencies toward control and manipulation, while those associated with blacks had to do with id-linked qualities of indulgence and gratification. In general, Bettelheim and Janowitz found the intensity of anti-Semitism significantly less than the white racism among the veterans they interviewed. But *The Dynamics of Prejudice* lacked the more critical social theory that Adorno brought to his analysis and thus was only a beginning in the psychoanalytic investigation of comparative prejudice.[58]

Aside from the two works just mentioned, studies of racism in the 1960s and early 1970s tended to abandon the modal personality/social character approach and instead formulated a typology of racial attitudes, such as Pierre van den Berghe's "paternalistic" and "competitive" racism or Joel Kovel's "dominative," "aversive," and "meta-racism."[59] This work was more specifically related to the social and economic context that gave rise to racist modes of thought than *The Authoritarian Personality* had been, and also tended to emphasize consciously held patterns of thought and behavior, although Kovel, a psychoanalyst, certainly emphasized the unconscious, particularly sexual, dimension of racism. Moreover, the up-shot of these studies was that racism was far from being a modern, urban, and industrial phenomenon, but was rooted, at least in the United States, in a rural, agrarian past. In addition, social character approaches, informed by psychoanalytic theory, had relatively little influence on studies of white racists. By focusing their attention on the victims rather than the perpetrators of white racism, Kenneth and Mamie Clark anticipated the particularist paradigm of the 1960s that concentrated on victims rather than perpetrators of prejudice.

Nor did studies of racism in the 1960s and 1970s really address the problem of obedience to totalitarian leaders or participation in the mass movements that they led. The whole problem of "mass psychology" and mass society in general seems to have been struck from the intellectual agenda. The most interesting post-1950s study of the problem of authority was Stanley Milgram's *Obedience to Authority* (1974), which tried to assess the conditions under which subjects would inflict pain on other human beings, but Milgram's work was divorced from the question of racism or anti-Semitism, that is, of prejudice generally, or mass politics. He did note that the subjects of his experiments who scored highest on the obedience scale proved also to be high scorers on the F-Scale used in *The Authoritarian Personality*. But Milgram begged off any psychoanalytic interpretation of these results when he wrote: "[W]e really do not know very much about how to measure personality." Besides, Milgram was much more impressed by the power of social role than character structure in predicting whether individuals would obey orders to inflict harm on others: "[I]t is not so much the kind of person a man is as the kind of situation in which he finds himself that determines how he will act."[60]

Finally, some of the New York intellectuals incorporated aspects of *The Authoritarian Personality* into their work. The startling fact to many of them, as it was to many students of prejudice generally, was that anti-Semitism failed to materialize as a major political force in postwar America, as Adorno et al. had implied it might. Specifically, McCarthyism and the new radical right never developed an anti-Semitic dimension. Such new right-wing phenomena were, if the lessons of *The Authoritarian Personality* and of "Elements of Anti-Semitism" are to be believed, a kind of anti-Semitism without the Jews. Projection, paranoia, and conspiracy were rife, but radicals and communists had replaced Jews as the source of danger. Indeed, what struck historian Richard Hofstadter about McCarthyism and the radical right was the refusal of their leaders or adherents to play politics in the normal way. Thus, according to Hofstadter, a new vocabulary of analysis was needed. To this end, he cited *The Authoritarian Personality* at the beginning of his essay, "The Pseudo-Conservative Revolt" (1955), where he identified the prime motivating force of the McCarthyite and radical right movements not as economic self-interest but "status anxiety." It was also significant that the term "pseudo-conservative" was drawn from Adorno's contribution to *The Authoritarian Personality*. Moreover, Fritz Stern, a colleague of Hofstadter's at Columbia University, associated pseudo-conservatism with the "politics of culture despair" that was one of the expressions of the revolt against modernity that lay behind National Socialist ideology.[61]

Strangely, the once urgent task of explaining the inexplicable, the mass murder of millions of Jews by Nazi Germany, seemed to fade in the 1950s only to revive with the Eichmann trial in Jerusalem in 1961 and then Hannah Arendt's provocative *Eichmann in Jerusalem* (1963). Rather, the focus, it is clear in retrospect, began to shift from concern with perpetrators of racism and anti-Semitism to a concern with their effects on the victims and, more importantly, how they understood their experience. Still, it remains to add that Adorno and Horkheimer look particularly prescient when, near the conclusion of "Elements of Anti-Semitism," they suggest that there is no longer a need—or market—for anti-Semitism, even though a free-floating mind-set of deep suspicion toward difference remains. The irony is that just as there seemed to be a unified theory of prejudice that explained racism and anti-Semitism, the historical focus shifted to the varieties of racism(s) and anti-Semitism(s).

4

Hannah Arendt: Race, History, and Humanism

What a piece of work is man! How infinite in faculty, in form and moving! How express and admirable in action! How like an angel in apprehension! How like a god! The beauty of the world! The paragon of animals! And yet, to me, what is this quintessence of dust? Man delights not me, —no, nor woman neither.

William Shakespeare

There is nothing one man will not do to another.

Carolyn Forché

If any single work made the term "totalitarianism" common currency after World War II, it was Hannah Arendt's *The Origins of Totalitarianism* (1951). Over the next decade or so, that text was at the center of the scholarly debate about totalitarianism inside and outside the academy. Although it is tempting to consider Arendt's book primarily as a specimen-text of the Cold War,[1] it is in fact much more important than that. For instance, *Origins* was for a number of years the most comprehensive and influential effort to come to terms with what came to be called the "Holocaust." Moreover, unlike other postwar analysts of totalitarianism and unlike the other theorists of racism examined in the preceding three chapters, except for W. E. B. Du Bois, Arendt linked the rise of totalitarianism within Europe to European colonialism and imperialism, particularly in Africa. As Arendt's biographer Elizabeth Young-Bruehl notes, Arendt uses "race imperialism" in the first two sections of the text, while the term "totalitarian" only begins appearing in the third section written in 1948–1949. In fact Arendt's working title was *The Elements of Shame: Anti-Semitism—*

Imperialism—Racism. Thus, Robert Young's contention in *White Mythologies* (1990) that only French and Francophone intellectuals such as Jean-Paul Sartre, Aimé Césaire, and Frantz Fanon considered fascism as colonialism "brought home to Europe" must be modified to make a place for Arendt.[2]

It is Arendt's focus on the role of imperialism in the origins of totalitarianism that justifies including *Origins* with the works we have examined by Myrdal, Adorno, and Sartre, as they sought to analyze and explain racism and anti-Semitism in the West. As Edward Said established in *Culture and Imperialism* (1993), European literary culture was shaped by the experience of imperialism from the early nineteenth century on.[3] Significantly, *Origins* includes fascinating discussions of Rudyard Kipling, Joseph Conrad's *Heart of Darkness*, and T. E. Lawrence's writings as explorations of the imperial encounter with racial and cultural "otherness" at the heart of the European imagination. She also devotes attention to Disraeli's and Proust's fiction as explorations of the precarious social situation of Jews in pre-World War I European society. *Origins* is more than a mixture of history, comparative politics, historical sociology, and phenomenology of total domination. It is also an attempt to answer the question of what it means to be human in light of the post-World War I collapse of European institutions and traditions and the emergence of totalitarian regimes in Germany and the Soviet Union.[4]

Arendt's personal, moral, and intellectual investment in *Origins* derived from her experience as a German Jew rather than as a disillusioned political radical. Although sympathetic to the fate of the left, a friend of Walter Benjamin, an acquaintance of Bertolt Brecht, and an admirer of Rosa Luxemburg, Arendt responded sharply to historian Gershom Scholem when, in the midst of the controversy over her Eichmann book, he accused her of being a typical German left-wing intellectual: "If I can be said to 'have come from anywhere,'" retorted Arendt, "it is from the tradition of German philosophy."[5] Born in Königsberg in 1906 of secular Jewish parents, Arendt studied philosophy and theology with Martin Heidegger and Karl Jaspers at Marburg and Heidelberg, respectively. After an eight-day interrogation by the Gestapo in Berlin, she fled Germany for Paris in 1933. There she worked for a Zionist youth organization and began to gather materials on the history of anti-Semitism and of European Jewry. Arendt's acknowledgment of her Jewish identity in these years was triggered by the growing crisis of European Jewry and the promptings of an older friend, the Zionist intellectual Kurt Blumenfeld. As she later reflected, she learned that "[i]f one is attacked as a Jew, one must defend oneself as a Jew. Not as German, not as a world-citizen, not as up-holder of the Rights of Man or whatever."[6] Her growing interest in poli-tics was also deeply influenced by her second husband, Heinrich Blücher, a self-educated, German gentile of working class origins who had been in-volved in the Spartacist movement in 1919 and was a member of the German Communist Party until the mid-1920s. They met as exiles in Paris in 1936 and were married in 1940. Eventually Arendt was transferred from Paris to the internment camp in Gurs in southern France. In the ensuing confusion she was able to leave Gurs and was reunited with Blücher and her mother. In January 1941, having obtained visas, the couple took the train to Lisbon, from where they departed for New York in May. Martha Arendt was able to follow soon thereafter. Most of the other inmates in Gurs perished in Auschwitz.[7]

It is worth emphasizing that Arendt's ideological loyalties were not ex-clusively forged by a left-wing political culture, since, as we have already seen, left-wing German-Jewish intellectuals were often deaf to the danger of Nazi-inspired versions of anti-Semitism. Because Arendt was never a Marxist, she never hesitated to acknowledge the historical importance of national, ethnic, religious, or racial movements and currents of thought. After arriving in America, Arendt reviewed books and wrote essays on Judaism, anti-Semitism, and the fate of Palestine, some of which were in-corporated into *Origins*. She firmly opposed any notion of collective German guilt and supported a bi-national rather than a Jewish state in Palestine, a position reflected in her analysis of the nation-state in *Origins*. As Young-Bruehl notes, Arendt's original proposal for *Origins* was for-mulated in 1945–1946 during the "most depressing period of the Blüchers' lives" when the full scope of the Nazi extermination policy was just be-coming clear. According to Arendt, "this [the extermination policy] was different. Personally, one could deal with everything else."[8] All this un-derscores the crucial point that she experienced the very European crisis that she explored in *Origins*.

Finally, there is the context of American intellectual life during the Cold War. Arendt was one of the key figures among the New York intel-lectuals, a group sometimes depicted in recent years as ardent Cold Warriors and smart McCarthyites. This is seriously misguided, since some of the members of this group were anti-Stalinists, hostile to McCarthyism, and also defenders of civil liberties. It is in this circle, which included rad-ical journalist Dwight Macdonald, socialist intellectuals Irving Howe and

Michael Harrington, anarchist and novelist Paul Goodman, literary critic Alfred Kazin, art critic Harold Rosenberg, and novelist Mary McCarthy, that Hannah Arendt should be placed. Arendt herself rejected the term "anti-Stalinist" since it suggested a grouping within the Marxist-Leninist camp to which she had certainly never belonged. She was anti-Marxist for political and moral, even theoretical, reasons and hostile to the Soviet Union because she considered it a totalitarian regime at least up to Khrushchev's accession to power in the 1950s. But she felt that the worst way to combat the ideology of communism was to make democracy or Americanism into a counterideology, around which people should be mobilized.[9] Arendt also differed from other postwar analysts of totalitarianism in becoming *more* politically engaged, even radical, rather than settling into anticommunist conservatism or a quietistic liberalism after the mid-1950s. In the ensuing years, she developed a theory of freedom and political action based on the desirability of increasing, rather than contracting, citizen participation in the public realm. Along with Goodman and C. Wright Mills, as much or more than Herbert Marcuse, Arendt was one of the theoretical champions of participatory democracy, which was so central to the civil rights movement and new left of the 1960s.

Two fundamental premises inform Arendt's *Origins*. One is that totalitarianism represents a fundamental break with the intellectual and political traditions of the West. As she writes in the original preface to *Origins*:

All traditional elements of our political and spiritual world were dissolved . . . the subterranean stream of Western history has finally come to the surface and usurped the dignity of our tradition . . . human dignity needs a new guarantee which can be found only in a new political principle.[10]

The second premise is that theories of historical inevitability, whether cast in terms of materialism or idealism, race or class, the forces of production, the unfolding development of *Geist* or evolutionary genetics, are both pernicious and wrong. Specifically, Arendt rejected the notion of what she called "eternal anti-Semitism," the Zionist idea that the Christian West had been and would always be hostile to Jews.[11] Her argument against inevitability was grounded in the simple but profoundly important fact of the continual appearance of new human beings in the world. Individual existence was, for Arendt, always a new beginning. Furthermore, Arendt refused to claim that there was anything inevitable about the rise of totalitarianism or about the Holocaust. That *Origins* itself was constituted by three separate, at times tenuously related, sections reflects her view that totalitarianism by no means flowed inevitably from what had come before it. But by rejecting historical inevitability, Arendt also seemed to question the validity of causal linkages altogether. As a result, it is hard, at times, to distinguish causes from foreshadowings and comparisons from prefigurations in *Origins*. Though I will return to the issue later, it is not clear whether, for instance, Arendt is claiming a causal connection between the enslavement and mass murder of Africans by Europeans (English, French, Germans, and Belgians) in the late nineteenth and early twentieth century and the emergence of the concentration/extermination camp system in Europe; or whether she intends the African experience to serve as a foreshadowing of the Holocaust, a hint of what was to come, but without strong causal links to it.

If history is not the narrative of causally linked forces, events, or ideas, what is it? For Arendt it is the story of human actions and events, most properly concerned with "new beginnings" that, to quote Walter Benjamin in another context, "blast open the continuum of history."[12] Of course, totalitarianism itself was a violent tear in the fabric of tradition, and thus the coming of the new does not only reveal the possibility of human freedom. *Origins* is informed by a somber vision of humanly created horrors, yet insists that things might have been different. Thus, from the wrenching experience of a fundamental break with the past, Arendt drew moderately hopeful conclusions. In the aftermath of the catastrophe, new beginnings and fresh departures were possible, though never inevitable.

The Historical Break

Arendt's focus in *Origins* falls roughly on the period between 1789 and 1945, with particular attention directed to the period extending from the Berlin Conference in 1884 to 1945. As already noted, her purpose was to analyze the component parts of totalitarianism without arriving at any grand, overarching conclusions about causal priority; rather, she thought it most important to identify the historical preconditions for the emergence of those elements. In the conclusion to the first edition of *Origins*, she seems to throw up her hands in bafflement and concludes that all the tendencies and trends that she has been analyzing are but "shadowy forebodings of Hitler's and Stalin's gigantic principled opportunism" (p. 431, 1st ed.). Aside from everything else, this was an atypical claim on Arendt's part, since a weakness of *Origins* was her refusal to attribute causal agency to either of these totalitarian leaders.

The historical phenomenon that I am most concerned with here is the one that usually receives short shrift in discussions of the rise of totalitarianism or of the Holocaust—European imperialism and colonial expansion. Although not a Marxist, Arendt identifies the expansion and the consolidation of empire as the historical phenomena that "politically emancipated" (p. 138) the various national bourgeoisies of the European colonial powers and saw them capture the nation-state for their economic self-aggrandizement. For Arendt, imperialism was the outcome of the alliance between surplus capital and surplus population, that is, "money" and "the mob":

> The new fact in the imperialist era is that those two superfluous forces, superfluous capital and superfluous working power, joined hands and left the country altogether. (p. 150)

Imperialism's most salient characteristic was its restlessly expansionist and domineering nature. With its triumph, "the conscious aim of the body politic" (p. 137) became closely linked to power and violence. This "expansion of political power without the foundation of a body politic" (p. 135) contradicted the commitment of the postrevolutionary nation-state to the equal rights of citizens and to republican institutions generally. Here, and elsewhere, Arendt had France in mind when she discussed the corrupting effects of imperialism on republican ideals, but clearly colonial rule ran contrary to the ethos of liberal parliamentary government and democratic ideals wherever they existed.

Besides identifying the abuses of power endemic to the imperial state abroad, her real point was that these gross violations of human and citizen rights involved in the blatant exploitation of subject peoples "boomeranged" (p. 206) back and undermined those same rights at home as a kind of "reverse colonization."[13] Expansion and domination "began with the application of bourgeois convictions to foreign affairs and only slowly [were] . . . extended to domestic politics" (p. 138). Establishing an economic and political imperium marked the onset of self-corruption and also involved the consolidation of imperial bureaucracies—what she named a "government of experts"—and of the secret police (p. 214). At times, expansion and domination seemed to be processes undertaken for their own sakes rather than out of any obvious self-interest, except continental or global domination.

Arendt yoked her analysis of the nation-state's expansionist tendencies to an analysis of the internal developments within the nation-state after the French Revolution. The title of the most powerful chapter in *Origins* tells the whole story: "The Decline of the Nation-State and the End of the Rights of Man." The post-1789 republican ideal was internally divided between a commitment to individual rights, on the one hand, and to the sovereignty of the people, on the other. Her essential point is that, over the course of the nineteenth century, the universalist vision within which individual citizen rights was central was displaced by an emphasis on the rights of the people as a whole. From this it was only a small step to defining "the people" in racial/ethnic terms. But, according to Arendt, this development was fatal, since

> the nation-state cannot exist once its principle of equality before the law has broken down. Without this legal equality, which originally was destined to replace the older laws and orders of the feudal society, the nation dissolves into an anarchic mass of over- and underprivileged individuals.[14] (p. 290)

Another important development was the emergence of a widespread hostility to existing state structures around the turn of the twentieth century. Pan-Slav and pan-German movements with their dreams of empires were not, according to Arendt, forms of nationalism, "if by the term we mean a loyalty to a stable political entity founding on equal rights for all citizens." Rather they showed a "contempt for the narrowness of the nation-state" and fed upon an "enlarged tribal consciousness" (p. 223). Such movements, she notes, aimed for a future when existing boundaries and the restrictions would be overridden. What linked the "pan" movements to racial thinking was their tendency to postulate a common essence or group "soul" that was to be "realize[d] fully in the future" (pp. 226–27, 236). In contrast with inclusive nationalisms based on universal rights inhering in individuals, central and eastern European nationalism conceived of rights as belonging to groups or to individuals as members of a "natural," that is, racial, group. Overall, Arendt's analysis of continental imperialism points to a crucial characteristic of National Socialism: a commitment to the triumph of the Aryan race rather than the German state as such.

When we factor in the traumatic impact of World War I, which created millions of "stateless," "homeless," and "rightless" peoples, the elements that "crystallized" to create the preconditions for totalitarian movements and then regimes become clearer. So-called "national minorities" were hardly better off than the stateless, since their rights depended on the good faith of their hosts and/or upon the international community. In neither case was meaningful protection forthcoming. The historical condition that struck Arendt so forcefully was the creation of millions of homeless and "superfluous" people. In a world of too many people without roots or loyalties, the conditions were ripe for political movements that defined themselves in terms of the expulsion or eradication of such excess population groups. The dissolution of a "class" society and the emergence of a "mass" society created a situation in which the move from social prejudice to legalized discrimination, then from expulsion to eventual extermination, was considered as serious policy. This situation "grew out of the fragments of a highly atomized society" marked by "isolation and the lack of normal social relationships" (p. 317). Though Arendt generally shunned social psychological speculation, the most obvious fact about the "masses" was their combination of "self-centered bitterness" and "selflessness . . . the feeling of being expendable"[15] (p. 315). Whatever the cogency of her mass society thesis as an explanation for the rise of totalitarianism, and few lend it much credence any longer, Arendt did not equate mass society, as so many conservatives did, with a society devoted to social and political equality. For her a "mass society" was one in which the legitimacy of institutional structures and cultural traditions had all but disappeared and individuals were bereft of a moral place in the world.

But this is where racism from the colonies and anti-Semitism in Europe converged, since both were involved in identifying groups for special treatment "in the name of race or class" (p. 306). What was also crucial in the development of racial totalitarianism was another "break" in the late nineteenth century—the shift from "race-thinking" to "racism," a shift that paralleled the commitment of the nation-state to imperialist expansion and the replacement of individual citizen rights by racialized group rights. According to Arendt, thinking in terms of race was relatively innocent prior to the onset of the imperial era. It was not yet "racist," if by the latter term we refer to an ideology that posits a fixed hierarchy of races. Race-thinking was compatible with the notion of a family of races, each having their proper place in the human community. Alexis de Tocqueville believed, for instance, "in the variety of races but [also] in the unity of the human species" (p. 176). She also insisted that the philology of Indo-Europeanism and "Aryanism" so prevalent in Germany was "innocent as innocent can be" and that science could not be held "responsible for race-thinking" (p.160), since scientific racism was not a cause, but an effect of, imperialist expansion and exclusionary anti-Semitism. Nor did Arendt have any use for historical claims that Hitler could be "explained" by Luther, or that the Hitler Jugend were anticipated by the German student movements of the 1810s. Racism and secular anti-Semitism were by no means the predestined fate of German thought.

Specifically, Arendt identified two dominant traditions of race-thinking in nineteenth-century Europe. The French variety, as illustrated in Gobineau's work, was essentially a substitute for the aristocracy then declining all over Europe. In this tradition, race was hostile to the nation-state. Arendt also noted that this sort of racism was closely linked to metaphors of decline and decay: "Doctrines of decay seem to have some very intimate connection with race-thinking" (p. 171). The French version of race-thinking helps explain why certain sectors of the French upper classes later identified with the Germans and supported Vichy cooperation with the Nazi anti-Semitic policies during World War II. On the other hand, the German race-thinking was originally intended to unify a disunited people rather than to divide an already existing nation-state and was thus more closely linked to nationalism. After 1815, it increasingly stressed "organic naturalistic definitions" (p. 165). Under the influence of Romanticism, ideas of "innate personality" and "natural privileges" (p. 167) emerged as attributes of Germans. Finally, by the end of the century, an "organic doctrine of history with its natural laws" and the "grotesque homunculus of the superman whose natural destiny it is to rule the world" (p. 170) had emerged.

But it was imperialism that provided the crucial context for transforming race-thinking into racism, since the various expansionist powers needed to generate an "ideological weapon of imperialistic politics." By the late nineteenth century, racism and anti-Semitism had emerged as the products of capitalist modernity in its expansionist phase. This modernization of racism and anti-Semitism involved three crucial developments. First, race-thinking was *ideologized* as a systematic worldview that could "attract and persuade" and "lead them [the people] through life" (p. 160). It was also *politicized* as the organizing principle of numerous political movements rather than just a personal opinion or social prejudice. Finally, racism and especially anti-Semitism shed much of their traditional religious justifications and, through the application of scientific theories such as Darwinism, were *biologized*. At the same time, Arendt insisted that there was no "immanent logic" linking race-thinking to racism, since the latter "sprang from experiences and political constellations which were still unknown" to the world in which race-thinking emerged. Indeed, Arendt made the stronger claim that racism would have been invented "even if no race-thinking had ever existed in the civilized world," although undoubtedly race-thinking "proved to be a powerful help." But, racism, as opposed to race-thinking, showed an "utter incompatibility with all Western political and moral standards of the past" (pp. 183–84).

If imperialism generally was one of the catalyzing factors in the emergence of totalitarianism, Arendt paid particular attention to the encounter, in central and southern Africa, between "civilized" Europeans and what appeared to the Europeans as scarcely human native populations. Informed by the spirit of Conrad's *Heart of Darkness* here and elsewhere, Arendt saw this confrontation as one with an almost absolute otherness, with what Hayden White has referred to as "arrested humanity."[16] It was, according to Arendt, the "fright of something like oneself that still under no circumstances ought to be like oneself [that] remained at the basis of slavery and became the basis for a race society" (p. 192) in South Africa. Most ominously, the European experience in South Africa led, by her account, to the first racialized society as such. There the Boers

> embarked upon a process which could only end with their own degeneration into a white race . . . having lost all consciousness that normally men do not earn a living by the color of their skin. (p. 194)

For Arendt, the lesson Europeans gleaned from their conquest was that "natural man," humans as they appear in the state of nature, had no natural rights that Europeans were bound to respect. Writing later in *Origins* of those who exist "outside the common world," she concludes:

> they are thrown back, in the midst of civilization, on their natural givenness, on their mere differentiation . . . since they are no longer allowed to partake in the human artifice, they begin to belong to the human race in much the same way as animals belong to a specific animal species. The paradox involved in the loss of human rights is that such a loss coincides with the instant when a person becomes a human being in general (p. 302).

In appearing to lack a settled place in the world, the indigenous peoples of Africa seemed also to lack some of the essentials of human existence. Most ominously, at least in retrospect, the above passage—which in fact describes the homeless/stateless peoples in post–World War I Europe and the inhabitants of the camp system—suggests that what happened in Africa foreshadowed what was to happen between 1933 and 1945 in Europe. Conrad's Kurtz's crushing injunction—"exterminate all the brutes"—was applied by Europeans to other Europeans. As Arendt notes in her 1946 proposal for what becomes *Origins*: "Conrad's Kurtz inspite [sic] of being a fiction character has become a reality in the Nazi character."[17] Whether the Europeans found or created a "state of nature" situation in Africa, it was a disaster for all concerned.

Driven by lust for gold and diamonds and for empire generally, Europeans in Africa produced superfluous natural products, made possible by the investment of superfluous capital and the labor of superfluous men. They began to think of themselves as gods meant to rule absolutely over the native populations. Though the Boers were still engaged in a recognizably economic enterprise, Arendt contends that imperialist expansion was driven by a mentality that transcended utilitarian calculation or economic self-interest. Not only did the expansionist mentality prefigure totalitarian forms of thinking, the racialized societies of the Belgian Congo, German South West Africa, and Dutch-British South Africa foreshadowed the essential nature of racist societies everywhere:

> no matter whether racism appears as the natural result of catastrophe or as the conscious instrument for bringing it about, it is always closely tied to contempt for labor, hatred of territorial limitations, general rootlessness and an activist faith in one's own divine chosenness (p. 197).

I will explore the role Africa played in Arendt's philosophical anthropology in the next section of this chapter, but here I want to examine objections to her claim for the great historical importance of Africa for Europe. One objection to Arendt's thesis is that she never really established specific causal links between colonial rule and the corruption of the various European body politics. Of the countries most heavily involved in African colonialism—Britain, France, and Belgium—it is hard to point to large-scale fascist or racist-imperialist political movements at home attributable to imperial experience in Africa. Germany's involvement in Southwest Africa, though relatively minor, did create a breeding ground for Nazi racism, and Mussolini's fascist regime did fight a war in Ethiopia in the 1930s. And, despite its system of legalized racism and a pervasive social racism, the United States, surely a "race" society before South Africa, did not develop a significant fascist-racist politics at home, though racist and nativist thinking was widespread up to World War II. Still, colonization of Africa had very definite negative effects in Europe. Some of the Algerian conflict of the 1950s and early 1960s was fought out on French soil, and almost led to a coup d'état, while Northern Ireland's agonies are still played out in London and other major British cities, not to mention in North Ireland itself.

On this whole matter, I would suggest that Arendt is best read as arguing not for strong causality but for historical prefiguration or foreshadowing. What happened in Africa, she seems to say, created an ethos in which total domination and mass extermination might more easily take hold in Europe. As she writes in summing up her "Race and Bureaucracy" chapter, "the stage seemed to be set for all possible horrors. Lying under anybody's nose were many of the elements which gathered together could create totalitarian government under racism" (p. 221).[18] The Belgian Congo and the genocide carried out by Germans in Southwest Africa against the Herero in 1904 *were* African precedents for genocide, facts she might have made more of. By focusing more attention on the Herero genocide, she could have established more direct links between the German colonial experiment in Southwest Africa, the racialization of German anthropology and social thought prior to 1933, and Nazi racial science and policy. Indeed, several individuals who were active in Southwest Africa were later instrumental in the development of Nazi racial policies, most strikingly, Hermann Goering's father, but also the scientist Eugen Fischer and social scientist Paul Rohrbach.[19] This is not to say that Africa was the only, or the chief factor, in creating the preconditions for Nazi extermination policies. But it does suggest that Southwest Africa was a kind of staging area for the development of racist science in Germany. Arendt could have further strengthened her case by attending to the way academic disciplines such as anthropology fed on, and in turn fed, the attitudes and policies informing the British and French colonial enterprises.[20] Besides the literary and cultural influence of the colonial experience suggested by Edward Said in *Culture and Imperialism*, European medicine, including psychiatry, developed specific etiologies and diagnostics for dealing with colonial patients and for colonial subjects in Europe. The United States, with its own internal colony in the South, presented perhaps the extreme case of a culture saturated with racial concerns and anxieties on the eve of World War I. Thus, I would suggest that Arendt under- rather than over-stated the pervasive impact of the colonial experience on the cultural life of Western Europe, North America, and the Antipodes.

Finally, there is the question of anti-Semitism. In the "Anti-Semitism" section of *Origins*, Arendt begins by challenging the conventional wisdom circulating in the post-Holocaust world. She rejects the Zionist idea of an "eternal anti-semitism" and also insists on the crucial distinction between "modern anti-Christian anti-semitism" and "the old religious Jew-hatred" (p. 7). Nor does she accept the scapegoat theory of anti-Semitism, since it implies that any other group could have been the object of Nazi hatred and also posits "the perfect innocence of the victim" (p. 5). She also rejects the related notion that anti-Semitism had been an "accident" or a "pretext" for economic or even political self-interest on the part of the Nazis (or other fascist parties). Finally, she focuses on the way that Nazi anti-Semitism and the "pan" movements were driven by a kind of envious imitation of the Jews: claims to "racial superiority" mirrored "Jewish claims for cho-senness"; Jews, like other stateless ethnic groups, were "without country and state"; and Jews, thought many, were guided by the secret cabal spoken of in the Protocols of the Elders of Zion (pp. 5, 239–43). Anti-Semitism "had the dubious honor of setting the whole infernal machine in motion" (p. 3) and was thus the "catalyzer" or "amalgamator" of the other forces and factors. It led the way toward, but was clearly not the only condition necessary for, the emergence of totalitarianism in Germany. It was clearly central to the Nazi vision of a "society of dying" and a "system in which men are superfluous" (pp. 427–28).

The story Arendt constructed about post-emancipation European Jewry—in reality her focus falls preponderantly on Germany Jewry—was a complex one. Rich Jews, she claims, had historically helped finance the emerging nation-state and had thus become identified with it. When, however, the existing state structures came under attack in the late nineteenth century, Jews were included in that attack, since they were identified with the political status quo. At the same time, Jews were losing their privileged status as international financiers and political mediators. Once those roles were lost, Jews became exceedingly vulnerable. (Arendt's analysis here reminds one of the cynical observation that the only thing worse than being exploited is *not* being exploited.) In general, this line of analysis bore a close resemblance to the one proposed by Adorno and Horkheimer.

But Arendt's real interest was in the relationship between politics and society as it bore on the fate of European Jewry, particular of middle-class Jews. As she writes,

> political anti-semitism developed because the Jews were a separate body, while social discrimination arose because of the growing equality of Jews with all other groups. (p. 54)

What European Jewry lacked, according to Arendt, was political experience and a tradition of political resistance. As a result, the "parvenu" desire to be accepted into gentile society took pride of place, and social acceptance was preferred to equal political rights: "[O]nly its enemies, and almost never its friends, understood that the Jewish question was a political one" (p. 56). In other words, post-emancipation Jewry should have recognized that political and legal protection rather than social assimilation was of prime importance. In typological terms, the proud "pariah," the Jew of marginal status, was preferable to the "parvenu" who yearned to be accepted into gentile society.[21] For Arendt, the significance of the Dreyfus affair in France was that it posed all the issues of the social versus the political, or the parvenu versus the pariah, in particularly clear form.

Arendt identified another radical break with tradition when she notes that over the course of the nineteenth century, "Judaism" or "Jewry," terms that referred to religious-institutional and demographic entities, respectively, gave way to "Jewishness." The latter was a "psychological quality," one that many Gentiles and Jews essentialized and by which they were either fascinated or repelled (pp. 66–74). Arendt draws chilling conclusions from this development. Once Jewishness became a "psychological quality," it was either a "virtue" or a "vice" (p. 83) and sometimes both. But, notes Arendt,

> Jews had been able to escape from Judaism into conversion; from Jewishness there was no escape. A crime, moreover, is met with punishment; a vice can only be exterminated. (p. 87)

Moreover, the insistence on *social* (as opposed to political) equality exacerbated "conflicts between groups" and made "differences become all the more conspicuous" (p. 54). In a complex way, the politicization of the "Jewish Question" in the last quarter of the nineteenth century was the response of gentile society to the Jewish desire to belong. Only the Zionists responded half-way adequately, claims Arendt, for they recognized that the central issue facing European Jews was not whether they were accepted into gentile society but whether they were protected legally and guaranteed access to the political process and/or could finally establish their own state.

Finally, Arendt's account of the triumph of racism over race-thinking, of the idea of ethnic-state over the citizen-body state, of biological over religious anti-Semitism, and of Jewishness over Judaism was a powerful tour de force. Again, Arendt's point was not that these historical forces and factors led by themselves to the emergence of totalitarianism in general or of the Holocaust in particular. Rather, she seems to want to explain why European Jewry was so unprepared, so vulnerable, when the Nazis came to power on an explicitly anti-Semitic platform and eventually embarked on their extermination project. Hers is an enormously suggestive effort to understand the political and social experience of continental Jewry between emancipation and extermination, particularly the degree to which European Jewry was not responsible for, but was historically complicit in, the horrendous process.

Race and the Death of Man: Toward a Philosophical Anthropology

I want to conclude my discussion by exploring Arendt's thesis that the emergence of totalitarianism marked a radical break with "the whole structure of Western culture with all its implied beliefs, traditions, standards of judgement" (p. 434, 1st ed.). The triumph of racism in Europe marked the demise of the idea of a unified human community and of Western humanism. With the human race divided by insuperable biological barriers, it was no longer possible to speak of a common human nature, condition, or *telos*. Against this background, *Origins* should also be understood as Arendt's intervention in the "humanism" debate initiated by Jean-Paul Sartre in his "Existentialism Is a Humanism" (1946), and continued most immediately by her two philosophical mentors, Martin Heidegger in his "Letter on Humanism" (1947) and Karl Jaspers in *The Question of German Guilt* (1947). As already mentioned, Arendt used history (not psychoanalysis, sociology, or phenomenology as such) as a way of illuminating the moral and conceptual crisis in humanism and of proposing a new way of thinking about human being in the wake of the collapse of the Western tradition. Rather, than evoking Being (as did Heidegger), championing subjectivity (as did Sartre) or placing undue hope in progress through rationality or proposing a conservative rejection of modernity, Arendt turned to historical experience as the starting point for an meditation upon what modernity revealed or obscured about the human condition. Though her impulses were conservative—she always emphasized the importance of institutional stability and authority, what might be called a vision of limits—she was never a conservative in a political-ideological sense.[22] The task, as she saw it, was to live in the present, not in the past or in the future.

Although Arendt was unambiguous about totalitarianism's radical break with the Western tradition, her private comments reveal a more nuanced view. In an exchange of letters with Karl Jaspers on the nature of evil in 1951, she notes that she had "the suspicion that philosophy was not entirely innocent" and added: "I haven't finally gone to all this effort to discover the elements of totalitarian forms of rule in order to exonerate the Western tradition from Plato to Nietzsche."[23] Specifically, she was struck by the failure of Western political thought to provide an adequate vocabulary of concepts to describe or explain totalitarianism. The three classical categories of forms of rule—monarchy, aristocracy, and democracy, and their perversions tyranny, oligarchy, and mob rule—failed to capture the unique features of totalitarian domination. Nor was modern political science's emphasis on utilitarian self-interest as the explanation for political behavior any more adequate, since the single most striking feature of totalitarianism in power, as not only Arendt but also Dwight Macdonald insisted, had been its tendency to act contrary to self-interest as normally understood. One of the distinguishing features of the totalitarian ethos was that "common sense has lost its validity" (p. 342); as a result, ideological consistency was more important than correspondence with reality or the ability to learn from experience. Totalitarian ideologies do not aim to illuminate but to transform reality. If nothing else in her work, this characterization of totalitarianism as "beyond" instrumental rationality or self-interest calls into question the claims of Adorno and Horkheimer, for instance, that modern domination is guided by instrumental reason in the service of capital, and it also helps capture the way in which the camp system differed from slavery, ancient or modern.[24]

In the same letter to Jaspers, Arendt also suggests that Christianity and Judaism failed to supply an adequate concept of the evil at the heart of totalitarian domination:

> [M]odern crimes were not provided for in the Decalogue. Or: the west-
> ern tradition suffers from the prejudice that the most evil that human-
> ity can do arises out of selfishness, while we know that the most evil

or radical evil no longer has anything to do with such humanly con-
ceivable sinful matters.[25]

Thus her introduction of the notion of radical evil near the end of *Origins*
is a provisional attempt to repair this fault in the philosophical and religious tradition. She ends her anatomy of total domination by outlining the
mechanisms whereby camp inmates were systematically deprived of their
"juridical," "moral," and unique, personal identity (pp. 447–53). Evil
seems to involve the attempt to change human nature by creating a purely
superfluous human being, characterized only by "animal reaction and fulfillment of function" (pp. 427–28, 1st ed.), and bereft of motivation, will,
or freedom. As she explains to Jaspers:

> What radical evil is I don't know, but it seems to me it has somehow
> to be linked with . . . the superfluity of human beings as such (not to
> use them as means, which leaves their humanity unaffected and only
> wounds their worth as humans).[26]

Thus what happened in the camps went beyond any recognizable form of
exploitation or instrumentalization of humans. It involved the systematic
attempt to fabricate not only corpses but to reduce individuals to the
"merely" human without the humanizing effect of culture. What the camps
produced were "specimens of the human animal" since "man's 'nature' is
only" human insofar as it opens up to man the possibility of being something highly unnatural" (p. 455). All this, for Arendt, was the result of
modernity's basic premise that "everything is possible." At the end of
modern history stood natural man, once again.

Still, Arendt's indictment of the Western tradition as guilty only of
sins of omission regarding totalitarianism and racism needs to be challenged. First, there is the tradition in Western thought, originating with
Aristotle, that assumes some people have a slavish nature and thus might
justly be enslaved: "[S]ome men are by nature free, and others slaves, and
that for these latter slavery is both expedient and right."[27] Though
Aristotle's position was not linked with race or cultural difference, his
idea that enslaving a person might be justifiable was an integral part of
the intellectual tradition. Furthermore, the idea that there were biological
differences among peoples that justified slavery and made extermination
easier had clearly emerged in the Western hemisphere by the seventeenth
century, much earlier than Arendt's focus on the "second" imperialism of

the late nineteenth century would suggest. And the (benign) idea of a family of races, which she linked to the Enlightenment, already encompassed differential/hierarchical orderings of various races well before the explicit emergence of nineteenth-century racial science. Indeed, one of the central concerns of the Enlightenment was to develop a taxonomy of the natural world, including humanity. Arendt was essentially correct to make a strong connection between racism and European expansion, but hierarchical racism, as opposed to horizontal race-thinking, emerged much earlier and much more decisively than she allowed.[28]

Arendt's exclusion of science from responsibility for racism is likewise highly dubious. Science is not some sort of platonic entity or natural kind; rather, it changes over time, adopting or abandoning positions according to prevailing views as they confront empirical evidence. What does seem to remain constant in modern science is the assumption that nature can be understood, dominated, and used for human purposes. The strength of the scientific tradition is its potential for self-correction, a capability that has become clear in challenges to scientific racism particularly in the twentieth century. But it is hard to see why a science that creates categories of racial classification that later turn out to be empirically untenable should be considered pseudo-science, just because they have been proven wrong or their effects have been horrific. We do not deny Newton's theory scientific status in its time just because it has now been in some contexts superseded. Nor is nuclear physics considered non-science because some of its outcomes are inimical to human or natural well-being.

Third, though Arendt always objected to the functional identification of secular ideologies such as Nazism or Marxism with religion, it is highly unlikely that the redemptive/emancipatory political ideologies of the twentieth century could have marshaled their appeal without the waning of these traditions of mass, communal religious belief. Moreover, Christianity has a tendency to divide the world into two distinct spiritual and moral camps and to develop its theology according to a binary logic. Such a protoparanoid worldview is also crucial to totalitarian ideologies. Finally, though Arendt's differentiation between traditional religious "Jew hatred" and modern anti-Semitism was immensely important when she advanced it, there has been a more complex (and stronger) connection between the two than she allowed. Biological anti-Semitism was a variation on, rather than a break with, religious anti-Semitism. One can imagine that Arendt's response to these charges would have been something like this: "All of this may be true, but none of these ideas, even at its worst, was a warrant for genocide or a prescription for the relentless dehumanization of human beings."

Whatever the case regarding the unprecedented nature of totalitarian genocide, Arendt was convinced that formulating a new basis for human dignity and solidarity was absolutely necessary.

> For man, in the sense of the nature of man, is no longer the measure, despite what the new humanists would have us believe. . . . [W]e shall have to create—not merely discover—a new foundation for human community as such. (p. 434, 1st ed.)

Her distinction between "create" and "discover" implies that rights are not "natural" or "inalienable": they are human artifacts. Second, in this passage, Arendt shifts her focus from human nature to human solidarity and human community. Humanity itself is the only source of human solidarity. Unlike existentialism, Arendt does not focus on the agonized and isolated individual as the site where the loss of meaning is most acutely registered. In her view, modern history had seen the systematic discrediting of all myths of origins and the loss of faith in anything that stood outside of history. There remains no way to ground human beings and solidarity in nature or history-as-tradition, much less in the Enlightenment faith in the "coming of age" of human beings and faith in "human nature" itself (pp. 434–37, 1st ed.). It was the ontological vacuum created by the loss of all these possible foundations for a human community that the idea of race sought to fill. But, for Arendt, race was no answer at all:

> For no matter what learned scientists may say, race is, politically speaking, not the beginning of humanity but its end, not the origins of peoples but their decay, not the natural birth of man but his unnatural death. (p. 157)

Arendt separated herself from most of the "end of humanism" thinkers by offering an essentially political answer to the crisis in European humanism.[29] Her answer is built on two contentions: first, "the condition for the establishment of rights is the plurality of men; rights exist because we inhabit the earth together with other men" (p. 437, 1st ed.). Individual plurality is in turn bound up with the idea that "the right to have rights . . . should be guaranteed by humanity itself"; that "the fundamental deprivation of human rights is manifested first and above all in the deprivation of a place in the world which makes opinions significant and actions effective"; and, finally, that "only the loss of a polity itself expels him [any human being] from humanity" (pp. 296–98). Such a "right to have rights" implies the rejection of any narrowly utilitarian grounding of rights in the claim that they are "good for" something or somebody (pp. 299, 437, 1st ed.). It also entails the idea that "crimes against humanity" are the kind of violation for which everyone must be responsible (p. 436, 1st ed.), since they violate the humanity shared by everyone. But again, rights are creations not discoveries, posited rather than inherent in the nature of things. They were not won through struggle for recognition per se, as in a Hegelianized model of rights acquisition, although they might on occasion have to be. Nor is she even claiming that the "fact" of plurality entails the existence of rights. Rather, she claims that plurality makes rights necessary in order to preserve the "space between" so vital for plurality. They are the condition of possibility for plurality.[30]

But in emphasizing the basic right to belong to a political space, Arendt rejects ethnic, racial, or religious criteria for political belonging or privilege within the political community.[31] Equality is a political rather than a natural "fact," and thus should not be a prerequisite for belonging to a political community. One of the worst things that a political community can do is to entrench a differential assignment of rights. It is, however, important to note that, in contrast with the expansive vision of politics that she later developed, her model of the polity, particularly in the first edition of *Origins*, was organized around an essentially defensive notion of rights. Indeed, after *Origins* Arendt never spoke of "the right to have rights," though she remained firm in the belief that the only protections we can even begin to depend on derive from a specific political community, that is, the modern nation-state or perhaps some federated system of political communities, none of which should enjoy absolute sovereignty. The crushing lesson of modern history was that to depend on international or transnational organizations, the good will of private individuals or of groups for enforcement of human rights had been a prescription for grief. Having failed once, no one could afford to depend on them a second time. Universalism without particular political entities to implement and enforce rights was impotent.

Finally, it is important to link Arendt's new basis for human solidarity back to her description of the European encounter with Africans in the late nineteenth century. Though she is reporting on the reactions of the European settlers to the otherness of Africa, Arendt seems at times to share their shock of nonrecognition:

> Europeans were faced with tribes which, as far as we know, never had found by themselves any adequate expression of human reason or human passion in either cultural deeds or popular customs, and which had developed human institutions to a very low level. (p. 177)

The "as far as we know" represents, I think, her authorial voice rather than just signaling a paraphrase of the thought processes of Europeans. She also describes the Africans as inhabiting a "world of folly," a place that "nobody had ever taken the trouble to change into a human landscape" (p. 191). They were

> human beings who, living without a future of a purpose and the past of an accomplishment, were as incomprehensible as the inmates of a madhouse. (p. 191)

They "behaved like a part of nature" (p. 192). Without a "political body" (at best they had large armies), they massacred each other in an "unreal, incomprehensible process which cannot be accepted by man and therefore is not remembered by human history" (p. 193).

At issue here is not whether Arendt recognized the human status of the Africans. She notes at one point that the "black men stubbornly insisted on retaining their human features" (p. 195) and observes that they were "becoming more and more aware of their humanity under the impact of regular labor and urban life" (p. 205). In the second edition of *Origins*, she refers to the denial of "rights" to Negroes in the United States and the impossibility of "action" when they are treated as examples of the natural category "Negro" (pp. 301–2). Nor is hers a Eurocentric position per se since she notes that there is simply "no excuse" for treating Chinese and Indians as though they were not human beings (p. 206). But her attack on the devastation wrought by imperialism in central and southern Africa is informed by something like the view, most commonly attributed to Hegel, that Africans, as stateless peoples, lack a full history or culture. (There is also a tradition in German anthropology that distinguished *Naturvölker* [primitive peoples] and *Kulturvölker* [people of culture].) Here Chinua Achebe's indictment of Conrad is to the point. According to Achebe,

Conrad traveled in the part of central Africa where the Fang people produced masks and sculptures that had such a great impact on Picasso and Matisse, and yet could attribute to the inhabitants of central Africa only the most primitive forms of thought or behavior. As Edward Said has noted of Conrad: "[H]e writes as a man whose Western view of the non-Western world is so ingrained as to blind him to other histories, other cultures, other aspirations."[32] Surely, that judgment should also be directed toward this "ethnocentric strain" in Arendt's thought in *Origins*. Indeed, at times *Origins* sounds like a rewrite of *Heart of Darkness* in the negative as well as positive sense. A major difference would be that in *Origins* the "horror" lies unambiguously in modern Europe not in the (allegedly) primal scene of Africa.[33]

I must confess bafflement at how Arendt could have expressed such views. One way of dealing with them would be to distinguish, as Jürgen Habermas does in another context, a thinker's "work" from his/her "Weltanschauung," the "philosophy" from the "ideology."[34] Such a distinction might prove useful in formal philosophical analysis, but it will not do as intellectual history. Arendt's characterization of African culture does not discredit her work as such, but it does, however, shed fresh light on several fundamental characteristics of her thought. First, as a "splitter" (not a "lumper") Arendt displays what Agnes Heller calls a "penchant for absolutizing her distinctions,"[35] a tendency closely linked with her hostility to reductionist modes of thought (such as Marxism or psychoanalysis or functionalism). Specifically, the distinction that underlies *Origins*—as well as much of Arendt's thought—is the deep opposition between the natural and the human, nature and culture. Her rejection of nature as a source of values or as an explanation of human thought or action was of a piece with her rejection of biological differences between people as politically irrelevant—and pernicious. And yet her commitment to the priority of culture to nature, of action to behavior, inclined her to denigrate cultures that seemed too close to nature, ones that had somehow failed to create a sophisticated political and cultural world. Indeed, in *The Human Condition*, she was to consign the satisfaction of biological needs and the labor that produced those basic satisfactions to an inferior place on the scale of human activities.[36] Yet Arendt, unlike Conrad, never suggested that Africa or Africans were mysteriously evil or seductive or that they actively corrupted the Europeans. Rather, it was what she referred to as "the dark background of mere givenness" (p. 301) and of life apparently lived without "the human artifice" (p. 300), the blankness of blackness as it were, that allowed the Europeans free rein in the face of the incomprehensible.

The only other explanation I can find for her negative characterization of African culture lies in the striking resonances between the massacre of millions of "natural" people of Africa in the late nineteenth and early twentieth century and the genocide visited upon the inmates of the Nazi camps, who had been stripped of any sort of protections of state or culture.[37] She may have transferred her anger, shame, and contempt for what happened to the Jews to contempt for what had happened to the Africans. If Orlando Patterson's characterization of life under slavery as "social death" is apt, then, for Arendt, the worst thing that could befall any people was "political death," extrusion from a human order.[38]

Unless we are certain that we are immune from those feelings to which Arendt fell prey, we should think through our attitude toward those whom we see degraded or enslaved as carefully as we should our attitudes toward those who enslave and degrade them. The temptation to hold the victims in contempt is very strong, just as Patterson notes that in almost all societies former slaves are looked upon with contempt, presumably for allowing themselves to have been enslaved, for preferring degrading life to honorable death. A witness to such a complex swirl of feelings, *The Guardian* reporter, David Beresford, once described the distressing, disorienting effects of observing the massive scene of death and dying in Rwanda in 1994:

> Dry-retching as I battled to take notes, I came away concerned for my mind, worried that I was learning a contempt for life through the discovery of the low value attached to it. A contempt which eventually must prove self-destructive.[39]

Finally, Arendt's analysis in *Origins* rested on two paradoxes, one I think she was aware of and one she was not. The first concerns the contradictory history of the nation-state. On the one hand, the nation-state was for Arendt the only possible political home in the modern world, the only entity that had a chance of protecting individual rights and preserving a human world of plurality. And yet its history had been an unhappy one of exclusion of ethnic and racial others in the attempt to achieve social/cultural homogeneity. The nation-state was both historically untenable and necessary, disastrous yet unavoidable. It was a particularist entity but one that was meant to preserve universal political and legal rights.

The other paradox involves Western humanism. One disturbing implication of Arendt's thinking is that the more intellectually "developed" a culture is, the more it is able to articulate a vision of common humanity, the greater is the temptation to differentiate among human cultures, to judge the relative achievements of various peoples and create a hierarchy of cultures. The confrontation with otherness seems to lead to the denigration of difference more often that it leads to respect for that difference. As a normative notion, humanism suggests discriminations among forms of life, whether within one culture or between cultures. Not the state of nature but the political realm is the realm of equality in Arendt's thought, while the social (and cultural) realm is the place where the differences of plurality are preserved. Thus, Arendt's own thought remained ensnared in the paradoxes of normative humanism, even as she took agonizing stock of the scene of European humanism's demise, beginning in Africa and ending in Auschwitz, and tried to develop a new basis for renewed human solidarity.

Part II

Modernization and Dominated Cultures

5

African American Culture
and the Price of Modernization

Negroes had never been allowed to catch the full spirit of Western civiliza-
tion. . . . [T]hey lived somehow in it but not of it.

Richard Wright

These were not really my creations; they did not contain my history; I might
search in vain forever for any reflection of myself. I was an interloper; this was
not my heritage. At the same time I had no other heritage which I could possibly
hope to use—I had certainly been unfitted for the jungle and the tribe. I would
have to appropriate those white centuries, I would have to make them mine.

James Baldwin

Historically, the discipline of sociology originated in the attempt to describe and explain the process of modernization. Shorthand conceptual-
izations of that process—the shift from *Gemeinschaft* to *Gesellschaft*
(Toennies), from status to contract (Maine), from mechanical to organic
(Durkheim), from traditional to rational (Weber), or from feudal to bourgeois (Marx)—have become clichés in the intellectual history of modernization. In the United States, modernization has referred to the transformation of an agricultural into an industrial economy and of a rural, folk
culture into a secular, urban culture. In contrast with the Marxist vision of
a classless society, liberal modernization theory assumed that, though role
differentiation and even social stratification would increase, the importance of race and ethnicity, not to mention religion, would fade as modernization proceeded apace. This assumption is evident in sociologist
Robert Park's schema that foresaw racial and ethnic conflict eventually
giving way to full assimilation, although clearly atavistic white prejudice
and black cultural "backwardness" would need addressing.[1]

123

Central to the American modernization process was the "Great Migration" of African Americans from the rural South to the urban North after 1914. There are two possible models to draw upon to describe the impact of this process on black Southerners come North. One stresses the process of "class formation," while the other emphasizes the process of "ghettoization" as reflected in the various histories of white ethnic groups. In fact, there is also an "exceptionalist" model according to which neither the class formation model nor the white ethnic model but a specifically African American model of ghetto formation is projected. In this model, white racial prejudice and black cultural difference prevent black migrants from becoming part of the white class structure, and thus they also fail to find political allies among the white working class. Nor did the African American experience in the North follow the white ethnic model, according to which ghettoization is succeeded by social and cultural assimilation into the dominant white society. Again, this was due to racial prejudice among white Americans and the aftereffects of the Jim Crow system in the South, both of which seriously hindered assimilation.[2]

On a global scale, "becoming modern" was seen as an objective, universal process, while "being modern" referred to the characteristics of the West that were held up as the ideal destination for the rest of the world. Other cultures could achieve in the future what the West already had achieved in the past and present, while subcultures within modern Western societies could become modern by shedding their particularist "folk" cultural traditions and loyalties.[3] Of course, the reality was something quite other. Modernization was a condition that the West had "invented" and then imposed on other cultures. Indeed, in postwar discussions of these matters, the terms "modernization" and "Westernization" were pretty much equated.[4]

The interwar years also saw race discredited as an explanation for cultural differences. But if race was not the explanation, one alternative explanation lay precisely in the area of culture. On this account, the West had been more successful in modernizing because of certain cultural values generated by its long and complex history. (Max Weber's "Protestant ethic" thesis is perhaps the best-known example of this type of cultural explanation.) But one problem with such an explanation was that it tended to explain cultural difference and levels of modernization by—cultural difference and levels of modernization. That is, it tended to assume as already existing what it set out to show as emergent in the modernization process. It was in such a context that the modern debate about the nature of African American culture was carried on. Both W. E. B. Du Bois and Alain Locke described American "Negro" culture as having significant, as yet untapped, strengths worthy of recognition, even celebration. Yet what Du Bois famously referred to as "double consciousness" was itself double-edged, since it suggested that black Americans were torn between the demands of the general American, that is, white culture, and the claims of their own cultural experience. Thus, one of the historical tasks of African American intellectuals was to reconcile their own "folk" cultural experience with modern American culture.

In this chapter, I want to look at four figures—Gunnar Myrdal, E. Franklin Frazier, Richard Wright, and James Baldwin—who articulated what now seems a largely negative, or at best ambivalent, view of African American culture. It is important immediately to state that these men were not white racists, racial/cultural conservatives, or self-hating African Americans. Far from it. The broadly progressive, that is, liberal and/or radical political credentials of Gunnar Myrdal and E. Franklin Frazier, Richard Wright, and James Baldwin are not in question. But it is important to note several things. As secular intellectuals in the Enlightenment tradition of rational critique of traditional, that is, irrational, culture, they (with the qualified exception of Baldwin) were suspicious of (folk) religion and premodern folk culture generally. Second, they were all in a broad sense integrationists, even assimilationists. Third, the emphasis on the shortcomings of African American culture was a consensus view among the black and white left well into the 1960s. The political left tended to be suspicious of those who celebrated the creative power of African American culture, since such celebrations diverted attention from the white society's role in creating and perpetuating racial segregation and oppression. It was only by the end of the 1960s that a consensus emerged, particularly among African American intellectuals, that African American culture was a culture of "creativity and resistance."

Finally, I want to suggest that the argument about the relative damage or creativity of African American culture has been badly stated. In fact, two sorts of phenomena were, and are, at issue. When the modernizers referred to black culture as weak or even pathological, they were usually referring to the inadequacies of its social institutions and organizations, especially the family. But when culturalists such as Melville Herskovits, Alain Locke, Zora Neale Hurston, and later Ralph Ellison and Albert Murray stressed the creativity and vitality of African American culture, they had in mind its expressive culture, that is the music, literature, painting, dance, and their underlying folkloric foundations. It was only in the 1960s that the view of black American culture as a source of cultural and *political* resistance to the dominant white culture triumphed. Prior to that, political resistance had little or nothing to do with cultural strengths or weaknesses.

Myrdal and the Pathology of Negro Culture

One of the most striking things about *An American Dilemma* was Myrdal's belief that black culture and institutions lacked the resources to play a major role in transforming the conditions of African American life. Indeed the much less political Robert Park paid more attention to black cultural consciousness than did Myrdal, the progressive sociologist. At the beginning of chapter 43 ("Institutions") in *An American Dilemma*, Myrdal asserts that the black "family, crime, insanity and cultural accomplishments" are "not focal to our inquiry," despite the fact that Myrdal had insisted that improving "standards of intelligence, ambition, health, education, decency, manners and morals"[5] was crucial to black progress. In fact, Myrdal was so little concerned with the cultural aspects of the American dilemma that the initial drafts of the two chapters dealing with Negro cultural and institutional life were written by one of Myrdal's assistants, Arnold Rose.

Not surprisingly, Myrdal was of the opinion that American Negro institutions "show little similarity to African institutions," thereby dismissing anthropologist Melville Herskovits's claim that African cultural survivals in the United States directly shaped the core practices and beliefs of black American culture. Myrdal generalizes the point when he announces the assumption behind, and the conclusion to, his inquiry:

> In practically all its divergences, American Negro culture is not something independent of general American culture. It is a distorted development, or a pathological condition, of the general American culture.

From this, he concludes that

> it is to the advantage of American Negroes as individuals and as a group to become assimilated into American culture. . . . This will be the value premise here . . . [that] in America, American culture is "highest" in the pragmatic sense (vol. 2, pp. 928–29).

In reading these passages, it is easy to miss the way Myrdal moves almost imperceptibly from Negro culture as "not something independent" to Negro culture as a "distorted development" and finally as "a pathological condition." The rhetorical escalation is considerable to say the least. Just after these passages, Myrdal acknowledges—and then sidesteps—the issue of cultural equality. He first grants the salutary effect of "the notion popularized by anthropologists that all cultures may be good under the different conditions to which they are adaptations" (p. 929). But he then gives his judgment a pragmatic spin: black Americans should forget the abstract issue of cultural equality and adapt to, by adopting, the dominant "American" (i.e., white) culture. As mentioned in a previous chapter, Myrdal deploys the binary opposition "general/local" to structure his normative argument. As always, the more general, the better; the more local, the worse.

That said, the normative standard Myrdal applied to the black family, schools, clubs, and churches was their success or failure in nurturing political change. In light of its later importance in the civil rights movement, Myrdal's dismissal of the black church as "an ordinary American church with certain traits exaggerated because of caste," and his failure to identify its potential to mobilize the black masses are striking. According to Myrdal, the modern black church has become "a more efficient instrument" for progress, but thereby its "relative importance . . . in the Negro community" is diminished. Only "the fighting [Negro] press" received good marks for its political militancy from Myrdal (vol. 2, pp. 873, 878, 908). Though Myrdal did detect stirrings of political discontent among African Americans, his main concern was to improve the quality of black political leadership so that it could forge political alliances with white groups. But a political movement targeted primarily at the Negro community seemed neither possible nor desirable. Myrdal treated Marcus Garvey with a certain wary respect but no great enthusiasm. The two lessons to be drawn from Garvey's rise and fall were that, first, support for the United Negro Improvement Association (UNIA) in the 1920s "testifies to the unrest in the Negro community"; and, second, "a Negro movement in America is doomed to ultimate dissolution and collapse if it cannot gain white support." "This," he concludes, "is the real dilemma" (vol. 2, p. 749).

And so it remains down to the present day. The parallel with the cultural issue is clear—the more general the political base and the goals are, the more chance there would be for significant change in the condition of black Americans. But Myrdal's position on these matters was hardly controversial at the time. There is no evidence that it was unpopular with his most trusted black associates Ralph Bunche and E. Franklin Frazier. Bunche was more politically radical than Myrdal, while Frazier was a figure of considerable intellectual independence. But concerning the strengths and weaknesses of black institutional culture, both men were in general agreement with Myrdal.[6]

How can we explain this near unanimity regarding the status of "Negro" culture circa 1945? First, contrary to Myrdal's reputation as an overly optimistic (and flattering) foreign visitor, neither black or white American culture emerged from his study unscathed. If black culture was imitative and black institutions politically ineffectual, the white culture and its institutions were disfigured by racist assumptions and compromised by divided moral commitments. Moreover, there was something to be said for *An American Dilemma*'s skepticism concerning the political potential of African American institutions and culture. African American life had been profoundly shaped—and scarred—by slavery and segregation. Specifically, black institutions suffered from the long-term effects of limited resources and had only sporadic historical success with political mobilization. Finally, it is important to note that Myrdal's motive was a constructive one. He opted for a critical perspective on black culture and institutions in order that they might develop greater political effectiveness.

In addition, most "progressive" social scientists (of both races) assumed the causal priority of social and economic factors in explaining human action and stressed politics as the key to change. Except for a figure like Du Bois, neither race nor culture as an explanation or a basis for opposition carried much weight. From the perspective of the 1930s and early 1940s, then, a focus on black culture was a serious diversion and would lend too much retrospective credibility to the Garveyite black nationalism of the 1920s, certainly no favorite of the progressive black intellectual establishment at the time. Frazier, for instance, profoundly disagreed with W. E. B. Du Bois's turn toward black self-sufficiency in the 1930s, attacking him in harsh terms for what he saw as a retreat from a head-on challenge to white society. Moreover, the celebration of cultural and racial differences smacked too much of the Nazi doctrines of Aryan racial and cultural superiority. In a world where a global, universalist perspective seemed the hope for the future, black cultural nationalism seemed hardly more compelling than the particularistic racial loyalties of white Southerners.[7]

Other factors were also at work. Myrdal himself had little interest in questions of culture, whether high, popular, or folk. Indeed, several critics have since stressed the inadequacy of Myrdal's "moralizing" approach, particularly when combined with his preference for a "rational mechanical, social-engineering remedy,"[8] a cast of mind not noted for its sensitivity to philosophical complexity or expressive culture. It is hard to imagine Arendt's *Origins of Totalitarianism* without the haunting echoes of Kafka, Heidegger, and St. Augustine, or to understand *The Dialectic of Enlightenment* without taking into account the sensibility of the interwar European avant-garde informing it. But no similar literary or philosophical reference points come to mind when reading Myrdal's two-volume work. At best, its philosophical orientation reminds the reader of John Dewey's earnest combination of social engineering and morality yoked to a Jeffersonian faith in enlightened reason.

Perhaps, this is what Richard Wright, one of Myrdal's champions and later a friend, was driving at in his introduction to *Black Metropolis* (1945). There Wright wonders how best to do justice to the complex realities of black urban life:

We have the testimony of Gunnar Myrdal, but we know that is not all. What would life on Chicago's South Side look like when seen through the eyes of a Freud, a Joyce, a Proust, a Pavlov, a Kierkegaard?

Ironically, considering his own deeply ambivalent attitude toward African American culture, Wright suggests that such a perspective would contradict the "socially inherited belief in a dehumanized image of the Negro" assumed by most whites.[9] Melville Herskovits and Alain Locke, who might have sensitized Myrdal to such matters, were marginal to the *An American Dilemma* enterprise, even though Herskovits's *The Myth of the Negro Past* was financed by the Carnegie-funded project.

It is also important to note the inherent limitations of a public policy approach to cultural issues. While the weaknesses of social institutions and issues of economic development can be addressed by the policy sciences, individual and group experience and the cultural articulations of that experience present considerably more difficulty. So accustomed to seeing black American life as a "problem," it was difficult for social scientists to focus on the strengths of the expressive and academic culture, where by the 1930s the African American achievement was impressive. But in devoting so little space to black culture, Myrdal and company implied that Negro Americans lacked cultural resources or moral reserves. More pointedly, Myrdal failed to make the connection between political mobilization and cultural consciousness or to paint a complex picture in which black American institutions were weak in certain areas, yet also had strengths to draw upon.[10]

Finally, Myrdal's cultural tone-deafness was closely related to his emphasis on the Enlightenment origins of America's political traditions. Myrdal was no crude positivist, and explicitly rejected value neutrality or objectivity in his dissection of America's racial dilemma. Indeed, Myrdal himself sketched out a partial critique of the Enlightenment sources. He notes that the Enlightenment tended to emphasize "equality in the 'natural rights of man' rather than equality in natural endowments," though he adds that "natural equality" and "moral equality" tended to be closely linked. Even more perceptively, Myrdal identifies scientific racism as one of the by-products of the Enlightenment. Due to the triumph of the idea of egalitarianism in the nineteenth century (De Tocqueville's "democratic" revolution), the enslavement of blacks could only be justified by appealing to ideas of black racial inferiority: "the dogma of racial inequality may, in a sense, be regarded as a strange fruit of the Enlightenment." Indeed, work in the history of racial thinking since the mid-1800s has generally supported Myrdal by showing that it was "scientific" racism that confirmed the natural inferiority of black people, while calling into question doctrines of single creation and the unity of the human species.[11]

This is *not* to claim that Myrdal was an adherent of scientific racism. The first volume of *An American Dilemma* explicitly rejected the scientific basis of racial inferiority and caste inequality. But Myrdal's study itself was caught in a classic ambiguity of rationality: substantive rationality as a shared human capacity was the foundation of human equality, while technical or instrumental rationality, embodied in the systematic procedures of empirical investigation, revealed significant differences between black and white achievement. A version of this ambiguity was present in the contemporary tension, already mentioned, between the "fact" of racial equality and the "fact" of cultural inequality. As James McKee has summed up the changes in racial and cultural thought in the interwar years, "[T]hey [sociologists] discarded the idea that black people were biologically inferior, but despite the arguments of anthropologists, they retained an image of them as culturally inferior."[12]

Just as his Enlightenment precursors had denigrated Africans as lacking a culture of rationality, Myrdal's own *Bildung*, grounded as it was in the Enlightenment, led him to consider African American life and culture too emotional, too disorganized, too backward, and too religious to be of much political use or to seem anything but an obstacle to modernity's triumph. By so emphasizing the normative status of the Enlightenment-derived American Creed, the cultural and political potential of the black Southern church was bound to appear meager. It was as though for 1930s liberals and social democrats of both races, Marx had been correct in his assertion that religion was the opiate of the masses. For Myrdal, the hope for rational change was bound up with the leadership potential of political elites, informed by social scientific knowledge, rather than invested in the mobilization of Southern black "folk" (or their culture) or of the black urban masses.

Yet it is important to remember that when Martin Luther King was an undergraduate in the late 1940s, he initially resisted the call to the ministry, so put off was he by the hyper-emotionality of the Southern black church. If King had this difficulty, how much more difficult must it have been for Myrdal and his associates a decade earlier? The "genius" of King and the civil rights movement was to forge a new sort of black political culture oriented toward general or universal goals but driven by values and practices embedded in the very black Christianity that Myrdal was so skeptical about. Rather than being a burden or hindrance, a drag or a drug, black Southern culture, especially religion, proved to be an invaluable resource in the struggle for black self-determination in the two decades after *An American Dilemma* first appeared.

E. Franklin Frazier: Modernization as Assimilation—and Beyond

If Myrdal was a relatively untroubled, once-born son of the Enlightenment, E. Franklin Frazier (1894–1962) was a more divided, complex, twice-born personality. According to Walter Jackson, Frazier's early intellectual life was marked by a tension between the appeal of socialism, including an "inter-racial working class alliance," and an attraction to a black nationalist perspective. The dominant focus of Frazier's mature work fell upon the centrality of social and economic change, while cultural issues received short shrift. Indeed, by the time the Myrdal-directed Carnegie project was getting underway, Jackson suggests that "Frazier abandoned any strategy of encouraging African cultural development. In an era of economic convulsions, cultural issues seemed to him of secondary importance."[13]

Frazier's no-nonsense "realism" was of a piece with his outspoken personality. As a kind of demystifier, he belonged to the same intellectual tribe as Thorstein Veblen; indeed, his classic sociological polemic *Black Bourgeoisie* (1957) deployed Veblenian concepts such as "conspicuous consumption" to excoriate the black middle class. Nor did he have much time for the culturalists, particularly those, like Herskovits, who stressed the African origins of American Negro life. As mentioned, he thought Du Bois's emphasis on intraracial cooperation in the 1930s was a capitulation to romanticism (a negative term for Frazier); and privately he was critical of his Howard University colleague, Alain Locke, as a "dilettante" and "vain as a popinjay."[14] His was also a thoroughly secular sensibility. Frazier viewed religion, particularly in its institutionalized form, as "primarily a conservative social force," while science (in Jackson's words) "offered humankind an alternative to religion and superstition and a means of understanding the laws of human society."[15] To be sure, Frazier's utopian positivism was more marked in his early writings and he came to appreciate the central role played by the church in African American life. But his early orientation testified to Frazier's grounding in an Enlightenment view of social progress through rationality. Frazier was no lonely or neglected figure. Indeed, "outsider" sociologist, Oliver C. Cox wrote scathingly of the way that Frazier's "professional career had to be contrived on the tight rope set up by the associational establishment. . . . He hardly confronted even tangentially a real power structure."[16] On the other hand, Frazier refused to take his distance from the anathematized Du Bois in the 1950s and considered him a heroic figure, despite the earlier, strenuous disagreements they had.[17]

Frazier's overall reaction to Myrdal's massive work was decidedly positive. His two reviews of *An American Dilemma* approved of Myrdal's identification of the American dilemma as a "moral problem," though he did wonder, as we have already seen, whether it was "on the conscience of white people to the extent implied in his statement."[18] But Frazier also heartily endorsed Myrdal's identification of the problem as one which white, not black, Americans had to take the initiative in solving. Frazier's other review of *An American Dilemma* in *Crisis* also praises Myrdal's "objectivity" in particular. By "objectivity" Frazier means the quality often associated with his own approach to the topic of race: "freedom from sentimentality and pathos in regard to the Negro." He approves of Myrdal's willingness to describe "the Negro community for what it was—a pathological phenomenon in American life," while also emphasizing that this pathological cultural formation arose from white-imposed "segregation." Nor, and here Frazier probably had Herskovits and also Du Bois in mind, does Myrdal "indulge in a lot of foolish talk about the peculiar 'contributions' of the Negro and his deep 'spirituality.'"[19] Overall, Frazier rejected any analysis of the plight of black Americans that diverted attention from social and economic ills for which white people had the responsibility.

In his correspondence with Myrdal, Frazier's hostility to the cultural argument comes through very clearly. Though Frazier contributed materials on African American recreation and leisure to *An American Dilemma* and Myrdal also used *The Negro Family in the United States* (1939) as a source on that topic, Frazier's most immediate contribution to the Carnegie project was as a reader of the first draft of the study. Overall, his criticisms were mild, to say the least. His chief substantive criticism concerned the concept of "caste." Like Oliver C. Cox, Frazier thought that the concept was too "static" to capture the nature of white-black relations and that it over-emphasized the difficulties rather than possibilities of black advancement. Myrdal was aware of the problems with "caste," but still insisted on using the term, since "race" lent a false sense of biological permanence to the differences between blacks and whites.[20]

More importantly, Frazier's objection to the emphasis on black cultural distinctiveness was related to his observation that a certain sort of white conservative thought that races "should maintain their purity just as flowers do" and "believe[d] that the Negro should develop race pride." The development of racial pride, it was hoped, would keep blacks from challenging segregation.[21] If anyone was responsible for diluting the effects of Herskovits's thesis in *An American Dilemma*, it was Frazier. In a letter to Arnold Rose, who had drafted the two chapters on black life and institutions after Myrdal's departure for Sweden in the fall of 1942, Frazier insisted that Rose had given too much weight to Herskovits's claims: "I would say there is some truth in the assumption about African origins rather than a 'great deal of truth.'" Frazier added in another letter to Rose in December of 1942 that "isolation" is "responsible for the incomplete assimilation of white man's culture." In the same letter, Frazier expands upon his reasons for rejecting the African origins thesis: "[I]f whites came to believe that Negro social behavior was rooted [in] African cultures, they would lose whatever sense of guilt they had for keeping Negroes down."[22] In sum, Frazier opposed any and all claims about African American culture that provided whites with an excuse for avoiding responsibility for America's racial problems.

The assumption about the inevitability—and therefore desirability—of black assimilation was part of what Frazier learned from his mentor Robert Park at Chicago. In general terms, the historical narrative informing Frazier's sociology, particularly his investigation of the Negro family, saw modernization as the telos of modern history. Frazier begins his story of African Americans in the "relatively simple pre-literate culture" of Africa, from where Africans were sold into slavery in the New World. Frazier did not reject all claims about the links between African culture and New World slave cultures. While there were "no traces of the elements of culture, the social structure" from Africa in the United States, the case was quite different in South America and the West Indies. For the black American, however, "traditions and culture . . . have grown out of his experiences in America," though Frazier noted in a 1934 essay that "the most conspicuous thing about the Negro is his lack of a culture." Frazier would even allow that fragments of African culture were still to be found in the United States. What was missing, however, were the "habits and customs," the "hopes and fears," and the "social organization" to make these fragments cohere into a distinctive African-derived culture.[23] In sum, it needed more than the discovery of artifacts or traces of African cultural practices to prove that African culture had had any persisting influence in the lives of Negro Americans.

Frazier's unyielding 1942 review of *The Myth of the Negro Past* rejected Herskovits's suggestion that those who disagreed with him suffered from "race prejudice" or "are ashamed of their past." Moreover, Frazier notes that Herskovits's speculation often outran his research. As a result, he (Herskovits) invokes "the spirit, the feel or the generalized attitudes" of Africans when "he is unable to discover African culture patterns" among American Negroes. Most seriously, Frazier argues that to posit a strong African influence on North American black culture "ruled out" black Americans' "spontaneous responses, imagination, and the acquisition of new habits and attitudes." But none of this prevented Frazier from joining the left-leaning, pro-Soviet, and anticolonial Council for African Affairs after World War II. He was also a strong supporter of African independence movements and donated his personal library to Ghana upon his death.[24]

The next "chapter" in Frazier's narrative of the black American experience focused on the emergence of a Negro folk culture under slavery, at the center of which was the matriarchal or maternal family structure. Here and elsewhere, Frazier asserts two somewhat different things at the same time. On the one hand, the patriarchal family is the norm in the dominant white culture and thus should be the norm for African Americans, too: "Where the assimilation of western mores went farthest and development of personality was highest, the organization of [black] family life approached most closely the pattern of white civilization."[25] Yet, the matriarchal family was a functional institution within the black Southern family-church-community. Blacks were certainly not genetically incapable of assimilating white culture and institutions; but they needed more exposure to them in order to encourage socialization and assimilation. Thus, there were two ways of judging the black family. Ideally, it should be patriarchal and approach the white European ideal. But in a stable folk culture, such as rural and small-town, black Southern life, the mother-centered family fulfilled its function. Overall, Frazier assumed that the purpose of the family in particular was to teach "impulse control" and that the patriarchal family provided the best prospects for inculcating that habit. This institutional weakness, manifested in illegitimacy and unstable families, emerged, first, in slavery, was exacerbated by the disruptive effects of emancipation, and was finally reinforced by the migration of Southern blacks to northern and western cities beginning in World War I. Social and geographical mobility, along with increased contact with the larger white culture, meant that illegitimacy "loses its harmless character."[26] As Frazier the social scientist presented such claims, they were less a matter of personal (moral) preference than they were facts of social life.

Thus, by the late 1930s the choices were stark. Frazier named Part 4 of his study of the Negro family "In the City of Destruction." There he takes a rare look at black cultural expression by focusing attention on the blues as the "record of the reactions of the uprooted folk to the world of the city" and "nostalgic yearnings for the sympathetic understanding and intimacy and security of the world of the folk which they have left behind" in "Feudal America."[27] Informing Frazier's analysis is a view that Ralph Ellison would particularly object to in Myrdal's study—that the blues are primarily a "reaction" to white oppression, important mainly as a symptom of a lost folk world rather than valuable in their own right. Yet the picture Frazier presents is not entirely bleak, since the new urban industrial situation might again stabilize and a "Brown Middle Class" emerge. Frazier's social radicalism meant that he also welcomed the process by which the Southern folk society gave way to an urban industrial society marked by class conflict. The result was the formation of a black proletariat in the urban centers of black migration and increased participation in the general culture:

> [T]he Negro, stripped of the relatively simple preliterate culture in which he was nurtured, has created a folk culture and has gradually taken over the more sophisticated American culture.

Modernization, in other words, was in the process of transforming African American folk culture and the institutional and social structure that had sustained it.[28]

Overall, two generalizations can be hazarded about Frazier's picture of African American culture. First, to say that Frazier had relatively little interest in the expressive culture of African Americans is to say, as already mentioned, that when he spoke of culture he actually had social institutions more than literature, history, philosophy, music, or the visual and the plastic arts in mind. Second, assimilation was, for him, the ultimate destination of the social process: the greater the exposure to the white/modern world, the greater the degree of impulse control. With a greater degree of impulse control (and hence stability) came a greater degree of assimilation. Just as the black family would/should come to resemble the white family, so would black culture come to resemble white culture and blacks would come to be accepted by whites. For Frazier, the race issue was secondary to the question of whether the emergent society was modern or not.

Since the debate about the nature and history of the black family began in the mid-1960s, Frazier's analysis of the Negro family has been identified as one of the main sources of Daniel Patrick Moynihan's "The Negro Family: The Case for National Action" (1965). Because of that connection, Frazier's work was also one of the main targets of Herbert Gutman's *The Black Family in Slavery and Freedom, 1750–1925* (1976). According to Gutman, Frazier had applied a "reactive model" of slave socialization and saw black American culture as "an imperfect imitation of the dominant culture." Where Frazier tended to see "disorganization" in family and kinship structures, Gutman and others saw a different sort of pattern with definite regularities. Though the black family did not replicate the conventional nuclear family, it was part of a "widespread, adaptive, and distinctive kinship system."[29] Undoubtedly, Frazier was too ready to see the black family as problematic rather than adaptive. Still, as already noted, Frazier always felt that to emphasize the adaptability of the black family would run the risk of exonerating whites.

The postwar years saw an important shift in Frazier's analysis of the negative effects of white racism and of modernization in general on black migrants in the northern cities. According to Daryl Scott, Frazier's prewar position was that the damage to black institutions, particularly to the family, did not imply that the personalities of it members had suffered damage. The problem was the "loss of moral values" not the "loss of morale or humiliation." Similarly, Robert McKee has noted that, to Frazier, pathology was a characteristic of the social process rather than a general condition and thus external to the individuals involved. Where the Moynihan Report offered a "social-psychological" focus, Frazier, claims Anthony Platt, focused on "economic, political and other cultural institutional factors."[30] But though all these accounts agree that there is a difference between a socioeconomic and a psychological approach to "damage," Scott, unlike Platt, contends that the postwar Frazier was much more willing to acknowledge the (social) psychological dimension of the damage that slavery and segregation had inflicted on African Americans.

This is a difficult issue to sort out. In his postwar methodological pronouncements, Frazier continued to focus on economic and social interests, social classes, and social structures as more important than individual or even social psychological states of mind. As he noted about the post-Reconstruction South, the origins of Jim Crow did not lie in "attitudes having their roots in slavery" or ones that "grew up spontaneously" through interracial contacts. Rather, its root lay in the "unresolved class conflict and the resulting political struggles among whites in the South."[31] And yet there were significant shifts in emphasis. Frazier's attack on the black middle class in *The Black Bourgeoisie* (1957) was accompanied by a new interest in black folk culture. Before World War II, Frazier depicted black folk culture facing disorganization and demoralization; after the war he increasingly compared folk culture favorably to the cultural inauthenticity of the black bourgeoisie. Indeed, the black bourgeoisie denied it folk roots and sought to "slough off everything that is reminiscent of its Negro origin and its Negro folk background" in its race to imitate the white world. Increasingly, Frazier held that assimilation on white terms and a neglect of black tradition were deeply suspect. Once one of the secular Enlightenment's most powerful spokesmen, Frazier now located the strengths of the burgeoning civil rights movement in the "religious experiences and culture of the Negro folk."[32]

But while Frazier demonstrated a new interest in black folk culture and traditions, he also embraced the view of slavery's destructive effects on the slave personality offered in Stanley Elkins's *Slavery* (1959): "[S]lavery was a cruel and barbaric system that annihilated the Negro as person." In addition, Frazier cited Abram Kardiner and Lionel Ovesey, *The Mark of Oppression* (1951) approvingly in *Black Bourgeoisie*. What became his best-known work adopted the focus on psychological damage that Daryl Scott has described. It ends with several chapters on the social psychological failings of the black bourgeoisie. A class ridden with a "self-hatred" and given to the "deprecation of the physical and social characteristics of Negroes,"[33] they bear a distinct resemblance to Hannah Arendt's Jewish parvenus. Generally, Frazier saw the future task of the civil rights movement and of black intellectuals as one not just of achieving political and constitutional rights but also of attempting to "bring about a transvaluation of that experience so that the Negro could have a new self-image or new conception of himself."[34] Thus, Frazier's stance at the end of his life foreshadowed the position many black radicals were to arrive at by the end of the 1960s. Politics promised a way to overcome, to anneal, the damage of the past. But political action would have to be built on a renewed acquaintance with the only authentic black tradition—that of the folk—once thought by Frazier to have been a necessary, even welcome, casualty of modernization.

Richard Wright: Between Past and Future

Richard Wright (1908–1960), it has been observed, was E. Franklin Frazier's novelistic counterpart. Indeed, Wright fully absorbed the lessons of contemporary sociology, which he learned in Chicago from the writings—and personal acquaintance with—Robert Park and the African American students there, especially Frazier, St. Clair Drake, and Horace Cayton. In addition, he readily endorsed the main thesis of Myrdal's *An American Dilemma* and later, as already mentioned, became good friends with the Myrdals.[35] Like Frazier, Wright shied away from any romantic claims about deeply shared spiritual or cultural essences among Blacks. And like Frazier, he was convinced quite early that traditional black culture of the South was an inadequate vehicle for black progress in the United States. Even when his nationalist tendencies were at their strongest, as in "Blueprint for Negro Writing" (1937), Wright insisted that "Negro writers must accept the nationalist implications of their lives, not in order to encourage them, but in order to change and transcend them."[36] If we replace "nationalist implications" with "the black folk culture of the rural South," we would have an accurate expression of Wright's lack of confidence in black Southern culture and its institutions. Whether as a member of the Communist Party up to 1941 or as an analyst of Third World affairs in the 1950s, he saw the central theme of modern history as the triumph of the modern over the "feudal" or "folk" or "traditional" past.

That theme is perhaps the central theme of all of Wright's American writing: the forced movement of African peoples from Africa to the plantation South and then in the twentieth century from the rural to the urban North (and South). This world-historical process, he wrote in *12 Million Black Voices* (1941), had been driven by a ruthlessly heroic humanism, the "higher human consciousness" of the "god-like men,"[37] who imposed the modern world on the indigenous societies of the New World and of Africa. Writing in 1945 to a friend, George Davis, Wright set forth his version of the story of modernity as refracted through the experience of African Americans. It was essentially the story of cultural destruction and then reconstruction. In that respect, it strangely echoes Frederick Jackson Turner's "frontier thesis" for Euro-Americans:

> But I want to take the Negro, starting with his oneness with his African tribe, and trace his capture, his being brought over in the Middle Passage, his introduction to the plantation system, his gradual dehumanization to the level of random impulse and hunger and fear and sex. I want then to trace his embracing of the religion of protestantism, his gradual trek to the cities of the nation, both North and South; and his gradual urbanization UNDER JIM CROW CONDITIONS and finally his ability to create a new world for himself in the new land in which he finds himself.[38]

But, Wright's was not an exceptionalist view of the African American experience; rather, it foresaw what modern history had in store for all traditional societies and folk cultures—abandonment of that folk past. To cling fast to the older ways of life was a counsel of despair and a guarantee of failure.

Yet, much of Wright's writing, including his fiction, sought to assess the spiritual costs of this historical trajectory toward modernity. In the essay "How Bigger Was Born," Wright claims that although fictionally Bigger Thomas (the central character in *Native Son* [1940]), is an individual, he is also a type: "There was not just one Bigger, but many of them, more than I could count and more than you suspect." Wright saw Bigger's life as one lived in proximity to, but excluded from, not just white society but the modern world in general. He and others like him lived "so close to the very civilization which sought to keep them out."[39] Bigger's bewilderment arises from the fact that "he had become estranged from the religion and folk culture of his race," and

> was trying to react to and answer the call of the dominant civilization whose glitter came to him through the newspapers, magazines, radios, movies, and the mere imposing sight and sound of daily American life.[40]

In general, Bigger's exclusion is, in Wright's mind, inseparable from the cultural contradictions of modern capitalism and the exigencies of modern urban existence: "[H]e was hovering unwanted between two worlds."[41] This was Wright's own reprise of Du Bois's theory of double consciousness.

Wright was also honest enough to suggest that types such as Bigger, whatever their race, were raw material for any political movement that spoke to their sense of exclusion and their yearning for wholeness: "I felt that Bigger, an American product, a native son of this land, carried within him the potentialities of either Communism and Fascism."[42] At the end of World War II, Wright still held to the idea that the failures of industrial and urban society, particularly its inability to disabuse the black American of the notion that "his hopes are hopeless," created a breeding ground for totalitarian movements of the left and the right.[43] Thus, the historical contradictions that threaten to tear Bigger asunder arise not just from economic deprivation or racial prejudice but also from the psychological and spiritual crisis of modern capitalist society. As long as the communist movement failed to recognize the appeal of fascism to the proletariat, or to realize that men such as Bigger could not be written off as mere *lumpen*, it would never be able to gain the proletariat's full support. All this was analysis in the dissident Marxist tradition of Wilhelm Reich and Erich Fromm; it was *Native Son* as a fictional rendition of *Escape from Freedom,* Southside Chicago-style.

Yet, Bigger was not just a blackface version of modern man in search of the soul that had been lost on the trip north. Wright was the least nostalgic of men. Being a black Southerner was rarely a positive thing for Wright, even though he was deeply grounded in that culture and had, for instance, written a number of blues lyrics. Wright could step back and note in "Blueprint for Negro Writing" that the two most important resources for the Negro writer were the "1) the Negro church; and 2) the folklore of the Negro people."[44] However, his own experience with African American religion had been, at least on the account given in *Black Boy*, an extremely unhappy one. When Bigger thinks to himself that "[t]he white folks like for us to be religious, then they can do what they want to with us,"[45] he is likely articulating something close to Wright's own deepest feelings about religion. The church and black Southern folk culture play a surprisingly small role in Wright's fiction. Even in *12 Million Black Voices* (1941), the closest Wright ever came to a kind of popular front exploration—even celebration—of black folk culture, Wright gives due recognition to the power and influence of the church and the religious spirit. Yet he concludes that "there are times when we doubt our songs; they are not enough to unify our fragile folk lives in this competitive world."[46] The implication was clear—the black folk culture/experience is inadequate preparation for life in the modern world.

Strictly speaking, Wright had not grown up in a stable folk culture at all, if such a thing has ever existed. Indeed, the terms "folk culture" and "folk history" have only the loosest of meanings when applied to Wright's situation. Barely surviving in an archetypal broken home with a mother and her relatives at its center, Wright could only see "the absence of fixed and nourishing forms of culture"[47] when he looked back on his early years in the South from which he had fled for his life. It was not just the racism and discrimination or the omnipresent threat of white violence that drove Wright from the South. Black Southern life itself stifled his intellectual and emotional development. In retrospect, the alternatives had been stark but clear for Wright. He could accommodate and go dead spiritually; or rebel directly against the white South and end up literally dead—or leave altogether. He opted, of course, for the latter.

This was the context for Wright's powerful indictment of Southern black life near the beginning of *Black Boy* (1945). There Wright identifies not only the inadequacies but also the pathologies of black Southern life, and how it was so misconstrued by outsiders, particularly whites, as vital and alive: "I saw what had been taken for our emotional strength was our negative confusions, our flights, our fears, our frenzy under pressure." The passage's extra emotional pathos and its edge of bitterness undoubtedly derive from Wright's encounter with his father, now an old "bleak peasant," for the first time in years. Through him Wright gauges the adequacy of black Southern culture: the black Southern family romance turns out to lack a central male authority at its core, either in fact or in recollection. Like Frazier, Wright insists that the weakness of that way of life is not an inevitable outcome of racial inadequacy; rather, it derives from the fact that "Negroes had never been allowed to catch the full spirit of Western civilization, that they lived somehow in it but not of it." Thus, as in *Native Son*, the core of the problem lies in black exclusion from the spirit of the dominant culture. But Wright shifts his considerations to another level by wondering whether the "cultural barrenness of black life" implies that "clean positive tenderness, love, honor, loyalty and the capacity to remember" are not "native with man" but must be "fostered, won, struggled and suffered for, preserved in ritual from one generation to another."[48] Put another way: culture is an achievement. Wright's dissection of the pathologies of black Southern culture yielded hard-won insights true to his own experience; but many of Wright's friends and readers, then and later, took exception to them.

It is only with this powerful passage from *Black Boy* in mind, particularly its contempt for those who romanticized black life, that we can begin to understand Wright's hostility to the work of Zora Neale Hurston, whom, in a 1937 review of *Their Eyes Were Watching God* he accused of "facile sensuality," of writing not for "the Negro" but "to a white audience whose chauvinistic tastes she knows how to satisfy." By imparting to her readers a minstrel version of black vitality and sensuality, Hurston, Wright suggests, was traducing the pain of black life. Nor was Wright really very much influenced or impressed by the Harlem Renaissance, with which Hurston was, of course, identified. By the end of the 1930s, he had still read little of the work associated with it; and in "Blueprint for Negro Writing," he casually alludes to it as "a liaison between inferiority-complexed Negro 'geniuses' and burnt-out white Bohemians with money." Recent attempts have been made to bridge the gap between Wright and Hurston—between Chicago School sociology and Boasian anthropology, between a proletarian and a nationalist emphasis, and between an emphasis on social conflict and the idea of a unified black cultural community. Several students of black literature have written convincingly of the need to modify the stark opposition drawn between the two figures. But finally, Wright and Hurston did rest their hope for the future on very different ideological and historical positions.[49]

As the passage from *Black Boy* indicates, the effect of exclusion was not only external to the "souls" of black folk. Wright was pointing to a deeper-seated impact that seemed to arise from the long history of oppression beginning with slavery. Already in *12 Million Black Voices,* Wright speculated quite prophetically about the effects of slavery on black Americans:

> [O]ur personalities are still numb from its long shocks; and as the numbness leaves our souls, we shall yet have to feel and give utterance to the full pain we shall inherit.[50]

Thus, the sequence of numbing, then release of pain, and the externalization of internal states and emotions offered the key to the psychology of African Americans; not just excluded in the present, but excluded from the beginning and, as a result, psychologically different. Such passages, written in the first half of the 1940s, also suggest that Daryl Scott's claim that emphasis on psychological damage was a post–World War II phenomenon should be accepted with caution.

Young Richard in *Black Boy* has enough intelligence and wit of his own to escape, at first, imaginatively through writing and reading and then by literally leaving the South. But Bigger Thomas's problem is that he possesses a consciousness that can scarcely get outside itself. The fact that the novel is told by a third-person narrator, one who moves in and out of Bigger's consciousness, points to the occluded nature of Bigger's own voice. But Bigger also stifles his own self-awareness out of a self-protective impulse: "He knew that the moment he allowed what his life meant to enter fully into his consciousness, he would either kill himself or someone else. So he denied himself and acted tough." It is Bigger's impulsive murder of Mary Dalton and the more calculated murder of his girlfriend Bessie that lead to his emergence as a self-conscious agent. Action does not follow from a change in consciousness; rather, a shift in consciousness is a consequence of his actions.[51]

Bigger is the prototypical "mass man," hardly necessary to anyone, and thus "superfluous" in somewhat the sense that Hannah Arendt characterized the victims of totalitarian regimes in *The Origins of Totalitarianism* (1951). Put another way, *Native Son* is about the process whereby Bigger ceases to be superfluous to others and to himself. Only by murdering a prominent young white woman does he come to "count" for anything, even if it is as a murderer and allegedly a rapist. This coming to "count for" something presupposes that he learns to think through his actions, "thinking" here being not so much a rational process as a process of acknowledging, "owning up to" his actions and their effects on others.[52] It is not, as the novel emphasizes several times, that Bigger feels particularly guilty for his actions; it is rather that he realizes for the first time that his actions have consequences, not only to himself but to others:

> He stood up in the middle of the cell floor and tried to see himself in relation to other men, a thing he had always feared to try to do, so deeply stained was his own mind with the hate of others for him.[53]

In arriving at some sense of himself "in relation to other men," Bigger becomes (more) human, not in the sense of fulfilling some ontological essence or realizing a biological capacity but in morally owning up to his own actions.

Wright's fictional discourse allows entry into the consciousness of its characters in a way that Frazier's sociology, concerned as it is with group behavior rather than with individual consciousness, with structures rather than motivations, and with institutions not individuality, does not allow. It was only with the post–World War II emergence of a powerful language of the self as developed by psychoanalysis and then re-applied to social reality (as in *The Authoritarian Personality*) that social science found a vocabulary with which it could identify and explore the psychological scars inflicted by oppression and exclusion.

James Baldwin: The Anxiety of Influence and the Dialectic of Damage

James Baldwin's relationship with Richard Wright was a tortured one. It is perhaps American literature's clearest example of what Harold Bloom has called the "anxiety of influence." Baldwin was shrewd enough to recognize this, for as he wrote in his moving eulogy to Wright, "Alas, Poor Richard," "He became my ally and my witness, and alas! my father. . . . I had used his work as a kind of springboard of my own."[54] Where Wright ruefully observed the inadequacies of his own father from a distance, Baldwin sought the approval of older men—his own stepfather, the painter Beauford Delaney, Wright, Elijah Mohammed—only to break with them, sometimes in his own mind and sometimes in reality. In the case of Wright, the "springboard" was the view that Wright wrote (merely) "protest novels"; and that this genre, of which Wright's *Native Son* was the most powerful contemporary example, was deeply flawed. Referring to Harriet Beecher Stowe's *Uncle Tom's Cabin*, one of his childhood favorites, Baldwin contends that the protest novel was, and is, addressed primarily to whites. It assumes that whites are the guarantors of black humanity and that protesting one's oppressed status is the best way to convince white people that black people were worthy of their support. The main problem, however, is that the image of black Americans presented in the protest novel, however different Uncle Tom is from Bigger Thomas, is one-dimensional: "Bigger," concludes Baldwin, "is Tom's descendent."[55] As each other's secret sharer, they mark out the spectrum of African American (male) possibility—benign forgiveness or mindless rage against the white oppressor. Particularly, Bigger Thomas is "that fantasy Americans hold in their mind when they speak of the Negro."[56]

Never a close reader of texts, Baldwin shrewdly widened his scope from the generic failure of the protest novel to Wright's failure as a spokesman to the white world, a charge that assumed that it was part of any novelist's brief, in this case Wright's, to become a cultural spokesman. In creating Bigger as the central figure in a protest novel, Baldwin claims that Wright failed to capture the complexity of the African American experience: "What the novel reflects—and it at no point interprets—is the isolation of the Negro within his own group and the resulting fury of impatient scorn." As a result, there is a climate of "anarchy and unmotivated and unapprehended disaster" in the novel. Echoing Henry James's pronouncement on the insufficiencies of Hawthorne's fiction arising from the thinness of nineteenth-century American culture and institutions, Baldwin charges Wright with perpetuating the view

> that in Negro life there exists no tradition, no field of manners, no possibility of ritual or intercourse, such as may, for example, sustain the Jew even after he has left his father's house.[57]

Baldwin goes on to note that "there has as yet arrived no sensibility sufficiently profound and tough to make this tradition articulate."[58] Clearly he was bidding to assume that role for himself.

The allusion to the experience of Jews as a point of comparison with black Americans here also points to one of Baldwin's dominant concerns throughout the 1960s. His basic position was reflected in the title to an essay of 1967—"Negroes are Anti-Semitic Because They're Anti-White." Yet several years earlier, Baldwin had developed a more complex line of analysis in "Harlem Ghetto." There, Baldwin stresses the simultaneous black religious identification with the Jews as a people in exile in "Egypt," and their anger at the way Jewish merchants and landlords in the ghetto exploit blacks: Jews "operate in accordance with the American business tradition of exploiting the Negroes." In addition, Baldwin notes that blacks also adopt "the subterranean assumption that Jews should 'know better.'" Finally, for Jews, America had traditionally served as a refuge from suffering, most recently from extermination by the Nazis, whereas, for African Americans, the United States was—and still is—the site of enslavement and oppression. Baldwin concludes his "Harlem Ghetto" essay with the judgment, "Georgia has the Negro and Harlem has the Jew," a comparison that fails to address the fact that Jews as whites are part of the national racial majority; conversely, blacks are part of the majority Christian population, while the Jews are a religious minority.[59]

Just as clearly as Baldwin rejected Wright's first, and best, novel, so he also felt compelled to respond to Wright's powerful indictment of black Southern folk culture in *Black Boy*. Although still ostensibly referring to Bigger, Baldwin's concludes "Everybody's Protest Novel" by suggesting that Bigger

> admits the possibility of his being subhuman and feels constrained, therefore to battle for his humanity. . . . But our humanity is our burden, our life; we need not battle for it; we need only to do what is infinitely more difficult—that is, accept it.[60]

This seems clearly aimed at Wright's assertion in *Black Boy* that those things that make us human "were [not] native to man" but had to be "fostered, won, struggled and suffered for, preserved in ritual from one generation to another."[61] Yet, for Baldwin, like Wright, the dominant literary influences were European and not African American, while growing up in Harlem meant that Baldwin was profoundly shaped by his experience in the black church, in which his stepfather was a preacher. Though Baldwin came to reject its message, he continued to remember the power of its rhetoric and music with considerable affection. To his credit, at this point early in his career, Baldwin also noted that Ralph Ellison "is the first Negro novelist I have ever read to utilize in language, and brilliantly, some of the ambiguity and irony of Negro life."[62] In a decade (1950s) when ambiguity and irony were literary virtues par excellence but the last two characteristics likely to be attributed to black American writing, Baldwin's comments on Ellison's achievement were not only high praise for the author of *Invisible Man* but also a way of calling attention to the complexity of black American traditions, never adequately conveyed by the spirituals or, say, performances of James Weldon Johnson's *God's Trombones*.

By 1964, Baldwin had become, in Robert Penn Warren's loaded phrase, "a voice." With the two volumes of essays, *Notes of a Native Son* (1955) and *Nobody Knows My Name* (1961), the enormously influential polemic *The Fire Next Time* (1963), and three works of fiction behind him, Baldwin assumed the role as the spokesman for Negro life that his early essays had called for. He fused, as Warren shrewdly saw, his own "interior life" with "the exterior fate of the country."[63] But in so doing, Baldwin confirmed the sense that his audience was as much a white as a black one, precisely the weakness he'd identified as central to Wright's protest sensibility. Liberal white America responded enthusiastically to Baldwin's jeremiads against that cast of mind that made it almost impossible for whites to get an accurate sense of American reality. White liberals in particular were "an affliction," insofar as they patronized Negroes by offering solutions to their problems, without having an idea of how black Americans experienced the world.[64] White Americans were also "innocents" in that they were profoundly unaware of how their own society and culture worked. Whites, asserted Baldwin in a radio roundtable in 1961, have

> always avoided knowing things—I'm afraid you have to call them tragic or black or deep or mysterious or inexorable—which are the very bottom of life.[65]

Later in the 1970s he would remember his early childhood attempts to think about white people:

> I had found white people to be unutterably menacing, terrifying, mysterious—wicked: and they were mysterious, in fact, to the extent that they were wicked: the unfathomable question being, precisely this one: what under heaven, or beneath the sea, or in the catacombs of hell, could cause any people to act as white people acted.[66]

Such judgments remind us that Baldwin was primarily a moralist not a social theorist or a conventional literary critic. In taking on the role of mediator between white and black America, critics accused Baldwin of being too concerned with white people and the white world.[67] But such charges confuse what, at its best, was Baldwin's concern for the fate of the republic with what was at times a glib, even sentimental, evocation of the power of love to heal the rifts between white and black Americans, as though he had made W. H. Auden's "we must love one another or die" into his personal categorical imperative. Baldwin might have learned from Martin Luther King's more down-to-earth understanding of Christian *agape* that "loving" white people did not mean black people had to like them. Baldwin did perhaps confuse the impersonal care and respect for the other that *agape* enjoined with the desire for emotional fusion characteristic of *eros*.

Baldwin's black critics were also undoubtedly suspicious of his desire to be "an honest man and a good writer." In the racially saturated atmosphere of the 1960s, Baldwin's earlier self-description sounds insufficiently "black":

> I have not written about being a Negro at such length because I expect that to be my only subject, but only because it was the gate I had to unlock before I could hope to write about anything else.[68]

Originally, that is, race was not the prime determinant but a relatively contingent factor about Baldwin's identity. If he entered the 1960s in triumph, he left it with his reputation in tatters, since such a universalist assumption proved one of the main casualties of that decade among African American writers and intellectuals. The irony, of course, is that Baldwin became trapped in his role as a black spokesman and never recovered either his pre-1965 reputation or, in fact, matched the achievement of his first decade, 1955 to 1965, as a published writer.

Baldwin was nothing if not aware of the hidden—and not so hidden— psychic injuries of race among black Americans. This undoubtedly hurt his standing among those who by the end of the 1960s were celebrating, rather than analyzing, blackness. If he broadly agreed with Myrdal that the American dilemma was a "white man's problem," as he surely did, he took on the role of national therapist, applying painful diagnoses to whites and attempting to heal the wounds that most black Americans, including himself, had internalized: "The American image of the Negro lives also in the Negro's heart." The fear of annihilation was also embedded in the black psyche. The black person, Baldwin writes, "can only acquiesce in the obliteration of his own personality," and blacks are "irreparably scarred by the condition of [their] life." The results are a population marked at some level by self-hate. "For who has not hated his black brother?" Baldwin once asked after having accused Wright of "despis[ing] . . . American Negroes."[69]

Like Wright, Baldwin possessed no formal educational qualifications beyond high school. But unlike Myrdal, Frazier, and Wright, he possessed an eloquence of style and voice, shaped by the homiletic traditions of the black church and reminiscent of Henry James's style stripped of much of its fussy quality and infused with a hortatory power. Still it *is* hard to read Baldwin's two books of early essays or *The Fire Next Time* as anything but very complexly rendered "protest" pieces, addressed as much to whites as to blacks, while all the while protesting against the obligation to protest. Baldwin himself came to sound predictable as though he could only write about one thing. Although he was steeped in African American religion and its music, he was otherwise not deeply read in African American literature. Increasingly, the rage and anger came through clearly—and easily.

And yet—despite Baldwin's emphasis on what had been done to and suffered by African Americans, despite all of his explorations of interior states and sensibilities, and despite the fact that his work had neither programmatic nor institutional implications, his analysis of black–white relations represented a real advance over Wright, Frazier, or Myrdal. It was not just that Baldwin was an elegant stylist and they were not; rather, the distinctive feature of Baldwin's analysis of black and white consciousness lay in the dialectical nature that he attributed to it. The presence of blacks in white America "has not only created a new black man" far different from the Africans he encountered in Paris and in Europe, but also "has created a new white man too."[70] This went beyond Wright's analysis and matched Du Bois's, where the dialectic is implicit but never emphasized. Indeed, it is hard to think of a place where Du Bois's account of the origins of black consciousness mentions, much less expands on, the way white consciousness is also modified by the black presence. For Baldwin it was clear that white Americans were just as much creatures of black culture as blacks were the creations of white European cultural realities. Both were, and are, Americans, joint creators and shapers of American culture.

In addition, Emily Miller Budick has noted a white misperception that Baldwin was quick to correct. Baldwin was never speaking as an outsider demanding to be let in. White intellectuals such as Irving Howe could accept Ellison and Baldwin as spokesmen for dissent from the margins. But Baldwin (and Ellison too) insisted that they were just as American as white Americans, and especially as Jewish Americans, were. It was the centrality not the marginality of black Americans that Baldwin and Ellison both emphasized and thus they rejected white cultural condescension.[71] Although Baldwin's probing of the black psyche did uncover considerable damage, his work finally transcended the "damage" school by contending that, first, white Americans had also been transformed—*and deformed*—by racial confrontation in the New World. The childish refusal of whites to face the facts of black life and their own lives indicated a kind of willed innocence. Second, Baldwin, like Frantz Fanon, would stress that not only contempt directed against the self, but also rage directed against white society was an integral part of the lives of the oppressed. Blacks were not just damaged victims; they might also become righteous avengers.

It only remains to note that an attentive reader of Wright's *Native Son* or of *Black Boy should* have arrived at pretty much the same conclusion regarding the provenance and power of black rage as Baldwin did. As Baldwin wrote of Wright in his eulogy, "Alas, Poor Richard": "The violence [in his work] is gratuitous and compulsive because the root of the violence is never examined. The root is rage . . . of a man who is being castrated."[72] But Wright *had* examined the roots of that violence and was fully aware of Bigger's need to repress the rage arising from a fundamental sense of his impotence: "[S]o he denied himself and acted tough." Wright too was, as already noted, fully cognizant of the "numbing" exacted by the experience of slavery—the painful release which, when it came, was likely to wreak havoc.

Overall, what Frazier, Wright, Baldwin, and, somewhat self-contradictorily, Myrdal pressed home in their work was that the "American dilemma" was not just a "white man's problem." In their view, the traumatic experience of slavery, the oppressive conditions of the Jim Crow South, the migration from the rural South to North, and the urbanization and industrialization of America had created a "Negro American" culture that was ill-suited to modern life. Thus, black progress in all aspects of life could only be made when black Americans had full access to the cultural and social institutions of white America, not when they clung to the folk culture of the black South or remained politically quiescent.

6

Culture, Accommodation, and Resistance I: Rethinking Elkins's *Slavery*

The pre-individual state is induced artificially like the regression to primitive states noted among cultured inmates of Nazi prisons.

Ralph Ellison

The only place where Negroes did not revolt is in the pages of capitalist historians.

C. L. R. James

It is difficult to think of another work by a post–World War II American historian that aroused more controversy than Stanley Elkins's *Slavery: A Problem in American Institutional and Cultural Life* (1959).[1] In this chapter, I want to steer clear of the ritual savaging that *Slavery* has received over the years. Instead I want to analyze Elkins's book in reference to several overlapping, post–World War II contexts. First, it must be seen as part of the effort to understand the "concentration camp universe" created by the Nazis. Indeed, the most innovative aspect of Elkins's account of slavery in North America was the way he linked the experience in the Nazi camps with the slave experience in North America. In applying the concentration camp analogy, Elkins's book also reflects the post-1945 concern with the relationship between dominated cultures and cultures of domination. Just what, it was asked with increasing frequency, had been the possibilities of resistance and revolt in Nazi Germany, in colonial Africa and Asia, and in slavery in the United States? Conversely, what

An earlier version of this chapter first appeared as "Domination and Fabrication: Re-Thinking Stanley Elkins's *Slavery*," *Slavery and Abolition* 22, no. 2 (August 2001): 1–28.

were the mechanisms of accommodation in such situations and what were the costs? Why, in short, had there not been more resistance to European colonialism, to North American slavery, or to the concentration camp system? Third, Elkins's work also treated slavery as a function of (capitalist) modernization, which was thus not only a vehicle of progress but also of domination. Not only did it generate institutions of domination, it also sought to create (or fabricate) human beings appropriate to those institutions, that is, to create "slaves by nature."[2]

In addition, I will focus on the radical shift in the reception of Elkins's *Slavery* over the course of the 1960s, a reception that increasingly reflected the emergence of a more positive conception of African American culture, changes in American conceptions of the Holocaust, and increasing tensions in African American–Jewish American relationships in that decade. I conclude with a brief look at the moral and philosophical issues raised by Elkins's *Slavery*, especially the questions of human nature and human freedom.

Contexts

Elkins's text is saturated with the post-1945 preoccupation with the relationship between the individual and society. This classic American, and perennially modern, issue dominated much of the intellectual discourse of the first couple of decades after the war. In countless publications, the nagging problem of conformity was taken up, a trend reflected in the academic currency of Alexis de Tocqueville's *Democracy in America* and the popular status of David Riesman's *The Lonely Crowd* (1950). Numerous works of anthropology and social psychology by figures such as Margaret Mead, Erik Erikson, and Erich Fromm explored the relationship between culture and personality in so-called "primitive" societies, while national and social character studies represented a kind of domestic anthropology of "advanced" societies. Mainstream psychoanalysis seemed to promise—or threaten— a way of reconciling the individual to society, while intellectuals as diverse as Lionel Trilling and Herbert Marcuse identified a utopian, nonrepressive dimension of Freud's model of the psyche that equipped the individual to resist the repressive nature of capitalism and the conformism of the postwar affluent society. Specifically, Elkins was greatly influenced by the earliest account of the effects of the concentration camp experience on the personality structure of the individual, Bruno Bettelheim's now well-known "Individual and Mass Behavior in Extreme Situations" (1943).[3] Bettelheim was, of course, a trained psychoanalyst; and the enormous influence of his article on Elkins (and many others), as well as his growing postwar popularity as an expert on autism and on child rearing generally, illustrates the extraordinary appeal of psychoanalysis itself as a master theory for understanding the individual/society relationship in the postwar years.

Yet Elkins approached the relationship between the individual and society by, first, examining not a "normal" but a "peculiar" institution, chattel slavery, which had long since disappeared from the United States (and the Western Hemisphere). He then compared slavery with another much shorter-lived institution that had only recently disappeared from Europe— the Nazi concentration camps. It is important to emphasize that Elkins never claimed that slavery was "like" the concentration camp system; rather, "the concentration camp [was] a special and highly perverted instance of human slavery."[4] Underlying this analogy was Elkins's central concern with the ways individuals adjusted to a "closed" system.

Despite somewhat similar concerns, Elkins only once mentioned the most influential postwar effort to understand the etiology of prejudice, *The Authoritarian Personality* (1950), while Arendt's *The Origins of Totalitarianism* (1951) was not mentioned at all. One can understand why Elkins found little reason to use *The Authoritarian Personality*: its focus fell on the sources of prejudice in potential perpetrators rather than on the effects of systematic prejudice on the victims. In retrospect, we can see that Elkins's attempt to understand the effects of domination risked making the victims somehow co-responsible for their victimization. That he was "blaming the victim" was to become one of the standard charges aimed at Elkins's *Slavery*.

A similar problem arose with Arendt's *The Origins of Totalitarianism*. In exploring the cultural and social psychology of post-emancipation European Jewry and of the uprooted masses in post–World War I Europe, Arendt sometimes gave the impression that the victims of totalitarianism had been complicit in their victimization. Certainly, Arendt's early work (including *The Origins of Totalitarianism*) noted the absence of strong traditions of political resistance, much less rebellion, among European Jews, that made it easier for the Nazis to implement their ideology of extermination. As we shall see in the next chapter, contrary to its reputation, Arendt's *Eichmann in Jerusalem* (1963) did not blame the Jewish people in general, but the Jewish leadership in particular, for facilitating the Final Solution. (As Arendt noted, no other European people actively resisted the Nazi terror either.) That said, Elkins's discussion of the way that slavery

in the United States reshaped the psyche of the slaves by allegedly strip-
ping them of their African culture would have profited from an explicit
comparison with similar processes in the Nazi camps, as presented in *The
Origins of Totalitarianism*.[5] There was more than a little similarity between the Elkins's *Slavery* and Arendt's Eichmann book, since both works
asked controversial questions about resistance to cultural and physical
domination.

Beyond that, Arendt and Elkins both assumed that what was most characteristic of human beings was not revealed in a hypothetical state of nature prior to cultural existence. Elkins made the point as follows:

> a man's humanity, such as he has, lies not in his naked essence but in
> his culture—and that when a corrupt culture has corrupted his "nature,"
> it is less than half a solution simply to strip away his culture and leave
> him *truly* naked. (p. 170)

This clearly echoed Arendt's philosophical anthropology:

> Actually the experience of the concentration camps does show that
> human beings can be transformed into specimens of the human animal
> and that man's "nature" is only "human" insofar as it opens up to man
> the possibility of becoming something highly unnatural, that is, a man.[6]

For Arendt, as we have seen, human beings in a pre-social state were
hardly human at all. Indeed, the camps had been experiments in reducing
humans to their most basic level of species-being, in a kind of perverted
state of nature within history. Thus, to strip an individual (or group) of its
culture was to radically dehumanize him or her rather than offering freedom from repressive restrictions.

Though the postwar decolonization process and liberation movements
were hardly part of Elkins's agenda, his analysis of the psychology of the
plantation slave bore a strong resemblance to analyses of the colonized
self. As we shall see, for instance, Frantz Fanon's rejection of Octave
Mannoni's explanation for the success of colonialism—that, at least in
Madagascar, an internalized ideology of deference to outside invaders was
part of the culture—revealed the explosive nature of the arguments about
decolonization, particularly as related to individual and group psychology.
Closely related to that Francophone debate in the first decade after 1945
was Richard Wright's confrontation with Leopold Senghor at the First

International Congress of Black Writers and Artists in Paris in September 1956. What was it in the cultures of Africa, Wright wondered, that had allowed the Europeans to conquer and colonize Africa so relatively easily? As the 1960s unfolded, similar questions were heard among black Americans; and one response was to contend that African American culture as it had emerged under slavery and developed in freedom was a prime source of resistance to white cultural domination.[7]

Just as important for understanding Elkins are the assumptions about slavery expressed in works such as *An American Dilemma*. One impetus to writing *Slavery,* Elkins admitted, was his sense that the study of slavery had reached a point of "diminishing returns" (p. 1) due to the hyper-moralism of the scholarship on the topic. Elkins's specific objection to Myrdal's study was that it fairly "crackled with moral electricity" (p. 23), an objection reflecting the influence of Elkins's mentor, historian Richard Hofstadter and his mid-1950s attacks on moralizing politics.[8] It was not that Elkins believed slavery to be anything but wrong; rather, assuming that, he wanted to focus on how slavery had shaped the slave personality. As evidence that this shaping had had a disastrous effect, Elkins accepted the "fact" that there had been no successful slave revolts in the United States. To understand this, in turn, he assumed that there was something called "the slave personality" and that it differed significantly between slavery in Latin America and slavery in the United States. Ironically in a book so concerned with the disastrous effects of institutions on human beings, Elkins himself offered a psychological rather than institutional analysis of life in slavery.[9]

Yet, in other respects, Elkins's *Slavery* fitted into the Myrdalian paradigm quite comfortably. Elkins assumed that a racial explanation for the "Sambo" personality was untenable (p. 89). And like Myrdal, Elkins doubted the claims of Melville Herskovits that African "survivals" in the New World had been of any great significance in forming North American slave culture, personality, and behavior.[10] In short, Elkins, like most other students of slavery, saw the slave system as part of capitalist modernization, the most important force shaping slave life in North America. Moreover, Elkins's focus on the *psychology* of slave dependence echoed Myrdal's location of the American dilemma within hearts and minds, though in Myrdal's case it was within white people. To be sure, Myrdal couched the American dilemma in moral terms, but the dilemma manifested itself in the psychological tension, that is, the guilt that it generated in white people.

But if Myrdal saw the race problem in American as a "white man's problem," Elkins seemed to suggest that under slavery there had been a "black man's problem," too. And Elkins, much more than Myrdal, stressed the peculiar configuration of the slave personality structure. He explicitly questioned Kenneth Stampp's claim in the *The Peculiar Institution* (1956) that "slaves were merely ordinary human beings, that innately Negroes are, after all, only white men with black skins, nothing more, nothing less."[11] By disagreeing with Stampp, he questioned the assumption that within slavery or once all institutional obstacles to black freedom were removed, slaves would act just like whites, as though their experience could be expunged from their memories and from their bodies. From this perspective, Elkins's position was closer than Stampp's to the next stage in the study of African American history—the discovery of a slave culture of creativity and resistance, even though Elkins dealt hardly at all with the culture of slavery.

The Elkins Thesis

At the heart of *Slavery* was Elkins's claim that the smooth functioning of slavery in the United States had depended on a plantation slave type called "Sambo" and that, furthermore, the lack of slave revolts in North American slavery could be explained by the preponderance of this slave type among the slave population. According to the characterizations of white Southern planters, Sambo was

> docile but irresponsible, loyal but lazy, humble but chronically given to lying and stealing; his behavior was full of infantile silliness and his talk inflated with childish exaggeration. His relationship with his master was one of utter dependence and childlike attachment. (p. 82)

Two things were crucial, observed Elkins, in forming the Sambo type. First, he contrasted the essentially "closed" system of slavery in North America with the more "open" system in Latin America. By "open," Elkins meant that in Latin America the institutional power of slavery had been checked by the "countervailing" power of the Catholic Church and the Crown (Spanish or Portuguese), both of which protected the slave against the "dynamics of unopposed capitalism" (p. 37).[12] However, slaves in the United States had been largely at the mercy of their masters, without institutional protection of church or state. What made the closed system so closed was the absence of countervailing institutional power to that of the master class. In such a situation, the imperatives of capitalist development, that is, modernization, could be implemented without any real resistance and the new slaves molded to meet the new system's needs.

Elkins's second—and more controversial—move was to argue that the Sambo personality had involved more than just "accommodation" (conscious hypocrisy). Instead, he was a "recognizable personality type" (p. 86).[13] It is here that Elkins brought to bear the analogy (as opposed to a comparison, which implied differences) with the Nazi camp system. He drew heavily on Bettelheim's contention that inmates came to accept camp authority figures (identification with the aggressor); mimicked their values (internalization); and took on childlike traits, including dependency (regression/infantilization). In other words, the Elkins thesis depended on the distinction between "internalization" and (conscious) "role-playing." The strong version of Elkins's thesis had it that internalization best captured the way in which people of African descent were turned into "slaves." But an appendix to all three editions of *Slavery*[14] offered a minimalist version of the Sambo thesis as well: "The main thing I would settle for is the existence of a broad belt of indeterminacy between 'mere acting' and the 'true self'" (p. 228). Such a "broad belt of indeterminacy" might be compared with Primo Levi's notion of a "grey zone" of concentration camp behavior that ran the gamut from conscious role-playing to internalization and included almost everything in between.[15] Although Elkins obviously felt that the two versions of the Sambo thesis were compatible, readers could be forgiven seeing quite significant differences between them.

Finally, Elkins not only connected slave life with camp life, he also stressed the analogy between the process of capturing, transporting, and breaking in Africans with what happened all over Europe as the *Reichsbahn* delivered millions of people to the concentration and extermination camps. The process of "shock and detachment" was, he wrote, "psychologically numbing"—the same term Richard Wright had earlier used to describe the effects of slavery when he wrote of "what this slavery has done to us, for our personalities are still numb from its long shocks" (p. 102).[16] In such a situation, the inherited values, traditions, and institutions of the slaves and the inmates lost any purchase on reality and both groups were at the complete mercy of their captors. As already mentioned, according to Elkins, neither race nor African culture(s) explained anything about the typical (North American) plantation slave personality. African cultures, noted

Elkins, were diverse and far from simple; nor were they dependency cultures. Nor, he claimed, had Latin American slavery produced a Sambo type. Thus, the contrast with Latin America and the analogy with the concentration camp experience converged to explain the Sambo type in the United States.

Critique/Criticism

Between the appearance of *Slavery* in 1959 and Ann J. Lane's *The Debate over Slavery: Stanley Elkins and His Critics* in 1971, there was a radical shift in the historiography of antebellum slavery. This shift was in part a response to the transformation in black consciousness and a revival of academic and popular interest in black history and culture. Elkins's book itself played a considerable part in the radical revision of the African American past, not because a school of followers extended or confirmed his thesis but because his work, after an initial period of acceptance, forced historians to reassess the nature of African American culture.[17] In that sense, *Slavery* fulfilled Elkins's original hopes for his book:

> It does not pretend to be a history, in either the extended or limited sense. . . . The present study is more properly a "proposal." It proposes that certain kinds of questions be asked in future studies of the subject that have not been asked in previous ones (p. 247).[18]

Had Elkins inserted this statement of intent in the main text of *Slavery*, he might have avoided some of the most vociferous objections to his book.

Before enumerating the criticisms of *Slavery*, it should be said that Elkins offered one of the bleakest accounts imaginable of slavery in the United States and, in fact, undermined his own claim to have avoided the high moralism of neoabolitionist historiography. His focus on the "dynamics of unopposed capitalism" as the main historical force shaping slavery in North America should have brought him considerable support from the left. But such support was blocked by Elkins's far from radical institutional analysis. In addition, one of the most influential voices joining the debate over slavery in the 1960s was the Marxist historian, Eugene Genovese, who characterized the slave society of the South not as prototypically capitalist but as seigneurial and premodern, a historical anachronism as it were.[19] And by stressing the way that slavery affected slaves at the very core of their being, Elkins made it more difficult to entertain the idea that the slave culture could be regarded as a carbon copy of the dominant European way of life.

Indeed, the black militant diagnosis of African American life in the 1960s could sometimes sound like an angry reprise of the Elkins thesis minus the social psychological vocabulary. Malcolm X, for instance, insisted that black Americans needed to launch a cultural revolution "to unbrainwash an entire people"; and that black Americans had to realize that "in hating the image [of Africa in the West], we ended up hating ourselves without even realizing it. . . . In America, they have taught us to hate ourselves."[20] Literary critic, Addison Gayle, Jr., came even closer to agreeing with Elkins when he linked role-playing and internalization in his observation that because African Americans have had to don a "minstrel mask . . . [t]he damage to the psyche is immeasurable."[21] Thus, the "damage" school was far from silenced in the 1960s, nor were its advocates exclusively drawn from the ranks of white liberals. Where the salient differences among various advocates of the damage thesis emerged was, and is, in the solution they proposed to this condition.

It should come as no surprise that the most immediate controversy over *Slavery* was aroused by the question of Sambo. But on this issue, the critics headed off in all directions. While some historians denied that anything like Sambo had existed at all, others contended *either* that, contra Elkins, there had been no Sambo type in Latin American and Caribbean slave societies *or* that Sambo was a universal type found in all slave systems. However, those who argued for the universality of Sambo tended to argue that, while there was a Sambo role, there was not a Sambo personality type under nearly all systems of slavery.[22] A second sort of challenge was that the Sambo type was only one of a number of slave types within North American slavery. Here John Blassingame's *The Slave Community* (1972) was invaluable in documenting a range of slave types and attitudes toward themselves and their masters in the antebellum United States.[23] Blassingame's use of slave testimony was also a reminder that Elkins cited no documents written or dictated by slaves or former slaves. Rather, the evidence for Sambo came from the white slave owners' written observations. This stood in stark contrast with the sources of Elkins's account of the concentration camp experience, which were supplied by former inmates such as Bettelheim or Eugen Kogon, not by camp commanders or SS guards.[24] Admittedly, most slaves were illiterate, while many camp survivors were drawn from intellectual, political, and religious elites. Still, Elkins could have easily used testimony about slavery from, say, Frederick

Douglass to counterbalance his dependence on Bettelheim's seminal formulations.[25]

A more sophisticated challenge to the Sambo thesis focused on the dialectics of slave self-formation. According to Eugene Genovese, an individual slave might display a capacity for resistance *and* for acquiescence, might act an Uncle Tom at one minute and become a Nat Turner the next. There was a variety, a "doubleness" to use the Du Boisian concept, within the individual slave as well as the slave population. Or as Genovese formulated it: "Sambo existed wherever slavery existed" but "he nonetheless could turn into a rebel."[26] The advantage of this dialectical model of personality formation was the way it combined internalization with a role psychology. The slave had internalized more than one role, to be sure, but a long and arduous process of overcoming the Sambo (or "Uncle Tom") role within the psyche was necessary. Bettelheim himself concluded his analysis of the camp experience by observing that "[t]hese same old prisoners who identified with the SS defied it at other moments,"[27] thus casting doubt on the total infantilization and identification with the aggressor among camp inmates. Elkins might have accepted such psychological complexity within slaves and still pointed to the lack of successful rebellions either among slaves in the United States or within the Nazi camp system as support for his thesis. Yet, internalization of dependency roles is hardly the only, or most plausible, explanation for the paucity of slave revolts. In most circumstances, a rational assessment of the situation by slaves revealed the slim chance of an uprising's success. It also needs adding, contra Elkins, that when the window of opportunity to strike a blow at slavery opened, slaves responded in large numbers. During the Civil War, they flocked to Union army lines, and by the end of the Civil War, over 180,000 black soldiers had enlisted to fight. These criticisms amount to the claim that Elkins overestimated the "closed" nature of the North American slave system and the strength or frequency of the Sambo personality. In certain respects, the most plausible alternative to the concentration camp analogy was based on sociologist Erving Goffman's work on "total" institutions such as prisons, which revealed more than the concentration camps about how slavery functioned, particularly how it shaped behavior.[28]

All of this in turn suggests two larger considerations, one rhetorical and one historical. Elkins's choice of the term Sambo clearly caught the reader's attention by alluding to a character familiar to many readers from such disparate sources as the children's story "Little Black Sambo," William Faulkner's *Intruder in the Dust* (1948), and Ralph Ellison's *Invisible Man* (1952), and from common usage among whites. In fact, Elkins had been struck by the public furor over the use of the term in Samuel Eliot Morrison and Henry Steele Commanger's *The Growth of the American Republic* in the early 1950s (pp. 82–83). But however it was glossed and explained, such a rhetorically loaded term understandably raised the hackles of many readers of both races and now seems needlessly provocative, considering the modifications that Elkins himself was willing to make elsewhere in his work. There was a world of difference between habituation to roles of infantile-like dependence and the claim that a large number of plantation slaves internalized their owners' negative judgments about them. As Blassingame suggested, slavery could hardly have survived had there been no powerful incentives rewarding acquiescence, however defined. But neither acquiescence nor the idea of brainwashing necessarily implied a deeply embedded structure of infantilization.[29] Or if Elkins had explicitly advanced the Sambo type as a kind of ideal type, what Genovese referred to as a "limiting case,"[30] then *Slavery* might have avoided some of the bitter reactions that it elicited.

In the end, positing a Sambo type as the product of a system akin to the concentration camp experience detracted too much from what Elkins wanted to claim. It conjured up a historically immediate horror that, in its massive incomprehensibility, all but foreclosed a nuanced treatment of slavery. Elkins was fully aware that Nazi camps were not only or primarily labor camps. (Nor are prisons primarily intended for economic production.) While racial slavery was first and foremost an economic institution, supported by a racist ideology, the Nazi system had not only a strong segregationist element, it had also by mid-1941 turned to the extermination of certain categories of inmates, above all, the Jews.[31]

But there were other problems with the analogy. Slavery had been part of the economic and social landscape of Western society, however intermittently, since the classical period and had of course been taken for granted in the world of the Hebrews. Modern slavery had reemerged gradually at the periphery of the European world at a time when it was not yet considered morally odious, however much it was to be avoided. It survived the emergence of religious and secular antislavery thought in the eighteenth century, but then became a target for moral reformers in the nineteenth century. The emergence of racism based on color—first, as a sign of status, then as a trope for permanent, negative traits and then as scientific doctrine—helped bolster an institution of declining economic rationality. The Nazi camp system, on the other hand, emerged suddenly and quasi secretly, within a twelve-year period, at the center of European civilization. But it had to be hidden or camouflaged. Anti-Semitism had a long religious history and more recent pseudoscientific underpinnings; but by the 1930s Nazi ideology conflicted with an emerging antiracist moral and scientific consensus in Europe and North America. Although most Germans had little problem accepting the Nuremberg Laws of the mid-1930s, which were modeled in part on the segregation statutes of the U.S. South, it is not at all clear that the inevitable next step was the Final Solution.[32] Thus, the Nazi concentration camp system, and then the mass exterminations, constituted a much more radical rupture with the existing moral-cultural consensus than did New World slavery. Many Nazi leaders, notes Seymour Drescher, were quite aware of the radical transvaluation of values that their project of extermination entailed.[33]

Translated into personal and group terms, life in the camps was a short and intense experience, while slavery as a system existed for around two hundred years in North America. Slavery was a lifetime experience and inheritable. Life in the Nazi camp system was also generally for a lifetime, but only in the grisly sense that millions of people died there "prematurely." It is gruesome to speculate what would have happened had the Third Reich lasted longer than twelve years. Would the camps have perpetuated themselves as part of a labor system, with extermination gradually diminishing in importance—or would the extermination process have been extended to other subjected peoples? Another major difference between the camps and slavery was that families, despite their extreme fragility, were maintained under slavery, while no families existed in the concentration camps (or in prisons). Also, under slavery, a sphere of intimacy existed in which slaves might even take on different roles with some minimal status and power attached to them. All this contrasted sharply with the radical attenuation, even disappearance, of "normal" life in the camps, including not only family but also sexual life.

Furthermore, Elkins emphasized that the transformational effects of slavery depended on the closed nature of the system rather than on extreme physical cruelty per se. But the Nazi attempt at total domination, joined with the goal of fabricating a new human type and exterminating masses of superfluous people, clearly depended on a state of constant physical and psychological terror. We simply do not know what sort of inmate personality, or cluster of modal personalities, would have emerged in the camps had they lasted longer. And it is hard to know whether the normalization of life under slavery, aided—or further undermined—individual or group autonomy. In contrast with U.S. slavery where the slave population reproduced itself after the cessation of the slave trade, the supply of inmates to the camps was inexhaustible right to the very end, and there was no reason for Nazi extermination policy to be curtailed.[34] But slavery was vital to the economy of the United States and, with the closing of the slave trade, slaves had to be treated with a certain amount of care.

Yet in some of the concentration camps, a variety of roles and even a degree of self-regulation were present. In the mid-1970s, another challenge was directed against Elkins's concentration camp analogy by Terence Des Pres. In the process of challenging Bettelheim's claim about the restructuring of personality and, by extension, the absence of significant resistance or solidarity among the camp inmates, Des Pres also criticized Elkins.[35] If the Bettelheim model did not work for the camps, then it surely did not fit slavery in the United States either. We can also now see that Elkins worked with a relatively simple notion of resistance and failed to spend much time making the historical case for the infrequency of slave resistance, including especially slave revolts. Again, Genovese's model of the slave personality could better account for various sorts of slave resistance. Yet Genovese's larger point was that something about slave culture made organizing and sustaining *collective* resistance to slavery, whether violent or not, extremely difficult.[36] It may be, then, that there was more resistance to slavery than Elkins allowed for, but that it did not, except in a few cases, lead to collective and violent expression. Certainly, the Caribbean and Brazilian phenomenon of maroon communities of escaped slaves was largely missing in the United States. Thus, where Genovese's model can explain both resistance and lack of collective revolts, Elkins's model makes it difficult to do the former.

Still, Elkins's Sambo thesis was potentially of radical usefulness. Within the late 1950s context of massive resistance campaigns against school desegregation in the South and widespread white Southern evocation of the glories of the Southern tradition, Elkins's study stripped the euphemistic cant from the historiography of slavery. Moreover, in making the slavery–concentration camp connection, Elkins's work should have provoked some consideration about what, once slavery in Europe and the Western Hemisphere had been abolished, caused the emergence of a virulent twentieth-century form of slavery under Nazism, Stalinism, and

Maoism, one that took the logic of domination and fabrication to their limits—and beyond. Still, the opportunity went largely without takers partly because the Cold War atmosphere hardly encouraged the grouping of capitalist modernization in the United States and Latin America, with National Socialist mobilization in Germany and with socialist development in the Soviet Union and China under the general rubric of "modernization."[37]

Finally, the Elkins thesis might be read as an account of the attempt to turn mainly West African people into "slaves by nature" and thereby create a new race. This image of the slave and of people of African descent as children was widespread in the nineteenth century. For instance, biologist Alfred Wallace characterized slavery as "adult infancy," while Louis Agassiz, a believer in polygenesis and in black inferiority, referred to the "submissive, obsequious, imitative Negro" and somewhat later observed that "they may be compared with children." Craniologist Samuel George Morton collected skulls in order to correlate brain size and intelligence. Among his more striking conclusions was that "American-born Negroes" were inferior to Africans, due to the debilitating effects of mixing white and black blood.[38] In all this, there was a certain anticipation, even prefiguration, of the ideology of group transformation so central to the Nazi attempt to create a "new Man." By concentrating on the way the North American slave system sought to reconstruct the personalities of the captive Africans, Elkins treated slavery in the United States as what sociologist Edgar Thompson has called a "race-making situation."[39] It was only when massive numbers of Africans were captured in order to labor for white Europeans that there was a need to turn them into a race with fixed traits and capabilities appropriate to being a slave. Since the vast majority of Africans lacked the desired qualities of "slavishness," those qualities had to be inculcated in the slaves and thus the attempt to fabricate a new slavish race. Overall, the American Negro "race" was created in, not brought to, the New World, especially North America.

Thus, Elkins's *Slavery* can be read as an exploration of the logic of the slaveholders' project under the conditions of unrestrained capitalism. Unlike Nazism or Stalinism, there was no sacred or canonical text nor a coherent ideology informing that project, not until at least the 1830s, when scientific racial ideologies stressing polygenesis and the dangers of interbreeding were developed on both sides of the Atlantic.[40] Elkins's book powerfully reinforced the view that the totalitarianisms of the twentieth century and slavery in the United States in the preceding century shared certain crucial characteristics.[41]

From Universalism to Particularism: The 1960s and Beyond

The 1960s provide another essential context for understanding the shifting reception of *Slavery*. One result of the frustration of the African American quest for recognition and the increase in Jewish self-consciousness in that decade was rising tension between African Americans and Jewish Americans.[42] The melting pot had failed to melt, it turned out. By the end of the decade, various ethnic groups (re-) emerged into self-consciousness and political visibility, having failed to exchange their ethnic loyalties for a more acceptable denominationalism of the sort described in Will Herberg's *Protestant-Catholic-Jew* (1955) and for the color-blind melting pot notion of the American Dream. Most crucial among Jewish Americans was the emerging interpretation of the Holocaust as the central event in the history of Western Jewry and not just a tragedy of European civilization in which Jews had suffered particularly horrendous losses. Helped along by the Eichmann trial in 1961 and Arendt's controversial *Eichmann in Jerusalem* two years later, Jewish Americans experienced growing anxiety about the survival of Israel, triggered by the Six-Day War in 1967, and feared an increase in anti-Semitism, particularly among African Americans.[43]

For their part, many African Americans felt a new urgency about group survival and embraced a protonationalist ideology of black pride and black consciousness. In that context, *Slavery* could be read as a cautionary tale about the fate of a people who had not defended themselves "by any means necessary." In addition, black writers and intellectuals began raising questions about the links between African Americans and Jews. If Jewish Americans detected a rise in black anti-Semitism, African American intellectuals such as Harold Cruse doubted that there ever had been any "special relationship" between the two groups and assumed that Jews were just as prejudiced as their white gentile counterparts. According to James Baldwin, black Americans were anti-Semitic only insofar as Jews were white. In his exchange with Irving Howe over the proper political and social role of the black writer, Ralph Ellison expressed regret that American Jews seemed to have identified so closely with white, gentile Americans. And poet LeRoi Jones (a.k.a. Amiri Baraka) turned viciously anti-Semitic by the end of the decade. For many black intellectuals, the new emphasis on the specifically Jewish nature of the Holocaust seemed a way of morally trumping the suffering of African Americans and the peoples of the African diaspora. Jewish intellectuals such as Arendt in her controversial article on Little Rock (1959) and Norman Podhoretz in his confessional essay "My Negro Problem—and Ours" (1963) handed out (mostly) unsolicited advice to black Americans. It was against this volatile background that Elkins's *Slavery*, written by a Jewish academic, was discussed, disputed, and increasingly dismissed as the 1960s came to a close.[44]

Comparisons between the white South and Nazi Germany, between black Southerners and European Jews, were not uncommon as the civil rights movement focused increased attention on the South. Civil rights journalist Pat Watters cut close to the bone when he concluded that white Southerners "do what the society has fashioned them to do. Evil is indeed banal. Eichmann, not Simon Legree, is the villain," while future civil rights activists Ed King and Joyce Ladner learned to draw the parallels between the Klan and the White Citizens Councils and Nazi groups from an émigré German sociologist named Ernst Borinski who was their teacher at Tugaloo College in Jackson, Mississippi.[45] But as the American dilemma became truly national, black intellectuals in the North also began comparing African Americans with Jews in Germany. Writing in the black nationalist magazine, *The Liberator*, late in the decade, Robert Staples's comments illustrate the mixture of black identification with, and a certain contempt for, Jews: "Blacks will not stand idly by and suffer the kind of punishment meted out to German Jews at the hands of the Nazis." A. Sivanandan, writing from London to *The Liberator*, sounded a similar note but also wondered whether the cultivation of group identity was a guarantee against anything: "The Jews in Hitler's Germany knew who they were, but it did not keep them from being a tacit party to their own annihilation." In 1969, Addison Gayle asserted in the same journal that "it was in the concentration camp environment that Bigger Thomas was born." Gayle returned to the analogy in a later piece when he bitterly observed that black Americans were supposed to expunge from their memories what they had suffered in America. But he wondered quite pointedly, "Can any Jews forget Auschwitz and Dachau?"[46]

But it is important to note that in his original article on the concentration camp experience, Bettelheim did not suggest any particular proclivity of European Jews to acquiesce in their own destruction.[47] The terms "Jew" or "Jewish" hardly turn up in the Austrian psychoanalyst's pioneering article of 1943. As already noted, between 1945 and 1960, there was a tendency to downplay the particularly Jewish nature of the Holocaust and of the camp experience. As Peter Novick writes,

> there was nothing about the reporting on the liberation of the camps that treated Jews as more than *among* the victims of the Nazis; nothing

that suggested that the camps were emblematic of anything other than Nazi barbarism in general; nothing, that is, that associated them with what is now designated "the Holocaust."[48]

In the two camps where Bettelheim was an inmate in the late 1930s—Dachau and Buchenwald—the camp population was by no means exclusively Jewish; nor were they extermination camps. Nor, as already mentioned, did Elkins assume that people of African descent were predisposed to accept slavery. Strictly speaking, his topic was the *slave* personality—not the *African* personality—as it emerged under extreme conditions. Finally, the important historical point is that, over the course of the 1960s, the focus of discussion shifted from induced dependency among concentration camp inmates and/or slaves to a comparison of the fate of Jews in *MittelEuropa* with that of people of African descent in the New World. In sum, the 1960s saw the racialization of accounts of resistance to domination.

Another tendency among black intellectuals such as Ralph Ellison and Albert Murray after the mid-1960s was to suggest that Elkins, E. Franklin Frazier, Kenneth Clark in *Dark Ghetto* (1965), and Daniel Patrick Moynihan in his "The Negro Family: The Case for National Action" (1965) were all saying roughly the same thing.[49] Specifically, black life was a "tangle of pathology," according to the heading of the fourth chapter of Moynihan's Report drawn from the work of Clark; the source of that pathology was located in slavery; and the black family, dominated by unmarried mothers, was an important cause and striking symptom of that pathology.[50] But Elkins's thesis differs from this other work in important ways. For instance, Elkins did not use Myrdal's term "pathological" to describe black culture, nor did he use terms such as "dehumanized" or "brainwashed" to characterize the slave. He did apply terms like "degraded" and "corrupted" to describe slave life and referred most often to the "infantilism" and "childlike" behavior of life in the closed system of slavery. Most often, Elkins stressed the way that North American slavery created "absolute dependency" (pp. 61, 86, 112, 130).[51] Nor did Elkins focus very specifically on the fate of the black family under slavery, the dominant concern of Frazier's *The Negro Family in the United States* and of the Moynihan Report. To be sure, Elkins spelled out the status of the black family under slavery quite clearly: "[T]he integrity of the family was ignored and slave marriage was deprived of any legal or moral standing." For that reason, Elkins added, there was next to "no guarantee against indiscriminate separation" of slave children "from their parents" (pp. 49–50, 54). Elkins also called attention to the lack of black father figures and to the presence of the white master as a "significant other" when he noted that "[f]or the Negro child, in particular, the plantation offered no really satisfactory fa-ther-image other than the master." Thus, he continued, "The mother's own role loomed far larger for the slave child than did that of the father" (p. 130). But while these factors were clearly important, Elkins did not ex-amine the structural or psychological stress points of the slave family in any detail. Somehow, the slave personality could be understood apart from any very specific analysis of the slave family.

Finally, the circumscribed nature of Elkins's claims becomes even clearer when we examine what *Slavery* did say about post-emancipation black life. Despite the temptation to extend the Sambo thesis to post-emancipation African American life, especially to the black family, Elkins himself was extremely reluctant to do so. He granted that the Sambo type would hardly have disappeared immediately: "It is hard to imagine its being reversed overnight. The same role might still be played in the years after slavery." Yet, he suggested that "[t]he day might come at last when it dawned on a man's full waking consciousness that he had grown up, that he was, after all, only playing a part" (p. 133). His point was a relatively simple one: with the destruction of the closed system of slavery, the via-bility of the Sambo personality (or role) also diminished and then ulti-mately disappeared. Appendix C to the second edition of *Slavery* particu-larly emphasized the importance of Reconstruction for the emergence of a reconstructed black sense of self. The "general effect," noted Elkins, "was to enrich and broaden the range of experience now open to the Negro and to limit still further the influence of his former master" (p. 245).[52] Finally, in his response to the articles gathered in the Lane volume, and specifically to Ralph Ellison's attacks, Elkins firmly denied that he "ex-tended the Sambo personality to present-day Negro Americans."[53]

Interestingly, the Moynihan Report mentioned Elkins only once in the main text and then by quoting extensively not from Elkins but from Thomas Pettigrew's summary of Elkins. That summary itself focused on the slave family, not on the dependent slave personality, and thus distorted the thrust of Elkins's study. Moynihan's position paper, as already men-tioned, referred to black life as a "tangle of pathology." Like Frazier, Moynihan focused not just on the experience of slavery but also upon the effects of the Great Migration to explain the rise of the black matriarchal family and high rates of illegitimacy among African Americans. This is

not to deny that Elkins's *Slavery* might, with some plausibility, be deployed as a kind of deep background for the Frazier-Moynihan thesis
about the black family. But it does Elkins's own intentions an injustice to
associate him too closely with that position.[54]

Finally, then, Elkins's *Slavery* appeared at a historical turning point.
During the 1960s, black critics and intellectuals began reacting against the
view of themselves as victims. At the same time, the feeling persisted that
the depredations of slavery and Jim Crow should be stressed in order to
convey to the white population the enormity of the crimes of slavery
against African Americans. But it was difficult *both* to assert the existence
of a Sambo type as a reaction to life in a closed system *and* to discover
something like a fully developed, quasi-autonomous slave culture and
functioning slave family. What eventually won out was an emphasis on
the positive, creative, and autonomous aspects of the African American
experience. Indeed, one of the rediscoveries of the decade was that there
had been—and still was—such a tradition to celebrate. Once this was established, Elkins began to look like the enemy rather than an ally. A re-
versal of polarities began to emerge: accentuating the positive in black
American culture became politically progressive rather than politically
suspect, as it once had been, while those who emphasized damage and dependency came to seem defeatist denigrators of all things black, even
racist, particularly if they were white.

Rephrasing the Issue/Ethical and Philosophical Implications

Finally, the argument in *Slavery* about the relative importance of internalization and role-playing raises not only social psychological issues, but
also the kind of issue that Arendt raised in *The Origins of Totalitarianism*
about the nature of human nature: what is inherent in it and what about it
can be changed. Since the 1960s, the critic who has engaged Elkins most
cogently at this level has been Orlando Patterson. In his wide-ranging
treatment of slavery, especially in *Slavery and Social Death* (1982),
Patterson quite clearly rejects the notion that

> any group of slaves ever internalized the conception of degradation
> held by their masters. To be dishonored—and to sense, however
> acutely, such dishonor—is not to lose the quintessential human urge to
> participate and to want a place.[55]

For Patterson, the most important fact about being a slave was not dependence and self-contempt, but the desire to assert dignity and honor. The experience of slavery created the desire for freedom. To be a slave was closely associated with being dishonored; to be free was, among other things, to have one's honor restored. In his view, internalization failed to jibe with human nature and the claim about human nature ("quintessential human urge") ruled out the Sambo personality by definition. Rather, as he wrote in a 1972 essay, for the slave "the clowning, the laziness, the childish adoration were all part of a deadly serious game."[56]

Patterson has recently clarified the issue by defining the disagreement between himself and Elkins in terms of the difference between infantilization (implying internalization) and dissembling (implying role-playing).[57] Yet, a theory of role-playing has its own problems. There is, for instance, the difficulty in explaining permanence of character and continuity of personality, not to mention self-consciousness, other than by resorting to concepts that beg all sorts of questions such as "habit."[58] The influence of the unconscious and the problematic status of remembering and forgetting are also hard to account for. Overall, role theory as an explanation for behavior is altogether too rationalistic. Everyone appears to be a conscious calculator of possibility, a devotee of rational choice. Taken to its logical conclusion, for instance, any consideration of slave revolts would seem irrational, since the chances of their success were practically nil. Perhaps they were—except when they were successful. Finally, to see slavery as an exercise in role-playing assumes that once the ensemble of roles has been destroyed or rearranged, old roles will not impinge on the performance of the new roles. If role theory does take the "after-life" of roles into account, it then needs something like the concepts of internalization, the unconscious, and even repression to explain the persistence of their a/effects.[59]

Nevertheless, Patterson's claim that slaves and former slaves experienced a sense of being dishonored leaves room for a degree of internalization or, at least, for the after-effects of role-playing. It is hard to read Patterson's *Rituals of Blood* (1998) where he uses the term "role devastation" and not wonder how that concept differs from internalization. Indeed, Patterson speaks of "anger and self-loathing" leading to "depression" among the black lower classes when "pathologically internalizing the perverse role assigned" them.[60] It is only a short step from a situation in which being dishonored is contained in the structure of the situation to believing that one's very being *is* dishonored. Whatever the case, however, Patterson need not deny the possibility of internalization when he also asserts that there is some "quintessential human urge" to participate in the determination of one's own fate. The former is a social psychological claim related to a specific historical situation, while the latter is a claim about human nature. Bigger Thomas, as I have indicated earlier, might be understood as the prime example of a (fictional) character whose whole existence leads him to question his fundamental sense of being dishonored, what Elkins might have referred to as "infantilized," when he [Bigger] realizes that he has not lost "the quintessential human urge to participate and to want a place."

It is difficult to know exactly where things stand more than four decades after Elkins's *Slavery* first raised the issues discussed in this chapter. But a few remarks might be in order. First, whatever theoretical language is used, it seems clear that something very close to internalization (and the more obvious related concept of identification) happens.[61] We know that children internalize the values of their parents; recruits to the U.S. Marines absorb the code of the Marine Corps and identify with figures of authority; and, more ominously, child abusers have often internalized the very attitudes and behavior that led to their own abuse and in turn lead them to abuse others. It would be surprising if slaves, of whatever sort in whatever system, failed to internalize some of the values and attitudes of those who controlled them. Indeed, the issue is not just internalization but whether slaves internalized values that undermined their capacity to resist slavery and to accept their master's low opinion of them.[62] Here the answer must be that some did, but not in the massive numbers and not so unambiguously as Elkins's Sambo thesis led us to believe.

Another conclusion would be that the dichotomy between internalization and role-playing, which most participants in the debate about the Elkins thesis have accepted, is a misleading, even false, one. (To his credit, Elkins has always recognized that the dividing line between internalization and role-playing was exceedingly fuzzy.) If the number of Sambo types was very small, the percentage of slaves who learned to play various roles vis-à-vis the master must have approached one hundred percent and probably included all adult slaves, or at least all adult slaves who survived very long. Indeed, the functional definition of a child or naïf or rebel, from the slave point of view, was anyone who had not learned the standard repertory of roles. Put another way, playing a role—"puttin' on ole massa," or just being a respectful and obedient slave—could, and did, lead to considerable psychological stress. In a certain sense, it was more damaging for self-aware slaves to engage in clownish behavior than it was for a "Sambo" to carry out his/her role. The loss of self-respect generated by role-playing and the resulting anger arguably caused more damage—or indicates the areas where damage was most likely to occur—than what Elkins was describing.[63] In other words, we may have been looking for damage in the wrong places.

But the historiography of slavery was not the only place where the question of accommodation to something approaching total domination was under discussion as the 1950s gave way to the 1960s. Similar questions were being asked about what was perceived as the failure of eastern European Jewry to effectively resist their ghettoization and then transportation to the death camps in Poland. In particular, crucial questions about resistance and accommodation emerged from the trial of Adolph Eichmann in 1961 and the publication of Hannah Arendt's *Eichmann in Jerusalem* (1963), along with the work of Raul Hilberg and Bruno Bettelheim. Overall, the Eichmann trial did not so much initiate as crystallize the public debate about these difficult matters, and it is to it that we will now turn.[64]

7

Culture, Accommodation, and Resistance II: The Eichmann Trial and Jewish Tradition

You see I cannot get over the extermination factories.

Hannah Arendt

The Trial was a way of giving public shape to a tormenting memory.

Harold Rosenberg

The past is never dead. It is not even past.

William Faulkner

Stanley Elkins's *Slavery* (1959) was so controversial because of its claim that the existence of a dependent slave type explained the paucity of slave revolts in the United States. Similarly, Hannah Arendt's *Eichmann in Jerusalem* (1963), along with political scientist Raul Hilberg's *The Destruction of the European Jews* (1961) and various pieces by psychoanalyst Bruno Bettelheim, grappled with what seemed to many a disturbing lack of Jewish resistance to the Final Solution. The Eichmann trial aroused great controversy within intellectual elites in the United States, Britain, Europe, and Israel. Initial reactions to the trial in America were quite mixed but the trial also penetrated popular awareness in the United States where a remarkable 87 percent of those polled in May 1961 knew what the Eichmann trial was.[1] Although Elkins generally ignored the psychology of the slaveholders, Arendt and Hilberg especially concentrated on the words, actions, and inferred mentality of the perpetrators, as expressed most notoriously in Arendt's claim that Adolf Eichmann exemplified the "banality of evil." Bettelheim's influential 1943 article on the transformation of inmate personality under extreme conditions was, as we have seen, the main source of Elkins's thesis, but played a much less direct role in his treatment of Eichmann.[2] Rather, Bettelheim and Hilberg, especially, attributed the lack of Jewish resistance to weaknesses (such as a "ghetto mentality") in the European Jewish tradition.

Unlike Elkins who was an American Jew, Hilberg and Bettelheim were Austrian Jews, while Arendt was born in Germany. Bettelheim spent from mid-1938 to early 1939 (six months in all) in Dachau and Buchenwald, while Arendt, as we have seen, was briefly jailed by the Gestapo in Berlin in 1933 and then later made her way to Portugal from France before arriving in the United States in 1941. Hilberg, who studied under Franz Neumann at Columbia and then taught for many years at the University of Vermont, came to America with his parents via Cuba in 1939 at the age of thirteen and was thus considerably younger than Arendt and Bettelheim. Just as Elkins was attacked with some vehemence, particularly by African Americans, for suggesting that slaves had accommodated themselves to enslavement, all three of the Central European émigrés were targets of strong, even virulent, criticism from other Jews. Indeed, Jennifer Ring has suggested that the extreme reactions to Arendt's book arose from several factors, one of which was that, as a woman, Arendt dared criticize the Jewish leaders during the war for not having been "manly" enough, as it were, to encourage and lead resistance to the Final Solution. More plausibly, Arendt's book indirectly challenged her New York intellectual colleagues' newly discovered Jewishness, something they had largely ignored when they were young, radical, and, as Dwight Macdonald put it, "hot for truth, justice and other universals" in the 1930s. Being Jewish was no protection against incurring the ire of fellow Jews or African Americans.[3]

There were other similarities—and differences—between Elkins and the three principals in the Eichmann controversy. Because he embraced concepts drawn from psychoanalysis and social psychology, Elkins was accused of insensitivity toward the slave experience, symbolized particularly in his use of the term "Sambo," and his neglect of the cultural achievements of slaves. Similarly, Arendt was condemned for the ironic, even sarcastic, tone she adopted in *Eichmann in Jerusalem*. Her erstwhile friend, historian Gershom Scholem, claimed that her book lacked a sense of tact (*Herzenstakt*) and displayed insufficient love for "her" people.[4] Thus, what members of each group admitted among themselves—anger (and shame) at lack of resistance to their enslavement and murder—was often denied when such opinions were placed under public, that is, gentile or white, scrutiny. Attempts by Arendt, Bettelheim, and Hilberg to explain the Holocaust by anything other than the history of anti-Semitism was seen by some as a way of exonerating the gentile world, while Elkins was accused of blaming the (black slave) victim. That said, although Elkins's explanation for the paucity of slave revolts in North America met with widespread opposition as the 1960s unfolded, he explained the acquiescence of slaves to their condition of enslavement—and left it at that. What created the greater furor around the work of Hilberg, Bettelheim, and Arendt, besides the fact that Arendt and Bettelheim published their work in general circulation magazines (e.g., *The New Yorker* and *The New Republic*) and with commercial publishers, was that they not only analyzed the cooperation of the Jewish ghetto leadership with Nazi rule, they judged that cooperation in harsh terms.

In general, then, by roughly 1960, the histories of slavery, colonialism, and the Holocaust were all coming under severe scrutiny, with a new—and often discomfiting focus—upon the involvement of the victims in their own domination, enslavement, and even extermination. These public controversies were more than temporary episodes in the mid-century history of intellectual and moral fashion, but were, rather, central to the moral history of the twentieth century in the West.[5] In Arendt's case, the controversy still simmers, as illustrated by historian Richard Wolin's recent claim that Arendt's Eichmann book was filled with "calumnies about the Jews" and that it "insinuat[ed] that, in certain respects, they [the Jews] were no better than the Nazis."[6] Nor, as I have already suggested, has Elkins's *Slavery* really shed its controversial status.

Specifically, the controversies aroused by Elkins's "Sambo" thesis and the Eichmann trial are important because they raised questions about the historical strengths and weaknesses of African American and Jewish cultures, respectively. Was there a flaw at the heart of the beliefs, traditions, institutions, and sacred texts of each culture (African, Jewish, African American) that weakened resistance to domination and encouraged acquiescence to slavery and the Final Solution? There were cruel historical ironies at work in all this. Though racial explanations had been discredited and prejudice against blacks and Jews steeply declined after World War II, both groups feared that any emphasis on group differences, even if explained in cultural and historical rather than racial terms, would encourage the revival of old stereotypes and represent a new form of "blaming the victim." Thus, both controversies showed that culture could be as controversial an explanation for group intentions and behavior as race once had been. A belief in racial equality was no panacea. There was one difference, however: a group's culture, in contrast with its race, could be changed. From this perspective, it is obvious that the common purpose uniting decolonization in the Third World, the rediscovery of African American culture and the emergence of the black power movement in the 1960s, and the founding of the state of Israel was the creation of a new political and cultural context for the transformation of once-dominated cultures. In each case, the presiding imperative was, "never again."

Between Secular Justice and Sacred History

The 1961 trial of Adolf Eichmann in Jerusalem represented a turning point in the way that the history of European Jewry was understood by Jews and gentiles alike.[7] Staged by the state of Israel for political purposes, it marked a new way of conceptualizing what by the early 1960s was coming to be called the Holocaust. Though the attempt to eradicate European Jewry had hovered in the consciousness of participants in the Nuremberg trials, until the early 1960s what was by then being called the "Holocaust" had been seen as part of a wider "administrative mass murder" (Arendt's term) in which not only Jews but several other groups (Poles, Gypsies, homosexuals) had suffered horrendous losses at the hands of the Nazis. According to this view, the Jews were "first among equals" among Nazi victims. But the Eichmann trial helped establish a new historical perspective in which the Holocaust became the central—and, for some, inevitable—event in the history of European Jewry. Concomitantly, Jews, by virtue of their absolute centrality in the Nazi *Weltanschauung*, became the special object of Nazi ideological hatred rather than "simply" one among several groups singled out for extermination or enslavement.[8]

It was in reference to the shifting significance of the Holocaust—and the need to bolster Israeli morale and to enlist world opinion on the side of Israel—that the Israeli government decided to make the trial of Adolf Eichmann, who had been captured in Argentina in May 1960, an object lesson in Zionist history. According to Tom Segev, Israeli Prime Minister David Ben-Gurion "had two goals: one was to remind the countries of the world that the Holocaust obligated them to support the only Jewish state on earth. The second was to impress the lessons of the Holocaust on the people of Israel, especially the younger generation." Put another way: "something was required to unite Israeli society" since by 1960 some of the initial fervor generated by the founding of Israel had been dissipated.[9] Furthermore, Israel was depicted as the only truly safe haven for Jews in an unremittingly hostile, gentile world. The incontrovertible lesson of the Holocaust was that ultimately Jews could depend only upon themselves for their survival, the further implication being the illusory nature of universal human rights and international solidarity. As a stateless people, a minority and/or refugees between the two world wars, Jews had looked to the formulation of transnational standards of justice as enforced by international organizations for their protection.[10] But the Zionist idea was that with the establishment of the state of Israel, Jews no longer needed to beg for help from an indifferent, even hostile, world; rather, they could find protection under Israeli law and in Israeli courts. Thus, Eichmann was charged not with crimes against humanity but with genocide against the Jewish people.

Ben-Gurion's government also undertook to rehabilitate, as it were, the Israeli image of Hitler's victims. During and after the war, *aliyah* (immigrant) Jews in Palestine, especially conservative ones, displayed considerable ambivalence concerning the European victims of anti-Semitism. They reasoned that European Jews should have seen what was coming and fled to Palestine before the war. But the Eichmann trial became the occasion for the public construction of a Zionist vision in which the Jews who perished in the Holocaust were recast as innocent victims and/or resolute heroes; indeed they were seen as proto-Zionists and thus "the great silence surrounding the destruction of the Jews" was broken.[11] To further encourage a positive image of European victims, the prosecution called "survivors" as witnesses against Eichmann. This stood in stark contrast to the Nuremberg trials where the documents and testimony of officials of the German government and of the Nazi Party constituted the primary source of evidence. The survivor experience, which was often only tangentially related to Eichmann's activities, was central to the prosecution's case. As the occasion for the first extensive use of survivor testimony, the Eichmann trial provided a therapeutic-legal theater for the survivors and served a therapeutic-pedagogic function for Israeli and world opinion generally.[12] Put another way, the historical narrative constructed at Nuremberg was "perpetrator" history, while the Eichmann trial was intended to create a "victim's" history of the Holocaust.

In all of this, it was perhaps inevitable that what several analysts have seen as a process of "sacralization" of the Holocaust would lead to the demonization of Eichmann and/or a significant overestimation of his importance in the Final Solution. Where, as Arendt pointed out, Eichmann's

defense tried to show that he had been but a "cog" in the machine of extermination, the prosecution erred in the other direction by considering
him its "actual motor" (pp. 11, 289). Only in this way did the Israeli government feel that it could dramatize the great lesson of the Holocaust.
Overall, then, the Eichmann trial, in both intention and effect, was a public incorporation of the Holocaust as the central event in Jewish history
and the strongest possible affirmation of the state of Israel. It is no wonder, then, that Arendt's *Eichmann in Jerusalem* aroused such an uproar in
1963, particularly in America, as did Bettelheim's work on the psychology of dependence and resistance, including his ringing defense of
Arendt's book, and as Hilberg's *The Destruction of the European Jews*
(1961) had already done a couple of years earlier.

In what follows, I want to explore the three areas where the work of
Hilberg, Bettelheim, and Arendt sought to resist the retrospective particu-
larization, monumentalization, and sacralization of the Holocaust (and the
state of Israel), along with the magnification of Eichmann's significance.
These areas are the Jewish resistance to the Nazis, the personality of Adolf
Eichmann and the question of evil, and the nature of the charges brought
against Eichmann. Though by no means in agreement on everything, the
thrust of their work taken together was not to particularize but to universalize, not to memorialize but to analyze critically, and not to sacralize but
to secularize the Jewish experience of the Holocaust by asking how and
why the Holocaust had happened without evoking the Zionist doctrine of
eternal—and murderous—anti-Semitism.

Resistance and Complicity

For understandable reasons, the debate over the degree of Jewish resistance to the Final Solution has been particularly intense. Although there
are comparisons to be made with the slave resistance/cooperation in North
America, one major difference is that whereas most slaves were born into
slavery, the vast majority of European Jews had known a time "before"
the Nazis, and thus were forced to develop a radically different attitude toward the Germans and German culture. While the differences between religious and secular forms of anti-Semitic ideology can be overdrawn, the
history of religious anti-Semitism was little or no help in understanding
the Nazi-inspired, secular-pagan anti-Semitism.[13] Moreover, the historical
experience of eastern European Jews was that the Germans were more
tolerable ruler-occupiers than the universally feared Russians.[14] Resistance

is itself a problematic term, for everything short of armed struggle, flight, and sabotage may reinforce, as much as it undermines, the system of oppression. And the desire to live dictates accommodation, as often as it leads to heroic resistance against domination and oppression.

In *Eichmann in Jerusalem*, Arendt delivered no blanket indictment of Jewish acquiescence, if for no other reason than that "no non-Jewish group or people had behaved differently" (p. 11). But the charge that the Judenräte (Jewish councils) had cooperated excessively with the Nazis was countered by some critics who maintained that the Nazis would have done what they wanted to do, whatever the resistance of the Jewish people in general or the Judenräte in particular had been.[15] In fact, it was Hilberg rather than Arendt who first offered a systematic delineation of the record of the Jewish councils in Eastern Europe. His *The Destruction of the European Jews*, a mammoth administrative-institutional history of the Final Solution, was a pioneering (and uncompromising) work in its emphasis on the ways that Jews, guided by the Jewish councils, actively cooperated in their own extermination or passively allowed the process to proceed with little resistance. The dominant impression conveyed by what historian Christopher Browning has referred to as a "truly great book" is that the Holocaust was the end result of a vast, highly rationalized system devoted to extermination, a paradigm case of instrumental rationality in the service of the production of corpses.[16] As Hilberg later asserted, it was not German "hatred" of the Jews, but the machinery of bureaucracy that best explained the magnitude of the Final Solution.[17]

On the matter of cooperation, Hilberg pulled no punches. In reference to the actions of the *Einsatzgruppen* in Eastern Europe and Russia, "it is significant that the Jews allowed themselves to be shot without resistance—in all the reports of the Einsatzgruppen there are few references to 'incidents'" (p. 209). Moreover, he asserted, "the great bulk of the Jews presented themselves voluntarily at the collecting points" for transportation to the extermination centers of the East once the process began, though some resistance did emerge when their "number grew smaller" (p. 316). And such resistance as there was, noted Hilberg, was not organized by Jewish councils. The significance of the Warsaw ghetto uprising lay not in its military success or lack thereof. Rather it was that

[i]n Jewish history, . . . the battle is literally a revolution, for after two thousand years of a policy of submission the wheel had been turned and once again Jews were using force (p. 318).

Discussing events in the Polish city of Lodz, Hilberg once again cited the historical-traditional constraints that had defined the Jews as a people: "[T]he ghetto inmates . . . were not capable of breaking with a historical pattern under which they had survived destruction for two thousand years" (p. 324).

Hungary in general and Budapest in particular were the worst. The Germans knew the war was lost, but even though both the Jews and the Allies knew what was coming, "mass deportations . . . were carried out openly" (p. 510). The Jewish council in Budapest was a "pawn in German hands" (p. 530); it "woke up too late to act" (p. 542); and thus reacted, according to an SS observer, "without resistance and in submission" (p. 541). Hilberg calculates that despite the resistance that was mounted by the Jews, the Germans and their allies suffered only "sixteen dead and eighty-five wounded" (p. 326). Most pointedly, he asks, "But were these people really fooled" or "did they deliberately fool themselves?" (p. 667). If two thousand years of adjustment to Christian domination provided a long-range explanation, Hilberg also suggested two psychological mechanisms that eased the cooperation of the Jews and their leaders in their demise. First is what he named the "bisection phenomenon," according to which a council would give up a certain percentage of people to the Nazis in order to save the rest—but only until the process began again when another "bisection" was necessary. The other response, something like collective denial, operated "to make the ordeal bearable, to make death easy" (p. 669). In light of all that had happened, the founding of the state of Israel, concluded Hilberg, was a "vast 'undoing' achievement" (p. 675), a way of overcoming a history of acquiescence to domination and extermination.

Hilberg certainly shied away from speculation and even, Browning suggests, moral judgments directed against the Jewish leadership.[18] However, Bruno Bettelheim approached the history of the Holocaust through his own personal experience and with the tools of his chosen profession, psychoanalysis. From his perspective, the camps functioned, as Primo Levi and Arendt also suggested, as "an experimental laboratory."[19] What went on there was the dismantling and then reassembling of the inmate personality structure, which up to then psychoanalytic theory had assumed was fixed in early childhood. Though working, as he later noted, without the psychological concerns of ego autonomy and identity developed by Heinz Hartmann and Erik Erikson, Bettelheim's main focus fell on the ways the inmates did or did not preserve their sense of self by splitting and self-observation.[20] The most common reaction was regression to a psychological state of childlike dependence on, and identification with, the camp guards and SS administration. Bettelheim also noted in a 1947 essay that the Nazis structured camp life along hierarchical lines and thus encouraged power struggles that undermined inmate solidarity. Under these conditions, it was all but impossible for the camp inmates to mount an organized rebellion, not just because of the threat of violent retaliation but also because of the way their consciousness and consciences had been modified.[21] Where Theodor Adorno and company would later identify a weak ego structure as characteristic of the "authoritarian personality," Bettelheim saw its mass emergence among inmates as well.

Although Bettelheim's early essays focused on the problematic nature of inmate ego strength and their dependent behavior, his 1948 essay, "The Victim's Image of the Anti-Semite," shifted to the problem of Jewish psychology and the psychology of anti-Semitism. Bettelheim did not mention *Anti-Semite and Jew* in this article, but much of what he says there reads like a response to aspects of Sartre's striking portrait of the dialectic between anti-Semite and Jew. In some respects, he affirmed Sartre's portrait of the inauthentic Jew. For Bettelheim, the Jews in the camps perceived the camp guards in superhuman rather than realistic terms, and thus acted in ways that confirmed rather than undermined anti-Semitic stereotypes. Because they overestimated the power and brutality of the SS, the Jews had a built-in excuse not to rebel. Even those who committed suicide, notes Bettelheim, failed to kill the guards before they died. (He noted the fact of German retaliation for such actions against surviving inmates,[22] but he added that even in the extermination camps, where all inmates knew they were scheduled to die, suicides seldom "took" a guard or guards with them.) While his 1947 essay on the class structure in the camps suggested that the struggle for power and privilege explained why inmates did not revolt against the authorities, the 1948 essay emphasized a failure of reality testing and an overestimation of the power of the SS, thus implying the existence of the dependent personality he had written about earlier. Still, in this latter essay, Bettelheim's relative optimism about the possibilities of treating others and being treated as an autonomous individual in the camp situation was striking—and bewildering.

Bettelheim differed crucially from Sartre on the nature of anti-Semitism. He considered the anti-Semite as fundamentally a normal person who happens to hold a particular set of prejudices: "[T]here is nothing peculiar about anti-Semites except their anti-Semitism" (p. 178). This was a surprising view coming from someone whose essential concern was with ego strength, that is, the individual's whole sense of himself. In his upbeat conclusion, he also rejects

> a gross image of the anti-Semite as one bloated with ignorance and sadism. Jews must surrender their stereotype of the anti-Semite as a person too inferior to take pains with, too powerful to be fought against, or too radically corrupt to be approached as a normal human being. Anti-Semites are, for the most part, average people—like Jews. And that is most encouraging (p. 179).

There was nothing here of Sartre's anti-Semite, whose whole world is devoted to the "creation" of the Jew; nor was the familiar psychoanalytic linkage between prejudice and a sadomasochistic orientation evident at all. By the late 1940s, Bettelheim's vision of life in the camps seems surprisingly benign, considering the hell on earth he had depicted in earlier essays. All this foreshadows the direction that Bettelheim's work would take in the 1950s as he gradually assumed guru status on matters having to do with contemporary society. The assumption underlying his *The Informed Heart* (1960) was that life in the concentration camps revealed something essential about normal life in modern, technologically oriented mass society. In both situations, the crucial task was to preserve and defend ego autonomy against the crushing forces of mass society. Put another way, in order to make his critical analysis of modern society stick, Bettelheim needed to make camp life less rather than more extreme.

In the 1960s, Bettelheim concurred with Hilberg's notion that the Jews had acquiesced because of long-standing patterns of thought and behavior, according to which the gentile authorities were always open to negotiation, and that it was best to wait out the storms of prejudice, pogroms, and even mass murder. In "Freedom from Ghetto Thinking" (1962), Bettelheim wrote of a Jewish "innocence tinged with ignorance" or a "deliberate innocence" motivated by the desire "to avoid taking action,"[23] and named this complex of beliefs, traditions, and folk wisdom "ghetto thinking" (p. 17). (He also contrasted it with the mentality developing in Israel that encouraged fighting back.) Ghetto thinking derived from

> inner feelings of resignation, in the careful eradication, over centuries, of tendencies to rebel, in the ingrained habit of believing that those who bend do not break (p. 22).

Though some defended such a stance for its nonviolence and thus made a virtue of "passivity in the face of persecution" (p. 21), Bettelheim wondered "why millions of Jews did not flinch from death but shrank from fighting for their lives," thereby displaying "an inability to act in self-defense on one's own *as a Jew*" (p. 21).[24] He admits the appealing features of ghetto culture—group solidarity and the capacity to endure privation, hardship, and oppression—but he rejects ghetto thinking for its refusal to learn from other oppressed people's histories and for failing to understand German intentions toward the Jews after 1937, by which time it was clear that there was no place in German-dominated Europe for Jews. Finally, he concluded the essay with a discussion of the Anne Frank case. Although claiming he was "critical not of the Frank family, not of Anne Frank, but of the universally positive reception given her *Diary* in the western world" (p. 24), the upshot of his discussion was to indict Jews such as the Franks for failing to plan a way out of their secret quarters in Amsterdam and preferring to wait passively for the end.

However, in a 1967 review essay of Jean François Steiner's *Treblinka*, Bettelheim criticized Steiner (and went beyond Hilberg) to insist that a crucial development in modern Jewish history helped even more to explain the lack of Jewish resistance. Over three generations, he maintained, the migration of Jews to the New World had cost European Jewry some of its most energetic and creative members. Western Jews, always accused of being "assimilated" and thus supposedly more gullible about gentile society, fled much earlier in the face of Nazi prosecution, while *Ostjuden,* the ghetto Jews, failed to flee in sufficient numbers and thus millions perished. From this perspective, it was not simply the two-thousand-year history of Judaism but specifically modern developments that had weakened Jewish leadership and Jewish traditions of resistance.[25]

In comparison with the positions of Hilberg and Bettelheim on Jewish resistance, Arendt's comments on the topic in *Eichmann in Jerusalem* were relatively brief and circumscribed. Because the topic itself had been ruled out of bounds at the trial, Arendt felt compelled to say something about it. Yet, she explicitly limited the scope of what she was undertaking in her Eichmann book. At times, she would claim that she was merely attempting to state the facts of the matter; at other times, she was more expansive. Indeed, two of the three major points of contention emerging from *Eichmann in Jerusalem*—Jewish resistance and the nature of evil—concerned topics she introduced "on the wing." Considering their importance, they were seriously underdeveloped. Nowhere did

Arendt speak in print of anything like "ghetto thinking." In fact, she was dubious about the term, as her reply to Bettelheim in *Midstream* (September 1962) made clear,[26] where she cautioned him against using such a term as a kind of "inverted chauvinism" (p. 86). She was also reluctant to fix a date after which all Jews should have fled Germany and Eastern Europe. There, as well as in the Eichmann book, she asserted that the behavior of the Jews in the camps and in the deportation process had been no better or worse than that of any other group. Where there were differences, she noted in the *Midstream* contribution, was in the behavior of the leadership of various European peoples. On that score, the Jewish leadership was sorely lacking, something about which Hilberg, she observed, had "put the record straight" (p. 86). Thus, her main charges in *Eichmann in Jerusalem* had already been announced in the early fall of 1962.

Here a brief look at Arendt's previous writings on Jewish resistance is revealing. In several essays and reviews during the 1940s and in *The Origins of Totalitarianism*, Arendt was far from uncritical of the Jewish record in political and military matters. During the war, she strongly supported organizing a Jewish army to fight in Europe in order that the "old mentality of enslaved peoples, the belief that it does not pay to fight back" might be eradicated.[27] Like Hilberg and Bettelheim, she felt that the significance of Israel lay in its effort to "wipe out the humiliation of Hitler's slaughterhouses with the newly-won dignity of battle and triumph of victory."[28] In her highly favorable review of Gershom Scholem's *Major Trends in Jewish Mysticism*, entitled "Jewish History, Revised" (1948), she admitted that Scholem's rediscovery of the mass movement led by Sabbatai Zevi in the seventeenth century had changed her notion of Jews as "not history-makers but history-sufferers" and "innocent victims."[29] There Scholem had demonstrated that Jewish history contained an episode of collective action, although the Sabbatian movement's eventual defeat (and Zevi's conversion to Islam) meant that the "people retired from the public scene of history" (p. 105). As she had written earlier, there had been two attempts in the diaspora at "direct political action. The first was the Sabbatai Zevi movement, . . . and Zionism is the second."[30] Consistent with this analysis, although with a nineteenth-century focus, was her claim in *The Origins of Totalitarianism* that post-emancipation European Jewry failed to develop the habit of thinking politically, since they were so concerned with social acceptance in the gentile world. Far from identifying this with "ghetto thinking," however, Arendt considered it a characteristic of the self-deception of assimilated bourgeois Jews of post-emancipation Germany.

In *Eichmann in Jerusalem*, her focus shifted to the Jewish leadership, specifically to the Jewish councils, to which she devoted all of nine pages. Early in the book, she reminded readers of what she had already emphasized in her writings of the early postwar period: the Zionist belief in the "eternal and ubiquitous nature of anti-Semitism."[31] In *Eichmann in Jerusalem*, she noted how such a belief had predisposed German Jews to begin early negotiation with the Nazis in time-honored fashion. However, she insisted that this was by no means of the same level of seriousness as the "later collaboration" of the Jewish councils. Still, as a precedent, it made it easier "to cross the abyss between helping Jews to escape and helping the Nazis to deport them" (pp. 10–11). Overall, then, if Arendt identified any one explanation for Jewish passivity and the readiness of the leadership to treat with their enemies, it was the Zionist belief in "eternal anti-Semitism." Such a historical constant bore a certain resemblance to the "long-established patterns" Hilberg wrote about, but it hardly implied the comprehensive nature of Bettelheim's "ghetto thinking."

The history of Arendt's stance on Zionism is a complex one. She worked for a Zionist youth organization in the 1930s in Paris and was favorably disposed toward Zionism as a movement that thought realistically about the possible destination (in both a literal and a metaphorical sense) of European Jewry. Yet, besides firmly rejecting the doctrine of eternal anti-Semitism, she doubted that the existence of Israel had resolved the problem of anti-Semitism as Theodor Herzl, the founder of modern Zionism, had hoped it would. By the mid-1940s, a "social revolutionary" Zionism had been replaced by a "nationalistic chauvinistic" movement whose plans—and their implementation—ignored the existence or rights of the indigenous Arab population.[32] A decade later she had come to feel that Israel, far from transcending the ghetto culture, was the scene of its displacement from Europe to the Middle East. "[T]he *Galut* and the ghetto mentality" was the way she described it to her husband, Heinrich Blücher,[33] an indication that she was not averse to such formulations in private. Clearly her conception of Zionism—the creation of a Jewish homeland in a bi-national state—had lost out to those who wanted a Jewish state. When it came to the Eichmann trial, then, Arendt's own attitude toward Israel was already highly ambivalent. Yet, critical though she was of the trial as a "show trial," she never disputed Israel's right to hold it.

Arendt's relatively brief discussion of the Jewish councils was explicitly based on Hilberg's account that had already revealed the history of the Nazi-created Jewish council in all "its petty and sordid detail" (p. 118). The only distinction that made any difference in discussing resistance, she asserted, was "not between Zionists and non-Zionists but between organized and unorganized people, and, even more important, between the young and the middle-aged" (p. 122). The prosecution avoided any discussion of the Jewish councils, she speculated, since otherwise "the clearcut division between persecution and victims would have suffered greatly" (p. 120).[34] About the Jews who manned the gas chambers and the involvement of "Jewish commandos" in carrying out the extermination process, Arendt could only write, "But this was only horrible, it was no moral problem" (p. 123). Once in the camps, conventional moral judgments failed to capture anything meaningful about the situation, since there were scarcely any meaningful choices to be made. Arendt also noted that, when cross-examined, Eichmann confirmed that "the Nazis regarded this cooperation [of the councils] as the very cornerstone of their Jewish policy" (p. 124). Finally, Arendt concluded with what was to prove to be an inflammatory summary:

> Wherever Jews lived, there were recognized Jewish leaders, and this leadership, almost without exception, cooperated in one way or another, for one reason or another, with the Nazis. The whole truth was that if the Jewish people had really been unorganized and leaderless, there would have been chaos and plenty of misery but the total number of victims would have hardly been between four and a half and six million people (p. 125).

Despite Arendt's heavy dependence on his comprehensive work, Hilberg later refused to distinguish between the Jewish leadership and the Jewish people: "The problem," he later wrote, "was deeper."[35] Contrary to what her critics asserted, nowhere did Arendt claim that the Jewish councils and the Nazis were equally responsible for the Holocaust. The councils' fault lay in not resisting more forcefully, thus making it easier for the Nazis to implement the Final Solution. But there is no denying that the effect of the work of Hilberg, Bettelheim, and Arendt was to undermine the notion that the Jews had proven themselves a heroic people during the Holocaust.[36] Their work comprised a "narrative," as Shoshanah Felman has remarked of Arendt's book, of "responsibility" not of "victimhood and heroism."[37] With this in mind, the outrage that Arendt, Hilberg, and Bettelheim triggered becomes more comprehensible.

Yet their critics deserve a hearing on several points. The first concerns the claim that the history and traditions of the Jewish people stunted their capacity to actively oppose the Nazis. Clearly, such an explanation needed much more fleshing out before it could be convincing as even part of the truth. But the general consensus among historians of the Holocaust is that the nature and extent of Jewish resistance, including the cooperation of the Jewish councils, is a much more complex matter than Hilberg, Bettelheim, and Arendt allowed. Historian Yehuda Bauer rejects Hilberg's "cogs in the machine" interpretation and even notes that, in an article from the 1980s, he clears the councils of blanket complicity.[38] Bauer does not deny that Jewish resistance failed by and large, but contends that the harsh judgment directed against the councils should be supplemented by an investigation of "their intentions and attitudes" (p. 128). Bauer's overall judgment is that some councils acted heroically and others fit Arendt's blanket indictment pretty closely, but "[m]ostly, however, they did neither" (p. 134). A few successfully played for time, hoping to stave off the day when all the ghetto populations would be deported. In most cases, however, this policy failed. Bauer's own judgment is that "there was a great deal of Jewish armed resistance, very much more than could have been expected" (p. 142). He also contends, however, that "it was not—it could not be—massive; quantitatively speaking it was marginal" (p. 136). Bauer also evokes Israel's struggle for independence as a refutation of the ghetto mentality thesis, but Israel's fight for its existence did not contradict the existence of a ghetto mentality in Europe as such, only the survival of that mentality outside of Europe. At any rate, Bauer ends agnostically by observing that "[t]he issue still awaits serious research" (p. 142), a bewildering conclusion to be drawn nearly four decades after the issue was first raised and in itself hardly a ringing endorsement of historians of the Holocaust. Finally, Bauer's position seems to be that because we know that the Jewish councils failed, any question as to whether more resistance might have been possible is irrelevant.

The attempt to judge the Jewish councils also raises the question of whether a historian should be concerned primarily with the intentions and motives or the *judgments* of historical actors.[39] As Susan Neiman has recently noted, *Eichmann in Jerusalem* represented a turning point in Arendt's thought. Beginning with it, she de-emphasized the intentions of actors, whether Adolf Eichmann or the Jewish councils, and focused rather on their judgment of the situation.[40] As Arendt wrote in an imagined address to Eichmann:

> We are concerned here only with what you did, and not with the possible noncriminal nature of your inner life and of your motives or with the criminal potentialities of those around you (p. 278).

It was such a stance that led many to see Arendt as too harsh in her judgment of the councils and too lenient in her condemnation of Eichmann. But to focus on judgments rather than intentions is not necessarily to be hard-boiled and insensitive. After all, the intentions of an Oskar Schindler were undoubtedly a murky mix of self-interest and altruism, while his judgment proved effective in saving a number of Jews from Auschwitz. Ideally, the historian should assess both intentions and judgments; but judging intentions should not be a way of ignoring what were often highly questionable judgments by the Jewish councils. When in response to Arendt's book, Gershom Scholem asserted that "I do not know whether they [the Jewish ghetto leaders] were right or wrong. Nor do I presume to judge. I was not there,"[41] one of the great modern historians whose work immeasurably enriched the history of Judaism, all but rendered the historians of the Holocaust superfluous and their task as hopeless.

Christopher Browning raised a related matter about the nature of judgment in his review of the revised edition of Hilberg's *The Destruction of the European Jews* in the early 1980s. According to Browning, his new edition sharpened the contrast with Arendt, since Hilberg conceived of the failure of the Jewish councils to have been a "perceptual, not a moral, failure." When Arendt's book appeared, Daniel Bell similarly noted that "what could have been left as historical fact or evaluation is converted by Miss Arendt into a moral judgment and opprobrium."[42] In the abstract, this distinction makes a certain amount of sense. Much of the time historians are not called upon to render moral evaluations of the individuals or groups about whom they write. But it is difficult to read the first edition of Hilberg's *The Destruction of European Jews* and imagine that he was not condemning the Jewish councils. The voice with which he records the facts and renders the judgment is also full of moral passion. Indeed, Hilberg's whole point was that being fooled was a form of culpability on the part of the Jewish leadership.

Eichmann and the Question of Evil

Although hostile reactions to the position on Jewish resistance taken by Hilberg, Bettelheim, and Arendt may seem excessive, it is not difficult to sympathize with them to a degree. But it is much more difficult to credit the anger aroused by Arendt's characterization of Eichmann and his actions as exemplifying the "banality of evil." The picture of Eichmann that emerges from Hilberg's *The Destruction of the European Jews* is relatively undeveloped, since Hilberg focuses on system, structure, and organization rather than character or ideology as crucial in the destruction of European Jewry. Eichmann's fingerprints are, as it were, all over the book, but Hilberg is not interested in the role of individual character or personality in the Final Solution, and thus Eichmann generally remains a cipher in the pages of his study. Later in his memoirs, Hilberg remarks about the banality thesis: "She [Arendt] did not grasp the dimensions of his deed. There was no 'banality' in this 'evil.'"[43] Of course, Arendt's thesis did not refer, in the first instance, to evil's banality but to the banality of Eichmann the man. Bettelheim, it should be added, had no problem with Arendt's description of Eichmann's "normality" or his "mediocre" personality and emphasized the "incongruity" between the deeds and the rather ordinary man who committed them.[44] For many readers, however, the way Arendt stripped Eichmann of his demonic stature seemed to trivialize the Holocaust and the suffering of the Jewish people.

Still, Hilberg was correct in one respect. Arendt also denied that evil itself, and not just Eichmann the man, was radical. In her response to Scholem's attack, she insisted that her conception of evil was that it

is never "radical," that it is only extreme, and that it possesses neither depth nor any demonic dimension. It can overgrow and lay waste the whole world precisely because it spreads like a fungus on the surface. It is "thought-defying." . . . That is its banality.[45]

As Arendt herself reminded Scholem, this represented a revision of the notion of radical evil she introduced, without really defining or developing, in *The Origins of Totalitarianism*. Whereas in *The Origins of Totalitarianism*, "radical evil" refers to the horrific *effects* of Nazi policy in creating superfluous populations upon which the camp experiments were carried out, not to mention the death camps themselves, the "banality of evil" refers, firstly, to the quality of Eichmann's *intentions or motives* and, secondly, to the nature of evil itself. If Eichmann's evil was not "deep," then his intentions are finally uninteresting. One learns little or nothing from investigating them. There is no better indication of Eichmann's failure to comprehend what he had done than his repeated response to the charges against him: "Not guilty in the sense of the indictment."

This question of how best to think about evil was also at the core of Lionel Abel's criticism of Arendt: her judgment of the councils and of Eichmann was fundamentally "an aesthetic one."[46] What "aesthetic" means in this context is not entirely clear, but it has something to do with Arendt's tendency to emphasize Eichmann's way of being in the world as revelatory of his essence as a person. According to Abel, that Eichmann could only speak or think in clichés seemed to worry Arendt more than what he had actually done. This was true but only in the sense that, for Arendt, Eichmann's flaw was not his anti-Semitism as such but his "lack of imagination": "He *merely*, to put the matter colloquially, *never realized what he was doing*." And later she wrote in her *Life of the Mind*: "It was not stupidity but *thoughtlessness*," an "absence of thinking" that most struck her about Eichmann.[47] Nothing about the content of his beliefs revealed how he could have played such a major role in the Final Solution. As a "man without qualities," there was no "there" there.

As Mary McCarthy and Dwight Macdonald noted at the time, the representation of evil as banal rather than grand was hardly a new departure. The representation of evil in the Western literary tradition was by no means confined to Milton's Lucifer as the Prince of Darkness or Melville's Ahab, figures of commanding intelligence and darkly attractive in their willed intention to violate the terms of human solidarity and God's law. Both Goethe and Dostoevsky had depicted the Devil as a rather unprepossessing figure: he was "shabby-genteel" in *The Brothers Karamazov*, noted Macdonald, and a wheedler in *Faust*.[48] From this perspective, Arendt's characterization of Eichmann and evil as banal undermined the melodramatic aesthetics—and erotics—of evil.[49] But she could only counter that tradition of melodramatic evil by first construing Eichmann in terms that avoided the melodramatic. Nor was Eichmann the only Nazi whom Arendt had portrayed in terms of commonplace, rather pedestrian, respectability. In 1945, she noted that Heinrich Himmler gave the impression of being a family man and a figure of bourgeois propriety rather than as someone of demonic stature. As she then wrote in *The Origins of Totalitarianism*, he was "more normal" than the other Nazi leaders. He was among those who insisted on "safeguarding their private lives," and not at all the "armed bohemian" or "sex criminal" or "crackpot" or "fanatic" or "adventurer" that other Nazis seemed to be.[50] Clearly, Eichmann was Himmler's successor in this role of the family man as *genocidaire*. But, Arendt never denied that Eichmann was evil, only that the man and the evil he committed were in no way interesting or profound. Indeed, Hilberg should have been the first to grasp this point, since the central theme of his massive work was the utter regularity (*Planmässigkeit*) with which the *Reichsbahn* was run in order to deliver millions to a hell on earth—and death.

Again, Arendt's peculiar, self-imposed limits on speculation meant that she failed to add that neither Himmler nor Eichmann exhausted the ways that evil might appear in the world. Reinhard Heydrich seems to have been a figure of consummate evil and an obsessive anti-Semite, for instance. Even Arendt's friends, philosopher Glenn Gray and Karl Jaspers, thought that Arendt had moved too quickly from "an instance of banal evil to a concept of evil generally."[51] Furthermore, Arendt's hostility to the psychoanalytic tradition kept her from seeing that certain concepts such as "splitting" or "denial," not to mention ambivalence, might have helped her understand Eichmann the man. On these and other related issues, Arendt's own intellectual and philosophical prejudices limited the reach of her analysis.

Finally, there is Eichmann's anti-Semitism. One fundamental criticism of Arendt's analysis of Eichmann was that she downplayed the role that anti-Semitism played in Eichmann's actions and in the destruction of European Jewry. Rather, for Arendt, his main flaw was that he was "a mindless bureaucrat."[52] However, Yaacov Lozowick has argued convincingly that Eichmann, whatever his pre–Nazi Party views, would have received a thorough indoctrination into radical anti-Semitism as a member of the SS, and thus it is highly unlikely that he would have been innocent of strongly ideological, anti-Semitic feelings. Even if we grant that not all Nazis were ideological anti-Semites, it is hard to make a plausible claim that Eichmann belongs among those who were unwitting or unwilling in these matters. We see, as Harold Rosenberg put it, Eichmann's "court room identity,"[53] but Eichmann in Jerusalem was a far cry from Eichmann in Budapest. Still, while Arendt may not have been right about Eichmann as such, she was onto something important in stressing the way that the modern system of administrative mass murder was more important than the ideological convictions of its administrators in implementing the Final Solution.

Again, anticipations of Arendt's position can be seen in *The Origins of Totalitarianism*. There she made clear that anti-Semitism was a "catalyst" for the emergence of Nazi totalitarianism and the concentration camp universe; it was not, however, the only force driving Nazi totalitarianism. Michael Marrus captures something essential about Arendt's position when he suggests that she was not interested in Eichmann, the "garden variety anti-Semite," but in Eichmann as the prototype of the new "totalitarian bureaucrat."[54] Whatever role eliminationist anti-Semitism played in propelling the Nazi project—and it obviously came to characterize the impulse behind the whole enterprise—individual administrators such as Eichmann did not need to have any great emotional investment in anti-Semitism. Anticipating Marrus, as it were, Bettelheim summed up the interpretive choices in his review of *Eichmann in Jerusalem*:

> If one regards the Nazi extermination of the Jews as a chapter in the history of anti-Semitism, then Eichmann and his kind are indeed the greatest anti-Semitic monsters of all—and this the court tried to establish. If, on the other hand, the "final solution of the Jewish question" was merely part of the master plan to create the thousand-year Reich, then Eichmann becomes a cog, sometimes an important one.[55]

Thus, for Arendt and Bettelheim, what was at stake in the Eichmann trial was not just the shape of the past, but the future itself.

From Universalism to Particularism

Finally, Arendt's analysis of the charges against Eichmann and how his trial was conducted has been the subject of considerable argument, particularly in recent years. Despite Arendt's ambivalence regarding Israel, she did not challenge the standing of the Israeli court to try Eichmann nor did she really object to the death penalty meted out to him. That said, Arendt would have preferred that the trial had been held outside of Israel under international auspices. But she recognized that there had been no realistic way for that to have happened.

Recent writing about the Eichmann trial from the standpoint of "narrative jurisprudence" has challenged Arendt's narrow focus on Eichmann's guilt or innocence as too formalistic and conservative in a legal sense.[56] For Mark Osiel, Arendt's criticism of the proceedings as a "show trial" captured, in a way she certainly did not approve of, what the trial, and trials like it, should have as their goal. Indeed, when Arendt objected that the prosecution's "case was built on what the Jews had suffered, not on what Eichmann had done,"[57] she was objecting to what Osiel and others think the trial should have been about. Two other crucial matters were in play as well. One was the relevance of survivor testimony, since, as already noted, the Eichmann trial was the first time that Jewish survivors of the camps had been called to the stand in the trials of Nazi war criminals. Arendt was dubious about the legal standing of such evidence, although she was occasionally moved by it. Thus, from the viewpoint of narrative jurisprudence, it was appropriate that the trial was constructed as a therapeutic opportunity for survivors.

Closely related to this was the third function of the trial: the reaffirmation of Israel's right to exist. Arendt's basic objection was to Israel's claim that it was all that stood in the way of the destruction of the Jewish people and saw its rejection of legal universalism and assimilation as "wrongheaded."[58] For the prosecutors, notes Lawrence Douglas, the survivor testimony provided "instances of the reconstruction of a people organized around a new national identity" and helped solidify Israel's position in Zionist teleology.[59] Arendt's objection to the therapeutic-educational function of the trial was somewhat strange. Insofar as the trial created a public-political space where various views and opinions were voiced, it fitted quite closely the Arendtian view of the proper context for a polity to reconstruct its own story and thus come to terms with the past.

Philosophically and legally, what most bothered Arendt about the trial was the decision to indict Eichmann for "crimes 'against the Jewish people,'" not for "crimes against mankind committed on the body of the Jewish people" (p. 7).[60] As she noted, the Nuremberg judges were never very comfortable with the concept of "crimes against humanity," and resorted to it as a kind of catchall, with the exception of the French jurist François de Menthon who understood it to refer to a "crime against human status." Arendt herself included under crimes against humanity such things as crimes against "human diversity."[61] Her own phrasing of the issue signaled her desire to combine the universalist spirit of Nuremberg with the particularity of the suffering of the Jewish people, a kind of incarnationist conception of what was at issue at the trial. As she wrote near the end of the book,

> only the choice of victims, not the nature of the crime, could be derived from the long history of Jew-hatred and anti-Semitism. Insofar as the victims were Jews, it was right and proper that a Jewish court should

sit in judgment; but insofar as the crime was a crime against humanity, it needed an international tribune to do justice to it.[62]

But this, of course, had been impossible, since one of the major assumptions behind Israel's decision to put on the trial was the inadequacy of moral and legal universalism. As Lawrence Douglas has noted, the Nazi and Nazi Collaboration Law of 1950 under which Eichmann was tried specified that "crimes against the Jewish people were not to be considered a mere subset of crimes against humanity." This was, according to Douglas, "*by design* a rejection of moral universalism."[63] It was this that disturbed Arendt, though, again, her failure to develop her own thinking on this matter hurt her case. While in *The Origins of Totalitarianism*, Arendt expressed deep disillusionment with the capacity of international law and universal rights to protect Jews and other stateless people in the interwar years, in the Eichmann book, she seemed to reaffirm the notion of the viability of a universalist moral perspective. Arendt might have claimed that, although it was the purpose of Israel to give Jews a state within which they had the "right to have rights" and to enjoy citizenship in a particular polity, those rights had universal status, deriving as they did from the right to have rights. Because Israel had defined itself as a "Jewish State," it was more difficult to link the particular with the universal.

Finally, then, Arendt challenged the particularist orientation of the Eichmann trial in two senses. First, she insisted that the explanation of the Holocaust had to move beyond individual or collective anti-Semitism as a sufficient explanation; and, second, she argued that Eichmann should have been tried on the charge of "crimes against humanity," with the incarnationist proviso ("against the body of the Jewish people"), rather than with genocide ("crimes against the Jewish people") as such. For her critics, then and since, Arendt's emphasis on the roots of the Holocaust in modernity rather than in the eternal anti-Semitism of the gentile world, on crimes against humanity rather than crimes simply against the Jewish people, and on a critical rather than a monumental version of Jewish history, was her ultimate betrayal. For those more favorably disposed to her, *Eichmann in Jerusalem* was a brave, though doubtlessly flawed, attempt to confront the failure of European Jewry to resist, more resolutely, the Final Solution, to rethink the nature of evil in the modern world, and to preserve a complex notion of moral universalism.

Generally, the efforts of Raul Hilberg, Bruno Bettelheim, and Arendt to take a critical stance toward the Jewish past rather than accepting the pieties about it, exemplify, as do the examples of Richard Wright and to an extent Franz Fanon, memory grown self-critical. But in rejecting the sacralization and monumentalization of Jewish history and tradition, they were fighting a losing historical battle. The post-trial growth of Jewish self-consciousness demonstrated that nationalist self-consciousness was not simply a reaction, at least in the American context, to the emergence of a similar tendency in African American thought. Rather, Jewish particularism had its own momentum, arising from the attempt of Jews in the United States, Europe, and Israel to come to terms with the Holocaust.

Part III
The Triumph of Cultural Particularism

8

From Roots to Routes: Wright and James

I'm black. I'm a man of the West.

Richard Wright

First, America, then Europe, then Africa failed him.

James Baldwin on Richard Wright

I am a Black European, that is my training and my outlook.

C. L. R. James

While Richard Wright came from the most impoverished of circumstances, C. L. R. James (1901–1989) had a lower middle-class, Trinidadian upbringing. By no means affluent, his father was a teacher and his mother introduced him to the world of books, primarily English literature, at an early age.[1] Both Wright and James left their homelands, never to return permanently, and made their way to the big city—Wright to Chicago and New York; James to London. There, they were "educated" in the Communist Party in Wright's case and in the Trotskyist movement in James's. Wright was to become a permanent exile in Paris after World War II, while James led a peripatetic existence his entire life. He came to America in 1938, remained there until he was expelled in 1953 and then returned to Britain. He spent the late 1950s and early 1960s in the West Indies, returned to teach in America in the late 1960s and most of the 1970s, and then spent the rest of his life in Britain. Neither man had a university degree, although James did teach at Harvard and at Federal City College/ University of the District of Columbia in Washington, D.C., in the 1960s and into the 1970s.

199

James was much more the activist and speaker than Wright. In the early 1940s, James spent some time organizing sharecroppers in Missouri and was one of the leaders of the Johnson Forest Tendency within Trotskyist circles in the 1940s. (James's party name was J. R. [Jimmy] Johnson.) Both were committed to the postwar liberation movements in the Third World; indeed, in the 1930s, James, along with George Padmore, Jomo Kenyatta, Ras MacKinnon, and others, helped establish an organization in London to work for African independence. Both visited Africa in the 1950s and wrote books about the one-time Gold Coast/Ghana of Kwame Nkrumah. In sum, they were members in good standing of the intellectual elite of what Paul Gilroy has called the black Atlantic.

In fact, Wright and James were friends and the latter's second wife, Constance Webb, wrote an early study of Wright. James had reviewed *Native Son* when it appeared,[2] but the two men did not meet until 1945, since the Trotskyist James and Wright, a member of the Communist Party until 1941, were ideological adversaries. James always tried to keep his ideological commitments separate from public comments on his black radical contemporaries. He wrote with great respect about W. E. B. Du Bois, even after the ageing black thinker had become a fellow traveler of Stalin's Soviet Union and joined the Communist Party. Similarly, James cast Paul Robeson as Toussaint L'Ouverture in the stage version of *The Black Jacobins* in 1936 and much later praised Robeson as "the most marvellous (sic) human being I have ever known or seen," despite Robeson's career as a fellow traveler of the Soviet Union in the post–World War II period.[3] After his first meeting with Wright in 1945, James wrote enthusiastically to Webb:

> He didn't know that I held the same views. Briefly the idea is this, that the Negro is a "nationalist" to the heart and is perfectly right to be so. His racism, his nationalism, are a necessary means to giving him strength, self-respect and organisation *in order to fight for integration into American society*. It is a perfect example of a dialectical contradiction. . . . He has worked to it artistically, I through history. But our conclusions are identical.[4]

Before Wright and his family moved to Paris in 1947, James was part of a New York group around Wright that included Ralph Ellison, Horace Cayton, Melvin Tolson, and others. Their plans to publish a literary journal never came to fruition. Both men were good friends of pan-African leader (and another former communist), George Padmore. James was a childhood playmate of Padmore (then named Malcolm Nurse), while Padmore and his wife, Dorothy, were primarily responsible for persuading Wright to visit the Gold Coast in 1953. Such links across oceans and continents testify to the intellectual cross-fertilizations that gave rise to what Cedric Robinson has called "Black Marxism."[5]

Both Wright and James have received increased critical attention in recent years. For instance, Wright's career between his departure for France in 1947 and his death in 1960 has been evaluated upward, particularly in Paul Gilroy's *The Black Atlantic* (1993).[6] Besides his long novel, *The Outsider* (1953), his books of cultural and political reportage, *Black Power* (1954), *The Color Curtain* (1956), and *Pagan Spain* (1957), along with the essays in *White Man, Listen!* (1957), provide a bridge between Wright's early writing and the wider world of the black diaspora. In this context, Wright's participation in the planning for the First Congress of Black Writers and Artists in Paris in September 1956, indicates his position as a key figure in the black diasporic community encompassing Africa and the West Indies, the United States, Britain, and France. In the decade and a half after 1945, Wright was probably the best-known black writer in the West.

Similarly, since his death in 1989, James has begun to receive the attention he long deserved. Though Gilroy fails to deal with James's thought in *Black Atlantic*—and acknowledges this shortcoming—James, even more than Wright, was the prototypical black diasporic intellectual. No single life in the twentieth century so exemplifies Gilroy's "roots/routes" pun, that is, that the black Atlantic experience was, and is, not about where you are from but where you are going. Gilroy also identifies the tropes of sailing and sailors, of the imagery of moving across oceans and establishing new cultural trade routes, as it were, as central to the black diasporic sensibility. From that perspective, it is no accident that James considered Herman Melville's *Moby Dick* the greatest American novel and published a study of Melville in 1953, *Mariners, Renegades, and Castaways*. A final irony is that James's still neglected study of Melville was written, in part, while James was held in Ellis Island for hearings that led to his deportation from America in 1953.[7]

In what follows, I want, first, to explore Wright's vision of the modern world in terms of the problematic relationship between race and culture and between modernization and tradition. My major points will be, first, that there is continuity between Wright's pre- and post-exile writings, precisely in terms of an exploration of the nature of modernization and modernity.

Second, I will explore Gilroy's claim that Wright's work was "simultane-ously an affirmation and a negation of the western civilisation that formed him." My conclusion is to place more emphasis on Wright's affirmation of the modern traditions of the West than his negation of them.[8] In contrast with the advocates of negritude, Wright insisted that the choice of modern Western humanism was the wisest one for Third World elites to make.

Similarly, I want to explore James's thought as he tried to reconcile a Marxist emphasis upon class with the claims of racial/ethnic nationalism between the mid-1930s and the mid-1970s. Never as preoccupied with race as Wright, James still had to work out the relationship among race, class, and nation, particularly since he was sent to the United States to develop the Trotskyist position on the "Negro Question." Much more than Wright (or Du Bois), James was fascinated by America's mass culture; and he developed a prototheoretical account of how it worked. Like Theodor Adorno, he considered such efforts to be a way of deepening not abandoning his Marxism; but, in stark contrast with Adorno and American critics of mass culture such as Clement Greenberg and Dwight Macdonald in the late 1930s and 1940s, James did not dismiss mass culture out of hand.[9] Finally, James's intellectual commitment was to the Western thought that had shaped him rather than to the African and African American culture that emerged in full force by the 1960s to make a claim on his allegiance.[10]

Back to Africa

Readers who expect Wright's *Black Power* (1954) to foreshadow the ide-ology of the black power movement in the United States will be severely disappointed. His skeptical, even querulous attitude toward the West African society of the Gold Coast (soon to be Ghana), made him often sound more like V. S. Naipaul than Stokely Carmichael or Amiri Baraka.[11] Nor is it entirely clear just what kind of book *Black Power* was intended to be. It contains a good bit of political reportage and analysis, particularly of Nkrumah's efforts to forge a national political culture in the face of re-actionary tribal loyalties. Linked with that is Wright's own anthropological-sociological analysis of African society and culture, which stresses the central role of religious tradition in the formation of the African person-ality. Finally, *Black Power* is a personal narrative of Wright's own efforts to come to terms with Africa, an attempt to figure out just what *attitude* he should adopt toward it and toward the claims of race and culture. *Black*

Power, like most personal narratives, gains as much as it loses from the tensions characterizing it.

The theme informing *Black Power* is familiar to those who know Wright's American writings—the necessity for a people caught between a traditional and a modern culture to choose the modern. Only by so doing could they overcome the loss of meaning, and of the institutions carrying that meaning, which had left them bereft of the capacity for purposive action. From Wright's point of view, the Africans in the Gold Coast were caught in much the same historical and existential dilemma as the black Americans in *12 Million Black Voices*, with Wright, once again, the sometimes troubled, sometimes dispassionate, sometimes hectoring, analyst. But there were differences between Wright's stance vis-à-vis the South and his attitude toward Africa. Wright was visiting the Gold Coast on the invitation of Nkrumah, but was clearly a stranger to Africa and just as clearly an emissary of Western culture. Throughout the early part of the book in particular, Wright regularly reports on his state of mind. Upon arrival, he is "excited" yet feels "disquiet."[12] More expansively, he notes "an unsettled feeling engendered by the strangeness of a completely different order of life" and experiences an "absolute otherness and inaccessibility" and a "vague sense of mild panic" (pp. 42, 44). Some of this panic seems to have been sexual in origin. Wright is obsessed with the naked bodies of Africans, particularly with the bare breasts of the women, and is also startled by the sight of two men dancing together, reactions that have led Kwame Anthony Appiah to assert that the dominant impression Wright conveys is "disgust."[13] Yet this negative reaction may also have represented a reaction-formation against the attraction Wright felt to what he saw in Africa where self-consciousness about the body was much less acute.

Because Wright encountered Africans on their own home ground, African culture plays a more prominent role in Wright's account of Africa than Southern black folk culture played in his representations of black Southern life. Where Wright recognizes himself in the figure of his father in *Black Boy*, he had to deal with an African reality quite literally foreign to him. In *Native Son*, Wright seemed to suggest that Bigger's fate was a possibility (not a reality) for all African American males. But in *Black Power*, *The Color Curtain*, and the essays collected in *White Man Listen!* Wright identifies not with the uprooted and dispossessed but with the "tragic elite" of the newly emerging nations of Africa and Asia. Considering his linguistic and cultural alienation from the African masses, this was hardly surprising.

From our vantage point, it is easy to overlook the importance of the Cold War shadowing all of Wright's nonfiction of the 1950s. Throughout Wright's post–World War II career, he had to pick his way through a minefield of political, ideological, and religious claims. Having broken with the communists in the first half of the 1940s, Wright was strongly opposed to the expansion of communism in the newly independent nations. As he noted in the introduction to *Black Power*, he found "Marxist instrumentalities of thought" useful, but this did not mean that he supported Soviet "programs or policies" (p. xxxviii). Yet, Wright never wavered in his belief that defeating European colonialism was the central historical imperative in Africa; nor was he ever guilty of downplaying its destructive impact or of emphasizing the beneficence of its intentions. "Hitler's clumsy dreams," he wrote scathingly, "were picayune when compared with the sanguine vision of these early English Christian gentlemen" who had incorporated themselves in 1663 to carry on the slave trade for "a thousand years" (p. 12). Besides, it was "only from Russia— not from the churches or the universities of the Western world—that a moral condemnation of colonial exploitation had come" (p. 33).

In sum, Wright sought to find a "third way"—*for* political independence in Africa and Asia but *against* Soviet or Chinese political domination of those countries after the departure of the Western colonial powers. In this respect, both *Black Power* and *The Color Curtain* were consistently anticommunist *and* anticolonial. In fact, his identification with the West was symptomatic of a split that had already taken place among African Americans after 1945. For popular front liberals and radicals such as Du Bois and Robeson, the Soviet Union represented the best postwar hope for anticolonial forces, while the West, including the United States, was hopelessly compromised by its colonial legacy. Du Bois, for one, had a hard time swallowing Wright's position. As he wrote to George Padmore, Wright's

> logic is lousy. He starts out to save Africa from Communism and then makes an attack on British capitalism which is devastating. How he reconciles these two attitudes I cannot see.[14]

Overall, in *Black Power* and elsewhere, Wright wrote remarkably little about economic matters; rather his focus fell upon the disastrous psychological and cultural impact of colonialism and the struggle for political independence.

In fact, Wright's position combined two subtle assumptions. First was the (Weberian) insight that both capitalism and socialism were modernizing projects informed by Enlightenment values of secular reason, a commitment to modern technology and hostility to the forces of tradition, particularly of religion. Both Marxism and capitalist development assume the "progressive" role of industrial and urban development in the traditional societies of the developing nations.[15] Second, Wright seemed to assume that colonial capitalism had occasionally been a force for creative destruction in the Third World. On this point, Wright implicitly echoed Marx's "pro-imperialist" analysis of colonial India where British domination had helped destroy the feudal institutions hindering development. For Marx communism was meant to be the successor, not the alternative, to capitalist modernization. Thus, a moral condemnation of capitalism should not, from Wright's vantage point, blind observers to its "progressive" impact in bringing "modern" values to traditional societies.

Wright also had to confront the ideology of negritude developed by Leopold Sedar Senghor and Aimé Césaire. According to this vision, all people of African descent shared certain essential characteristics. As Wright sees it, negritude entails the view that

[w]e have a *special* gift for music, dancing, rhythm and movement. . . . We have a genius of our own. We were civilized in Africa when white men were still living in caves in Europe. (p. 6)

If this were the case, however, "there ought to be something of 'me' down there in Africa. . . . But I could not feel anything African about myself" (p. 45). This failure to experience the mystic chords linking race and culture in Africa lay behind his later confrontation with Senghor and Césaire at the First International Congress of Black Writers and Artists in Paris in September 1956.

Although Wright left Africa with his commitment to nonracial explanations of cultural differences intact, it was not without a certain amount of soul searching. He could not ignore the "strange but familiar" (p. 73) group movements, obviously "ring shouts," which he remembered from his youth in Mississippi. Confronted with this phenomenon, he first questions his belief that racial explanations lack explanatory value and, then, tentatively takes up Melville Herskovits's controversial view that ring shouts were "African survivals," the product not of genetics but historical-cultural transmission. At this point in *Black Power*, Wright circles rather than resolves the issue. But he does recognize that black Americans often denied any links with Africa, not just because of the normal desire to assimilate into American culture but also because for "so long had Africa been described as something shameful" (p. 73).

The aspect of *Black Power* that I particularly want to explore here is Wright's discussion of the "African personality" and the importance of religion in its construction. When analyzing African urban life, Wright tends to blame Christianity for having created in Africans an endemic suspiciousness, a lack of self-confidence and a certain "childlike" (p. 118) overestimation of their ability to conceal their true feelings. Wright attributes such characteristics to the fact that Africans inhabit a "half-way world" (p. 167). British colonialism, with the help of Christian missionaries, created "millions of detribalized Africans living uneasily and frustrated in two worlds and really believing in neither of them" (p. 72). The results are "[e]roded personalities" and "psychological damage," the products of a Christianity that had "rendered them numb to their own dearly bought vision of life" (p. 169). Not only did Christianity have destructive effects, the missionaries themselves were "prodded by their own neurotic drives" (p. 168). Significant here is Wright's use of "numb," the same term he used in *12 Million Black Voices* to describe the effects of slavery on black Americans. What Wright is developing in such passages is an African variation on Du Bois's "double consciousness," while his notion of a "half-way world" also anticipates V. S. Naipaul's later analysis of former colonial societies as "half-made."

This line of analysis is supplemented by the impressions he gathered in a less densely populated part of Accra. There Wright observes that Africans seem to merge with the earth as a kind of autochthonous force and concludes with the

> intuitive impression that these people were old, old, maybe the oldest people on earth, and I felt a sense of melancholy knowing that their customs, laboriously created and posited for thousands of years, had been condemned as inferior, and shattered by a strong and predatory nation . . . but surrounded by a new order of life, they didn't and couldn't believe in them as they once had (p. 76).

At this point it is important to note that Wright proposes a *political* solution for this massive psychological and cultural alienation. To do this, he applies a mass society analysis to the new African historical reality.

Nkrumah's "mass nationalist movement" is founded on the intimate relationship, sealed with an oath, between the leader and the masses and
marked by large chanting crowds. It is "a new kind of religion. They were
politics *plus!*" (p. 61). Nkrumah "fused tribalism with modern politics" to
replace the tribal culture and religion destroyed by the British (p. 65).

It is not always clear in Wright's account how much of African political culture is the product of colonial penetration and what is indigenous to
it. When Wright journeys to the interior of the country, a trip that echoes
The Heart of Darkness with its intimations of cannibalism and reveries of
violence, he finds not only much that is strange, but also much that echoes
the reality of the cities. The fact that "[t]hey [Africans] cannot really con-
ceive of a political party except in the form of a glorious leader" (p. 294)
derives from the intense personal loyalty to the tribal chief. It is while in
the backcountry that Wright arrives at his solution to the race versus culture problem, for he comes to see that the African way of seeing the world
is "a natural and poetic grasp of existence" and thus a "basic and primal
attitude(s) toward life" (p. 295). Remnants of such a worldview will sur-
vive, even when one-time inhabitants of a traditional society are transferred to a modern environment. It is not specifically racial but shared,
Wright seems to be saying, by all indigenous, premodern traditional cultures. Wright's analysis also shows the way that a folk cultural analysis,
in this case of African folk society, can easily lead to the view that African
culture is timeless and primordial.

Still, Wright was convinced that this primordial cultural vision, however fascinating or appealing, ill prepared a people to deal with the modern world. It was not a matter really of simplicity versus complexity, although at times Wright does characterize traditional Gold Coast society as
simple. Rather, as he suggests at one point, the African of the village is,
if anything, "too civilized" (p. 282), too weighed down by rituals, beliefs,
and forces. All of this testifies to "the omnipotence of thought" in traditional African society (p. 248). What is needed is not a more complex culture but one in which the orientation has shifted from images to concepts,
from concreteness to abstraction, from immersion to detachment, and
from a past to a future orientation.

Specifically, Wright's analysis rests on the conviction that "jungle life"
has failed to "develop a hard and durable ego" in the African (p. 293). The
African self is characterized by something like what psychoanalytic theory calls primary process thinking in which the boundary between "reality"
and "dream" is constantly effaced and confused (p. 216). It is "sensuous,

loving images not concepts; personalities, not abstractions; movement, not form; dreams, not reality. . . . System is the enemy of the tribal mind; action proceeds on the basis of association of images;" (p. 294).

Interestingly, Wright's analysis reveals a mentality that advocates of negritude identified as prototypically African. In other words, Wright and the ideologists of negritude did not differ on the nature of the African personality but on its viability under modern conditions. Wright concludes with a somewhat ominous and prophetic injunction to Nkrumah to impose "firm social discipline" (p. 388). In more drastic terms, Wright insists that "AFRICAN LIFE MUST BE MILITARIZED!" (p. 389); not, he hastens to add, for purposes of war making but to supply the "form, organization, direction, meaning, and a sense of justification to those lives" (p. 389). Before Africa could become modern, it had to become disciplined.

In retrospect, what is most telling about Wright's analysis of the (West) African situation was his failure to suggest what specific forms of self-government might be adopted, how the power of the leader and his retinue might be curbed, and how political participation, beyond the mass rallies, might be encouraged. Also, a sense of urgency about developing independent institutions of civil society to replace the older tribal structures and thereby reducing the dependence upon strong leaders, while inculcating in the population the habit of self-government, is missing. Instead, Wright stresses the critical role of political elites, and especially the political leader, in mobilizing the population for independence, a standard recommendation in theories of political development during the Cold War. The message to Kwame Nkrumah was straightforward: "It's a secular religion that you [Nkrumah] must slowly create" (p. 392). Osagyefo Nkrumah got the message.

The Politics of Culture

The mid-1950s were a time of political ferment and high optimism in the Third World. In April 1955, Wright journeyed to Indonesia to cover the conference of leaders from the nonaligned nations of Africa and Asia. Though Bandung represented a major effort to escape the bipolar Cold War alignments, Wright's trip was, ironically, funded by the Congress for Cultural Freedom, later revealed to be subsidized by the CIA. Wright got assurances that he would be free to express his opinions and this demand was apparently respected. Wright's report from Bandung in *The Color Curtain* (1956) focused on the public rhetoric of political leaders rather than pursuing the sort of self and cultural analysis he offered in *Black Power*. At Bandung, most of Wright's attention fell upon Asian societies and Asian leaders, particularly China's Chou En-Lai, who, in Wright's opinion, performed very skillfully at Bandung.

Bandung clarified several matters for Wright. He became increasingly convinced of the irrelevance of the older categories of left and right for Third World dreams and realities, while being struck by the overwhelming importance of race and religion. About this, Wright was far from happy, since it implied a rejection of the secular universalism at the heart of the modernizing vision he proposed. Third World leaders detested the West and then mimicked its worst features. Moreover, he felt compelled to present an alternative vision to these racial and religious appeals. Here, Wright was much more conciliatory to the West than he had been in *Black Power*; and his answer to the following question was basically an affirmative one:

> Is this secular rational base and thought-feeling in the Western world broad and secure enough to warrant the West's assuming the moral right to interfere without narrow, selfish political motives?[16]

Such a Western-derived commitment to modernity would encourage "rapid industrialization" and the "shaking loose of the Asian-African masses from a static past" (p. 220). What Wright referred to as "Japanese fascism" had combined modern science and technology with particularist racial and religious ends in a quite sinister fashion (p. 218), while communism in power, whether in Stalin's Russia or in Mao's China, exemplified a "secular religiosity of horror and blood" (p. 221). These alternatives were clearly unacceptable.

Although never as interesting as his more complex and wide-ranging book on Africa, *The Color Curtain* clearly articulated the main concerns of Wright's thought until his death—the contest between the secular humanism-universalism of the West and the particularist ideologies of religion, race, and culture for the loyalty of Third World political and intellectual elites. It was the First International Congress of Negro Writers and Artists held at the Sorbonne, September 19–22, 1956, that provided the forum where the debate about these matters was carried on, perhaps for the first time, face-to-face among black writers and intellectuals.[17] The Congress was the brainchild of the journal, *Présence Africaine*. Wright had been associated with the journal since its founding in 1947 and was a member of the planning committee for the Congress. As Michel Fabre has noted, however, Wright was always closer to Sartre's *Les Temps Modernes* than to *Présence Africaine* edited by Alouane Diop of Senegal. For Wright the latter journal was primarily the outlet for Francophone Africanists; and it was oriented more toward cultural pan-Africanism than political nationalism, more open to the African humanism of negritude than to the Western humanism that Wright preferred. (In addition, Wright also suspected that there were those at the Congress who wanted to hijack it for the cause of communism.)

At the Congress, which included sixty-eight participants from eight African colonies, five Caribbean islands, India, and the United States, Wright had the unenviable task of mediating between the moderate American delegation and the more radical French-speaking Africans and their Francophone allies. Many of the alleged differences between Anglophone and Francophone cultures proved all too true, even among men of color. (As Wright pointed out, there was a woeful lack of women at the Congress.) Those trained in France tended to be more politically and culturally radical and were enamored with an idealized version of traditional African culture. The contributions of the English-speaking delegates had a more empirical and historical focus, were reformist in tone and substance—and often uninspiring. In fact, the American delegation hardly addressed cultural or literary issues at all.

That Du Bois had been denied a visa by the State Department and thus could not attend the Congress did not help; nor did the fact that a more radical delegation envisaged by Wright, one which might have included poet Melvin Tolson, E. Franklin Frazier, historian J. A. Rogers, Chester Himes, William Gardner Smith, and Ralph Ellison failed to pan out. There was even talk that Josephine Baker would make an appearance (as a speaker not a dancer) and that Langston Hughes might also participate. In the event, Hughes and James Baldwin attended but only as observers. All this may explain the lack of a certain political and cultural sophistication among the eventual black American delegation of John A. Davis, Horace Mann Bond, James W. Ivy, William Fontaine, and Mercer Cook. In addition, Wright worked under the threat of expulsion by the French government if he denounced French control of Algeria, which was gathering increasing attention. Also, Wright had been under surveillance since the early 1940s by the FBI and other agencies of the U.S. government and feared that his passport would be lifted if he were too vocal in his criticisms of American foreign policy or white supremacy.

Besides delivering a somewhat shorter version of "Tradition and Industrialization," which was later collected in *White Man, Listen!* Wright posed two crucial questions from the floor after the initial session of the Congress. Wright began his intervention by objecting quite sharply to Du Bois's telegram to the Congress, which impugned the motives of the American delegation. Because the State Department had granted passports to its delegates and had refused one to him, Du Bois suggested that the American delegates were stooges of the U.S. government. But the immediate provocation for Wright's first question was Leopold Senghor's address, "The Spirit of Civilisation, or the Laws of African Negro Culture." After outlining what he saw as the essential spirit of African culture, Senghor concluded that "The spirit of African Negro civilisation . . . animates the best Negro artists and writers of today, whether they come from Africa or America."[18] Much as he had admired the speech, Wright responded with "a sense of uneasiness" as he listened to it:

> I wonder where do I, an American Negro. . . where do I stand in relation to that culture? . . . I cannot accept Africa because of mere blackness or on trust. . . . Is it possible for me to find a working and organic relationship with it? (pp. 66–67)

Senghor's brief response merely reiterated the claim that Negro American writing and culture were in essence part of "the African heritage" and that specifically *Black Boy* was "an African American recital" (pp. 73–74). Such a response was hardly surprising since Senghor's African essentialism presupposed what it set out to show—the underlying spiritual affinities among all peoples of African descent.

Negritude's other main spokesman, Aimé Césaire, offered a brief contribution to this exchange by stressing that just as French, German, and Italian cultures were all part of European culture, so the various black diasporic cultures were part of a larger African culture (pp. 72–73). Césaire's own full presentation "Culture and Colonisation," delivered the next day (September 20), included Negro Americans within the African world, not because they shared an African essence but because they

> occupy . . . an artificial position that can only be understood within the context of a colonialism that has certainly been abolished but whose after-effects still persist down to the present day ("Culture and Colonisation," p. 93).

Césaire's response had the virtue of taking into account the role of history and economics in shaping diasporic consciousness rather than simply positing a transhistorical pan-African spiritual unity.[19] Still, John Davis of the American delegation responded sharply to Césaire's analysis. He insisted that American Negroes wanted "complete equal status as citizens" not "self-determination in the belt" (p. 217).[20] The clear implication was that America's black population did not consider itself part of the colonial world that sought national self-determination. Black Americans wanted "in" not "out."[21]

Wright's "Tradition and Industrialization," the last formal presentation of the Congress, forcefully restated the message of *Black Power* and *The Color Curtain*. Wright insisted that there were specifically Western values and modes of thought, deriving from the Reformation and the Enlightenment, which had created individual consciousness and conscience in the Westerner. This tradition of thought and feeling provided an alternative to the lack of definition that characterized the African personality as Wright had depicted it in *Black Power*. He also noted the paradox that the protests of the Westernized elite against Western colonial hegemony were themselves derived from Western values. Thus, dialectically, the dominant culture generated the tools for self-criticism and self-examination. Wright's two-page, prefatory comment to his paper at the Congress was not included in the version reproduced in *White Man, Listen!*, but it contained his disavowal of the black nationalism of his "Blueprint for Negro Writing." That position had been appropriate in a time of great hostility against "American Negroes," observed Wright, but it "was a reluctant nationalism, a proud and defensive one" ("Tradition and Industrialization," p. 355). With changes in the racial climate in America, Wright hoped that "that nationalism of itself will be liquidated" (p. 355). He assured his audience, however, that black nationalism was still valid in places where white rule had yet to be thrown off.

Wright posed a second, potentially explosive question on the first day of the Congress, one that implied a scathing view of the African culture that Senghor and others so celebrated. Behind his question lay not only Wright's own experience but also his reading of French psychoanalyst O. Mannoni's *Prospero and Caliban: The Psychology of Colonization*, which appeared in French in 1950 but had only been translated into English in 1955. In fact, Wright's review of Mannoni's controversial study, which suggested that the culture of some non-European peoples primed them for acceptance of European domination, appeared in *The Nation* of October 20 only a month after the Paris Congress adjourned. In turn, that review was incorporated almost word for word into Wright's "The Psychological Reactions of Oppressed Peoples," a paper first given in Germany shortly after the Congress, and also included in *White Man, Listen!* Wright's question undoubtedly reflected Mannoni's analysis of the native's "dependency complex," which was referred to several times during the Congress:

> Might not the vivid and beautiful culture that Senghor has described not been—I speak carefulfly (sic), choosing my words with the utmost caution, speaking to my colleagues, hoping that you will understand my intentions—might not that beautiful culture have been a fifth column a corps of saboteurs and spies of Europe? . . . . The ancestor cult religion with of all (sic) its manifold, poetic richness that created a sense of self-sufficiency. . . . Did that religion help the people to resist fiercely and hardily and hurl the Europeans out? I question the value of that culture in relationship of our future. I do not condemn it. But how can we use it[?]. . . . I have the feeling, uneasy, almost bordering upon dread, that there was a fateful historic complement between a militant, white christian Europe and an ancestral cult religion in Africa. (p. 67)

Besides the dependency thesis, Mannoni, like Arendt in her *The Origins of Totalitarianism*, to which Wright also made reference in his review of *Prospero and Caliban*, emphasized the European rage to dominate African societies and to discover some larger purpose in that collective activity. Rather than the heroic figures he once suggested the Europeans were, Wright, echoing Mannoni and Arendt, wrote scathingly of "neurotic, restless Europeans" who created a world that "would permit free play for their repressed instincts."[22]

Disappointingly, Senghor failed to respond to Wright's question about the complicity of African societies in their own destruction, while Césaire reacted by insisting that there should be no either/or choice between the traditional culture of Africa and the West. In retrospect, it is striking that no one at the Congress offered an alternative scenario of how Europe was able to bring sub-Saharan African under its control.[23] Besides historian of negritude, Cheikh Anta Diop, one other participant at the Congress might have responded to Wright on this issue. But the thirty-one-year-old, Martinique-born psychiatrist, Frantz Fanon, chose not to. Fanon's thought was clearly in the process of evolution in the mid-1950s and he was just three months away from leaving his post as a psychiatrist in Algeria to take up full-time political work for the FLN (National Liberation Front) in its struggle against the French. His own speech at the Congress "Racism and Culture" failed to address the question of possible complicity of African culture in its own defeat, except to reject both blind assimilation of Western values and unthinking celebration of the African past. Perhaps the situation simply was not appropriate or perhaps Fanon was in awe of Wright, whom he (Fanon) had not met before the Congress but from whom he professed to have learned much. Fanon had written Wright a letter of homage in 1953; but Wright, according to Michel Fabre, never read entire books in French, and had not read *Black Skin, White Masks* by the time of the Congress.[24] Whether Wright and Fanon became better acquainted at the Paris Congress remains unknown.

Still, Wright's review of Mannoni left no doubt that the Europeans were the aggressors in the colonies. Though Mannoni does not have to be read as "blaming the victim," it is a tendency to which his work has lent itself. In fact, the same might be said of Wright's *Black Power*, which also emphasizes the strong streak of dependency—in the form of the need for strong, authoritarian leaders—in West African culture.[25]

Finally, Wright's vision of the complex relationship between history and cultural change must be confronted. On the one hand, Wright always assumed that Third World elites had a choice about the decisions they were called upon to make. Otherwise, he would have hardly spent the last years of his life urging those elites to choose the West intellectually but to reject colonial political control, in the name of self-determination. In that sense they were free, as were the advocates of negritude, to adopt an alternative understanding of what cultural values were best for Africans to adopt. But it is difficult to determine whether Wright thought that the values of the modern West were better in themselves or whether they were of most adaptive value for the survival and flourishing of the newly emergent nations. Overall, it is hard to escape the conclusion that Wright had little feeling for African or any non-Western cultures.[26] The glorification of the African past or celebration of black Southern folk culture seemed almost an irrelevancy to Wright. At the same time, as mentioned, Fanon was moving toward a similarly skeptical position regarding negritude, not to mention his rejection of conventional Western humanism. Rather, some sort of revolutionary humanism was desirable. Against both the advocates of negritude and Fanon's revolutionary humanism, Wright was implicitly suggesting that there was no virtue in recommending the impossible or undesirable just because it is "ours" rather than "theirs"—or vice versa. He might even have agreed with the spirit of the remarks offered by an African father to his son as quoted in V. S. Naipaul's *Finding the Center* (1984): "I am not sending you to school to be a white man or a Frenchman. I am sending you to enter the new world. That's all."[27] Whether that *is* all was, and is, another matter. Though Wright was concerned enough with the promise of Africa to visit there and try to understand it, he was also one of the last African American intellectuals to express skepticism about the viability of the cultural heritage of Africa. (Ralph Ellison, who never went to Africa, expressed such skepticism but generally in private.[28]) Ironically, by the time that black American intellectuals had taken up the cause of black cultural and political consciousness in the late 1960s, the intellectual elites of Africa had largely followed Fanon in opting for a national rather than pan-African political-cultural consciousness.

James and the Creation of a Revolutionary Tradition

C. L. R. James arrived in Britain from Trinidad in 1932. The ensuing six years were ones of prodigious intellectual and artistic productivity. The main themes of his work in that decade, culminating with *The Black Jacobins* (1938), set his intellectual, political, and cultural agenda for the next half-century. During these six years, besides writing about his great love, cricket, in British newspapers, James published *The Life of Captain Cipriani* (1932), three chapters of which were excerpted as *The Case for West Indian Self-Government*, and his only novel *Minty Alley* (1936), a pioneering work in West Indian fiction. He also directed Paul Robeson in *The Black Jacobins*, a 1936 stage version of James's not yet published study of the slave revolt in Saint Domingue; composed *World Revolution, 1917–1936*, a Trotskyist narrative of the decline of the Leninist ideal since 1917; and finished *The Black Jacobins*, along with *A History of Negro Revolt* in 1938. As mentioned, he also took a leading role in organizing the International African Service Bureau (IASB), which organized protests against the Italian conquest of Ethiopia in 1935, and involved himself in the burgeoning anticolonial movement in London. Clearly, his political involvements grew organically from his intellectual and artistic work—and from his own experience.

The *Black Jacobins* is one of the classics of Marxist historiography. Specifically, as James later acknowledged, the influence of W. E. B. Du Bois's *Black Reconstruction* (1935) permeates the book. James, along with Du Bois and Carter Woodson, was one of the pioneers of black diaspora historiography.[29] Also like E. P. Thompson's *The Making of the*

English Working Class (1963), Du Bois and James focus on the development of political consciousness as much or more than the social and economic forces that constrain action. Against the tendency of Stalinist historiography to see American slaves as raw material for, but not agents of, their own liberation, James announced in 1949 perhaps the central theme of his entire body of work, the concern with collective action:

> Any history of the Civil War which does not base itself upon the Negroes, slave and free, as the subject not the object of politics is ipso facto a Jim Crow history.[30]

In *The Black Jacobins*, James combines the novelist's skill in probing personality and character, particularly Toussaint L'Ouverture's, with the historian's concern with specificity. James's style is engaged and impassioned; often epigrammatic and pithy; and always incisive.[31] Indeed, his book is a vivid reminder that Marxism was—and is—most compelling when it is cast as a narrative of great social and historical conflicts rather than when it claims to be a "scientific" analysis of social and economic forces. Marxist historiography at its best also reminds us that human progress, far from automatic, is won through struggle; and that struggle involves a struggle for recognition and the risk of life on the part of a large number of human beings. James's version of the Marxist grand narrative tells the story of how black slaves in Saint Domingue, one of the most brutal of modern slave systems, ceased being objects of, and became subjects in, their own history. James's book is a prime example of what Seymour Drescher refers to as "history-as-rhetoric" and "history-as-scholarship."[32]

In light of our concern with the way that James positioned himself in relation to European tradition on the one hand and his engagement with the destruction of European colonialism, on the other, one of the most interesting things about *The Black Jacobins* is the way that he locates the uprising in Saint Domingue both in the context of the Enlightenment-inspired universalist tradition and of the early French Revolution. By doing so, he refuses to see it as just "a huge riot" in the jewel in the crown of the French colonial empire or as just a black/African phenomenon. This view of Haiti as crucial to the success of the revolution in France is apparently still relatively rare in the histories of the French Revolution.[33] James also insists that the Haitian Revolution, the first successful slave revolt in the Western Hemisphere, is a prefiguration of the impending African struggle for independence. As James later remembered, he saw the Saint Domingue uprising at the time "as the preparation for . . . the revolution in Africa. . . . It was written about Africa. It wasn't written about the Caribbean."[34] And in *The Black Jacobins*, James notes how in the 1770s "well-meaning persons talked of the iniquity of slavery and the slave trade, as well-meaning persons in 1938 talked about the native question in Africa or the misery of the Indian peasant."[35] Finally, in referring to Toussaint's period of waiting before joining the struggle in earnest, James also makes the African connection: "[H]e and his brother slaves only watched their masters destroy one another, as Africans watched them in 1914–1918, and will watch them again before long" (p. 82). Finally, James concludes *The Black Jacobins* by noting the contradictions at the heart of European imperialism:

> Imperialism vaunts its exploitation of the wealth of Africa for the benefit of civilisation. In reality, from the very nature of the system of production for profit it strangles the real wealth of the continent—the creative capacity of the African people (p. 377).

Thus, the revolutionary tradition was not simply the property of the "white" man, but was appropriated and transformed in the colonies by the rebelling slaves. James's work was monumental history in the service not of reaction but of revolution, its heroes drawn from the masses not the classes.

In what follows, I will be less concerned with the historiographical status of James's pioneering work—though his book is still acknowledged as the place to start in understanding the Haitian Revolt—than with it as an expression of James's central theoretical and political concerns, especially its links with the European traditions of revolution. One of James's themes in *The Black Jacobins* is a meta-historical one familiar to students of Marxism: the issue of determinism versus freedom. Marx expressed it most clearly in *The German Ideology* when he wrote that "life is not determined by consciousness but consciousness by life" and more complexly in *The Eighteenth Brumaire of Louis Bonaparte*:

> Men make their own history, but they do not make it just as they please; they do not make it under circumstances chosen by themselves, but under circumstances directly encountered, given, and transmitted from the past.[36]

The possibility of "making history" was not only a historical theme; it was also a rhetorical leitmotif running throughout the book. Clearly "riffing" on Marx, James writes: "Men make their own history. . . . But if they could

seize opportunity they could not create it" (p. 25). In discussing the range
of Toussaint's possibilities, James again evokes circumstances: "The revolution had made him." He then cuts back against the grain of that thought
a few lines later by emphasizing Toussaint's indispensable role in the
process: "[I]t is impossible to say where the social forces end and the impress of personality begins. It is sufficient that but for him this history
would be something entirely different" (p. 249).

Generally, James seems to evoke the dialectic between action and constraints, as a way of warning against judging historical actors, whether
Toussaint or his great world-historical adversary, Napoleon, in too facile
a fashion. Both men were creatures of historical circumstances; neither
should be easily condemned or unreservedly praised. As the revolution developed after 1791, Toussaint and his followers had one overriding goal:
to avoid re-enslavement. Expressed more positively, the abolition of slavery
became Toussaint's primary goal, which largely explains Toussaint's willingness to make and break alliances with all the European (and North
American) powers involved in the Caribbean. In other words, human beings can never choose or determine the exact terms under which they act;
nor can their values and ideals remain isolated from historical circumstances or situational considerations.[37] Thus, James was too subtle a historical thinker to plump for either total freedom or iron determinism in his
history of the slave uprising between 1791 and 1804. His response to this
perennial issue in historical thinking made his re-creation of the context
of contending social, economic, and political forces all the more compelling. That said, James's later development emphasized the emergence
of group political action as his great political theme. In this, his Marxism
was a far cry from the scientific socialism and economic determinism of
the Stalinist orthodoxy in the interwar years.

A second major concern of *The Black Jacobins* is the relationship between race and class and, related to that, an analysis of the internal social
structure of the slave population. Historically, both issues were problems
for twentieth-century Marxism, which privileged the industrial working
class over the peasantry, much less the slave class, as the agent of historical change. That is, class trumped race and ethnicity as the central category
of historical analysis. James "solved" the first issue by analyzing the slaves
as *both* peasants and as proletarians. He begins chapter IV as follows:

> The slaves worked on the land, and, like revolutionary peasants every-
> where, they aimed at the extermination of their oppressors. But working

and living together in gangs of hundreds on the huge sugar-factories which covered the North Plain, they were closer to a modern proletariat than any group of workers in existence at the time. (pp. 85–86)

In some ways, this issue was the easier to resolve, since the Revolution in Russia also had to recognize the crucial importance of the peasantry. But the same issue arose in the post–World War II struggles for national liberation where the industrial working class was small and weak but the peasantry and *lumpen* proletariat were large and potentially powerful. This later led James to recognize the crucial importance of Frantz Fanon's work in abandoning the industrial working class, whether in Europe or in the colonies, as the prime agent of historical change.

Still, James's resolution of this class issue was perhaps a bit too neat. He finesses the race/class problem rhetorically but without resolving it theoretically. Indeed, James was to spend much of the 1940s seeking to work out the relationship between class and race in Marxist theory and in social reality. For instance, he notes that

[h]ad the monarchists been white, the bourgeoisie brown, and the masses of France black, the French Revolution would have gone down in history as a race war. But although they were all white in France they fought just the same. (128)

While abstractly true, James's claim is nevertheless a bit evasive, since the claim for the equal importance of race and class is not that white people will never fight each other. It is rather that when whites are faced by the opposition of a considerable number of people of color, they (whites) will generally close class ranks against them rather than fighting among themselves.

James did have a point to the extent that people of color on Saint Domingue—black slaves, free blacks, and mulattos—were rarely, if ever, aligned with one another, divided as they were by class and status, especially by the categories of slave and free. As he writes at one point, "It was now a war with the racial divisions emphasizing the class struggle" (p. 359). Indeed, James captures the complexity of the situation when he writes:

The race question is subsidiary to the class question in politics, and to think of imperialism only in terms of race is disastrous. But to neglect the racial factor as merely incidental as [sic] an error only less grave than to make it fundamental. (p. 283)

Thus, what united Du Bois, Wright and James as black Marxists was their rejection of the absolute priority of class over race in analyzing or explaining group action. As of 1938, and generally thereafter, James assigned co-equal causal importance and psychological efficacy to race and class consciousness.

But the relationship between Toussaint and the masses of former slaves seems to have most intrigued James, despite the orthodox Marxist commitment to the causal priority of historical circumstances over individual will.[38] James's depiction of the rebelling slaves is decidedly partisan, though not without complexity. Because they were fighting for their liberty, the slaves were more strongly motivated than their French counterparts: "The masses were fighting by instinct" (p. 348). By this he meant not that they were fighting irrationally but that they were fighting for their lives and with the determination not to be re-enslaved. Interestingly for future historiographical developments, James notes the prevalence of African-derived religious observances and rituals among the slave population, the majority of whom were African born (p. 108).[39] That said, according to James, one of Toussaint's great achievements was his success in shaping his troops into an organized fighting force: "Toussaint alone . . . was in those early months of 1792 organizing out of the thousands of ignorant and untrained blacks an army capable of fighting European troops" (p. 116). Overall, though James clearly celebrates the courage and rationality of the masses, he just as clearly emphasizes their need for the organization that European civilization had to offer, not only in military but also in economic and social life. In emphasizing the need for work discipline and the retention of large sugar plantations as units of production, "Toussaint's revolution," suggests Eugene D. Genovese, "called for the 'Europeanization' of Saint-Domingue."[40]

James also readily admits the cruelty and destruction wrought by the revolting slaves. But he points out that "[f]rom their masters they had known rape, torture, degradation, and, at the slightest provocation, death. They [the slaves] returned in kind" (p. 88). They were, he also notes, "surprisingly moderate. . . . They did not maintain this revengeful spirit for long. The cruelties of property and privilege are always more ferocious than the revenges of poverty and oppression" (pp. 88–89). Such issues are hard to adjudicate from our historical vantage point, if for no other reason than that different standards of personal cruelty prevailed then. Both sides practiced what seems to us as considerable inhumanity. On the other hand, there were no massive aerial bombardments of civilians; no cluster bombs or napalm; nor were gulags or concentration camps established. Race war was the "invention" of the Europeans, not the Africans.

Toussaint is James's great man in history, a materialist version of Hegel's world-historical figure, and the pan-African answer to Hegel's elevation of Napoleon to world-historical status. For all of his personal strengths—ambition, intellect, self-discipline, character, administrative, and organizational ability,

> he [Toussaint] accomplished what he did because, superbly gifted, he incarnated the determination of his people never, never to be slaves again (p. 198).

And more complexly, if obscurely,

> [i]n him, born a slave and the leader of slaves, the concrete realisation of liberty, equality and fraternity was the womb of ideas and the springs of power, which overflowed their narrow environment and embraced the whole of the world (p. 265).

It is not that Toussaint imposed his personal qualities and goals on his followers; rather, they dovetailed with theirs. At least, that was true for a time. But Toussaint's tragedy, according to James, lay more in his attitude toward his followers than toward his adversaries.

> His error was his neglect of his own people. They did not understand what he was doing or where he was going. He took no trouble to explain. It was dangerous to explain, but still more dangerous not to explain (p. 240).

As a result, Toussaint's followers came to feel that he was too conciliatory toward the whites. Later, James reaffirmed this judgment by comparing Toussaint with Nkrumah in the way both men "lost contact with the people," a perennial theme in the history of modern revolutionary struggle.[41]

This brings us to the final two themes of *The Black Jacobins* that link that work with James's future thinking about race and culture. The first is the assumption that the success of a colonial revolt depends on a revolution in, or at least the disruption of, life in the metropolitan colonial power. Indeed, there was a certain amount of truth to this assumption, since the first successful colonial liberation struggle broke out during the French Revolution. It was the confidence of the bourgeoisie that had been engendered by the wealth gained from the slave colonies, linked with the spread of ideas such as the rights of man and the confusions engendered by revolutionary turmoil in Paris that created the possibility of a successful slave uprising in Haiti. James was almost certainly remembering too that the success of the Bolshevik Revolution was dependent upon the disruptive effects of World War I.

The final great theme of *The Black Jacobins* focuses on tension between the generally preliterate slave culture of the French colony and the need to learn and develop the ideas and techniques, the cultural resources, of Europe. What made this conflict most agonizing was, of course, the former slaves' hatred of slavery and of their former slave masters. But how, at least initially, could the former colony have European civilization without the Europeans? James stresses throughout that Toussaint knew that the revolutionary cause needed the skills and expertise of the remaining white planters and skilled middle classes: "[T]hey [the whites] alone had what San Domingo society needed" (p. 290). It is not, James claims, that this was a mistaken policy. Rather, Toussaint failed to make sufficiently clear either to his lieutenants or to his troops that his conciliatory attitude toward whites was for that reason alone. More generally, the reason for Toussaint's failure was that he suffered from a too complex, rather than a too simple, cast of mind. His complexity of purpose contrasted sharply with the single-mindedness of leaders such as Dessalines whose commitments to "French civilization were of the slenderest. . . . Toussaint's failure was the failure of enlightenment, not of darkness" (p. 288). But, again, this was "the truly tragic character of his dilemma" (p. 291). Toussaint wanted the destruction of slavery and then independence; yet he needed the French, their skills, and their ideas. The French Revolution "had made him what he was. But this in the end ruined him" (p. 290).

It is important to emphasize that James never faulted Toussaint for his commitment to Enlightenment ideals. Rather, the flaw lay in his failure to develop the political consciousness of his followers and to use their growing confidence, the discipline they had learned from fighting, and their absolute commitment to liberty to maximum effect. It would be Dessalines who eventually cut the Gordian knot by massacring whites, a policy that was adopted again before independence was achieved. Independence from France came at the cost of desolation and destruction. As James notes,

> The massacre of the whites was a tragedy; not for the whites. . . . The tragedy was for the blacks and the Mulattos. It was not policy but revenge, and revenge has no place in politics (p. 373).

Overall, the prospects for a prosperous, free Haiti were slim from the start and sustained revenge against whites only served to "brutalise and degrade a population. . . . [T]he unfortunate country, ruined economically, its population lacking in social culture, had its inevitable difficulties doubled by this massacre" (p. 374). Just over a quarter-century later, James repeated his verdict on the fatal turn in the Haitian experience: "For this divorce from Western Civilization Haiti has paid dearly." According to Eugene Genovese, land reform policy broke the back of Haitian sugar production; Haiti was dominated by a "centralized authoritarian state" and lacked a bourgeoisie to check the concentration of power or to manage affairs. The fate of Haiti was sealed for the rest of the century—and after.[42]

Alone in America: 1938–1953

James's decade and a half in the United States was a period of fundamental intellectual development—and reassessment. The deeper that he involved himself in sectarian disputes over Marxist doctrine, the more he fell in love with American popular culture and the New World generally. After the early 1940s, James went "underground" to evade the immigration authorities and assumed the nom de plume of J. R. (Jimmy) Johnson. He traveled widely around the country, and while recovering from periodic ulcer attacks became fascinated by the popular culture of capitalism, particularly radio, film, and the newly emerging television industry. He also read widely in "serious" American literature, particularly of the nineteenth century and published, as already mentioned, the book on Herman Melville, *Mariners, Renegades and Castaways* (1953).

Overall, James's intellectual and political development between the late 1930s and the late 1950s followed several interlocking paths. He undertook a fundamental reassessment of Marxist theory, especially the Leninist conceptions of revolution and party, developed an approach to the Negro question for the Trotskyist movement, and also worked toward an "Americanization of Bolshevism." Anna Grimshaw and Keith Hart claim that "[f]or James the black question lay at the core of the American question."[43] This is true insofar as the presence of the former slave population helped define American exceptionalism. Yet in his own thought, James never really established a convincing link between black American and general American culture. For James, the Negro question was a social problem with a political component and ultimately an economic solution. But he neglected the cultural component of the Negro question and African

Americans never figured very prominently in his analysis of American literary history or popular culture.

James joined the Trotskyists while in Britain; and it was at their behest that he went to America in 1938. In April–May, 1939, he visited "The Old Man" (Trotsky) in Mexico and argued at length with him about the best strategy for advancing the cause of African Americans. I will return to the position that James developed on this matter later. The Trotskyist Socialist Workers' Party (SWP) split over U.S. entrance into the war; and James left with Max Shachtman to form the Workers' Party (WP). Soon, along with Raya Dunayevskaya and Grace Lee Boggs, James formed the nucleus of the "Johnson-Forest Tendency" within the WP and spent the 1940s playing ideological-organizational tag with both the SWP and the WP.

Underlying what now seem to be boring scholastic disputes were serious matters of concern for Marxist theory and practice.[44] A particularly crucial issue for the Trotskyist left was whether to support the capitalist powers (Britain, France, and the United States) in their alliance with the Soviet Union against Hitler. It was not enough to justify siding with the Allies as a matter of *realpolitik* or as a war of nonideological self-defense. Rather, two questions were crucial—would support for the Allies help them strengthen their control over much of Asia and Africa, and was Stalin's Soviet Union still a "workers' state" and thus worth defending in its own right? For James, the Comintern's post-1935 Popular Front rapprochement with Western capitalist democracies and its directives to soft-pedal criticism of colonialism abroad and America's Jim Crow system at home confirmed his contempt for Stalin and Stalinism. But, in the early 1940s, Trotsky precipitated a crisis among his supporters by urging that critical support be given to the Soviet Union in the war, even though it was a "deformed" or "degenerated" worker's state. However, James and his colleagues in the Johnson-Forest Tendency sat out World War II, as did New York intellectuals such as Dwight Macdonald. James's refusal to support the Soviet Union contrasted sharply with W. E. B. Du Bois's and Paul Robeson's public support of the Soviet Union during and after the war, not to mention Robeson's call for the persecution of Trotskyists opposed to the war. Along with Wright, James demonstrated the possibility of taking a principled Marxist position against imperialism and colonialism without supporting the Soviet Union.

More important for our purposes is James's gradual postwar abandonment of the Leninist idea of the Communist Party as a vanguard party, that is, as a special political elite formation acting on behalf of the proletariat but without seeking mass membership from the proletariat. As Robert Hill has suggested, Trotskyists considered themselves the real Leninists and guardians of the true communist heritage against the depredations of Stalin. But for James, the elitist position, even of the Trotskyists, was increasingly hard to stomach. The idea of a vanguard party and the notion of the state, which for James was practically synonymous with rule by bureaucracy, were the two great hindrances to democracy. For most Marxist-Leninists, even Trotskyists, the new society was still "the society of the Party and the Plan."[45] Although political parties might be necessary or at least inevitable, contended James, they should be mass rather than elite organizations. What Marx had envisaged as socialism was, as James wrote in 1958,

> first of all a society of a new mode of labor, of new social relations of production, of workers' councils in every branch of national activity.[46]

Implicit in James's rejection of "vanguardism" was his distaste for any sort of elite direction of political action. His position also represented a powerful, if indirect, democratic critique of Du Bois's notion of the "Talented Tenth," that self-chosen black elite who were to guide the affairs of African Americans along the path of progress. Beyond that, James's increasing commitment to radical democracy led him to question the opportunistic role of intellectual elites in politics or cultural life generally.

Overall, in the Jamesian vision of politics (and culture), power properly originates with the people and spreads outward and upward rather than being imposed from the top down. As indicated in the passage just cited, the paradigmatic political form for James was the workers' council, which constituted a clear institutional break with both parliamentary democracy and (Stalinist) democratic centralism. In his *American Civilization* (1950), an often fascinating, if only abstractly realized, study of American culture, he championed popular taste and creativity against the bureaucracy, against the intellectuals who "go with the power,"[47] and against the heavy hand of the welfare state. In general, the American contribution to radicalism was not the idea of freedom or equality but the belief that everyone had the right to develop their "individuality" through the "struggle for happiness." Presenting a Tocquevillean view of America, not as exceptional but positioned at the cutting edge of contemporary history, James viewed the United States as the next site for the development of socialism.

James's political thinking came to rest upon the democratic promise of worker "self-activity," the pursuit of political goals and the development of individuality through common political activity. Echoing contemporaries such as the communitarian anarchist, Paul Goodman, or neorepublican political philosopher, Hannah Arendt, James thematized the grassroots political activity of the workers' councils as they emerged as the key institutions in the Hungarian Revolt of 1956. Behind that contemporary model stood the classical example of the Greek polis,[48] in which the political and aesthetic-cultural power was lodged in the hands of the citizen body. The citizens not only voted and held office, but were also critic-judges of the great tragedies performed at the public festivals. For James, Athens represented a polity in which power and imagination, politics and culture, were united rather than sundered from one another. It remained the great moment in the history of politics and of the possibility of democratic culture.

In his own time, James apotheosized "the experience of the Gold Coast revolution, of Montgomery, Alabama, and in the Hungarian Revolution"[49] as crucial events in the history of democratic self-rule. Rather than being the creations of intellectuals or vanguard political parties, these movements originated among the people and outside the existing channels and structures of politics. Like Arendt, he judged the Hungarian Revolution as "the decisive turning point in modern history."[50] Those who made history there, not just workers but people from all walks of life, chose a system of workers' councils as the vehicle for self-rule rather than establishing a new ruling bureaucracy or a unified political party. Not surprisingly, James later greeted Solidarity in Poland with great enthusiasm. But except for the letter in which the line just cited occurs, James never discussed the emerging civil rights movement in America in any detail. (His knowledge of the movement seems to have been largely based on a conversation with Martin and Coretta King in London in 1957.) More fatefully, James's work remained unknown to the young radicals of the Student Nonviolent Coordinating Committee (SNCC) in the period when they were engaged in grassroots organizing and working with communities to develop their own leaders and to formulate the issues that mattered to them. As of the late 1950s, James was one of the few modern Marxists—or black Marxists—to develop an explicitly participatory democratic vision of politics and to suggest new forms such as workers' councils to preserve the possibility of political action. Clearly, the Haitian Revolution was still hovering in the back of his consciousness.

A final break with Leninist revolutionary theory (and with his position in *The Black Jacobins*) came when James abandoned the belief that Third World liberation movements depended on prior revolutionary upheaval in the metropolitan world. Undoubtedly encouraged by the Nkrumah-led Ghanaian independence movement between 1947 and 1957, James wrote in a letter to his colleagues in America in 1957:

> I shall ... break completely with, or rather develop qualitatively the theoretical premises of the *Black Jacobins* and the Leninist theory of the colonial revolution. The African revolution (as a process) is no longer to be seen as supplementary to or subordinate in the revolution in Western Europe.[51]

Two years later, James explained his break by citing the failure of the European workers to overthrow European governments before, during, or after World War II:

> Everyone, revolutionaries and conservatives expected the war and out of the war, revolutionary upheavals. . . . [N]owhere had the proletariat of the metropolitan powers overthrown the imperialist state. The actual struggle of the Africans now had to depend on themselves alone.[52]

Finally, there is the Negro question. James's thinking on race in the 1940s and 1950s was divided between explicit discussions in left-wing Trotskyist publications and his avoidance, or at least deflection, of it in his literary and cultural writings. His book on Melville scarcely touches on race, except in reference to Nazi totalitarianism, and certainly never thematizes it.[53] Nor, even more strangely, does the "Negro problem" play a very large role in James's unpublished *American Civilization*. All told, James devotes eleven of its 292 pages to a rather inconclusive discussion of race. This is not exactly to say that James minimizes its importance. He notes that it is the "number one minority problem in the modern world" and "on par with the labor and the women's question" in importance. Tellingly, for James, it is "not the state but the mass of the white population" that perpetrates most of the crimes against America's Negro population.[54] The system is kept in place by a "vast and complicated and powerful . . . system of interrelated interests" and thus "there does not exist in the U.S. any government to put them [anti-discrimination] laws into force." Moreover, some Negroes have been co-opted by the system and have "a vested interested in segregation itself."[55] But James, like most other observers of the African American scene in the postwar world, missed the potential for political action among black Americans.

James spends several pages of *American Civilization* analyzing the abolitionist movement. In keeping with the importance of active involvement by slaves in their own emancipation, James emphasizes that "any kind of analysis of the Abolitionist intellectuals must therefore begin with the slaves" (p. 85), with the most important of those intellectuals being Garrison, Douglass, and especially Wendell Phillips. Second, James stresses the "American-ness" and the radical nature of abolitionism, which needed "no assistance from any alien tradition but from the very genius of the country." In their commitment, absolute determination, and dogmatism, the abolitionists were reminiscent of "the early Christians, the Puritans, and later the early Bolsheviks" (p. 91). Overall, James stressed against Herbert Aptheker that the slaves were not merely raw materials for the abolitionists; nor were the abolitionists a mainstream, popular-front type of movement but an uncompromisingly radical one. The abolitionists showed that there was revolutionary potential among both the American masses and the intellectuals, if it could but be mobilized.[56]

Besides his social and political analysis, James describes Richard Wright and Chester Himes as Negro writers who "represented the extreme peak of *American* revolt against the intolerable psychological burdens placed upon individuals in every part of the modern world."[57] From this perspective, the fate of the Negro American seems to be representative rather than unique. But where Richard Wright showed the bewildering effects of capitalist popular culture on Bigger, James was more open to mass culture in America, without differentiating between its effects on white and black Americans. James's theory of culture emphasizes the way that mass culture not only reflects the frustrations and disappointments but also expresses the hopes and dreams of the people. Both Wright and James were unusual among radical black intellectuals in understanding and analyzing the importance of popular culture in shaping popular consciousness. But James was much more sanguine about its effects.

What made his relatively inconsequential discussion of race in *American Civilization* even more peculiar was that James's essay, "The Revolutionary Answer to the Negro Problem in the United States" (1948), provided a strategic blueprint for tapping the radical potential of African Americans.[58] Trotskyism found itself in a dilemma circa 1940. On the one hand, it did not want to simply duplicate legal and political reformist efforts of, say, the NAACP. On the other hand, the Trotskyists neither supported the Communist Party's post-1935 Popular Front policy of downplaying the race issue in the name of a center-left coalition against fascism;

nor had they ever really supported the "black belt nation" of the Comintern position from 1928 until the mid-1930s. Thus, the Trotskyists were unwilling to go down the nationalist route with the Garveyites. Though not compromised by untenable past positions, the Trotskyists were left with very little room to maneuver.

In the decade between his discussions with Trotsky and his 1948 article, James's thinking developed along the following lines.[59] The basic plight of American Negroes arises from the contradiction between their "increasing integration into production" and their continuing "exclusion from democratic privileges." Although the problem is both economic and political, James's position is that Negroes should not fall under the direction of white-controlled organizations, whether Marxist or not. Rather, they should have a separate organization with goals of its own, avoid "racial chauvinism," and begin with "day-to-day demands." In the short run, racial considerations may outweigh cross-racial solidarity, but

> [b]lack chauvinism today is merely the natural excess of the desire for equality and is essentially progressive while white American chauvinism, the expression of social domination, is essentially reactionary.[60]

This statement from 1939 was, some ways, an anticipation of Sartre's characterization of negritude as "anti-racist racism," though it recognized the difference between racial and racist consciousness.

That such an organization was not explicitly socialist did not worry James; in fact, he cited Trotsky to the effect that even the demand for self-determination of Negroes should be supported, despite the fact that their ultimate goal should be "integration into American society." Still, the Negro, "more militant than ever," is "logically and historically and concretely. . . headed for the proletariat." Indeed, James contended in 1943 that the Negroes' "independent struggles form perhaps the most powerful stimulus in American society" to the proletariat. As "the most oppressed and most discriminated against" of the working class, Negroes should be in the "very vanguard of the working class struggle for socialism."[61] One thing was clear to James—American Negroes could not find an answer to their struggle for political and economic rights within American capitalism. All that said, James never contended that organized American Negroes should appeal only to other working class black people or only to black people with socialist credentials. Even though James thought Garvey's ideas were rubbish and that he was a "race fanatic" who reminded him of Hitler, James was nevertheless fascinated by Garvey. He believed in the necessity of "going over the literate and vocal intellectuals" to capture the support of the Negroes who responded to "the Garvey movement," "the Divine movement," and those who gave their money and energy to the black church.[62] Rather than rejecting all ideological deviations from nonracial radicalism, he envisaged a kind of racial Popular Front and showed at least some awareness of the political potential of religious movements, although not particularly in the South. Overall, "racial chauvinism," nationalism, and even religion were way stations, not dead ends, on the road to working class solidarity and eventual integration.

In retrospect James's position in the 1940s on the Negro question combined shrewd insight and a certain unreality. Though he mentions white chauvinism a couple of times, he never explores it in depth nor suggests just how the white working class might eventually see a convergence of their interests with American Negroes or why the latter should want to join them in an alliance. Nor is it clear how a radical, although strategic, separate-but-equal organizational policy would fail to encourage, rather than suppress, black racial chauvinism. The kinds of contortions that James and other Marxists put themselves through are obvious, for instance, in James's 1943 claim that the "movements which seek 'to drive the Jew out of Harlem or the South Side' have a valid class base." The danger is, he notes, that despite "their fundamental progressive basis," they "can be exploited by fanatical idiots, Negro anti-Semites, or self-seeking Negro business men."[63] Though one might agree that this type of black action was not anti-Semitic as such, it is hard to see such reasoning as anything but playing with fire. Fortunately, it was a line of thought to which James did not return. Along the way, James came to recognize that the North American context was different from that of late eighteenth-century Saint Domingue or the Caribbean in general. Because people of African descent were a minority and were all assumed to be "black," cross-racial alliances were much more difficult, while dark-skin solidarity of a Garveyite sort was a dead end.

Again, what was most lacking in his articles and essays of the 1940s was an explicit focus on Negro cultural life. In this he was closer to Wright and Frazier than to Hurston or Locke. His firm belief as expressed in *American Civilization* was that

[t]he Negroes are Americans. There never was a minority which was so much flesh of the flesh and blood of the blood of the majority. In

language, religion, social culture, education, training, perspectives, the Negroes are nothing else but American. . . . The Negroes do not seek any special privileges, constitution or statehood.[64]

Clearly, James rejected the Herskovits thesis and any other claims about African-oriented consciousness among Negro Americans: "He [the Negro] has no culture but Anglo-Saxon culture."[65] There was, then, little in James's work as of the mid-1950s to encourage a cultural nationalist position.

In general, then, James seems to have been interested in the question of racial consciousness insofar as it referred to political matters among Negro Americans rather than to cultural expression. Little in his work indicates any deep engagement with black music, whether the blues or the spirituals and gospel music. He seems also to have been religiously "tone deaf" and thus uninterested in black American religious culture, except as it provided a potential pool of recruits for political movements. As he quite candidly wrote later:

> I lived in the United States for twenty-five years, and I had no idea that this kind of community could be built in the southern Black churches; but of course this was the source of Dr. King's power. It would not be the same in the West Indies.[66]

Yet clearly James's call for a provisional, protonationalist organization with inclusion in the larger white society as its ultimate goal did make a good bit of sense. Such a call recognized the psychological need for black Americans to organize and fight for equal rights rather than being subordinated to a class-oriented Marxist organization. Overall, from *The Black Jacobins* on into the 1960s, James firmly rejected separatist positions based on racially or culturally exclusive criteria.

Identities: Race, Culture, and Nation

James's position on race, culture, and national identity was both complex and coherent, but his sense of himself as a black man developed relatively late. In 1971, he remembered attending an exhibition of African art in London in the early 1930s, at which time he "began to realise that an African, a black man, had a face of his own." Such experiences, along with his friendship for Paul Robeson, who "taught me a lot about black people," helped James realize that there was a fundamental black aesthetic that provided an alternative to the standards of white European aesthetic judgment.[67] Constance Webb also remembered that in the 1940s,

> C. L. R. had given very little thought to himself as a black man, until he reached the United States. And he was not obsessed with the problems as were American Blacks and southern Whites, all of which gave him a special quality.[68]

Interestingly, in a letter to Webb in 1948, James refers in passing to "the deeply British instinct, hammered home in books, in education, in conduct and example: push *yourself* away."[69] Thus, James identifies himself as "British" rather than "West Indian" or "Negro." As Anna Grimshaw later observed of James, "[T]he race question is rarely discussed as a personal experience."[70] That said, James's reluctance to make race the defining fact of his identity made it easier for him to move between cultures with considerable ease.

James also insisted in understanding the human condition as mediated through the thought and culture of the West, however much it was inflected by particularist commitments. I have already noted his clear preference for Toussaint's commitment to the universalist ideals of the French Revolution over Dessalines' racially exclusive policies and actions. As far back as his first writing on West Indian self-government in 1932, James describes the population of the West Indies, which was 80 percent black, as "essentially Western and, indeed, far more advanced in Western culture than many a European community."[71] According to James, the indigenous aboriginal culture of Trinidad had been wiped out; and he seemed indifferent to the African survivals still extant in Trinidadian culture. Rather, he emphasized, especially in *Beyond the Boundary* (1963), that he and his associates had fundamentally been late Victorian intellectuals:

> We lived according to the tenets of Matthew Arnold, spreading sweetness and light and the best that had been thought and said in the world. . . . Intellectually I lived abroad chiefly in England.[72]

It is also significant that James's own "opening" to the fact of his blackness was practically simultaneous with his political radicalization and took place in Britain, not in Trinidad. Only by leaving the West Indies did James come to his radical vocation and a certain racial self-awareness. Over time, James became more aware of another racially inflected aspect of his identity. Writing in the early 1960s about the reggae singer the Mighty Sparrow, one of the great creative figures in West Indian popular culture, James concluded: "We are Western, yet we have to separate what is ours from what is Western, a very different task."[73] Yet it is important to note that even here the "we" James refers to had a national not a racial reference. He spoke, he would say later, "as a West Indian. This has nothing to do with my race. It has, however, much to do with my nationality."[74]

Negritude engaged James's interest to a degree, but only to a degree. In his "A National Purpose for Caribbean Peoples" (1964), James notes the debt that colonial literatures owe the literature of the nation to which they "belonged." But he also calls attention to the contribution that "outsider" writing makes to that same metropolitan literature. In the 1960s, James generously championed West Indian writers such as Vic Reid, George Lamming, Wilson Harris, and especially the early V. S. Naipaul.[75] What he valued in their writing was a kind of inclusive realism that gave voice to all sectors of West Indian society and represented them without idealization or condescension. Though he was conversant with the landmarks of European and American literary modernism, he always kept modernism at an arms length, since it was, he thought, too alienated from its own origins. It was a symptom not a solution.

But in that same essay James shifts his attention from the literary-critical register of realism to the modernism of Aimé Césaire's poetry of negritude, particularly his *Cahier d'un retour au pays natal*, which appeared in 1939, just a year after *The Black Jacobins*. There, as well as in his 1963 Appendix to *The Black Jacobins*, "From Toussaint L'Ouverture to Fidel Castro," James pays less attention to negritude's formal and aesthetic qualities than to its origins and significance. His claim that negritude "is not an African concept at all. It is a West Indian concept. It cannot be African. An African is a native of Africa; what is he going to do with *negritude*?"[76] hardly bears sustained scrutiny, since it ignores the contributions to the ideology of negritude of Leopold Senghor and Cheikh Anta Diop or of the Harlem Renaissance. But James's more defensible point is that Africans have identities as members of tribes or nations. Only with difficulty can they see Africa as a unitary symbol or mythical site, since they live "in" rather than "from" or "for" it.

Needless to say, James's thinking on these matters derived in part from his own experience. The paradox of identity is that individuals have to migrate in order to return; they must take their distance in order to get closer. Césaire had to escape, through the imagination, from Martinique to Africa in order to understand that he was a West Indian—which meant, for him, someone of African descent. As James puts it, "[S]alvation for the West Indies lies in Africa, the original home and ancestry of the West Indian people."[77] But, James also makes the interesting point in "From Toussaint L'Ouverture to Fidel Castro," that the raw materials of negritude are as much West Indian as pure African. Speaking of the period between independence from France and World War I, James observes that

> [t]he Haitians did not know it as Negritude. To them it seemed purely Haitian. . . . Left to themselves, the Haitian peasantry resuscitated to a remarkable degree, the lives they had lived in Africa.[78]

The implications for James's own sense of cultural identity are also difficult to determine. On the one hand, his comment represents a modification of his own assertion from the early 1930s that there were no remnants of African culture still extant in the West Indies. (Undoubtedly, the middle-class status of James's parents had much to do with his own lack of connection with the folk culture of Trinidad.) Later in America he immersed himself in mainstream popular culture, not the black folk culture of the South, or of the South come north. Always on the move, one whose roots were in texts rather than places, James was above all a contemporary man, for whom the materials (though not the poetics) of negritude were too traditional (Senghor) or too limiting (Césaire). Yet, James's analysis is also to the point insofar as it suggests that the "Africa" evoked by negritude was not a pristine culture or even a "real" place at all. In this respect, James should have said that Césaire's *Cahiers* was not about Africa but about a certain idea of Africa. No more nor less than Picasso's African masks was Césaire's Africa the "real thing." Césaire had created a mythical Africa to serve a certain therapeutic cultural and political purpose. As James wrote in summary:

> *Before they could begin to see themselves as free and independent people they had to clear from minds the stigma that anything African was inherently inferior and degraded.* The road to West Indian national identity lay through Africa.[79]

But, neither race nor skin color was the whole story for West Indian identity. As James emphasizes, particularly in *Beyond the Boundary*, to be a person of African descent in Trinidad was to say little or nothing significant about that person's social or cultural status. The cricket club you played for had a lot to do with what color you were, which, in turn, was complexly linked with class and status. One can of course find the experiences in *Beyond the Boundary* that lay behind his Marxism and his emphasis on class over race in *The Black Jacobins*. His fascination with the black–mulatto conflict on Saint Domingue in the 1790s clearly was an extension of his own efforts to decode the grammar of race and color, so much more complex in the West Indies than in North America. In addition, as V. S. Naipaul has so powerfully reminded us, a sizable Indian population in Trinidad was also made up of people of color, that is, non-European, but not, of course, of African descent. To add to the complexity, one of the early leaders of the Trinidadian struggle against colonialism was Arthur Andrew Cipriani, a white man of French descent. To complicate matters even further, the enemy of James the Marxist was the bourgeoisie. But for James, the radical spokesman for West Indian independence, the absence of a commercially, politically, and intellectually sophisticated black middle class was a major problem for newly independent developing nations.[80] And yet, it was far from inevitable that James would choose a political position that emphasized class over race and nation over both. Finally, it is not hard to imagine that Marxism originally appealed to James because its universalist vision, mediated by the class struggle, was a way around the particularism of race or ethnicity. If color, race or ethnicity had played that mediating role, the way to universality would have been much more difficult to negotiate.

This background undoubtedly helps explain his position on black power in the late 1960s when he was teaching in the United States. Although politically in sympathy with his fellow West Indian Stokely Carmichael, James rejected a racially exclusive understanding of black studies and instead urged the study of history per se.

> I do not know, as a Marxist, black studies as such. I only know the struggle of people against tyranny and oppression in a certain social and political setting.[81]

Earlier in the same piece, he resists linking skin color with bravery fighting against slavery and the slave trade:

> not because their skins are black, or any special bravery of blacks. It is that men who are fighting for freedom and to whom freedom is a reality

fight much better. . . . This is the history that black people and white people and all serious students of modern history and the history of the world have to know. To say it's some kind of ethnic problem is a lot of nonsense.[82]

This makes James sound a bit more hostile to black studies than he really was—he also insisted that he would help teach it at Federal City College in Washington, D.C. Still, in the midst of the late 1960s rush to prove one's radical black credentials, it took a certain courage for James, for the first time recognized as a founding father of black radicalism, to assert this skepticism about, but political support for, black power.

Overall, for James, as for Richard Wright, the culture of Africa in general and the vision of negritude in particular remained somewhat alien, but political independence and socioeconomic reconstruction for Africa were of the highest priority. Just as James identified the prominent role that West Indians played in developing the concept of negritude, he also emphasized, though not without exaggeration, the West Indian contribution to African political independence. The two great West Indian figures in the growth of African political self-consciousness were, according to James, Marcus Garvey and James's childhood friend, George Padmore. If *The Black Jacobins* is James's reconstruction of the first racially inflected revolution for colonial independence, James's last book *Nkrumah and the Ghana Revolution*, published in 1977, was his valedictory to the whole question. It is a measure of James's honesty that the 1977 edition contains the original 1960 text, full of high praise for Nkrumah, and then adds to it a series of critical letters to Nkrumah, several articles in which James tries to analyze the failure of the Ghana experiment, and an article by Lenin. The whole book—and James's lifelong commitment to revolution—remains all the more poignant for containing the following dedication:

> To FRANCIS
> in never to be forgotten memory.
> Like Cromwell and Lenin, he
> initiated the destruction of a
> regime in decay—a tremendous
> achievement; but like them, he
> failed to create the new society

Francis was the name that James knew Kwame Nkrumah by when they first met in the United States.[83] To a much greater extent than Wright,

James was intimately connected with Ghana's struggle for independence. While living in New York, he had befriended a young Gold Coast student, Francis Nkrumah and referred him to Padmore when Nkrumah left for London in the early 1940s. In 1945, the Fifth Pan-African conference was held in Manchester, at which time Padmore and Du Bois merged their efforts and were joined by Nkrumah. Under Padmore's (and James's) tutelage, Nkrumah was groomed to return to the Gold Coast to lead the independence movement.

For James, the great promise of Nkrumah and his movement lay in two areas. First was the modernity of his efforts. "There was," writes James, "nothing backward about the Ghana revolution. It was a revolution of our times." Moreover, the movement created the ideal type of the modern body politic—"the disciplined community obeying its own laws." Second, there was the nature of Nkrumah's self-conception and his ideas. He was "the exact opposite, antithesis, negation of a tribal chief" and "the fine flower of another garden altogether, the political experiences and theoretical strivings of Western civilization." Once in the Gold Coast, Nkrumah, according to James, took his campaign to the people: "He did not speak down to them." According to James, "This was politics in the Greek-city sense of the word. It embraced the whole man, symbolized the beginning of a new stage of existence." Like the later civil rights movement in the U.S. South, Nkrumah's movement used Christianity and its music/songs to rally the spirits and transform the consciousness of the people. General strikes worked with considerable effect. The result was that the British brought Nkrumah into government in 1951. In 1957 independence was celebrated.[84]

Although *Black Power* recounts Wright's journey to the hinterlands of the Gold Coast, James never left Accra. Indeed, the weakness of his book—and perhaps of its vision of Africa—lies in the absence from it of the people of Ghana.[85] There is none of Wright's eye for detail and the sheer difference of African life. Though Wright's reactions to African village culture often seem awkward, even embarrassing, he never forgets that Africa *is* another culture, not a Lancashire cotton mill town, the U.S. South, the West Indies—or the Greek polis. It is as though James had forgotten how to write like a novelist or journalist or like the great historian he had been in *The Black Jacobins*. The political and historical analyses of the failure of Nkrumah's revolution are there. But the experience is missing.

Intellectually, James knew all this about Ghana and Africa. He appended two of his newspaper articles about Ghana from a Trinidad newspaper. In them, he observes that "Africans are not a primitive and not a Western people. Their whole historical experience makes them see and feel their world differently." But just for that reason, the great temptation had been to push on through: "[Y]ou drive for westernization, modernisation" but "every economic advance means social disruption." Nkrumah succumbed to the great temptation of revolutionary leaders—he failed to recognize the validity of parliamentary opposition, tried to do too much, and eventually violated civil liberties with impunity. The alternatives, writes James, were not clear. Somehow "Africans had to work out a way that was neither the way of the West nor the way of the East," as he records the late Nyasaland leader, Chisiza, as saying. James concludes with the cultural question, which is ultimately a philosophical one: "[T]he plans for economic development [must be] part of a deep philosophical concept of what the mass of the African people need. That is where Nkrumah failed." It is perhaps also where James—and the West—failed.[86]

James spent the last years of his life in London's Brixton neighborhood. At his modest flat, he still received guests and counseled friends, still read and thought and listened and watched indefatigably. His was a remarkable career of personal and intellectual adventure; and he is perhaps the most appealing of the black Marxists or of the Marxist thinkers of the last century generally. No one, I suspect, knew better than James the difficulties of trying to combine the universalist vision and the particularist struggles, the traditions of Europe with the culture of the black Atlantic. Unlike Wright who died on the eve of the era of black power, James was forced to confront the wave of black cultural and political nationalism that emerged in the latter half of the 1960s. As we have seen, his ambivalence regarding the politics of race and culture was considerable, yet he seems to have worked out a way to be sympathetic with the impulse toward political and cultural self-determination without becoming captive of a racially exclusivist vision. Overall, it is hard to imagine a life more committed to living with such difficulties with integrity, passion, and openness.

9

Negritude, Colonialism, and Beyond

To de-westernize in order to universalize, such is our desire.

Alioune Diop

It is around the people's struggle that African-Negro culture takes on substance, and not around songs, poems or folklore.

Frantz Fanon

Ambivalence toward negritude is evident in the work of both Richard Wright and C. L. R. James. For all their commitment to achieving black equality in the United States and African independence, they failed to see the immediate relevance of a cultural ideology that sought to revive the values and traditions of people of African descent. Their basic position seems to have been that cultural reconstruction was not entailed by political decolonization. In contrast with James and Wright's concerns, the years between the First and Second World Wars saw the growth of interest in black diasporic cultures in the United States, in the Caribbean, and in France. Martinique's Aimé Césaire used the term "negritude" in his epic of the black diasporic sensibility *Cahier d'un retour au pays natal* (1939) and elsewhere, but negritude only emerged as a full-fledged cultural ideology in the early post–World War II years.

Of crucial importance for its emergence was the founding in 1947 of *Présence Africaine* under the editorship of Alioune Diop, a younger man than negritude's major spokesmen Césaire, Leon G. Damas, and Leopold Sedar Senghor. Though not exclusively devoted to the propagation of negritude, *Présence Africaine* became the chief forum where issues involving negritude were aired.[1] Césaire's *Cahier* also began receiving serious attention after the War and was translated into English in 1947 by

Lionel Abel. Then, in 1948 Senghor published *Anthologie de la nouvelle poesie negre and malgache de langue francaise* with Sartre's essay "Black Orpheus" as its introduction. These three intellectual "events" signaled the heightened importance of negritude among African and diasporic black intellectuals in the West.[2] The choice of the term negritude itself was intended as a provocation. As Césaire makes clear in *Cahier*, the use of "negre" was an act of defiance, a challenge to respectable usage, which employed genteel terms such as "hommes de coleur" or "noir" to refer to people of African descent. Thus, using "negre" was roughly equivalent to using the term "black" or even "nigger" rather than "Negro" in English. Negritude might be translated as "blackness" or "niggerness."[3]

Negritude was an overwhelmingly Francophone phenomenon and its spokesmen (practically all were men) were Antillean and African literary intellectuals, though some would insist that it was more a West Indian than an African formulation.[4] In addition, Cheikh Anta Diop (1923–1986) of Senegal developed an African historiography beginning in the 1950s. The central thesis of Diop's work was, first, that the origins of African *and* European culture lay in Egypt and, second, that "ancient Egyptian and Pharaonic civilization was a Negro civilization." With this, he rejected both the ideas that Egypt was Asian or Berber (Europeanized North African) in origin and that the culture of West Africa was different in origin from that of Egypt.[5] Diop's thesis assumed that cultural diffusion from Egypt took a southwest-ward path into West Africa but that a later technological decline led to the European domination of West Africa and the establishment of the trans-Atlantic slave trade.[6] On the other hand, the northern path of diffusion explained the great achievements of the classical Mediterranean civilizations of the West, particularly Greece's.

Though Diop stressed the continuities between Egypt and West Africa, Egypt and Greece, he also posited a typological distinction between the cultures of the South and those of the North, between Egyptian Africa and northern Europe. Aryan cultures were nomadic in nature and thus patriarchal, while African cultures were agricultural and matriarchal; where the state structure in Egyptian Africa had been "unitary" and "cosmopolitan universalist," Greece was made up of contentious and xenophobic city-states; and, finally, the northern mentality was given to pessimism and the glorification of the warrior, while African cultures were more optimistically inclined and never cultivated the warrior ethos to the extent that the European did. "We therefore see," writes Diop, "in passing from the south to the north all cultural values are overthrown and become as opposite as the poles."[7] But, if the two cultural types were so different, how could contact between the two have led to a fruitful development rather than to a fragmented or self-undermining culture? Nor was it clear why Egyptian culture failed to continue the dynamic development that had made it the source of the cultures of Africa and Europe.[8] In short, how cultural diffusion worked was never very satisfactorily explained in Diop's work.

Diop's North–South divide, suggested in 1959 at the Second Congress of Black Writers and Artists in Rome, was already politically present in his idea of pan-Africanism, the goal of which was the development of a complex political/cultural unity, expressed in a "General History of the Continent," a common language, an indigenous art, and an industrial capability based on an Africa rich in "energy and raw materials."[9] It was not clear the extent to which Diop was a historical particularist, who saw the future of Africa as separate from the rest of humanity, or a universalist, who hoped for a historical and cultural convergence between Africa and Europe. His diffusionist theory would seem to suggest a fundamental unity of human culture, at least of European, Near Eastern, and African cultures, while his North-South typology seemed to imply separate political and cultural development within the ancient world.[10]

In Senghor's hands, negritude was marked by an ambivalent relationship to European thought and culture. He starkly contrasted Europe and Africa in one of his most familiar formulations: "[R]eason is Hellenic and emotion is Negro."[11] Yet, Senghor softened the binary opposition in his 1956 address to the First Congress of Black Writers and Artists in Paris: "European reasoning is analytical, discursive by utilization; Negro-African reasoning is intuitive by participation."[12] But the dichotomy between African and European culture also implied that African cultural values were, at least originally, superior to the European ones. Thus, Senghor's negritude attempted not only to rescue but also to privilege "Africanness" in the face of the European political, economic, and cultural domination of Africa. Finally, and ironically, the very process of drawing the stark distinction was itself part of the organicist, antimodern tradition of European thought that sought to retrieve what had allegedly been lost with the triumph of modernity. In other words, Senghor and others used European antimodernist thought against Europe.

All this is to say that the negritude movement was far from simple in its origins or goals. Indeed, when philosopher Paulin Hountondji later formulated his strong critique of ethnophilosophy, a concept closely related to the negritude idea, he used the work of Césaire to criticize the Belgian priest Placide Tempels's *Bantu Philosophy* (1945), but then also identified negritude, as developed by Senghor, as one of the ideologies that was complicit with colonialism.[13] Lilyan Kesteloot's literary history of negritude in 1963, the first major study devoted to the topic, identified "[n]egritude's central premise" as "the existence of a cultural relationship among peoples of the black world,"[14] a characterization that resembles Senghor's claim that negritude refers to the "ensemble of black Africa's cultural values" and was compatible with Césaire's reminiscence:

> Therefore we affirmed that we were Negroes and were proud of it, And that we thought that Africa was not some sort of blank page in the history of humanity; and finally, the idea was that that Negro past was worthy of respect—that its values were values that could still bring important things to the world.[15]

To this orientation toward Africa, as an experience and as a trope, should be added the influence of French symbolist and surrealist poetry and, above all, the influence of the Harlem Renaissance on both Senghor and Césaire. Not only did these Francophone intellectuals become acquainted with writings of Langston Hughes, Alain Locke, Claude McKay, Jean Toomer, and others in print, they also met them when they visited Paris, as they often did, in the interwar years.[16] Finally, as one student of negritude has observed, negritude was also divided between Senghor's interest in discovering (and celebrating) the actual institutions and traditions of African life, while Césaire was much more concerned with exploring the "subjective" consciousness of blackness and thereby its links with Africa.[17]

There was also a political dimension to negritude, what Césaire later referred to as "resistance to the politics of assimilation."[18] Césaire in particular developed this political dimension, thus illustrating David Macey's suggestion that negritude be divided between, on the one hand

> a celebration and endorsement of specifically black-African culture and values; on the other, there is the cry of revolt voiced by the wretched of the earth.[19]

Whereas the "cry of revolt" characterized Césaire's position, Senegal's Senghor was much more concerned with celebrating the superior spirituality and energy of the African worldview. In 1968 Leon Damas, the third but most neglected member of the founding triumvirate of negritude, brought the cultural and political dimensions of negritude together when he remembered that in the mid-1930s,

> the black man was seeking to know himself, that he wanted to become an historical actor and a cultural actor, and not just an object of domination or a consumer of culture, . . . we accepted the word *negre* as a challenge.[20]

Questions of race, color, and "blood" were never far from the center of discussions of negritude. The Marxist Césaire was hardly comfortable with the language of "blood" and other hints of racial essentialism found in the literature of negritude, though he did occasionally resort to it, particularly in his poetry.[21] More commonly he rejected biological explanations, as witness the following lines from *Cahier*: "negritude, not a cephalic index any more or a plasma or a soma but measured with the compass of suffering," which he unpacked, as it were, two decades later when he noted that "a greater unity between the men of the black race" exists but "not because of skin, but because of a community of culture, history and temperament."[22] Still, "blood" is one of the central tropes in *Cahier*. It sometimes refers to the bodily substance that has been shed in the course of a history of oppression and rebellion, while at other times, it is the trope for group kinship or race. Put elliptically, Césaire can be read to say that what makes black people "kin" is their having shed blood together throughout their history. Overall, Césaire was more reluctant than Senghor to identify black commonality with race or skin color, except as such physical characteristics point to a shared historical experience of capture in Africa and enslavement in the New World.

For Césaire, diasporic Africans were products of an agonizing history rather than related organically to an ahistorical, pastoral Africa imagined by Senghor. *Cahier* contains relatively few evocations of Africa as a source of heroic examples for those living in the black diaspora. As Césaire insists sardonically and unheroically:

> No, we have never been amazons of the King of Dahomey, nor Princes of Ghana with eight hundred camels. . . . We do not feel the itch of those who used to hold the spear in our armpits. . . . [T]he only undeniable record we ever broke was at endurance under the whip.[23]

And then later:

> And in the midst of all this I cry hurray! My grandfather is dying, I cry hurrah! The old negritude is gradually cadaverising.[24]

Clearly the poet's return to Martinique is no rediscovery of a new world Eden; rather, his focus falls on the poverty of a ramshackled society that is nevertheless ready to affirm itself.

Césaire's complex vision is also reflected in the form, voice, and thematic content of *Cahier*. It mixes prose and poetry, straightforward condemnation and celebration with sarcasm and irony, hope with despair. Indeed, *Cahier* will remind American readers of Walt Whitman's celebration of "the people" and Allen Ginsberg's visionary incantations. The difference is that Césaire's vision is angrier and more embattled, his language more tortured, than Whitman's, while *Cahier* more clearly includes a historical and political dimension than Ginsberg's work does. Motifs referring to the body and to sexual potency, particularly to male phallicity, abound. Though it transcends the category of protest poetry as such, *Cahier* has a strong protest element to it.[25]

On the other hand, Senghor's vision posits an imaginary, almost timeless Africa. Yet he came to see the ultimate goal as one of "reconciliation" between negritude and Western culture and the realization of a universal humanism,[26] although the terms of assimilation had to be set by people of African descent not by Europeans. As he insisted at the First Black Writers and Artists Congress in 1956: "[W]e must not be assimilated, we must assimilate."[27] The model for African socialism lies not in the modern present or utopian future, but in the traditional African village organized around communal property. It is this aspect of Senghor's thought that helps explain why some varieties of negritude drew upon the antimodernist work of certain suspect figures in French thought—Arthur Comte de Gobineau, Maurice Barres, and Teilhard de Chardin. As already mentioned, Senghor's negritude was an African-inflected version of romantic organicism, which emphasizes the group over the individual, race and culture over class, the irrational over the rational, the unconscious and mythical over the conscious and rational, images over concepts, and art and religion over science and technology.

Césaire's brand of negritude, wedded as it was to Marxian/socialist critique of present-day colonial societies, opposed Western capitalist "modernity" in the name of revolutionary socialism rather than a premodern, pastoral ideal. Indeed, both wings of negritude and almost every-one else in the African diaspora after 1945 agreed on the idea of "African socialism," no matter what the origins of this anticapitalist impulse were.[28] For Césaire, alienation and oppression had more to do with Western colonialism than it did with modernity as such. For all his indictment of Western colonialism, he makes relatively little place for a search for African roots or spiritual stability. If Senghor's version of negritude tends toward the reactionary and romantic, Césaire's seeks to combine aesthetic modernism with political/social modernity. His surrealist emphasis on the juxtaposition of disparate images mirrors the unevenly developed cultural life of the colonies where traditional and modern, indigenous and European, clashed. *Cahier* stands as one of the few examples of a modernist literary text that articulates a "progressive" social and political vision, despite having chosen "surrealism" over "socialist realism," as Amiri Baraka once succinctly noted.[29]

In 1956, the uneasy coexistence in Césaire's thought between Marxism and negritude finally broke down. But just before it did, he mounted an explicit attack on Western colonialism, especially the United States in his *Discourse on Colonialism* (1955). There Césaire claims that "Hitlerism" in Europe was merely colonialism applied to European whites, what he, echoing Arendt, calls "the boomerang effect of colonization." Culturally, the epoch of fascism and Nazism showed the "barbarism of Western Europe . . . only surpassed—far surpassed, it is true—by the barbarism of the United States."[30] For Césaire, the Soviet Union and the proletarian revolution constituted the wave of the future that would leave behind the two concepts "invented by the bourgeoisie in former times and launched throughout the world," the first of which was "man," that is humanism, and the "other was the nation."[31]

Yet in October 1956, Césaire resigned from the French Communist Party, though it was not directly related to the Soviet invasion of Hungary. In a public letter to the Party's General Secretary, Maurice Thorez, Césaire revised his view of the prospects for a revolutionary future. Where his *Discourse on Colonialism* had apotheosized the Soviet Union as the hope of the future, Césaire spoke now of the "abyss of dismay, of pain, and of shame" that Khrushchev's revelations of the crimes of Stalin had opened up at the 20th Party Congress earlier that year. Césaire also condemned Moscow's iron grip over national communist parties and attacked the French Communist Party (PCF) for its failure to condemn Stalinism and for giving the French government "full powers" to execute its policies in

Algeria.[32] Ultimately, suggests Césaire, the interests of the international communist movement and those of colonial peoples "are not purely and simply identical." The colonized should no longer be permanently subservient to the Party line. Communism had fallen prey to "thinking of our countries as fields for missionary endeavor and of mandated territories," thus subordinating African needs and interests to those of the "world's proletariats," that is, the proletariat of Europe. Rather, Césaire contends "that Marxism and Communism [should] be harnessed into the service of colored peoples, and not colored peoples into the service of Marxism and Communism."[33] While African American intellectuals such as W. E. B. Du Bois and Paul Robeson continued to stress the vanguard role of international communism and the Soviet Union in the struggle against Western colonialism, Césaire had decided that the Soviet Union and Marxism-Leninism represented more of the same Eurocentric attempt to control the pace of revolutionary change in the Third World. The best place to look for change, was in "Black Africa, the dam of our civilization and source of our culture, it's to her I look for regeneration of the Antilles; not to Europe."[34]

Finally, Césaire recognized that by abandoning the communist movement, he would be accused of a "strait particularism" but insisted that he did not want to "become lost in a fleshless universalism."[35] His resignation from the PCF pointed to what he saw as the ultimate incompatibility between orthodox Marxism-Leninism and negritude and, more prophetically, to one of the reasons for the eventual failure of Soviet Communism in the Third World. Communism was a European rather than an authentically worldwide movement. Indeed, Césaire confronted the same question that once faced Toussaint L'Ouverture: should revolutionary forces in the colonies wait for their marching orders from metropolitan radicals and subordinate their interests to those of the industrial proletariat?

Paris: September 1956

Just a few weeks before Césaire's resignation from the PCF, a crucial event in the cultural politics of the Third World took place: the First International Congress of Negro Writers and Artists at the Sorbonne, September 19–22, 1956. For many, the First Congress was the cultural counterpart of the Bandung Conference held the previous year in Indonesia.[36] As we have seen in the previous chapter, the task of the Congress was to explore the possibilities of cultural independence from, but cultural coexistence with, the West. The contributions of Césaire and Senghor revealed quite clearly the differences in the two men's conceptions of negritude. Senghor, in keeping with the ostensible cultural, as opposed to political, orientation of the Congress, assumed that "cultural liberation" was "an essential condition of political liberation."[37] His contribution, "The Spirit of Civilization or the Laws of African Negro Culture," set forth the case for African difference with clarity and grace. The Negro, he suggests, is a "man of Nature" who deals with the world primarily in "sensual" terms. But this does not mean that Africans are "devoid of reason." Rather, "his reason is not discursive; it is synthetic," not "analytic through utilization" but "intuitive through participation." Drawing on Tempels's *Bantu Philosophy*, Senghor identifies African being with a "vital force" that "animates every object which is endowed with a sentient character." Beyond that, however, "all creation is centred on man." African metaphysics is thoroughly humanistic, that is, focused on human beings.[38]

Senghor also sketched in the prototypical African social structure underlying the African worldview: the clan and family provide the basis for the tribes, who taken together make up the kingdom. Since arts and crafts are inseparable, no viable distinction between use, beauty, and goodness makes sense: "The truth is that the African Negro assimilates beauty to goodness, and especially to effectiveness." "Image and rhythm, these are the two fundamental features of African Negro style," while music is dominated by rhythm not melody.[39] Painting stresses "repetition" by "color contrast," thus creating a rhythm, while deploying colors "without shadow effects."[40] Nor is there any essential difference between art and knowledge: "The act of knowledge is an 'agreement of conciliation' with the world." Overall, Senghor concludes with the resounding claim that

[t]he spirit of African Negro civilization consciously or not animates the best Negro artists and writers of to-day, whether they come from Africa or America.[41]

To that he adds:

And if it is also said that this African Negro culture resembles that of ancient Egypt, and of the Dravidian and Oceanic peoples like two sisters, I would answer that ancient Egypt was *African* and that Negro blood flows in imperious currents in the veins of the Dravidians and the Oceanics.[42]

Though I have already analyzed Wright's challenge to his position, Senghor's depiction of black African culture did not go unchallenged by other participants at the Congress. J. S. Alexis from Haiti spoke for the various diasporic communities when he challenged Senghor's assumption that all cultures of Negro peoples shared in the essential spirit of African Negro culture, thus implying that Senghorian negritude represented a kind of African cultural imperialism. Alexis wondered about the relationship of national cultures, such as Haitian or South African, to that of African culture. Surely, he concluded, it is necessary to "pose the problems of culture in the light of national independence,"[43] a statement that anticipated the theory of national culture that Frantz Fanon proposed at the Second Congress in Rome in 1959. Later in the discussion, Alexis asserted that there was no "overall one single African Negro culture," despite the fact that African elements are present in, for instance, the cultures of Brazil, the United States, and Haiti. Anticipating his formal address later in the conference, Césaire sought to reconcile the positions by noting that just as there is a general European or Western culture that contains French, Spanish, and German cultures among others, so African culture contains distinct but related diasporic cultures.[44] Senghor conceded at bit on these issues but insisted that the "classics [i.e., the models of cultural achievement] for American Negroes . . . can only be found in Africa."[45] Overall, then, Senghor assumed not only a complex unity of African worldviews in Africa but also a continuity of spirit or essence between Africa and the diasporic communities.

But though Senghor and Césaire agreed that peoples of black Africa constituted a complex cultural unity, Césaire's explanation of this unity differed sharply from Senghor's. According to Césaire, what united the various diasporic communities, including Haiti and the United States, with each other and to Africa was not a spiritual or cultural essence but the "colonial situation." He explained the inclusion of the United States and Haiti in the following terms:

> In other words, if you are not in a colonial situation, you are in a situation which, as Senghor just now very rightly said, is a *sequel* of slavery—and therefore, in the last analysis, a sequel of the colonial regime.[46]

Césaire's simple but powerful explanation was all the more striking considering that Senghor's presentation had hardly mentioned the term "colonialism," much less how it might have modified traditional African society. Césaire also imagined a condition in which a "new civilization" was possible that "will owe something both to Europe and to the native civilization."[47] With that he recognized that whatever cultural synthesis might emerge in the future, it would look different from the pure, ideal type of either culture. But Césaire also insisted on a complex kind of coherence in which the disparate materials making up the new culture had to be experienced as a cultural unity. That is, however heterogeneous the cultural elements, they had to be "lived internally as homogeneity."[48] Césaire also historicized the notion of Negro unity by emphasizing the priority of politics to culture; or at least their co-equal status. (Senghor, it should be remembered, assumed the priority of culture to politics or economics.) That is, the "political status" and the imposition of capitalist imperatives upon a people or a nation have "cultural consequences."[49] This is so because political and economic hegemony, whatever its other effects, stifles the indigenous culture. Finally, bringing the two lines of thought together, Césaire argues that it is only when a "people is free," that is, when its cultural choices are uncoerced, that a new sort of culture can come into being that will combine elements from disparate cultures. Overall, the significant difference between Césaire's and Senghor's approach lay in his (Césaire's) identification of African Negro culture as much with the diaspora populations as with the African homeland. With his emphasis on the historical intervention/imposition of European rule to disrupt premodern, African pastoralism, Césaire also anticipated Fanon's emphasis on the crucial importance of politics, that is, the national question, for the question of culture and also pointed to something like Gilroy's "the Black Atlantic."

Even though Césaire's presentation made a plausible case for a certain unity of peoples of African descent, it bothered some of the participants, particularly the members of the U.S. delegation. Not only did they wonder, as we have seen, how Negro Americans might really be said to participate in the essence of negritude in cultural terms, Howard University's Mercer Cook was also worried by the political slant to Césaire's remarks. In his intervention from the floor during the discussion period, Cook spoke of how he had asked Alioune Diop "if this meeting was a cultural congress or a political congress" and was assured it was the former. Cook went on to express his bewilderment at Césaire's speech:

[W]hat am I doing in this outfit [sic]. Mr. Césaire has certainly said that we American Negroes have a semi-colonial status; but since 7 o'clock

I feel less and less at one with my African compatriots. And that trou-
bles and hurts me greatly . . . We are discussing colonialism; is it because other questions on other aspects of culture are only pretexts for
this Congress?[50]

Another member of the American delegation, John Davis, affirmed the
"Negro cultural heritage," but wondered what followed from Césaire's attacks on colonialism. Was there, he wondered, any practical alternative?
Beyond all the calculations of political advantage, ideological loyalty, and
patriotism, the American delegation's questions about the relevance of the
category of "colonialism" to the situation of Negro Americans and to
Haiti, revealed the problem with positing a political and cultural commonality among people of African descent and pointed to the pitfalls of
the colonial analogy when applied to the situation of black Americans.

Though it is difficult to recapture the mood of the Paris and Rome
Congresses, it is safe to say that intellectuals of African descent were far
from agreement on the meaning or value of negritude as an ideology *or* as
a strategy in the late 1950s. Indeed, a distinction between ideology and
tendency, vision and strategy, might be useful as a way of differentiating
among the various functions of negritude between the end of World War
II and the mid-1970s. From this perspective, the Césaire wing of negritude
tended to adopt negritude as a form of cultural and political intervention
but not as a closed ideology, while the Senghorians set more stock by
negritude as a coherent theory of self, society, and history.[51]

Negritude under Interrogation

The piece most responsible for bringing negritude to the attention of white
Western intellectuals was Sartre's long essay "Black Orpheus" of 1948.[52]
In his essay, Sartre sought to explain the black "other" to white Europeans.
Sartre had already commented briefly on the significance of black writing
in his *What Is Literature?* (1947). There he observes that "one can imagine a good novel written by an American Negro," even though it is filled
with hate, since that hate is the vehicle for demanding "the freedom of his
race" but not the enslavement of whites. But, it is not "possible to write a
good novel in praise of anti-Semitism" since anti-Semitism seeks to de-
prive the Jews of their freedom.[53] With this distinction, Sartre anticipates
the controversial point in "Black Orpheus" where he identifies negritude
as a form of "anti-racist racism," a form of racial consciousness that ulti-

mately seeks to go beyond and abolish itself. In *What Is Literature?* he also writes of the way Richard Wright's career exemplifies the simultaneous discovery of the black writer's vocation and his subject as a writer, thus assuming, as Irving Howe later did in his essay in defense of Wright against James Baldwin and Ralph Ellison, that the first subject of black writing is the experience of being black and oppressed. Sartre goes on to offer his own Gallic version of Du Bois's double consciousness thesis: "Each work of Wright contains what Baudelaire would have called a 'double simultaneous postulation,'" since his writing is directed toward two reading publics and thus takes on double meaning.[54]

In assuming the role of self-designated mediator between the ideologists of negritude and white Europeans, Sartre's piece demonstrated all the ambiguities involved in that extremely tricky role. If hermeneutics is always ambivalently positioned between serving and mastering a text, between striving for a faithful rendition of a text and having "designs" on it, this is doubly the case when a citizen of a colonial power seeks to convey to white Europeans what "the colonized" say and mean to each other. Having perhaps become more aware since *Anti-Semite and Jew* of the pitfalls of speaking for the "other," Sartre opens by urging his white readers to realize that the tables have been turned. Blacks are now writing, as well as fighting, back: "I hope you—like me—will feel the shock of being seen" (p. 5). With this, Sartre assumes a capacity for action on the part of people of color that he had not attributed to Jews in *Anti-Semite and Jew*. He also makes a much stronger effort to penetrate the psychology of the black poet, but wonders about his capacity and, implicitly, his right, as a white man, to claim to understand the meaning of the black experience: "[A] white man could hardly speak about it suitably, since he has no inner experience of it" (p. 24). Overall, Sartre's essay announced that the black "other" can no longer be considered opaque because of supposed limitations in his ability to feel or think. It is more that his/her thoughts have become intentionally impenetrable to whites.

Still, none of these concessions prevented Sartre from pronouncing on the new ideology of blackness in Senghor's anthology. The essay itself is lyrical, at times dithyrambic, in contrast with the analytical stringency of *Anti-Semite and Jew*. Though its topic is ostensibly the aesthetic of black poetry, it easily slips into an analysis of the aesthetics, ontology, and politics of black existence in general, justifiable in Sartre's own terms since: "Negritude is, in essence, poetry" (p. 39), and poetry is a way to "reveal the black soul" (p. 11). The picture that Sartre paints of black existence includes many of the stereotypes whites attribute to black people—a more immediate access to (phallic) sexuality; in general "a certain affective attitude toward the world" (p. 25); and a "comprehension through instinctive congeniality" (p. 27). Their way of being in the world contrasts sharply, notes Sartre, with the white working class whose relationship with the world, including with nature, is primarily instrumental. For the white worker, "Nature is matter for him" and "[m]atter has no song" (p. 8).[55] Black poets also suffer from a double alienation—from their own native country and from Africa itself—and that explains the predominance of "themes of return to the native country" (Césaire), "re-descent," and "quest," and also the Orpheus trope (p. 13). Moreover, since negritude poets use the language of their colonial oppressors, in this case French, they must deploy that language itself to undermine the oppressors' physical, linguistic, and psychocultural domination. But central to Sartre's analysis are, first, the *image* of the black Christ as much as of Orpheus, a sacrificial figure whose passion permeates his existence; and, second, the *concept* of negritude, as a "moment of negativity" that will eventually be surpassed in the dialectical movement of history.

Famously, Sartre refers twice in the essay to negritude as the "antiracist racism" of the new Negro. With that, he brings together the trope of self-abnegating passion with the concept of dialectical transition and conceptual self-undermining:

> In fact, Negritude appears like the up-beat [unaccented beat] of a dialectical progression: the theoretical and practical affirmation of white supremacy is the thesis; the position of Negritude as an antithetical value is the moment of negativity. But this negative moment is not sufficient in itself, and these black men who use it know this perfectly well; they know that it aims at preparing the synthesis or realization of the human being in a raceless society. Thus Negritude is *for* destroying itself, it is a "crossing to" and not "an arrival at," a means and not an end. . . . With what pride as a *man* he will strip his pride as a Negro for other men! (pp. 36–37)

For Sartre, then, black people have replaced the proletariat as carriers of historical development, but that historical role will disappear, whatever the subjective objection of the black poet or black people in general to this process of self-surpassing might be. The universal man becomes particular and is incarnated, first, in the proletariat and now as a black; but the particularistic incarnation must eventually be surpassed in order that the universal man can reemerge.

Here several questions central to the critique of negritude over the next two decades need discussion. As in *Anti-Semite and Jew*, though in a less pronounced fashion, Sartre assumes that antiracist racism, that is, negritude, like all particularisms, will eventually disappear, thus leaving race and ethnicity without a role or meaning. For Sartre, what should emerge is a concrete universalism in which racial and ethnic particularisms have been subsumed rather than abolished. But as Emmanuel Eze has wondered, suppose history is not a dialectical development but a process in which opposites clash without a third term or stage into which thesis and antithesis can be sublated?[56] From this perspective, Sartre's dialectic is a utopian hope rather than a historical or ontological inevitability. Another problem is that Sartre never defines what he means by "anti-racist racism." In fact, what he refers to as "racism" could better be called "racial self-consciousness"; it is not racism in the sense of treating whites in a discriminatory fashion and viewing them as evil or inferior in any biological or ontological sense, but rather a form of heightened racial awareness. If Sartre had been clearer on this point, it might have allowed him to understand how racial consciousness might still exist in the third stage without implying an essentializing racism. Indeed, Eze notes that Sartre has it both ways to the point of self-contradiction—racial consciousness will eventually disappear, but how is not clear, since white racism derives from skin color rather than the position of blacks in the labor process or an economic system.[57] The negative impact of skin color thus seems to be transhistorical and permanent.

A couple of later developments in the dialectic of race and history should also be noted. First, by the 1960s in the United States and in South Africa somewhat later, the thesis in the dialectic was not "white supremacy" but universalism or humanist equality. In many cases, black intellectuals unmasked universalist perspectives as white European hegemonic values, but without supplying any alternative version of universalism to take its place. Though most African American intellectuals who were influenced by negritude or adopted black nationalist perspectives steered clear of a biological essentialism, in emotional terms an antiracist racism was increasingly a temptation as the 1960s proceeded. Again, without a third stage to which the dialectic might lead, a perpetual racial/cultural conflict tended to replace the dialectic pointing leading to historical reconciliation.

The emergence of the concept of "colonialism" in Sartre's thought was also of great significance. What is surprising in surveying the literature of negritude, including Sartre's "Black Orpheus," is the silence about colonialism per se; it seems everywhere assumed but rarely made explicit. This is perhaps due to the fact that the proponents of negritude were primarily men of letters and rarely social or political theorists. Yet, as Sartre and others came to realize, negritude remained primarily a subjective phenomenon, a literary one as it were, while the system within which it arose in and against which it was a sometimes explicit, but always implicit, protest needed a full description and analysis. Though this, it might be said, was just the point of Césaire's contribution to the 1956 Paris Congress, he never fully explored colonialism in his writings. Nor did Sartre's disciples in these matters, Albert Memmi and Frantz Fanon, analyze colonialism empirically as a historical phenomenon so much as they conceptualized it in preparation for such an analysis. Thus, the work of Sartre, Memmi, and Fanon was a kind of propaedeutic to the historical/empirical study of colonialism.

Almost a decade after his "Black Orpheus" essay, Sartre again focused on colonialism, but more analytically, as the title of his 1956 essay asserted: "Colonialism Is a System." Colonialism is not a "series of chance occurrences" or "the statistical result of thousands of individual undertakings."[58] For instance, the psychology of the various roles and positions in the colonial system would need analysis. Individual psychology did not simply reflect the formative experiences of early childhood, but was shaped by the system of roles that one occupies as an adult. According to Sartre, a colonial system creates two fundamental roles: the "native" and the "colonist." Colonialism "fabricates 'natives' by a double movement which separates them from their archaic community" and "creates masses but prevents them from becoming a conscious proletariat."[59] As a result, natives no longer have their own culture as a resource; nor can they act politically with others. But colonialism also does something similar to the European colonizers: "For the colonist is fabricated like the native; he is made by his function and his interests." For example, the ideology of "Algerian nationalism is not simply a revival of ancient traditions; old attachments." The colonist abandons the republicanism of the homeland, though only half realizing it: "Republicans in France . . . they are, in Algeria, fascists who hate the Republic but who passionately love the Republican army."[60] In fact, Sartre might have developed this point about the constructed nature of all ideologies in his discussion of negritude.

Neither negritude nor pan-Africanism was a simple revival of traditional African culture either. They were instead reinterpretations and reconstructions of past traditions by black diasporic intellectuals living in France and thus often alienated from their roots.

The final crucial feature of colonialism as a system was, for Sartre, its violent nature. Violence and terror were not mere side effects of, but integral to, colonialism. Echoing Césaire (and Arendt), Sartre writes in the preface to Fanon's *The Wretched of the Earth* that the violent reaction against colonialism on the part of the colonized is originally

> the settler's but soon they will make it their own; that is to say, the same violence is thrown back upon us as when our reflection comes forward to meet us when we go toward a mirror.[61]

Or as he writes in *The Critique of Dialectical Reason*:

> [T]he colonialist reveals the violence of the native, even in his passivity, as the obvious consequence of his own violence and as its sole justification.[62]

Albert Memmi's *The Colonizer and Colonized* (1957) offered a more nuanced model of colonialism than either Sartre or Fanon did. In his analysis, Memmi develops a complex analytical typology and role psychology and also explains the logic of colonialism as a system. One reason for a certain detachment on Memmi's part was that, as a Tunisian Jew, he was neither fully in the colonizer's camp, since he was not a Christian, nor was he entirely at one with the colonized, since he was part of a religious minority in an overwhelmingly Moslem world and of one that had embraced European culture. Thus, he lacks Sartre's passionate, largely uncritical engagement as a fellow traveler of colonial revolt, but neither is he one of Fanon's wretched of the earth or their ideological spokesmen. For instance, Memmi's analysis of "The Colonizer Who Refuses" identifies the crucial dilemmas encountered by left-wing Europeans living in the colonies. They enjoy the privileges of the ruling minority but support equality; or, as used to be observed about French left-wing intellectuals generally, they live right and vote left. Memmi notes the conceptual/political difficulties that left-wing colonials had in acknowledging the centrality of "nationalism" rather than the class struggle in the ideology of colonial revolt, and they are embarrassed by the crucial role that "terrorism" and "religion" play in that revolt.[63] In other words, to the European sympathizer with the struggle for independence, the ends are recognizably left-wing but the means often seem more akin to those of fascism with its emphasis on the national, even racial, struggle, and on the positive role of violence. What in Europe was presented in universalist terms was in the colonies hitched to particularist goals, something that, as we have seen, Richard Wright realized when he analyzed the Bandung Conference after his visit in 1955.

Memmi's contributions to a theory of colonialism were twofold. Besides being a system, creating new identities for its inhabitants, and having violence at its core, a "consubstantial part of colonialism" is racism, since the colonialist is "unsure of his true nationality" and must rationalize his privileged position.[64] Racism perfectly serves this purpose insofar as it justifies the "gulf between" the two cultures. In other words, colonialism creates, more than it builds on, racist attitudes of the European minority. Second, for Memmi, the colonized has two options—"assimilation" or "revolt."[65] Since the logic of colonialism dictates the impossibility of the former, the only option is to revolt. Memmi's concept of "defensive racism" on the part of the colonized also bears a strong resemblance to Sartre's "anti-racist racism." It is "neither biological nor metaphysical, but social and historical."[66] The colonized "begins by accepting himself as something negative" and then, by reversing the colonizer's judgment, "everything he represents, becomes perfectly positive elements."[67] There is, however, always an element of doubt in the self-assertion of the colonized, since s/he realizes that at some level it is a "reaction" against, and thus remains a function of, the dominant ideology. Finally, concludes Memmi, in a formulation that could have applied as well to the analysis of negritude, the colonized must "cease defining himself through the categories of the colonizer."[68]

While the comparisons between Jews and Blacks generally remain underdeveloped in Sartre's or Fanon's thought, Memmi's short essay "Negritude and Jewishness" of 1968 suggests a way to clarify the situation of the two dominant minorities in the West. He notes that French (unlike English) has only one word, *judaisme*, to encompass three interrelated different ideas: Jewry (*judacité*), the "group of Jewish people"; Judaism (*judaisme*), "the whole of the teaching, institutions, and beliefs of Jewry"; and Jewishness (*judeité*), "the fact or manner of being a Jew."[69] His point is that negritude needs to be broken down into the three similar components—the population, the tradition/ideology, and the collective psychology—in order to help clarify the debate about negritude. Specifically, he suggests that, as black people acquire their own several nations, the idea of negrity (Jewishness), such as proposed in pan-Africanism, will gradually disappear. Moreover, the "still largely negative" nature of negritude, that is, as a critique of the dominant white world, will also tend to disappear,[70] since the positive achievements of black nations will emerge more clearly. Finally, Memmi also suggests the need to distinguish among types (and intensities) of prejudice directed at Jews, blacks, and colonized people generally: "The oppression of the Jews is not the same as that of the black man, nor as that of the colonized nations." But to Memmi, this suggests that the notion of an undifferentiated humanism is untenable insofar as it "neglect"[ed] the "concrete."[71] Finally, Memmi differs sharply from Sartre in insisting that "the differences must be luckily acknowledged"[72] and preserved without abandoning the universalist/humanist ideal.

Within and Beyond Negritude

The theorist of colonial revolt who most clearly embodied and analyzed the complex relationship between negritude and anticolonialism was, of course, Frantz Fanon (1925–1961).[73] It is common to divide his intellectual career into two distinct phases with *Black Skin, White Masks* (1952) dominating the first phase, and *The Wretched of the Earth* (1961) marking the culmination of his second phase. Of the two, *The Wretched of the Earth* exerted a greater influence in the 1960s, both in the Third World and in the United States, but since the mid-1980s *Black Skin, White Masks* has received the bulk of attention. Though linked by the common (Sartrean) notion that the oppressed (however designated) is the creation of the oppressor, there are significant differences between the two books. The focus of *Black Skin, White Masks* clearly falls on individual identity as it emerges in a racialized culture. Fanon's central concern is with how to understand the extremes of self-alienation experienced by individuals of a racial minority, and how self-alienation can be overcome and action may become possible. Significantly, the issue of colonialism as a system scarcely arises in it, although it is clearly part of the background condition for Fanon's analysis of the racialized self. The important exception to this is Fanon's critique in chapter 4 of O. Mannoni's concept of colonialism, which I mentioned in connection with Richard Wright in a previous chapter. The difference in the positions of Mannoni and Fanon might be summed up as follows. According to Mannoni, colonialism triggered a deep dependency complex in the psyches of native peoples, while Fanon believed that colonial domination, imposed by force of arms, created that dependency culture. In his critique, Fanon asks why, if the "colonial situation" is the starting point of Mannoni's analysis, "does he try to make the inferiority complex something that antedates colonization?" The effect of this claim is to place responsibility for the native's supposed "dependency complex" upon a preexisting, indigenous dependency culture rather than upon the French invaders.[74] In the dreams of the natives of Madagascar, 80,000 of whom were killed in the brutal war with the French between 1947 and 1949, Fanon claims that he found not sexual fantasies but fears of their torturers. Finally, by way of concluding his attack on Mannoni, Fanon invokes a variation on Sartre's famous analysis: "[I]t is the racist who creates his inferior."[75]

The Wretched of the Earth is much more focused on group political identity and action in the service of national liberation. Most controversially, Fanon claims there that revolutionary action, specifically violence, possesses a therapeutic, self-cleansing effect, just the reverse of what is assumed in *Black Skin, White Masks*, where a therapeutic effect is what is necessary to free the colonized to act. If *Black Skin, White Masks* is a response to Sartre's *Anti-Semite and Jews*, *The Wretched of the Earth* grows out of Sartre's *Critique of Dialectical Reason*.

Violence and terrorism in Fanon's work are particularly important to consider, not least because they have been de-emphasized in recent discussions, one might almost say "rehabilitations," of Fanon. One way of contrasting his two main texts is to say that where the violence analyzed with such intensity in *White Skin, Black Mask* is located largely within and directed against the unhappy black consciousness, in *The Wretched of the Earth*, violence is politicized and directed against the colonizer, its main purpose or function being the therapeutic impact on the colonized. Much of the irony and sarcasm of *White Skin, Black Masks* derives from this self-lacerating racial consciousness. Fanon agrees with Sartre and Memmi that violence and terror are endemic to colonialism. Indeed, colonial rule *is* institutionalized violence. From this it follows that the counter-violence of the colonized against the colonizer is not only militarily justified but also morally acceptable and psychologically necessary. The Algerian revolution, the struggle with which Fanon was most intimately acquainted, was a particularly violent war, according to Robert Young.[76] Terror—the application of disproportionate violence against civilians taken singly or in small groups and often in crowded urban settings—constituted an integral part of the military strategy of both sides. Just as Fanon claims that violence could have a therapeutic, cleansing effect in helping the colonized overcome their sense of inferiority and in creating solidarity among the freedom fighters, the French Army employed torture not just to gain vital military information, but to destroy the sense of self of the prisoners and to intimidate the colonized population.[77]

But it is also important to note a—or perhaps "the"—crucial characteristic of the theories of colonialism developed by Sartre, Memmi, and Fanon—an emphasis on the *essentially* violent nature of colonialism, the *essentially* racist nature of colonialism, and the *essentially* systematic nature of colonialism. By creating models that stress the fixed nature of colonialism, they seem to detach it from the possibility of change. Faced with a model so resistant to reform, it follows that opposition to the colonial system could justify adopting "any means necessary."[78] The problem with the essentialist model of colonialism is that it has difficulties accounting for the fact that there may be an "outside" or "beyond" colonialism for both colonizers and colonized, and they may even have personal relations with one another. Moreover, it is difficult to make sense of the claim that colonialism stultifies and distorts the indigenous culture in any obvious way.

The extent to which Fanon was himself caught up in the iron logic of anticolonialism is not entirely clear. Certainly he was passionately committed to the cause of Algerian and Third World independence. During the Algerian conflict, Fanon had no qualms about advocating the use of violence as an instrument of policy against the colonizer and their native collaborators. He argued, for instance, that violence

is closely involved in the liquidation of regionalism and of tribalism. The nationalist parties show no pity at all toward the caids and the customary chiefs. Their liquidation is the preliminary to the unification of the people.[79]

Christopher Miller's lapidary gloss on Fanon's words is: "Fanon's response to local resistance is to call out the firing squad."[80] And yet, Fanon himself maintained the integrity of his role as a psychiatrist by treating French and Algerian patients and even members of the French army and of the police. According to his own logic, this should have been politically and morally forbidden. Second, such actions as Fanon recommends were quite common not only in anticolonial struggles, but also in the various resistance movements in Europe under German occupation. Quislings and collaborators were as fair game for resistance fighters against Nazism as complicit tribal chiefs were for Algerian or Vietnamese freedom fighters. If this was a policy of inhumanity and terror, it was not at all foreign to the West. Where the trap closes on Fanon and the advocates of ideological violence on both sides is that, though counterviolence seems to be the most radical gesture imaginable against the systemic violence of colonialism, in fact, its perpetrators remain trapped in the system of violence. "Tit for tat" and "an eye for an eye" tend to escalate rather than reach some appropriate limits. This is particularly corrosive and destructive in situations where conditions of civil war obtain and civilian populations are divided, since violence on both sides makes the prospect of coexistence after the end of hostilities exceedingly difficult.

To understand the way that Fanon linked colonialism and negritude, it is essential to look at his essay, "On National Culture," one of the central chapters in *The Wretched of the Earth*. The chapter itself is forty-three pages long, the last twelve pages of which were delivered at the Second Black Writers and Artists Congress in Rome in 1959, as "The Reciprocal Bases of National Cultures and the Struggles for Liberation."[81] The Rome speech and its longer version in *The Wretched of the Earth* were so significant because in them he abandons cultural pan-Africanism and negritude and casts his lot with the ideology of national liberation as the basis for a national culture, what David Macey refers to as a "nationalism of the will."[82]

To understand Fanon's evolving attitude toward negritude, chapter 5 of *Black Skin, White Mask* ("The Fact of Blackness") must also be examined. There Fanon offers a quick personal history of his involvement with negritude, one that walks a tightrope between high seriousness and high sarcasm. He moves breathlessly from the way "I began to flush with pride" at Senghor's writing about Negro art, embraced the feelings of "bitter brotherhood" and racial pride, and learned from Victor Schoelcher of the glories of the African past.[83] At this point, Fanon recalls that when he read Sartre's "Black Orpheus," he "needed to lose myself completely in negritude." Reading that essay also made him realize that "I *needed* not to know" that "my blackness was only a minor term."[84] But though the occasion for bitter regret, Fanon comes to understand Sartre's claim that Marxism or the universal is the "logical conclusion of Negrohood,"[85] since it becomes a way of escaping from the unsatisfactory alternatives of skin rejection or affirmation. Thus, already in *Black Skin, White Masks*, Fanon all but rejects negritude, grudgingly accepting Sartre's view that it is the transition stage toward the universal. He also wonders what concrete use the (Diopian) knowledge of the glories of the black African past will have in the lives of black people:

Let us be clearly understood. I am convinced that it would be of the greatest interest to be able to have contact with a Negro literature or architecture of the third century before Christ. I should be very happy to know that a correspondence had flourished between some Negro philosopher and Plato. But I can absolutely not see how this fact would change anything in the lives of the eight-year-old children who labor in the cane fields of Martinique or Guadeloupe.[86]

Indeed, a monumental view of the black past leads to a sense of entrapment:

But I as a man of color, to the extent that it becomes possible for me to exist absolutely, do not have the right to lock myself into a world of retroactive reparations.[87]

At the First Congress in Paris, Fanon, on the verge of resigning his position in the psychiatric hospital in Algeria and entering full-time political work, delivered what seems now a fairly unexceptionable address, "Racism and Culture." He notes that the old biological racism "is changing into a cultural racism" with the glorification of "Western values" pitting "Cross against the Crescent," and also echoes Sartre's point about the way colonial domination effectively transforms the indigenous culture of the colony into something "closed, fossilized" and "mummified."[88] More controversially, he asserts that racism should no longer be seen merely "as a disposition of the mind, a psychological flaw" but rather as "structural"; that is, racism is not best understood as the product of an individual or collective psychopathology. In other words, colonialism itself creates racism (and racists), as its form of "inferiorisation" of the indigenous population. Fanon also strikes a blow at French pride by insisting, as did Memmi a year later, that "a colonial country is a racist country" and that "[t]here are no degrees of racism." Nor are there different kinds of racism: "Jewish racism is no different from Negro racism."[89] With these pronouncements, Fanon places France in the same category as the United States, Britain, Belgium, and other colonial powers that were considered more racist than France at the time and in effect formulated an early version of what would be later known as "institutional" racism. There is no evidence that questions were addressed to Fanon's paper and apparently he left just after delivering it.[90]

Finally, as mentioned, Fanon's affirmation of national culture and his rejection of negritude and pan-Africanism were announced in *The Wretched of the Earth*. Even there he acknowledges the drive to show "that a Negro culture exists" and that negritude is "the emotional if not the logical antithesis of that insult that white men flung at humanity."[91] But as the Algerian War escalated and Fanon assumed a directly political role in the struggle, advocates of negritude such as Madagascar's Jacques Rabemananjara and even Senegal's Senghor sided with France against Algerian demands for independence. This suggested to Fanon the complicity of negritude with colonialism or at least its failure to develop a critique of it. It was this specific political failure, his earlier questioning of the effective link between cultural achievement and present oppression and the general tendency of negritude to emphasize skin color over historical and cultural differences that led Fanon to consider the search for an essential African culture "a blind alley."[92]

Rather, what was needed was a commitment to a specific national culture that emerged from the *present* struggle for national independence:

> A national culture is not a folklore, nor an abstract populism that believes it can discover the people's true nature. . . . A national culture is the whole body of efforts made by a people in the sphere of thought to describe, justify, and praise the action through which that people has created itself and keeps itself in existence.[93]

In the context of the armed struggle for independence, an emerging national culture transcends tribe, race, or ethnicity and is inseparable from that struggle. As he develops the analysis elsewhere in *The Wretched of the Earth*, neither the native bourgeoisie nor the struggling proletariat can lead the struggle for national liberation, for they are not socially, politically, or historically in a position to do so. For this reason, it makes little or no sense to see Fanon as a Marxist in *The Wretched of the Earth*, if he ever was one. Thus, *The Wretched of the Earth* not only records Fanon's rejection of negritude as a revolutionary creed; he also abandons Marxism and bourgeois humanism generally. Contra Sartre, negritude is not a transitional stage to color-blind universalism but the stepping stone to a national consciousness and culture that transcends race and ethnicity without dissolving all specificity into an abstract end-of-history where state—and nation—wither away.

In general, then, Fanon sought to escape the older, discredited notions of Western humanism in whose name cultural colonization had been justified. For Fanon, it was not enough, as Robert Bernasconi has pointed out, simply to reverse things and attach the label of humanism to black domination over whites. In both cases, humanism would be "defined against a subhuman other." What was needed was a new humanism that "liberates both colonized and colonizer."[94] It was not just a change in legal or political status, that is, from slave to free or from subject to citizen, but a self-transformation that had to take place, through violence if need be. Thereby both "colonizer" and "colonized" would be destroyed. Once accomplished, a new humanism/universalism that "resides in this decision to bear the burden of the reciprocal relativism of differing cultures, provided only that the colonial status is irrevocably excluded"[95] could emerge. What he envisioned, then, was an acceptance of cultural relativism based on universalist assumptions. Because all humans are of equal worth and status, so too are all human cultures.

Racism and Anti-Semitism

But there is a contradiction in Fanon's thought on the matter of sameness and difference. In *Black Skin, White Masks*, Fanon insists that all racism is the same; that "a given society is either racist or it is not"; and that national, regional, class, or educational distinctions make no difference in judging someone or something to be racist. Indeed, as he asserts in his analysis of Mannoni, the "differences between the anti-Semitism of Maurras and that of Goebbels are imperceptible."[96] In general, then, "All forms of exploitation are identical because all of them are applied against the same 'object': man." He asserts, "Anti-Semitism hits me head-on. . . . I cannot dissociate myself from the future that is proposed for my brother."[97] Yet other places in that same text and in *The Wretched of the Earth*, Fanon emphasizes the differences among racisms and national cultures, potential or actual. His chapter "The Negro and Psychopathology" in *Black Skin, White Masks* notes the differences between the way Jew is seen and the way the Negro is understood, even though he states in "The Fact of Blackness" that "an anti-Semite is inevitably anti-Negro." But in "The Negro and Psychopathology," he claims that while the Jew is "attacked in his religious identity, in his history, in his race, in his relations with his ancestors and with his posterity," it is "in his corporeality that the Negro is attacked. It is as a concrete personality that he is lynched. It is as an actual being that he is a threat."[98] This would suggest that all forms of racial essentialism are not the same, including those of Maurras and Goebbels. Anti-Semitism, as Fanon observes, sees the Jew as an "intellectual danger" while the Negro is a "biological danger," though he adds later that "[b]oth of us stand for evil."[99]

How this apparent contradiction might be resolved is not clear. One might argue that when Fanon posits the identity of all forms of racism, he is advancing an essentially moral argument based on human solidarity— that all racisms are wrong because they degrade or denigrate certain categories of human beings. In that sense, racism is the quintessence of anti-humanism. But when he calls attention to the different forms of racial prejudice, he is calling attention to specific historical, cultural, and psychological differences in the way that hostility to equality is expressed. But it is still not clear that national cultural differences can avoid, for very long, being recast in a hierarchical order, if some idea of universal rights that transcends national rights is not adopted. What prevents a new nation from privileging certain racial, ethnic, or religious groups over the other? (That may have been the basis upon which the struggle was carried on in the first place.) Fanon gives no principled grounds for ruling out particularist commitments as the foundation for a new national culture and no reason to think that racial, ethnic, or religious loyalties will easily be exchanged for universalist commitments.

At least in the United States, negritude's focus on skin color as signifying deep cultural differences has proven more enduring than Fanon's identification of the nation as the carrier of political and moral universalism. Yet, the Senghorian sense of negritude as a coherent, total ideology has also lost its capacity to compel assent. This is due in part to the manifestly mythical or "imaginary" (in the Lacanian sense) nature of the pastoral form of negritude, one that projected "a warm, maternal, security-providing Africa."[100] The title of Abiola Irele's essay, "In Praise of Alienation," captures something of this reaction against negritude. Irele notes that, for Hegel, alienation, the loss of a unified way of life, is not primarily the personal and historical disaster it is often imagined to be. Rather, it is "the moving power of the historical process."[101] Whether Africa could have joined the movement of history at other junctures or even guided it in other directions is another matter, but there is little doubt that Senghor—as opposed to Césaire—posited a unified African sensibility in which the modernist distinction between fact and value or among the aesthetic, the practical, and the cognitive realms had not yet become operational. As a contrast ideal, this vision of an organic society had obvious appeal and provided an often-powerful position from which to critique the modern world shaped by European power. The problem was, and is, that a traditional society and culture cannot be reimagined and then reinvented without considerable violence to historical reality. Yet Fanon's effort to justify a national, rather than a racial or ethnic, culture with the universalist assumption of equality has proven almost as difficult to make a reality in the former colonial world.

10

The Cultural Turn: Rediscovering African American Culture in the 1960s

We must integrate with ourselves.

Larry Neal

You deal as accurately as possible with idiomatic particulars, but you're trying to get the universal implications.

Albert Murray

The 1960s saw something like negritude, or the spirit of negritude, come to the United States. In that decade African American culture was rediscovered—and rethought—after around a quarter century of dormancy. Objectively, of course, the tradition of black thought and culture was always "there." Its *Ur*-text was W. E. B. Du Bois's *The Souls of Black Folk* (1903), and the writers of the Harlem Renaissance laid down many of the central themes and ideas. In the interwar years, anthropologist Melville Herskovits, a former student of Franz Boas, devoted his efforts to exploring the African roots of diasporic cultures in the Western hemisphere, while his one-time assistant, Zora Neale Hurston, collected the folklore of Southern Blacks and of the Caribbean and wove it into the texture of her fictional world.

Indeed, the oft-remarked rediscovery of the local and the regional roots of American culture(s) during the Depression was far from an exclusively "white" concern. Despite the collapse of the Harlem Renaissance by the mid-1930s, African American artists and intellectuals, supported in their efforts by organizations ranging from the New Deal's WPA to the

Communist Party (CPUSA), spent much of the decade exploring the folk sources of African American expressive culture.[1] But as we have seen, some black intellectuals suspected that to emphasize the achievements of that culture was to play into the hands of white supporters of the racial status quo who wanted to avoid political, economic, and social reform. Whatever the case, the idea that African American culture possessed a history and integrity of its own was certainly muted from around 1940 well into the 1960s. If African American cultural self-awareness did not exactly go underground in that period, neither did it publicly flourish in the two and a half decades after the 1930s. Ironically, certain forms of jazz and popular music with a strong black dimension to them spread among the white population, while losing their cultural constituency among African Americans.

Why a heightened black cultural self-consciousness reappeared in the 1960s is not entirely clear. James C. Hall, for instance, names the African American response to the decade as an "antimodern" one by which he refers to the black "sense that American culture was sterile, secular, and disturbingly immune to the tragic lessons of history."[2] This black "counter-statement," as Albert Murray might say, to mainstream, "white" notions of progress was created by the whipsaw effect of increased African American self-assertiveness growing out the successes of the civil rights movement, combined with frustration at the slow pace of change in the wake of those same successes. The result was a flood tide of books by African Americans reviewing and redefining African American culture from almost every perspective. As white critic Richard Gilman noted, this new black writing took its distance from conventional (white) aesthetic and humanistic precepts: "[W]e can no longer talk to black people, or they to us, in the traditional humanistic ways."[3] The point of this new black writing, according to Gilman, was not to make connections across racial lines, much less to transcend color consciousness. It was precisely to strengthen black consciousness by speaking to other people of color rather than protesting to white people about the way blacks had been treated. It seemed to be less and less the case that black and white intellectuals or artists in general shared traditions of judgment or spoke in the same universalist idiom.

In what follows, I want to examine three important, yet quite different moments in this African American cultural turn—Harold Cruse's cultural nationalist *The Crisis of the Negro Intellectual* (1967) and its companion volume, *Rebellion or Revolution* (1968); the emergence of the black arts and black aesthetic movements as set forth in Larry Neal and LeRoi

Jones/Amiri Baraka, eds., *Black Fire* (1968), and Addison Gayle Jr. ed., *The Black Aesthetic* (1971); and the cultural vision of Ralph Ellison's *Shadow and Act* (1964) and Albert Murray's *The Omni-Americans* and *The Hero and the Blues* (1973). These thinkers and others like them reacted against the universalist, largely color-blind assumptions about race and culture that had dominated thinking since World War II. Yet, they were far from agreement with one another. For that reason, I want to explore differences as well as similarities among them, with particular attention to the political indeterminacy of this cultural turn of the 1960s.

Harlem on My Mind

The position that Harold Cruse staked out in the 1960s clearly rejected the modernizers' position, according to which African American culture was either downgraded or to be transcended. At the same time, Cruse's work was a welcome antidote to many of the nationalist polemics of the late 1960s in part because he was just as critical of black intellectuals, and occasionally more so, than he was of white ones. Nor was Cruse afraid to show his critical acuity or knowledge of African American intellectual, literary, and cultural history. His central thesis was that the great failure of the "Negro intellectuals" lay in their unwillingness to forge a coherent vision or philosophy of an autonomous black culture. This had been true of the Harlem Renaissance writers and intellectuals and remained true up to the time of (his) writing.

Cruse's own background remains obscure.[4] He was born in Petersburg, Virginia, in 1916, but spent his formative years in New York City. He had experience in CPUSA circles before World War II and then served in the U.S. Army in England, Algeria, and Italy. After the war, he wrote for *The Daily Worker* and was involved in Party debates on culture and aesthetics in the late 1940s and early 1950s. As head of the Harlem Writers' Club in the late 1940s, he challenged the Party's commitment to the aesthetics of socialist realism, and left the Party in 1953 because it "had no program for American blacks," especially in the realm of cultural policy.[5] In 1960, Cruse visited Cuba in a group that included LeRoi Jones, Julian Mayfield, Sarah Wright, Richard Gibson, Robert F. Williams, and John Henrik Clarke. Yet, rather than being drawn back into the communist orbit, Cruse began developing a radical nationalist position, taught history at Amiri Baraka's (a.k.a. LeRoi Jones) arts projects in Harlem, and wrote occasionally for the new left–oriented *Studies on the Left* and also for black publications such as *The Liberator* and *Black World*. From 1968 until his retirement, he held a post at the University of Michigan.

The phases of Cruse's intellectual development are not entirely clear. No longer a Marxist by the early 1960s, he still wrote with his former comrades very much in mind. E. Franklin Frazier received high praise for his independent-minded analysis of African American life; clearly Cruse's "Negro intellectuals" made up the cultural wing of Frazier's black bourgeoisie. Cruse also lauded Richard Wright for introducing the "national-ist" theme in "Blueprint for Negro Writing" (1937), and defended Ellison's *Invisible Man* against the attacks of CP intellectuals when it first appeared. Though a co-worker with Baraka on Harlem cultural projects, his problem, according to Cruse, was his "hatred of whites" and his com-mitment to a racial ideology that "tends to be narrow."[6] Sociologist and theoretician of the new left C. Wright Mills clearly influenced Cruse's theory of culture; and it is not fanciful to imagine that Cruse wished to do for the black left something analogous to what Mills had done for the white new left in-the-making in the late 1950s—free it from what Mills called "the labor metaphysic" and from the integrationist-assimilationist ethos.[7] For Cruse, the African American left needed to be more than the colored auxiliary of the white left or the ideological vanguard of the civil rights movement.

But the precursor most clearly informing Cruse's work was the proto-nationalist W. E. B. Du Bois of *Dusk of Dawn* (1941) rather than more ob-vious nationalists such as Marcus Garvey or Malcolm X or even the pro-tonationalist, Booker T. Washington. Much of Garvey's message, claimed Cruse, was really aimed at West Indians, while Washington, though call-ing for group economic development, lacked anything like a dynamic vi-sion. Malcolm X had the "nationalist appeal but not the program; Du Bois had the program but not the nationalist appeal." However, Du Bois had come closest to understanding the problem as one of "integration" versus "nationalism," but he "could not interpret his data into new conceptions of social reality."[8] In the argument that led to his departure from the NAACP in the 1930s, Du Bois offered a vision of African American life that transcended what Cruse later called the "non-economic liberalism" of the NAACP and the economism of the assimilationist Communist Party.[9] Whether seen as part of Du Bois's "talented tenth" or as the intellectual wing of Frazier's "black bourgeoisie," black intellectuals had clearly not been doing their job. Cruse's point was not that the black intellectual elite was bad because it was an elite; rather, it was that the black elite had failed to fulfill its proper function of articulating a vision of the African American experience.

Cruse's own version of that experience concentrated, first, on the need for African Americans to organize a black political party and to recast constitutional rights in group rather than individual terms. This was necessary due to the failure of the "integrationist ethic" despite a "Constitution [that] recognizes the rights, privileges and aspirations of the individual." America's "political institutions recognize the reality of ethnic groups only during election contests." As he wrote later in *Crisis*, "the Constitution, as it now stands, does not recognize the legal validity or rights of groups, but only of individuals." In fact, as early as 1960, Cruse was writing that "[e]thnically, America has never been an open society and has never been a 'melting pot' for the races,"[10] a clear anticipation of Daniel P. Moynihan and Nathan Glazer's *Beyond the Melting Pot* (1964). Economically, Cruse echoed Du Bois's call in *Dusk of Dawn* for African Americans to develop their own economic institutions, including cooperatives, and also to encourage private enterprises run by an energetic and talented black bourgeoisie. The major failing of the black middle class, according to Cruse, was its timidity rather than its rapacity.

Above all, black Americans must control the sphere of cultural production and dissemination by "gain[ing] ownership of cultural institutions,"[11] including print and electronic media, publishing houses, and recording companies. Only if black Americans controlled these institutions could they create a group consciousness adequate to the pluralistic realities confronting them. Thus Cruse's thought is based on the fundamental assumption underlying much of the cultural turn of the 1960s—the primacy of the cultural realm in reshaping American life and institutions. Echoing Mills, Cruse notes that "white labor is not going to overthrow" capitalism. For that reason, neither economics in general nor cross-racial political alliances in particular are of highest political priority. Historically and pragmatically, the case for privileging culture over economics or politics was far from absurd, since it was particularly in the area of popular culture that the achievements of African Americans were most striking. Yet, strangely, Cruse could also write that "the American Negro is culturally underdeveloped because America is undemocratic culturally. . . . The Negro has been robbed of his cultural identity in America."[12] However these two claims fit together, Cruse's main point was that black cultural achievement had to be conceptualized, and then, formulated as a coherent tradition.

Not surprisingly, the whole focus of Cruse's work of the 1960s fell on what was unique to black Americans rather than what they shared with white Americans. Imagining himself a cynical Lorraine Hansberry presenting white people with the kind of drama they wanted, Cruse lashed out at the popular universalism of the postwar era: "[W]e'll become what they call human and universal, which in the white folks' lexicon and cultural philosophy means 'universal white.'" To depend on the individual or on universal values to guide social reconstruction was a way of disguising the social and cultural primacy of the group over the individual in America: "'Universality,'" he insisted, "cannot be used to mean the negation of one's own ethnic origins or the art ingredients or the cultural qualities of those origins."[13]

By the 1960s, Cruse had also largely abandoned a class analysis (except when examining the internal structure of the African American community). Instead he advocated a "revolutionary nationalism." Black Americans were "colonial being[s]" and their collective life marked by the problem of "underdevelopment."[14] By 1967, he had dropped the colonial analogy as well. Always trying to think against the grain, Cruse preferred to characterize African Americans as a "nationality" or as an "ethnic group" rather than in racial terms. Not "class warfare," but "disequilibrium in the economic, cultural and political status of ethnic groups" was, he argued, the issue that needed addressing.[15] Cruse explicitly challenged the idea that black Americans should assimilate into the larger white society. The United States was not a nation of individuals but rather a "nation dominated by the social power of groups, classes, in-groups and cliques—both ethnic and religious." It was "a nation of nations."[16] Underlying Cruse's analysis was also the assumption that black Americans were ready to respond to a nationalist message.

But Cruse's indictment of the "Negro intellectual" was accompanied by a vehement attack on white Communist Party intellectuals. Beginning in the early 1930s, they had, he insisted, steadfastly blocked all efforts by black Party members to develop black political or cultural consciousness as a complement to the reigning class orientation of Marxist theory. Specifically, he claimed that the intellectual history of the CPUSA was a history of "Jewish dominance" among Party intellectuals, running from the influence of novelist Mike Gold in the 1930s to that of historian Herbert Aptheker in the 1960s. Over the years, Party organs such as *The Daily Worker* or *The New Masses* had printed numerous articles on Jewish life, Zionism, and related matters, but very few, Cruse charged, on black culture or black identity. To have allowed them to appear in the late 1930s, remembered Cruse, would have been to conjure up "the horrible nationalist spectre of a Garveyite inner-party plot."[17] Further, in his essay "My Jewish Problem and Theirs" (1969), an obvious riposte to Norman Podhoretz's "My Negro Problem—and Ours" (1963), Cruse rejected the idea that American Jews were more sympathetic to black Americans than other white Americans were. Already in *Crisis*, he had emphasized that American Jews of whatever background "have no real problem, political, economic or cultural" in America.[18] Overall, Cruse's work, along with more obvious events such as the Ocean Hill–Brownsville community control controversy and the New Politics Conference of 1967, illustrated and widened the breach between Jewish and African American intellectuals as the 1960s drew to a close.

Cruse was also something of an African American "exceptionalist," in that he doubted that the experience of Afro-Caribbeans or Africans had much political pertinence for African Americans. Garvey's problem with skin color had arisen out of a much different situation in the West Indies where it was more closely correlated with privilege and color demarcations were clearer.[19] There was simply too much color diversity among black Americans for Garvey's color politics to be anything but divisive. Thus, it was not only Jews whom Cruse saw as imposing an alien experience ("the horror of the European Jewish holocaust"[20]) on American realities. The spirit of pan-Africanism was foreign to him, though Cruse later seemed sympathetic to the idea that African Americans had to focus on the importance of black culture in the way that Senghor had done in developing his idea of negritude.[21] Thus, Cruse's position might be described as negritude "in one country."

Cruse's iconoclastic work also contained other nuggets of controversy. He dismissed the idea that violence, whether threatened by Robert Williams in North Carolina or by the Black Panthers in the Bay Area, was revolutionary per se. In Williams's case especially, violence was "defensive," and was quite compatible with an integrationist position. Nor did Cruse wish to identify black nationalism with the hatred of whites, as the Jones/Baraka position seemed to entail. White exclusion from black organizations and movements was justified as a coherent strategy of black advancement, not as an aggressive rejection of inter-racialism.[22] He was, as noted, dismissive of socialist realism as a fusion of "black bourgeois sentiments and left wing ideology." It encouraged, he asserted, "a very prissy, neo-Victorian, pseudo-revolutionary social ethos," and had led critics such as John O. Killens to attack Ellison's *Invisible Man* for not presenting black people as, in Cruse's words, "beautiful, pure people."[23] Figures as different as playwright Lorraine Hansberry and Paul Robeson were scored by Cruse for advocating the integrationist vision and falling prey, in Robeson's case, to "misapplied internationalism."[24] Again and again, Cruse returned to the glaring failure of Negro intellectuals to develop a conceptually sophisticated cultural analysis and vision relevant to their own experience in America.

How does Cruse's work, particularly *Crisis*, look three and a half decades later?[25] One problem is that, for all its insights and bracing critical tone, Cruse's work rarely transcends the level of polemics. It is less a new vision of black American culture than an urgent call for the development of such a vision. It lacks the detailed exploration of positions to be adequate as an intellectual history of modern black America, yet neither does Cruse propose a theoretical model to link the spheres of culture, economics, and politics conceptually rather than on an ad hoc basis. As one critic has noted, Cruse neglects the "corporate" nature of media domination and thus his call for a black takeover of the means of cultural production contains little or no serious institutional analysis. By emphasizing the centrality of culture, Cruse strangely underplays economic and institutional factors.[26] Nor does Cruse ever really propose an aesthetic of his own. An attentive reader might have wondered whether Cruse's nationalist perspective entailed generic, formal, and thematic choices as constricting as the straitjacket imposed by the CP's socialist realist and agitprop aesthetic. In other words, it is far from clear whether Cruse's was a principled objection to political criteria for art or whether he merely opposed the specific terms of ideological correctness advanced by the CP intellectuals and their allies.[27] Overall, Cruse's assumption that there is *a* black cultural philosophy would suggest that there are also certain preferred modes of black aesthetic expression.

Furthermore, though Cruse's shift from a discourse of class and race to one of ethnicity and nationality was refreshing in the 1960s, he—like almost everyone else—failed to clarify the basic categories and the relationship among them. If the categories were religious, as in Will Herberg's Protestant-Catholic-Jew schema, where then did African Americans belong? They were hardly just evangelical Protestants with black skins. If the terms were ethnic—Cruse's WASP, black, Jew—then where did American Catholics belong? And if the groupings were determined by skin color identification—red, white, black—where did Jews belong?

There was something to be said for considering African Americans as an ethnic group rather than describing them in "imaginary" racial terms.[28] But there were problems as well. If black Americans were an ethnic group, their experience contradicted that of all other ethnic groups in the United States, since African Americans had not come to America voluntarily. Indeed, the resistance to black demands from European ethnic groups, that is, so-called "white" ethnics, was much greater than any of these groups expressed toward each other.[29] And in calling African Americans a nationality, Cruse must have been aware that the historical tendency has been for nationalities to "want out," that is, work for self-determination, while in the United States and the Western Hemisphere, with the exception of Quebec, nationalities tend to consider themselves minorities or ethnic groups who "want in" on equal terms. If black Americans wanted out, that hardly squared with Cruse's observation that "the masses of our people have not yet said they want a revolution. They want equal rights."[30] Though Cruse criticized Stokely Carmichael and Charles Hamilton's *Black Power* (1967) as reformist in nature, Cruse's own work vacillates between a radical nationalist vision and a strategy for hard-boiled ethnic politics with a militant patina to it.

A particularly bothersome aspect of Cruse's perspective was his relentless focus on the CP in Harlem in the 1930s and 1940s. For a work that made broad claims about twentieth-century black intellectual and cultural life, Cruse's historical sample was exceedingly narrow. Whatever the difficulties of African American radicalism in this century, Cruse's suggestion that its failure lay largely with what had transpired in cultural debates within the CP in Harlem is strange—to put it mildly.[31] Basically, Cruse raised two separate, though closely related, issues. First, he criticized the refusal of the Party between the 1930s and the 1960s to encourage the development of a black nationalist consciousness; and, second, he specifically charged Jewish Party intellectuals with taking the lead in stifling that development. As background, it is important to keep in mind that between 1928 and 1945, the CPUSA, always responding to Comintern/Cominform dictates, first adopted the policy of black "self-determination." The "Negro Question" was an aspect of the "colonial question" to be addressed by the "black belt nation" thesis of the Party up to the mid-1930s. But beginning with the Popular Front phase in 1935, the CP recast American Negroes as a (national) minority, whose goals now became social and political equality and whose political strategy entailed a black-white working class alliance. With the introduction of the Popular Front policy, focused as it was so exclusively on antifascism, criticisms of Western imperialism were soft-pedaled.[32]

In the postwar years, especially after 1948, the Party crumbled under external anticommunist pressures and from internal tensions, particularly a campaign within the Party against "white chauvinism," which led, according to Joseph Starobin, to "bitter internecine battles." In this period, a somewhat different position on the Negro question emerged. In this view, "national liberation movements" in the Third World "were "replacing the struggle of the working class as a whole as the true revolutionary force." This position represented a kind of throwback to the "black belt nation" idea, though articulated in global rather than regional terms. Clearly, this version of the nationalist position was anathema to Party orthodoxy.[33] As Starobin notes, Cruse's disillusionment with the Party came precisely during the late 1940s when the Party rejected this nationalist position, which Cruse was to later advocate in the 1960s. Overall, then, Cruse's claim that after World War II the black nationalist position was rejected by the Party was broadly true.

But the Jewish issue is much harder to sort out. For one thing, we do not know how many party intellectuals or leaders were Jewish as opposed to gentile and whether they split along ethnic-religious lines. As C. L. R. James observed in 1969: "The Communists have a line that in Switzerland, Albania, in India, in China, in Moscow, in London, in Paris, that has nothing to do with Jews. That is the Stalinist line." Specifically, according to Mark Naison, several somewhat contradictory things must be considered. First, even during the "black belt nation" period, interracialism within the Party was encouraged. Second, Party membership lists from the 1930s fail to indicate ethnic backgrounds; if anything, skin color not ethnicity was the focus. And, third, black nationalists emerged as rivals to the Party in Harlem by 1934. At that time, though there was some talk of the Jew as "neighborhood exploiter," there was no denigration of Jews within the Party.[34]

This situation changed between the mid-1930s and 1942, the period when Cruse was first involved in Party affairs. Contrary to the thrust of Cruse's remarks, Naison emphasizes that, though the Popular Front policy called for interracial and cross-class alliances, the tendency in Harlem was still to encourage interest in African American culture and history.[35] Yet, Naison does note that Jews may have been overrepresented in the Party by the early 1940s. With the rise of Nazism and growth of anti-Semitism at home, not only did the Party begin to pay more attention to combating anti-Semitism, it also stressed the universalist rather than particularist dimensions of its ideology. Some evidence, says Naison, "invokes the image of the Jewish Communist as exploiter," thus indicating that Black-Jewish tensions within the Party had begun to emerge in the prewar period when Cruse had been active in the Party in New York.

All things considered, Cruse's attack on Jewish communist intellectuals still lacks enough evidence to be convincing. Outside the CP, Jewish academics such as Franz Boas and Herskovits were instrumental in encouraging interest in the African roots of black American culture, while Herbert Aptheker, whom Cruse does mention very critically, emphasized the importance of African American history in his master's thesis on Nat Turner and, as already noted, criticized Gunnar Myrdal for omitting slave revolts in his account of the Negro American experience. Even if there were some justification for his charges, as Naison indicates there *might* be, this would scarcely warrant Cruse's making the African American–Jewish conflict the central explanation for the failure of the black left in America. In other words, if Cruse's scope had been more inclusive, the role of Jews as Party intellectuals in Harlem could have been seen from a wider perspective. As Cruse presents the case, Jews were, in familiar (European) fashion, both models for how African Americans should organize and, in Emily Budick's terms, "virtually demonic." Nor could Cruse see that Jewish cultural pluralism in America was not a Zionist as much as it was an assimilationist position.[36]

Overall, Cruse's elevation of the cultural sphere over the economic and political spheres reflected a basic trend of 1960s radicalism.[37] Yet, one of the major shortcomings of Cruse's work was his serious neglect of black Southern folk culture in his vision of African American culture. Since approximately half of black Americans still lived in the historic South as of the 1960s and almost all African Americans originally hailed from the South, the origins of black culture were there rather than in the urban areas of the North. Ellison's *Invisible Man* should have told him that, if nothing else. Moreover, by neglecting the Southern roots of northern black life, Cruse could scarcely explain why Martin Luther King's wing of the civil rights movement garnered so much support, while neither the NAACP nor the Communist Party succeeded in mobilizing black people in either region. The only thing of interest that Cruse found to say about all three organizations was that they were "integrationist" in orientation. But as one critic of Cruse later noted, "integration" can mean quite different things according to whose integrationist position is being considered and in what context.[38] All of this is to say that Cruse missed the chance to analyze how the politics of culture worked itself out in a specific historical instance. Had he done that, it might have suggested that the black Protestant church in the North, along with the nation of Islam, were better placed to mobilize the black population than revolutionary nationalist organizations or a black political party was. Nowhere more than here does Cruse reveal his ideological grounding in the old left's suspicion of religious institutions and movements as reactionary.

Where all this leaves Cruse on the question of African American culture is harder to answer than it might appear. On the one hand, his emphasis in *Crisis* fell not so much on black American culture as on the need for a self-conscious conceptualization of its meaning and purpose(s). Yet until "Negro" intellectuals took up that assignment, he seemed to say, African American culture would remain in a state of confusion, and even underdevelopment, and closer, in some respects, to Myrdal's conception of a derivative black American culture than one might expect. But for Cruse—as for Fanon—it was not a matter of reviving traditional or folk culture as such. Rather, the task of a black intellectual elite, a cultural "talented tenth," was to formulate a new nationalist perspective on that black culture, past and present.

(Black) Nationalist Realism

Ironically, what Cruse had called for in *The Crisis of the Negro Intellectual*—the formulation of a cultural nationalist perspective—was emerging just as his book appeared. On the popular level, the unique qualities of black American culture, many felt, were captured by one term—"soul." An experience, emotion and concept, all in one, soul encompassed the indefinable but recognizable black *Volksgeist*, the spirit infusing black culture, particularly at the popular level. Soul was "all of the unconscious energy of the Black Experience"; the American version of negritude and "the folk equivalent of the black aesthetic."[39] Just when African American intellectuals began to engage specifically with negritude is difficult to say. The *Negro Digest* (later *Black World*), edited by Hoyt Fuller, included a flurry of articles, reports, and symposia on Africa in general and negritude specifically in the mid-1960s. This was partially explained by the pre- and post-event coverage of the First World Festival of Negro Arts in Dakar, Senegal, in April 1966. Indeed, Senghor himself contributed to a roundtable discussion of negritude in May 1965, while other African writers such as Wole Soyinka expressed his view that negritude was more a slogan than a substantive vision. In June 1964, St. Clair Drake published a lengthy article in *Negro Digest* explaining the importance of the American Society of African Culture, a spin-off from the Society of African Culture that grew out of the Paris Congress in 1956. There Drake tried to head off any idea that negritude was based on a "mystique of race or blood" as opposed to "a core of common experiences, a skein of common values, and a common identification which unite 'men of culture of African descent.'" John O. Killens wrote in May 1966 that "Afro-Americans and Africans have a community of experiences vis-à-vis the white man" and, like Drake, avoiding any talk of blood or race as such.[40] Clearly a move was afoot among black American intellectuals not only to cease measuring their culture by "white" standards, but also to expand the reach of black American culture to include its African origins. Overall, the black arts movement, informed by the black aesthetic, was the cultural wing of the black power movement. It sought to conjoin politics and literature, that is, the search for power and a literary aesthetic that would justify that power.

Two collections—Larry Neal and Amiri Baraka's *Black Fire* and Addison Gayle, Jr.'s *The Black Aesthetic*—were central to this project of aesthetic and cultural recuperation. In particular, *Black Fire* reflected the generational dimension of the newly emerging black arts movement, with the majority of its contributors born in the 1930s and 1940s. Though Gayle's volume of essays included twenty-nine and *Black Fire* had seventy-seven contributors (besides essays, poetry, fiction, and drama were included), surprisingly, only four writers contributed to both collections. Moreover, the early 1970s were the last time that this generational conflict could be couched in overwhelmingly male terms and involve men almost exclusively. Two of *The Black Aesthetic*'s contributions and only eight of the seventy-seven contributions in *Black Fire* came from women. The third salient characteristic of the two anthologies followed, at least in part, from the generational and gender bias—the strident, polemical, and often belligerent tone of many of the contributions. It was all bare knuckles and no holds barred. As a one-time academic associate of the black aesthetic group, Houston Baker, Jr., later wrote:

[I]t is now incumbent to read the sixties under the sign "power." . . . Bullet words and paramilitary posturing were read as signs of black "power."[41]

Underpinning the anthologies were three fundamental assumptions. The first was that black writers and intellectuals should no longer be concerned with what white people thought; rather, the black masses should become the main audience for black writing. The day of protest literature addressed to white people was past. The second, more radical assumption challenged both the Du Boisian vision of double consciousness and the goal of an integrated society. As Gayle noted in his "The Function of Black Literature at the Present Time":

> For here we stand, acknowledging those truths we would not admit at the beginning of the twentieth century: that the problem of the color line is insoluble; that the idea of egalitarian America belongs to the trash basket of history, and that the concept of an American melting pot is one to which sane men no longer adhere. In light of such realities, the literature of assimilationism belongs to the period of the dinosaur and the mastodon.

But Larry Neal had already taken aim at the double consciousness when he wrote in *Black Fire* that the "literature of the young has been aimed at the destruction of double-consciousness" and very shrewdly turned the integrationist motif to black purposes when he proposed that "[w]e must integrate with ourselves."[42]

Third, poet Don L. Lee was more specific—and graphic—in spelling out what these abstract pronouncements entailed:

> We must destroy Faulkner, dick, jane and other perpetuators of evil. It's time for DuBois, Nat Turner, and Kwame Nkrumah. As Frantz Fanon points out: destroy the culture and you destroy the people. . . . Black artists are culture stabilizers; bringing back old values, and introducing new ones. Black Art will talk to the people and with the will of the people stop impending "protective custody."[43]

In fact, several salient characteristics of the new nationalist cultural attitude are apparent in Lee's statement—the existence of a trans-Atlantic, cross-cultural tradition of black thought and action; the idea that artists are the prime creators of values; and the belief that art is for the people not for elites.

With these background assumptions in mind, four concerns of the black aesthetic are worth highlighting. First, just as with Cruse, the racial nationalism expressed in the black aesthetic charged that humanism and universalism were really expressions of white Eurocentric values. Wrote John O. Killens: "I am convinced that when Western man speaks of universality, he is referring to an Anglo-Saxon universality, which includes a very meager sector of this young and aging universe." This Western ideology implied, according to Hoyt Fuller, that "to be important, writing must have universal values, universal implications; it cannot deal exclusively with Negro problems."[44] Though some of the black writers still spoke of formulating a new black humanism, Baraka being one of them, most seemed to feel that humanism and universalism had been discredited by Western hypocrisy.

If universal truths of experience were the goal of art in Western aesthetics, the black aesthetic identified "blackness" or "the black experience" as the proper vehicle and content of black art. Black art should immerse or "saturate" (to use Stephen Henderson's term) itself in the black experience. It should, wrote Fuller, "reflect the special character and imperatives of the black experience."[45] But the nature of blackness was not exhausted by the black American experience; rather, as John Henrik Clarke asserted, the African heritage "must be reclaimed if American Negroes in general and Negro writers in particular are ever to be reconciled with their roots."[46] Baraka, undoubtedly the central figure in the development of the black arts movement, wove the African and American experiences together when he described the complex nature of the black American experience, as reflected in black music. Working here from a Herskovitsian perspective, as he had in his *Blues People* (1963), he notes that

> [b]lack music is African in origin, African-American in its totality, its various forms (especially the vocal) show just how the African impulses were redistributed in its expression, and the expression itself became Christianized and post-Christianized.[47]

A complex unity, rather than "double consciousness," was the best way to characterize the black experience in America.

Second, specifically, blackness (or soul) was often essentialized, though rarely biologized. As John O'Neal, one of the most Afrocentric critics, wrote: "Black as a physical fact has little significance. Color, as a cultural, social and political fact, is the most significant fact of our era." Yet, O'Neal finished his article by asserting that "[w]e [Europeans and Africans] come from different blood." However, in *Home* (1966), Jones, contrary to his claims about complex unity, noted that "the Black Man is played on by special forces. His life, from his organs, . . . is different and for this reason racial is biological, finally. We are a different *species*."[48] White racists could not have expressed it more forcefully. On the other hand, Jones, echoing Herskovits, could also argue that whites and blacks differed in terms of body movement and physicality without assuming some deep biological differences: "[A] white man could box like Muhammad Ali, only *after* seeing Muhammad Ali box. He could not initiate that style. It is no description, it is a culture." That is, the differences were cultural and psychological, even spiritual: "[T]he will of expression is spiritual."[49] Once the black style was codified and institutionalized, it could be taught and learned by anyone. Overall, culture trumped biology in the thinking of the black aesthetic movement, though there were slippages here and there and a careless biologism occasionally crept in. It was as though the history of romantic folk organicism was repeating itself— culture was continually slipping over into race; heterogeneous cultural wholes morphed all too easily into homogeneous racial essences.

Third, a third tenet of the black aesthetic, one familiar to those experienced in the cultural/class wars of the 1930s and to those schooled in the history of romantic nationalism, assumed the popular origins and purposes of art. Art is "from the people and for the people," asserted Ron Karenga; the "people" being everything that the "middle class" or "bourgeoisie" was not. The meaning of "bourgeoisie" in black cultural thought was a confusing mixture of Marx, Frazier, and a bohemian contempt for all those hostile to advanced thinking on racial matters. According to Neal, the black aesthetic "speaks directly to black people," and thus rejects "'protest' literature" and avoids what Jones referred to in connection with James Baldwin as "the cry, the spavined whine and plea" for white attention.[50] Finally, the black aesthetic had no truck with either the agonized, alienated modern artist or "l'art pour l'art" allegedly so central to European aesthetics. The artist wrote (or painted or composed) within and on behalf of the black community rather than beyond and against it.

Specifically, art should serve two primary purposes. According to Karenga, art "must reflect and support the Black Revolution."[51] Just as importantly, art should correct the distorted black image that the white world has imposed on the black people. Besides overcoming double consciousness, Killens also wondered, "Who will uninvent the Negro?" One way to do this, he suggested, was to find or develop "our own myths and legends to regain our lost self-esteem."[52] It was in this connection that the recently assassinated (February 1965) Malcolm X played such a crucial role for black intellectuals. Larry Neal spoke for many when he wrote:

> We feel a Malcolm in a way that a Roy Wilkins, a King, and a Whitney Young can never be felt. Because a Malcolm, finally interprets the emotional history of his people better than the others. . . . He was the conscience of Black America."

For Addison Gayle, Malcolm was the "first acknowledged prophet of our era to preach the moral decadence of Western Civilization," while Carolyn Gerald described Malcolm in a special issue of *Black Digest* in 1969 as "the epic hero of our struggle. . . . His significance, far more than histori- cal, is mythological."[53] It was this expressed need for a monumentalist aesthetic, one which apotheosized black heroes as embodiments of the people's will, that explains why many black intellectuals reacted with such outrage against William Styron's critical modernist portrait of Nat Turner in *The Confessions of Nat Turner* (1967). Overall, the black aesthetic functioned as a kind of group therapeutics, its main purpose being that of transforming individual selves and reconciling them with a community primed for revolutionary action.

But of course there were villains in the epic black struggle for a new consciousness. On the black side, there were so-called "Negroes" who had not yet become "black" and remained part of the "bourgeoisie." Two other terms of opprobrium, especially for Baraka, were "faggot" and "pervert." Because the white "attitude toward sex in general is diseased," association with white people led to "a softening of the black man and woman." The dominant theme of Eldridge Cleaver's brutal polemic against James Baldwin in *Soul on Ice* had to do with the close connection that Cleaver detected between Baldwin's homosexuality and his alleged desire to be white and/or to curry favor with the white world. In this whole area, Baraka and Cleaver expressed a kind of racialized Reichian vision, de- rived in part from Mailer's "The White Negro," in which robust, male het- erosexuality becomes an index of the natural and the authentic. Perversion, then, was a political as well as a sexual and psychological category.[54] White people were also regularly excoriated as "beasts" or "devils" or, more familiarly, as "crackers," while white men were often referred to as "boys." White "liberals" were the all-purpose whipping boys, the quin- tessential trimmers who wanted somehow to preserve their position, while advocating token changes for black people. The heroic epic of the emergence of black consciousness was actually a melodrama in which the conflict between black and white was literally a white and black one.

Fourth, black art was also defined by certain formal and aesthetic qualities. The prime mode of black American expression, most thought, was music. As Neal saw it, "The key is in the music. Our music has always been far ahead of our literature," a judgment echoed by Ron Wellburn's "Our music is the foremost expressive quality of our being." Thus, although the Du Bois of double consciousness was rejected, the Du Bois who identified black music as the only creative gift that America offered to the world, was reaffirmed.[55] Of particular interest in this context was the deep ambivalence toward both sacred and secular Southern music, that is, toward the spirituals and the blues among cultural nationalists. Peter Labrie brought a much-needed historical and sociological perspective to the discussion when he identified "a large rapidly growing black population who are indigenous to city life." They "have had no direct contact with the rural South," particularly with the "belief structure" of both the black church and the white Southern power elite. Calvin Hernton echoed Richard Wright, with a Fanonist (or perhaps Maileresque) inflection to his analysis, when he described young blacks "possessed with the psychology of the damned." They are produced in "the ghettos in the big cities of the South and the North" with the potential to become the "dynamos of oppression" or "the volcanoes of liberation." These young people, Hernton concluded ominously, "shall be gods, answerable to no one."[56] Clearly, the art of the black ghetto would be very different from that which had been produced in the South.

More provocatively, Ron Karenga went so far as to assert that "we say the blues are invalid" now; they are "not functional" in the political and cultural struggle, though they once may have been. Writing in a little magazine, *Nommo*, in 1969, Don L. Lee concurred:

we ain't blue, we're black.
(all the blues did was
make me cry)[57]

This negative judgment of the blues had already been voiced by Clay, the black character in LeRoi Jones's *The Dutchman* (1964), when he explodes at Lulu, the white woman on the subway who taunts him about his sexuality and the authenticity of his blackness: "If Bessie Smith had killed a few white people, she wouldn't have had to sing the blues."[58] In this view, then, the older Southern blues culture had substituted musical expression for collective political action, passivity for actual resistance, and bemoaning one's fate for changing one's condition.

This view was far from universally shared by the intellectuals involved in the black arts movement. Baraka at his most militant would hardly have bought the dismissive judgment of his character Clay. It was left to Larry Neal directly to address Karenga's "sincere but misguided statements about the blues" as "teaching resignation." On the contrary, Neal claims, they are the "blackest part of the Black Man's voice."[59] Finally, Baraka posited an underlying spirit or essence to all African American music. What unites African American musical expression is "the deepest feel of spirit worship." Indeed, the "differences between rhythm and blues and the so-called new music or art jazz . . . are artificial, or they are merely indicative of the different placement of the spirit."[60] Once again the existence of a unified black soul kept apparently disparate artistic expressions from losing touch with one another.

But the other source of black cultural unity, particularly in music, was Africa. Ortiz Walton traced the differences between white and black music in America to the distinctive heritage brought from Africa. He noted that, historically, European music had been highly rationalized, fixed, and specialized in performance via a notational system. This made it (somehow) more easily exploitable by "capitalistic commercial endeavor." By contrast, the African aesthetic was grounded in "improvisation," emphasized the "functional and the collective," and assumed the necessity of group participation.[61] Somewhat analogously, Jimmy Stewart identified "two distinctive aesthetic traditions" in America, while granting that there had been "considerable borrowing" back and forth between them. For Stewart, the black approach to creativity assumed that "the creative process [is] a movement *with* existence," while "white cultural art forms" are somehow contrary to the nature of things. Crucial in the white aesthetic is "the thing," while in the black aesthetic it is "the procedure" or the process that is central.[62] Overall, the nature of the binary opposition between black and white music was clear. Wherever the provenance of the two kinds of music, the binary oppositions always fell out the same.

Finally, there was an institutional dimension to the black aesthetic that clearly echoed Cruse's concerns and built on the charges leveled by the black critics of William Styron's *The Confessions of Nat Turner*. Darwin Turner explored the problems that black writers had with getting published, and noted particularly the underdeveloped state of black literary criticism. Ron Wellburn insisted that black people should be "protecting black music and culture" not merely "defending it."[63] Writing in *The Liberator*, Walter Lowenfels radicalized the analysis by contending that all this was "part of a genocidal attack on nonwhite people" and thus "not solely a literary affair." James Emanuel, one of the most thoughtful contributors to either volume observed that there was "racism in the literary establishment," which included critics, commercial publishing houses, and university presses. Emanuel did note that African Americans had "the burden of discovering and preserving" their literary culture rather than continually blaming whites for neglecting it.[64]

Finally, contributors to both volumes insisted that it was time to abandon the European canon of authors and criteria of aesthetic judgment and replace them with writers and standards more attuned to the black experience. Indeed, Gayle took the issue of the black versus white (European) aesthetic literally by unpacking one of the West's master tropes—light versus dark. In doing so, he pointed to the way that, culturally, "light" has been valorized over "dark" and enlisted Nietzsche, the modernist West's great deconstructor of morality, to justify the call for "a new table of laws."[65] Ultimately, the black aesthetic implied a new black ethics and politics, indeed a new black ontology.

Even on its own terms, the formulation of the black aesthetic raised as many questions as it answered. Similarly to Cruse, its formulators posited a uniform black experience from which a single black aesthetic could be forged. Those who dissented from it were branded as traitors or insufficiently militant rather than as speaking, for instance, from a different social or position or historical vantage point. This pointed to the lack of a structural explanation for differences in vision and value in the new cultural nationalist ideology. The only oppression that counted was racial oppression; the only structures that divided people were racial structures and assumptions. Race was reified and mystified in both directions. White people had the mysterious power to sap strength and pervert natural impulses; in fact, contact with white culture created a kind of black cultural pathology rather than enriching black life as Frazier and Wright had hoped.

Still, there was nothing any more dubious about the call for a black aesthetic and a black arts movement than there had been, as Gayle himself noted, in the efforts of Ralph Waldo Emerson and other white writers of the nineteenth century to develop peculiarly American modes of cultural expression. Both were species of romantic cultural nationalism.[66] But there was a definite tension within the new black nationalism between the

call for a transvaluation of all cultural and aesthetic values and the populist desire for a new, more accessible art. There were, perhaps, ways to
reconcile the two impulses, as in Fanon's idea of a transformation of values arising from a popular revolutionary movement. But the tension was
very much present in practice, since there was as much thinking *for* as
from the people in the various essays collected in the two anthologies.

There were other problems. Some contributors focused on the open-
ended, improvisational nature of black art, particularly in music and poetry. It was generally accepted in black aesthetic circles that (white)
European art was incapable of developing a less constricted, more open-
ended style. Yet the evidence hardly supported this claim. The prenation-
alist LeRoi Jones clearly acknowledged the Beats along with poets such
as Charles Olson and Robert Creeley, Federico Garcia Lorca, William
Carlos Williams, and Ezra Pound as figures who had helped open up his
poetry. As Jones wrote in 1959: "The only 'recognizable tradition' a poet
need follow is himself." The only use of tradition is to "broaden his own
voice."[67] Since it would be difficult to maintain that the formal qualities
of Jones's poetry changed radically after his transformation into a nationalist poet and polemicist, one can only conclude that the open-ended and
improvisational quality of his poetry was inspired as much by the (white)
modernists as by an aesthetic derived from African American culture.
Pound's famous modernist injunction to "make it new" was hardly a plea
for formal orthodoxy. Indeed, it was just the experimental quality of much
modernist writing that made it often seem so difficult.

This in turn points to another tension within the black aesthetic. In the
Anglophone tradition, political art has tended to deploy straightforward,
formulaic modes of expression, at their clearest in propaganda and agitprop, a kind of kitsch realism. If the art championed by the black aesthetic
were to be politically effective, its experimental nature would, arguably,
need to be minimized. But, as even Jones noted, postwar avant-garde jazz,
in its effort to avoid too-easy assimilation and popularization, turned away
from the "people" and became coterie music. In doing so, it drew upon
certain traditions of avant-garde European music and appealed to highly
educated audiences. Such music was no longer "functional"; no one could
dance to it any longer.[68] Thus, the most innovative music issuing from the
black community was hardly very accessible or popular—and increasingly
less so. Thus, posing an opposition between closed and open structures in
all art forms raised as many problems as it solved. No clear implications
about the political uses of art seemed to follow from the contrast. In fact,

it was hardly tenable to neatly distinguish African and European modes of music in a situation of such cultural hybridity.

Overall, many of these problems seemed derived from the trap of binary oppositions. Once a binary was set up—and the style of thought adopted by many of these nationalist intellectuals was nothing if not dualistic: the tendency was for characteristics once rejected as stereotypical to reemerge as positive virtues. At various points in the two anthologies, African Americans are described as uniquely musical or soulful, spiritual, or sensual; less up-tight and repressed than whites; possessing a communal spirit rather than plagued by anomie and rampant individualism. All in all, the black pole of the binary usually ends by expressing the modernist protest against modernity—the attempt to abolish alienation and its African American counterpart, double consciousness.[69] Behind the protest against modernity was the desire to efface the differences between politics and aesthetics, public and private, and the whole modern separation of realms. But for the most part, the black aesthetic really only inverted rather than transcended the "white" aesthetic and thus remained trapped within the existing (Western) binaries.

What is also obvious in retrospect is that the approved forms of aesthetic (or moral) expression had narrowed rather than broadened by the late 1960s. The macho swagger and bluster marking the pronouncements of Baraka drowned out his own (and others') sense of humor and even self-mockery. His voice became a shout or yell. He and his supporters made frequent use of profanity, as though it were an adequate substitute for articulate outrage or anger. The smoothness of the "soul" sensibility at its best was hard to find in the writings of the black aestheticians. Indeed, much of what was attractive about the artistic and cultural styles of black Americans was jettisoned rather than embraced.

All this leads back to the issue of the stereotyping of the white "other," the ritualized insult delivered against all sorts and types of whites. Such ritualized rhetoric reflected and encouraged a laziness of thought and feeling and quickly descended to the most morally disreputable dimension of the Western tradition, resurrecting the "Jew" and the "fag" as the principal figures of opprobrium. This is not to say that other white ethnics, particularly the Irish and Italians, avoided Baraka's rhetorical wrath; or that he didn't also use the term "nigger" with numbing frequency. But lines such as "dagger poems in the slimy bellies/of the owner-jews" or "Another bad poem crackling/steel knuckles in a jewlady's mouth/Poem scream poison gas on beasts in green berets" simply cut too close to the moral and historical bone.[70] Even now, it is difficult to know how to react to such lines, except to be dumbstruck by the moral vulgarity and the coarseness of spirit informing them.[71] What was dangerous about Baraka's lines was that they *did* function as blows, as he hoped his poetry would. They were examples of language as action rather than argumentation or imagination. As part of the modern literature of insult and the pornography of poetic-political violence, his writings were, if anything, more pernicious than the anti-Semitic utterances of Eliot or Pound, since he was quite conscious of the historical reality that these images inevitably conjure up.[72]

Later (in 1980), Jones/Baraka repudiated and tried to explain the anti-Semitism of his poetry and prose of the late 1960s and early 1970s. He described his own experience growing up in Newark and then as a young poet in New York: the strong influence of Allen Ginsberg, both a Jew and a homosexual; his marriage to Hettie Cohen, a Jewish woman whom he divorced after the assassination of Malcolm X; and the political ideology of extreme Muslim groups and general anti-Zionist opinion. Surprisingly, he directly links anti-Semitism with black nationalism: "Anti-Semitism grew in the Black Liberation Movement as we moved further into cultural nationalism." Baraka insisted throughout the article that it was primarily white people he hated; it was as though Jews were not only white; they were hyper-white, the very quintessence of the whiteness he came to detest. As he concluded: "I did not think I hated specific Jews"; it was "momentary and never completely real."[73] Thus, we have a mixture of candid analysis and the standard clichés of the repentant bigot.

It would be wrong, however, to identify the entire black arts movement with Baraka's views. But few who later sought to take the measure of that movement ever addressed the issue of Jones's anti-Semitism or his gay "bashing" very directly. (Baraka has not, as far as I know, ever recanted his antigay sentiments.) By "address" I do not mean "apologize for," so much as I mean "discuss" its source and function in Baraka's thought in particular or in black cultural nationalism generally. For instance, deriving from a black American culture—and I would stress the "American" as much as the "black" part here—in which the life of the mind and high art have been associated with effeminacy, it is not surprising that Baraka and his associates picked out the people of the book and the sexually deviant— here one thinks of the relatively large number of gay writers among the leading members of the Harlem Renaissance—as the enemies. Age, class, sexual preference, ideology, and culture all conspired together to produce the enemy.

A critique of the anti-Semitic and antigay tendencies of black nationalism might also derive these tendencies from the cult of power and violence
at the heart of the black power sensibility. This is not to deny that black
Americans needed political and cultural power, then or now. But the obsession with power in the late 1960s became an end in itself and equated
with violence. It became the way to anneal the deep ontological hurt suffered by African Americans. The irony is that Baraka recapitulated all the
worst forms of thinking manifested in fascism, Nazism, and racism, the
political, moral, and cultural pathologies developed to the highest pitch in
the modern world. He was never more a man of the West, never more a
"good European," never more ideological and closed off from experience,
than when he fulminated against Jews and "fags."

There were some contributors to *The Black Aesthetic* who combined effective critiques of white culture and the American literary/cultural complex with powerful doses of self-examination. James Emanuel, for instance, characterized the siege mentality informing the new cultural
nationalism as the result of "enforced inbreeding of beleaguered minds
(literary ones included), emotionalized by desperation" and expressive of
a "repressive provincialism."[74] He, like Darwin Turner, cautioned against
the dismissal of all black literary precursors as dupes or fools. That warning was justified, for what is striking about the contributions to both *Black
Fire* and *The Black Aesthetic* is the apparent lack of any intimate knowledge of black American literary or intellectual history, not to mention the
Francophone tradition of negritude. Though short selections from Alain
Locke, Langston Hughes, W. E. B. Du Bois, and Richard Wright, among
others, are included in the anthologies, it is impossible to put together a
coherent picture of the Harlem Renaissance or to understand the importance of Wright or Hughes, Baldwin or Ellison from any single essay or
all of them taken together. This is understandable for a generation reacting against its precursors and trying to create a space in which its own
voices could emerge. But the ironic effect was to reinforce the conventional wisdom that there was hardly any black literary or cultural tradition
to be revived.

Already in 1962 before his nationalist phase, LeRoi Jones described
Jean Toomer, Wright, Ellison, and Baldwin as barely approaching the
standards of white middle-class fiction, while later in 1970 Addison Gayle
dismissed Ellison, Baldwin, and James Weldon Johnson as part of the literature of assimilation rather than pioneers of nationalist consciousness.[75]
But it was, again, left to Larry Neal to provide some perspective on the

matter. Despite the political differences between most black radicals and Ellison at the time, Neal generously acknowledged Ellison's pioneering role in putting readers and writers in touch with the wealth of black folklore. As Neal noted, Ellison was one of those black writers who had urged blacks to "learn the meaning of the myths and symbols which abound among the Negro masses" long before it became fashionable.[76] Only Dudley Randall's sketch of three decades of black poetry in *The Black Aesthetic* offered more than a nod toward black American literary history, while of new developments in African American historiography, there was scarcely a word.

Even less explicable, since it involved nonliterary forms of black expression, was the failure to engage with, much less discuss, the rich tradition of African American visual arts. The painting of Horace Pippin, Aaron Douglas, Jacob Lawrence, William Johnson, Romare Bearden, and Beauford Delaney, to name a few, constituted a rich tradition that was both accessible to "the people" and visually sophisticated in a stylized modernist way. Whole swatches of African American music, including a coherent account of the history of jazz, went practically unmentioned, though perhaps Jones's *Blues People,* written prior to his nationalist phase, might count in a pinch. And though the editors and contributors of *Black Fire* and *The Black Aesthetic* can hardly be blamed for not anticipating the explosion of African American women's writing in the early 1970s, much less the rediscovery of Zora Neale Hurston and the other women writers of the Harlem Renaissance, the overwhelming tone and mood of the new nationalist realism, was, as I have tried to indicate, resolutely masculine, even macho.

Undoubtedly, much of what the black aesthetic/black arts movement undertook needed doing. Insofar as it moved beyond previous black forms of expression, it was a valuable movement. But insofar as it stressed the argument with others to the exclusion of the argument with themselves, emphasized race as such rather than shared racial experience, it may have delayed, as much as it furthered, the re-emergence of a vital African American cultural tradition.

South toward Home

If James Baldwin was the best-known black American writer by the mid-1960s, Ralph Ellison (1914–1994) was the most highly regarded by critics, primarily for his novel, *Invisible Man* (1952), and his book of essays,

Shadow and Act (1964). His close friend, Albert Murray, like Ellison a one-time student at Tuskegee, had a career in the Air Force behind him when he published his first book, *The Omni-Americans,* in 1971. Taken together, the two men developed a powerful vision incorporating the African American experience into America's democratic culture. They were, as Henry Louis Gates has observed, "part of a single project," one that placed the black (or Ellison would have said "Negro") experience at the heart of the American experience. For both men, claims Gates, "America, roughly speaking, means 'black.'"[77]

Ellison and Murray also belong, albeit uneasily, in the African American literary/intellectual tradition of Du Bois, Locke, Sterling Brown, and Hurston, although the two friends hardly acknowledged the authority or influence of these somewhat older figures. In 1941, Ellison, still in the left-wing orbit of the *New Masses,* spoke harshly of the Harlem Renaissance's "exoticism and narrow Negro middle class ideals." Murray, much later, suggested that the Renaissance figures were too much the supplicants of white tastemakers and financial patrons: "I didn't find any of those writers to be at the depth I required at the time." To Murray, the Harlem Renaissance writers simply didn't match up to the best of the European modernists. Locke's anthology of the Harlem Renaissance, Murray later claimed, "was sandlot stuff compared with Eliot, Pound, Mann, [Proust] and Joyce."[78] Nor did either man show much interest in the African origins of black American culture. Like Harold Cruse, Ellison and Murray were Negro American exceptionalists, always working in the American grain and with little more than a casual public interest in Africa or the Caribbean.

Considering his long-standing interest in African American folklore, Ellison's dismissal of Hurston's work in 1941 for "ignoring the folk source of all vital American Negro art" and for being addressed to a "white audience" seems wrongheaded. Her work, he wrote, "retains the blight of calculated burlesque that has marred most of her writing."[79] Hurston, even then, was marching to a different drummer, including an ample use of dialect in her writing. Gender politics may also have played a role; and Hurston's association with the Harlem Renaissance and the fact that she enjoyed white patronage may have made her seem an insider to challenge rather than a colleague from whom Ellison might learn something.

Yet, Hurston's work anticipated no other writers so much as it did Ellison and Murray. All three emphasized the richness of African American folklore and reflected its importance in their fiction. None was politically predictable, certainly not according to left-wing and/or nationalist ideological standards. And all three rejected what Hurston called the "sobbing school of Negrohood" and the social scientific emphasis on black victimhood. Indeed, Hurston's objections in *Dust Tracks in a Road* (1942) to the view that "black lives are only defensive reactions to white actions" anticipated Ellison's remarkably similar rejection of Myrdal's view of black culture. If Hurston's self-dramatizing and insouciant personal style was too much for Ellison, who tended to take himself awfully seriously, the exuberant, outgoing, and dapper Murray style was not a million miles away from Hurston's. Hurston's focus on black folklore also encompassed the religious dimension of black folk life, an aspect of which neither Ellison nor Murray paid much attention. In the black folk tales that Hurston "transcribed," God often appeared as a not very bright white man, often a slave owner, while blacks were depicted as wily and gullible. As with Jewish humor, it was never clear whether one should laugh or cry in response. With her work, as with Sterling Brown's, who made ample use of African American blues forms in combination with Euro-American poetic traditions, it is easy to confuse what Henry Louis Gates Jr. refers to as the "simplicity" of the black folk tale and dialect poetry (at its best) with "simplemindedness," gaiety and high spirits with emotional shallowness and lack of irony. Still, it remains a puzzle—and something of a minor literary tragedy—that Hurston simply never elicited the sympathy or respect of Ellison or Murray.[80]

Despite very conscious attempts to shape their own literary genealogies, Ellison and Murray belong in a recognizable tradition that saw African American culture as rich rather than impoverished, and adaptive and creative rather than merely pathological. Ellison's by now oft-quoted question (from 1944 but not published until 1964) could have been asked by any of them:

> But can a people (its faith in an idealized American Creed notwithstanding) live and develop for over three hundred years simply by *reacting*? Are American Negroes simply the creation of white men, or have they at least helped create themselves out of what they found around them?[81]

What differentiated this view from the efforts of Cruse or the black cultural nationalists was the deceptively simple belief that a "good enough" black American culture and cultural self-awareness existed already. No new ideological or conceptual framework needed formulation; nor did American Negro culture need cleansing of white and/or bourgeois impurities. The main task, Ellison and Murray seemed to be saying, was to call attention to the existence of a black "vernacular" tradition, which was also part of the general American democratic culture.

For them, an intimate acquaintance with Negro American culture revealed not an ontology of blackness, but a mixture of European and American, black, white, and red cultures undergirded by universal archetypes. Hybridity was just one sign of its "democratic" nature. Murray expressed this view most forcefully in *The Omni-Americans* (1971) when he called America a "nation of multicolored peoples," for whom the problem is not "ethnic differences" but the "intrusion of such differences into areas where they do not belong." Put another way, America was a "mulatto culture;" and all Americans were "omni-Americans . . . part Yankee, part backwoodsman and Indian, and part Negro."[82] This was in many ways classic American cultural pluralism, *e pluribus unum*, with an African American rather than Jewish inflection.

But though the two men stressed the overarching importance of an American democratic culture, they never denied that black Americans possessed a specific, even distinctive, repertory of cultural forms, motifs, and traits. Ellison identified the dominant characteristics of "American Negro Culture" as

> a body of folklore, in the musical forms of the spirituals, blues, and jazz; an idiomatic version of American speech (especially in the southern United States); a cuisine, a body of dance forms, and even a dramaturgy. . . . Some Negro preachers are great showmen.

Still, Ellison emphasized that Negro culture was ultimately part of a larger, more inclusive entity:

> Nor should the existence of a specifically "Negro" idiom in any way be confused with the vague, racist terms "white culture" or "black culture"; rather it is a matter of diversity within unity.[83]

Finally, this hybrid American culture was informed by something that sounded much like Myrdal's "American Creed": the "moral imperatives . . . implicit in the Declaration of Independence, the Constitution and the Bill of Rights" that stood at the center of the "consciousness and conscience" of the classic American writers. Unacknowledged political philosophers for the nation, these writers united public and private, individual and collective, by "inform[ing] our language and conduct with public meaning, . . . they provide the broadest frame of reference for our most private dramas."[84] Overall, then, the Ellison-Murray position reinstated the universalist vision jettisoned by Cruse and the black cultural nationalists, but articulated it through black vernacular culture. All this was a delicate balancing act, an exercise in having it both ways, because both ways were needed. As Murray later observed: "You deal as accurately as possible with the idiomatic particulars, but you're trying to get the universal implications."[85] The great wager of their work taken together was that you could get "there" from "here."

Another fundamental difference separating Ellison and Murray from Cruse and the black arts group arose from the former two men's emphasis on the Southern origins of black American culture. (Murray was from the Mobile Bay area, while Ellison was from the southwestern frontier of Oklahoma, though his ancestors came from the Carolinas.) In fact, not long before his death, Ellison observed:

> My grandparents were slaves. See how short a time it's been? I grew up reading Twain and then, after all those Aunt Jemima roles, those Stepin Fetchit roles, roles with their own subtleties, here comes this voice from Mississippi. It just goes to show that you can't be southern without being black, and you can't be a black southerner without being white. Think of LBJ. Think of Hugo Black.[86]

Contrary to Ron Karenga, Ellison and Murray saw the "blues genre or idiom"—for them, a whole way of being and not just a kind of music—as a creative response to slavery and Jim Crow rather than a form of acquiescence. The blues idiom is not, insists Murray, a "crude, simple-minded expression of frustration and despair" but a way "to make human existence meaningful" through "confrontation" with, and "improvisation" upon, experience. The move from folk cultural to popular cultural and then to high cultural forms is a process of "extension, elaboration and refinement of the vernacular into a higher level." Each level has its appropriate strengths and weaknesses, though finally "fine art is the ultimate extension, elaboration, and refinement of the fundamental rituals" of a people.[87]

Art derives, according to Murray, from two sources. It is, first of all, the "stylization" of the experience of the artist and of a "given group of people."[88] Yet each work of art is also a "counter statement" to previous works of art. For those reasons alone, no art is really "realistic" or "naturalistic." Overall, the aesthetics of confrontation, improvisation, and stylization can be understood in the following way:

> [W]hat makes a blues idiom musician is not the ability to express *raw emotion* . . . but rather the mastery of elements of esthetics peculiar to U. S. Negro music. . . . [Blues musicians] derive most directly from styles of other musicians . . . whose *"primitiveness"* is to be found not so much in the *directness* of their expression as in their pronounced emphasis upon stylization.[89]

But art is also more than just stylized expression or counterexpression. Murray echoes J. O. Killens in emphasizing the "epic" dimension of art. Its function is to tell stories about the "exploits of epic heroes" not to retail "case histories" rehearsing individual and collective victimhood; it should "provide a basis of action" not "produc[e] guilt" in the manner of a Wright or a Baldwin.[90] The most effective and powerful art draws upon underlying archetypal patterns such as the "myth of the birth and death of the hero" or archetypal figures such as the "trickster." Murray's own dismissal of Styron's *The Confessions of Nat Turner* focused on the way Styron took a black "epic hero" and turned him into a "White man's Negro (specifically, Mister Stanley Elkins's) Sambo." In Styron's version, Nat Turner was a sexual neurotic, not a freedom fighter.[91]

Two things are of particular interest here. First, there is the contrast that Murray posits between stylization and the primitive, an observation that helps illuminate much twentieth-century African American art, based as much of it is on the high stylization of the black folk experience. The second thing is that the universalist vision of Ellison and Murray takes, paradoxically, a romantic form. It stresses not shared rationality or rights, but common human participation, across cultures and particular groupings, in universal patterns of feeling and of action, grounded in the unconscious and articulated through myth and art. "Every hero in every story," asserts Murray, "is nothing if not a symbolic individual. . . . He may be inadequate for his mission, of course, but even so he represents mankind."[92] Thus, all particularistic art is at the same time grounded in universal motifs and patterns.

Overall, for Ellison and Murray, art ultimately should serve as a way of reintegrating the individual into the group. Nothing if not modernist in their explicit choice of literary precursors—Malraux, Mann, Hemingway, and Faulkner, to name the most prominent—the political and social role they attributed to art was quite at odds with the modernist tradition of alienated art and artists. Though this would seem to put Murray and Ellison in the same camp with the formulators of the black aesthetic, neither Ellison nor Murray assigned to art a revolutionary or nationalist role. Whatever role artistic expression plays in reacquainting African Americans with their own cultural roots, it should, according to Ellison particularly, strengthen the already existing, but always imperfect, democratic culture of the United States.

In that sense at least, and contrary to their own rhetoric, Ellison and Murray were thoroughly political writers, even though in the early 1960s Ellison sought, in a famous riposte to Irving Howe, to distinguish art as a "public gesture" from art as a "political" gesture, a distinction without much of a difference to it, unless Ellison meant to equate "political" with a specific party line or political ideology. Subtler was Ellison's claim that "protest is an element of all art, though it does not necessarily take the form of speaking for a political or social program." Still, it is hard to square Ellison's general rejection of art's political dimension with his explicit claim that literature should revitalize "the mood of personal moral responsibility for democracy which typified the best of our nineteenth-century fiction" and thus strengthen the democratic culture of possibility.[93] Nor was this merely an early view of Ellison's. In the introduction to the 1982 edition of *Invisible Man*, Ellison wrote that since democracy needs "conscious articulate citizens," novelists must be involved in the "creation of conscious articulate characters."[94] Art, in this view, was in the service of the republic and writers served as civic pedagogues. To put it crudely, but not entirely unfairly: because Bigger Thomas wasn't a good citizen, he wasn't a good fictional character.

Finally, both men expressed an ongoing (and sometimes tiresome) hostility to social scientific accounts of black life and its institutional inadequacies. Besides Ellison's rejection of Myrdal's pathology view of black culture, Murray took Myrdal, Kenneth Clark, Stanley Elkins, and Daniel Patrick Moynihan to task for peddling "the folklore of white supremacy and the fakelore of black pathology." Murray's point was that "interpretations of human behavior in the raw require as least as much respect for the complexity of human motives as the interpretation of a poem or play or a story."[95] Beyond that, Murray feared that the image of blacks as victims, far from eliciting white sympathy, would lead whites to treat them as, at best, objects of pity and, at worst, as objects of contempt. Ellison saw his art as a protest against the determinism allegedly assumed by social scientists. Creation, and then making that creation "public," was already a clear manifestation of freedom and equality. Art's justification lay not in convincing others of the necessity for freedom or justice. It already was its own justification insofar as it exemplified what it meant to be free, to live in a world of possibility.

The Ellison-Murray position is hard to criticize, since it clearly avoids the rhetorical and ideological bluster of the black aesthetic position, while retaining a sensitivity to African American cultural expression. As already mentioned, even Larry Neal was generous in his praise of Ellison's pioneering role in identifying the black folk origins of African American art. Still there are problems. Aside from the fact that the Ellison–Murray position is almost always "gendered" as male, their emphasis on art's role in providing models for emulation comes close to the view that all art should tend toward allegory or moralizing. Similarly, in grounding artistic creation in archetypal patterns, Ellison and Murray make it difficult (though not impossible) to recognize, much less approve of, art that deliberately alienates itself from a common world.

It is in this context that their treatment of Richard Wright is so revealing. At times Ellison and Murray criticized Wright in a manner similar to those white Southern literary patriots who rejected Faulkner's characters as unrepresentative of the South. More ironically, they could also sound like the CP critics who charged Ellison's *Invisible Man* with defaming black Americans. Murray, for instance, describes *Native Son* as "for all its naturalistic detail, a generalization about Black America's behavior as a whole. . . . People who are forced to live in subhuman conditions develop subhuman traits." But, continues Murray, "MOST DO NOT." Bigger Thomas was not "sufficiently representative" and the plot complications fail to "adequately symbolize the eternal condition of man."[96] In short, Murray thought the novel was too negative and its protagonist too limited in character and consciousness.

This line of criticism followed directly from Murray's belief in the didactic purposes of art. In one respect, it did fit with Wright's intentions for Bigger as a social type (if taking Wright's intentions into account is important): "[T]here was not just one Bigger, but many of them, more than I could count and more than you suspect."[97] But that is not to say that Wright intended Bigger to illuminate the human condition in general or to embody the essence of what it meant to be an African American male.

Rather he was the product of a specific historical situation. By universalizing and allegorizing character and plot, by seeing all artistic creation as tending toward allegory or philosophical anthropology, Murray, trapped by his own logic, came very close to a prescriptive aesthetics for African American writing.[98]

Ellison's relationship with Wright was more complex, since it involved both a literary and a personal relationship. For instance, Ellison denied that Wright was a literary "ancestor" while affirming him as a literary "relative," even for a time a "personal hero."[99] More interestingly, Ellison's attitude toward Wright and the possibilities of black Southern life changed significantly over the years. On most accounts, Ellison's rejection of Myrdal's characterization of American Negro culture represents Ellison's settled opinion on such matters. Thus, Ellison's general criticism of Wright's representation of African American life as needlessly bleak and barren is a variation on his criticism of Myrdal. Yet a careful reading of Ellison's "Richard Wright's Blues" (1945) reveals a quite different attitude toward Wright and black Southern life than the one we are used to. The essay's overall conceptual framework uses (Wilhelm) Reichian concepts such as "armored," while Ellison's term "channelization," for example, is a rough synonym for "sublimation" and is central to his analysis of the oppressive nature of black Southern life offered in the essay. The essay's general point is that the lives of black Southerners reveal "the full extent to which the Southern community renders the fulfillment of human destiny impossible." From the white side, this is accomplished through racial discrimination, exclusion, and intimidation, while, from the black side, "preindividual" values rein in any individual who threatens to "become the agent of communal disaster." Moreover, according to Ellison: "This preindividual state is induced artificially, like the regression to primitive states noted among cultured inmates of Nazi prisons." But Ellison rejects the view that Southern blacks are "simple" and/or straightforwardly passionate. They are anything but unrepressed hedonists and have, claims Ellison, all sorts of implausible characteristics attributed to them. With this essay in mind, one can understand a little bit better why Ellison might have found Hurston's picture of black Southern life too idealized, too pastoral.[100]

Several aspects of this essay of 1945 deserve comment. First, Ellison clearly rejects any view of black folk culture as an organic or natural form of life; rather, it is organized around a sustained reaction to the oppressive white society. Second, and most startling, Ellison's analysis obviously drew on Bruno Bettleheim's account of his experience in Dachau and

Buchenwald. In this it anticipates the comparison that Stanley Elkins later made between the effects of slavery upon the slave and the effects of the concentration camp upon its inmates. The irony is, of course, that by the 1960s Elkins had become a bete noir of both Ellison and Murray. This is not to deny Ellison the right to change his mind, but it is to make the point that drawing the link between the condition of black Southerners and that of camp inmates seemed neither far-fetched nor insulting to Ellison in 1945.[101]

But Ellison did depart from Elkins and Bettelheim in emphasizing the way that oppressive conditions had made black Southerners more rather than less complex beings. The South failed to provide the intellectual resources for black people to articulate or refine such complex emotions. Only when they left the South could they discover the language to match their emotions. As Ellison put it in reference to *Native Son*'s central character, the problem was how to "translate Bigger's complicated feelings into universal ideas. . . . Between Wright's skill and knowledge and the potentials of mute feelings lay a thousand years of conscious culture."[102] It is precisely in this context that Ellison cites Wright's indictment of black Southern culture from *Black Boy*. As of 1945, Ellison insists that the passage is "the strongest affirmation that they [black Southerners] have the capacity for culture."[103] Along with Frazier and Wright, Ellison seemed to believe that the problem was the exclusion of blacks from the dominant culture and society.

Remarkably, Ellison's 1945 essay also rejects the criticisms of Wright that he (Ellison) later directs at *Native Son*. Some "complain that Wright has omitted the development of his own sensibility" and that *Black Boy* "presents too little of what they consider attractive in Negro life." Both criticisms, Ellison goes on to say, "miss the very obvious point" that the prevailing environment south of the Mason-Dixon line crushes those positive elements which have as little possibility of "prevailing . . . as Beethoven's quartets would have of destroying the stench of a Nazi prison."[104] Besides, Ellison adds, art depends as much on selectivity as it does on a stenographic representation of reality in order to make its larger point. As of 1945, Wright's achievement, according to Ellison in eerie anticipation of his own *Invisible Man*, was to have "convert[ed] the American impulse toward self-annihilation and 'going-under-ground' into a will to confront the world." For those who escaped to the North, there was sometimes "personality damage" that was "not the disintegration of a people's fiber, but the failure of a way of life."[105] The context within which black personalities were damaged was precisely the social context that Wright created so powerfully in *Native Son*.

A decade and a half later, Ellison's assessment of Wright had shifted markedly. In 1961, Ellison described Wright as too "ideological" and too much a "social determinist." This reflects, he went on, a "difference in our concept of the individual" and a disagreement over Wright's "conception of the quality of Negro humanity."[106] But it was in his exchange with Irving Howe in 1963–1964 that Ellison's views of Wright were most polemically charged. Smarting from Howe's charge that he and Baldwin had abandoned Wright's literature of political engagement, Ellison resorts to the ultimate put-down. Wright, he suggests, "began with the ideological proposition that what whites think of the Negro's reality is more important than what Negroes know it to be." In addition, Ellison drastically simplifies his earlier view of what Bigger Thomas represents: "a near sub-human indictment of white oppression." Finally, Ellison offers what is by now the familiar observation that "Wright could imagine Bigger, but Bigger could not possibly imagine Richard Wright."[107] Although this seems like a crushing criticism of Wright's fictional judgment, upon reflection, it is hard to imagine it as a general principle by which any fictional character should be judged, particularly a modernist one.

Ellison's critical demotion of Wright was matched by an assessment upward of the possibilities of black life in Mississippi, the South, and the nation. Ellison now contends that "there is a *fullness* even a richness here—and here *despite* the realities of politics, perhaps, but nevertheless here and real . . . even in Mississippi."[108] While "Richard Wright's Blues" treated Wright as an escapee from the concentration camp universe of the South, now Ellison saw Wright, along with the black opera diva, Leontyne Price, as demonstrating the rich possibility of black life in the South. Ellison once again quotes Wright's description of the "bleakness of black life in America," but he now distances himself from it with a rhetorical question: "Must I be condemned because my sense of Negro life was quite different?" He follows this question with an assertion intended to trump Wright's position once and for all: "keeping faith would never allow me to even raise such a question about any segment of humanity."[109] With that, Ellison all but claims that Wright doubted the humanity of black Americans.

Finally, in 1971 Ellison once again took up the task of "Remembering Richard Wright." He wrote quite appreciatively of *Native Son* as "one of the major literary events in the history of American literature," a judgment that echoed Irving Howe's more dramatic (and generous) description of the effects of *Native Son*: "The day [it] appeared, American culture changed forever."[110] But Ellison did add, with considerable understatement, "even though at this point I have certain reservations about its view of reality." He also praises Wright's sense of daring, for being as "courageous and as irresponsible as Jack Johnson," and for his generosity to the young Ralph Ellison. But, Ellison cannot help adding that Wright "didn't possess the full range of Afro-American culture."[111] But, then, who did?

My larger point here is that neither Ellison nor Murray really did justice to Wright's intensely felt account of the black experience.[112] By insisting that all literary representations should be normative projections of human possibility, they came close to denying Wright the freedom to experiment, to "improvise," as it were, to represent other ways that African Americans had dealt with their condition. Ellison (almost) said it best when he suggests that *Native Son* was "one man's essay in defining the human condition from a specific Negro perspective at a given time in a given place."[113] This seems a most appropriate way to historicize *Native Son*, but even then Ellison cannot quite let go of the notion that the definition of the human condition is at stake in any piece of fiction. Under such moral and philosophical weight, any fictional project would run the risk of collapsing.

There are also problems with the blues aesthetic/ethic developed by Ellison and Murray. By emphasizing the archetypal, they made it difficult to distinguish between the presence of archetypes in a work of art and their aesthetic or critical function. They seemed, by and large, to miss the modernist's ironic use of myth and symbol as a way of highlighting the difference between the original and the modernist reinterpretation, between, say, *The Odyssey* and *Ulysses*. Murray came close to recognizing this in *The Hero and the Blues* when he notes that "mythological substructures" work as "historical puns" or "mnemonic devices" to enrich a text, but they are not the main point of a work of art.[114] But if this is the case, it is hard to see why he and Ellison made such a big deal about archetypes in the first place. Moreover, it is not clear from their account whether different cultures have their own unique set of presiding archetypes, myths, and symbols. This issue has often been raised in reference to Jungian notions of archetypes and implies that for Jung the differences among races are shaped by the different archetypes they have at their disposal. Finally, though improvisation, creativity, and flexibility may be valid characteristics of both an aesthetic and an ethics, it is hard to be very comfortable with so closely identifying an aesthetic with a moral vision, artistic achievement with ethical evaluation.

Moreover, the emphasis on common, underlying patterns in art tends to wash out what Jerry G. Watts has referred to as the "caste/class" differences in aesthetics.[115] It is difficult to analyze a "folk" culture in terms of class-cultural differences when the concept of folk culture by definition excludes significant class divisions. In other words, there is something too static about their picture of black American culture; specifically, it fails to incorporate historical change or transformation. Though Ellison wrote fluently about the jazz tradition as it reestablished itself in the North, and Murray even ghosted an autobiography of Count Basie, neither man had a story, much less a theory, of how all this might play out—or had played out—over time in the North. They failed, in other words, to develop a "countersociology" of African American culture that would identify those core institutions of black life north of the Mason-Dixon line or west of the Mississippi (or in southern cities) which had—or had not—preserved black Southern folk culture. The work that the Lafargue Clinic in Harlem carried out was one pointer, but though Ellison wrote a short essay on it in 1948, a social psychological approach to black life in the North was precisely what the two men so scorned by the 1960s. On these matters, Wright was every bit as culturally sophisticated and historically self-aware—and rarely tempted by what Jerry Watts calls the "folk pastoralism" that marks the work of the two men (and of Hurston).[116] Nor with the exception of a dissident Jewish sensibility did either man ever seem to modify his pluralist vision of America to accommodate the impact of Italian and Irish immigrants on American culture, much less in later years to factor in the new ethnic cultures from Asia and Latin America.

But what follows from the fact that America is a mulatto or hybrid culture? Overall, Murray and Ellison are cases in point of the observation that a celebration of black American culture does not necessarily imply a politically radical position. Though Murray does talk a bit in *The Omni-Americans* about the need for black power (more than for black pride), neither man discusses the significant power differentials between the two races as the two cultures have interacted. Without a clearer sense of how power works in America, it is hard to make their theory of American democratic culture, as one in which Negro American culture has an honored place, stick. Put another way, if social scientists lose the character and texture of life as they develop their abstract models of society, the literary/cultural approach of Ellison and Murray fails to do justice to the institutional and structural constraints on individual and group expression. Merely dismissing social science as "fakelore" will simply not do. Their failure to provide much sense of institutional constraints in and on black American culture makes Harold Cruse's emphasis on the necessity for African Americans to control the means of cultural production and dissemination all the more prescient and valuable.

Specifically, as the examples of Hurston, Ellison, and Murray indicate, a full appreciation of African American culture, from its "folk" to its "high" forms, was hardly synonymous with political radicalism. Both men were hostile to black political and/or cultural nationalism and also gave President Johnson and the war in Vietnam their qualified support. Murray, a retired Air Force officer, seems to have valued Johnson's social liberalism—and his strong support for civil rights, even though—or because—he was a Southerner. "That is exactly what we need," Murray once observed, "some mean old crackers on our side for a change."[117] But Ellison and Murray never saw American Negro culture as oppositional in large part because it was already part of the complex mix that constituted the dominant culture. Put another way, their emphasis on individuality and the virtues of cultural creativity and improvisation did not necessarily entail political solidarity or dissent.[118]

Culturally, the only way to make sense of the differences among those who rediscovered (and developed) the positive aspects of African American culture in the 1960s is to see the Murray–Ellison position as one of *discovering* or *uncovering* an already existing Negro American tradition. By contrast, Cruse and the black arts/aesthetics group sought to *re-create*, *invent*, or at least develop a new self-consciousness about a black cultural tradition. Where both positions differed from the modernizers is that they did not seem to worry that interest in African American culture would somehow let white people off the hook by neglecting conventional political and social analysis.

Overall, Ellison and Murray's focus on the fact that the particular and the universal must be encompassed in cultural analysis and production was extremely valuable. Without the particularism of the vernacular and the idiomatic, a universalist perspective lacks purchase on concrete experience. But without those same universal moral, aesthetic, and epistemological perspectives, particularism threatens to become exclusive and essentialist. For all their criticism of Myrdal, Ellison and Murray ended by making a vernacular Negro culture part of a general American culture informed by the values of the founding political values of the nation.

Conclusion

Although the intellectual and cultural history of post-1960s developments in racial and cultural thought remains to be written, the relative triumph of cultural particularism, at both an elite and a popular level, was one of the crucial prerequisites for the emergence of identity politics in the late 1970s and of multiculturalism by the late 1980s and early 1990s. These developments were also propelled by the post-1965 influx of millions of immigrants from (especially) Latin America and Asia. As a result, by the mid-1990s, David Hollinger had concluded that the white-black racial binary had been replaced by a five-sided racial-ethnic relationship among European Americans, African Americans, Native Americans, Asian Americans, and Hispanics.[1] Indeed, cultural "hybridity," a concept that lies somewhere between the "melting pot" and the "multicultural" models, has become the most interesting way of describing contemporary American culture and society. As a way of concluding, I would like to do two things: first, reflect on the salient points that have emerged in tracing the shift from universalism to particularism as the dominant orientation in thinking about race, ethnicity, and culture; and second, to focus on three areas where much more thinking about these matters remains to be done.

Reflections

One important matter that has remained implicit up to this point is that modern racism and anti-Semitism were almost exclusive concerns of the political left rather than the right. To be sure, the German left only haltingly recognized the seriousness of Nazi anti-Semitism; while American liberals and progressives were often tone-deaf to, and even shared in, racist ideologies prior to the early 1940s, and the European left in general was slow to see that the anticolonial struggle demanded its support. Yet it is difficult to think of any case in which postwar political conservatives led political or intellectual attacks on racism, anti-Semitism, and colonialism. This does not mean that all political conservatives were racists, but insofar as conservatives seek to conserve existing institutional and cultural realities, they will be wary of challenging received prejudices of any sort; and insofar as they are suspicious of secular modernity, they will tend to reject Enlightenment-derived views that emphasize human equality of rights, that is, universalism. More tellingly, most of the intellectual critics of racism, anti-Semitism, and colonialism, were members of the groups—people of the African diaspora, Jewish diaspora, or Third World—that remained objects of racial, religious, and cultural prejudice. Myrdal and Sartre, along with Gordon Allport, were exceptions, but there were not many others.

A second, more explicit point of this study was to assess the variety of explanatory approaches to the question of why people become "racists," a term I use here to include white racism, biological anti-Semitism, and other forms of essentialist categorization. Gunnar Myrdal, Oliver Cox, and W. E. B. Du Bois (in one of his incarnations) emphasized the social and economic function of racism, while Jean-Paul Sartre offered a phenomenological description of anti-Semitism as a way of being in the world rather than as one belief among others held by a particular person. (Sartre tried rather unconvincingly to relate this to the capitalist mode of production as well.) Theodor Adorno and Max Horkheimer of the Frankfurt School emphasized the psychological impulses behind prejudice and authoritarian behavior and articulated them in terms provided by psychoanalytic theory. Underlying this psychoanalytic approach was the assumption that the authoritarian personality was a unique product of capitalist modernity. Hannah Arendt, though never a Marxist, emphasized capitalist imperialism as one of the realities behind European racism and anti-Semitism in the late nineteenth and early twentieth centuries. The growth of Nazi anti-Semitism was also encouraged by the failure of political and social assimilation of European Jewry after emancipation. Two overall points are of particular interest. First, except for Arendt's work and Sartre's analysis of negritude, most of the thinkers canvassed here were resolutely Eurocentric and thus failed to pay the attention that Du Bois and Aimé Césaire did to the importance of Western expansionism in the history of racism. As Sartre, Albert Memmi, and Frantz Fanon all emphasized, colonialism created racism rather than the reverse. Second, none of the approaches convincingly integrated "subjective" (psychological) and "objective" (social and economic) factors in their explanations of racism, though Myrdal succeeded as well as or better than the others.

A third impulse uniting most of the thinkers in this anti-racist tradition was the intuition, bordering on a firm conviction, that "color-coded" racism and biological anti-Semitism could be linked in explanatory and/or phenomenological terms. Only Myrdal and C. L. R. James foreswore the temptation to bring them together. The Swedish social scientist noted as of 1944 that anti-Semitism had been growing but was convinced that most Americans believed that all ethnic groups were ultimately assimilable.[2] Nor did James ever address the subject of anti-Semitism and, like Myrdal, had little or nothing to say about Nazism. Yet, despite the universalist assumption about human equality, the epistemological, psychological, historical, and ideological roots of racism, anti-Semitism and Eurocentrism proved to be quite disparate.

More controversially, why and how African and black diasporic cultures *seemed* to adjust to the culture of their occupiers and slave masters and European Jewry *seemed* to acquiesce in the process of the Final Solution were nagging preoccupations after 1945. By the early 1960s the issue began to be publicly discussed—and often denied—in various plausible and implausible ways. Clearly, this extremely painful issue called into question the growing celebration of the cultures of racial, ethnic, and religious minorities during that decade of global ferment. (Undoubtedly, the two views—minority cultures as damaged or dysfunctional versus minority cultures as healthy and autonomous—fed one another as well.) Again, two points are of particular interest. One that is still debated concerns how much difference the shift from racial to cultural explanations for group difference actually made—and makes. Another is that judgments of a minority culture's strengths and weaknesses are by definition controversial, even if proposed, as was the case with Arendt, by a member of the culture under examination.

Finally, related to the question of how to judge the "performance" of cultures under exigent conditions were the specific issues that arose in relation to African American culture in the three decades prior to the 1970s. The most interesting, at least to this writer, is the "fact" that those who saw modernization as desirable or as inevitable, whether under capitalist or socialist auspices, looked on folk or traditional cultures with considerable skepticism. This was so not despite, but because of, their political progressivism. It was only in the 1960s that thinkers linked the "progressive" cause with cultural nationalism and cultural exceptionalism. Second, my own modest suggestion in assessing the health/pathology of cultures in general and of African American culture in particular is that a distinction needs to be made between the intellectual-expressive culture and the basic institutions of a group. There is no necessary link, no tight fit at least, between intellectual-cultural achievement (in art, dance, literature, music, philosophy, etc.) and the strength of basic institutions, ranging from the family all the way to the political organs of the polity. From this perspective, Myrdal-Frazier-Wright *and* Ellison-Murray-Cruse-Baraka may both have been correct. African American expressive culture had a range of impressive achievements to its credit, but some of its basic institutions, notably the family, were exceedingly fragile.

Unfinished Business
The Rise and Fall of Racism

One of the most important, but also most neglected issues has to do with the reasons why thinking about race and culture between the early 1940s and the early 1970s underwent a shift from universalism to particularism and then from racial to cultural explanations of group difference? One might, for example, focus on a shift in moral perception, a Myrdalian moment as it were, by pointing to the way that the Nazi genocide directed against European Jews and other minorities, the tradition of lynching and racial brutality in the South, and the political and cultural domination of colonized people created an intellectual and moral revulsion against racist theory and practice. An answer from the realpolitik perspective, at least in America, would suggest that after 1945 the U.S. government came to realize that it had to confront its racial problems at home, if it were to gain the support of the increasingly restive colonial peoples in Asia, Africa, and the Caribbean as they made bid for independence. The answer might also be traced back to the revolution of rising expectations among the racially oppressed and colonized around the globe (and among the remaining Jews in Europe and in Palestine). Oppressed peoples everywhere began to organize to eject colonizers and to take political and cultural control of their destinies. I am certain that these explanations based on conscious intentions are important, but they also beg the larger question of just why intellectual, moral, and political arguments against race and racism began to have historical efficacy when they did. One answer would be that these conscious reasons built on and interacted with one another to create a critical mass of opinion that made racism and colonialism morally and politically disreputable.

Another way to pose the question would be to ask about economic factors rather than moral and political intentions. Some of the theorists of prejudice I have examined—for instance, the authors of *The Authoritarian Personality*—understood racism as deeply irrational, a form of social or personal pathology. Yet to those who see things in terms of economic systems and motivations, including Marxists, racism can look quite rational, that is, functional in terms of the system within which it operates. From this perspective, there was nothing irrational about the way racism had functioned historically to justify the establishment and maintenance of slave systems in the Western Hemisphere. Thus, my question should be rephrased as, "Why did racism come to seem economically counterproductive or irrational at a certain historical juncture?" Even though Marxism has lost much of its power to convince, we still tend to give precedence to the material over ideal, to economic rather than intellectual or moral explanations for historical developments. Specifically, we tend to assume that there is a close causal connection between capitalist modernization and the rise and fall of race and racism. If so, what is it?

The problem with the modernization thesis is that it explains too much and too little. European industrial development, as especially the Black Marxists emphasized, depended not only upon the exploitation of an industrial proletariat but also upon the creation of a slave system and slave class in the Western Hemisphere. The emerging ideological justification for New World slavery, especially in North America, was that Africans were a different order of human beings, a racialized version of Aristotle's slaves-by-nature. This racist ideology served to justify enslavement in a "white" society that, by the late eighteenth century, was growing increasingly egalitarian in its view of itself. Indeed, Alexis de Tocqueville and, more recently, Hannah Arendt have suggested that the simultaneous decline of the aristocracy and the rise of racism in European society was no accident. Having lost one way to organize society (birth and status), another was needed (race and cultural differences).

There is a problem, however. While modernization may explain the origins of the ideology of white racial supremacy (and the scientific revolution may explain the prestige attached to scientific racism), it fails to explain the origins of virulent, anti-Semitism in the Middle Ages. Although what George Fredrickson refers to as "color-coded, white-over-black variety" racism is clearly a modern phenomenon,[3] anti-Semitism (not simply theological anti-Judaism) had its roots in medieval Europe. To be sure, the conventional story has it that Jews became involved in the money economy of Europe because they were non-Christians.[4] Over time, families such as the Rothschilds acquired enormous economic power and attracted considerable resentment because they seemed to be profiting from a capitalist system that adversely affected so many others. To make matters more complex, Arendt also contended that anti-Semitism emerged in its specifically racial form just as the economic position of European Jewry was weakening in the late nineteenth century. It was in this context that August Bebel offered the mordant observation that anti-Semitism was "the socialism of fools." Modern anti-Semitism was articulated in economic as well as religious-cultural and racial terms, but economics was by no means the fundamental explanation for anti-Semitism or the basic motivation of the anti-Semite. The religious, cultural, and collective psychological roots of anti-Semitism both antedated and survived its economic expression.

In the first half of the twentieth century, the modernization thesis gets even more complicated. In this period, modernization, whether under private or state aegis, for profit or for use, undermined as much as it underpinned ideologies of racism. Because consumer capitalism needs broadly based purchasing power, wage and job discrimination based on race, religion, or ethnicity stops making economic sense. One reason behind the Carnegie Corporation sponsorship of Myrdal's project was the fear that the racial discrimination would hinder the growth of the U.S. economy. Thus, by the 1940s, if not before, racism, legal discrimination, and structural inequalities increasingly came to seem irrational and dysfunctional. With this in mind, it is easier to see why racism and race-thinking came under fire after World War II. It was not so much that those in power consciously saw that racial equality was crucial to a flourishing economy, but more that rational opposition to structures of discrimination collapsed. This meant that the way was open for a counterattack against racism on scientific, moral, psychological, and political grounds, the focus of my attention particularly in Part I.

Yet, simultaneously with the gradual yet genuine weakening of racist ideologies in one part of the West, an explicitly anti-Semitic regime came to power in Germany, the most intellectually and culturally sophisticated nation of Western Europe. Modernization was particularly disruptive of traditional German society and was a main causal factor in the growth of late nineteenth-century racism and anti-Semitism, what Fritz Stern once identified as the "politics of cultural despair." (As Arendt claimed, the experience and ideology of imperialism also injected the fatal poisons of repressive rule and racism into the European political and cultural bloodstream.) The difference between Germany and the rest of Europe was one of the things that the *Sonderweg* thesis—the idea that Germany's modernization was quite different from that of the rest of Western Europe and the United States—was supposed to explain. The German road to modernization not only went through Prussia; it also picked up considerable freight in Nuremberg. One of Arendt's most striking points in *The Origins of Totalitarianism* was that the implementation of the Final Solution was both economically and militarily irrational.

After World War II, just as the colonial empires were on the verge of collapse and ideologies of universal equality, independence, and democratic self-rule were gathering support in the West, the largely Francophone negritude movement began emphasizing how different the spiritual and intellectual legacy of Africa was from that of Europe. It is also important to remember that just as the "First" World was abandoning racist and colonialist ideologies, South Africa established an exceedingly rigid apartheid system in 1948, which lasted down to the early 1990s. Similarly, just as the whole edifice of the Jim Crow system was on the verge of collapse in the U.S. South in the mid-1960s, the radical wing of the civil rights movement and black radicals outside the South embraced black consciousness and black power. Racial consciousness developed a positive historical and cultural pedigree. Uneven development indeed!

All this suggests that an economic explanation of racism, whether expressed in terms of individual motivations or of systemic functions, rarely captures the whole truth. Political ideologies emphasizing individual and group self-respect are as important as appeals to, or satisfaction of, economic interests. Structures of meaning and feeling are as important as class structures. Hegel and Freud, as much or more than Adam Smith and Karl Marx, illuminate the psychology of insurgency and rebellion, resentment and envy, dehumanization and reification of the "other." Something like a collective reaction formation that leads an insurgent group to embrace the very terms—for instance, racial and cultural difference—by which their own domination has been justified seems to go with the territory. What Jean-Paul Sartre named "anti-racist racism"[5] was perhaps the form that the dialectic of history assumed in the early postwar years. As Du Bois's work makes clear, race-thinking endures long after race has lost its scientific credibility because it provides a basis for individual and group identity. From this perspective, racial-ethnic politics was the invention of the late nineteenth century rather than the late 1970s America.

Racism as Essentialism

As already emphasized, an intellectual history of the modern West's rejection of race and racism reveals a multiplicity of types of prejudice. Though I am sympathetic to the universalist perspective, I also am convinced that prejudice assumes a variety of forms with overlapping characteristics, but different origins, dynamics and, most obviously, different objects of prejudice. This is one reason that I have avoided making comparisons in this study between, on the one hand, racism and/or anti-Semitism and sexism and homophobia on the other. All forms of prejudice, as Elisabeth Young-Bruehl has emphasized, are not alike.[6] This is particularly true of white racism and anti-Semitism, the two most important forms of prejudice in the modern West. One way to describe the differences between them is to use terms borrowed from psychoanalysis. For instance, Young-Bruehl has linked anti-Semitism with obsessional character traits. It is often accompanied by paranoia, phobias about pollution, and disturbances of superego functioning. Color racism, on the other hand, mimics hysterical character traits of acting out or projecting repressed desires onto "lower" people, and is linked with id-related imagery. Young-Bruehl contends, for instance, that the white racist wants to keep people of color/desires "in their place," while the anti-Semite wants to get rid of the Other who threatens "from above," as it were. Clearly, these are typologies rather than empirical descriptions, but they are suggestive enough to illuminate the vastly different, but equally inhospitable, terrains of modern racism and anti-Semitism. Her typology suggests, for instance, that what is lacking in most of the theoretical work that I have discussed is a "theorized" distinction between anti-Semitism and color racism.[7]

If we exchange a psychoanalytic for a historical/sociological perspective, some of the central distinctions among types of prejudice in *Race, Culture, and the Intellectuals* become clearer. For instance, George Fredrickson's analysis of racisms in terms of modernization is particularly cogent. Fredrickson notes that in the late nineteenth century, people of African descent were considered unsuited for modernity and therefore inferior, while Jews were more often considered carriers of a hypermodernity that endangered traditional forms of life: "[I]f African Americans were not modern enough, German Jews were too modern."[8] Yet, it should also be remembered that *Ostjuden* (Eastern European and Russian Jews) were often adjudged hopelessly traditional and ill-suited to the modern world not only by Christians but also by more assimilated Jews. This is a point that Adorno and Horkheimer emphasize (perhaps too much so) in their "Elements of Anti-Semitism" in *Dialectic of Enlightenment.*

This submodern/hypermodern opposition suggests the reason why Jews have also often been identified with universalism as well as modernity. Lacking a homeland, they were seen as rootless purveyors of universalist dreams and utopian visions of an abstract, rational, and hence destructive nature. Known euphemistically as "rootless cosmopolites" in Stalin's Soviet Union, Jews asked too much of the gentile world: they strained its capacity for moral and intellectual rigor to the breaking point. Conversely, black diasporic cultures, whether positively or negatively assessed, have been linked closely to body imagery and to sexuality as the quintessence of the embodied and the embedded. Negatively considered, people of African descent have been associated with a temptation to regression and desublimation, which threatens the precarious gains of civilization.

A final, crucial difference between Jews and blacks is the one that thinkers from Albert Memmi to Paul Gilroy and Laurence Thomas have emphasized—the lack of what Thomas calls a "narrative" behind black diasporic identity, that is, the absence of a specific ideology of black diasporic life.[9] Historically, there has been no single religious tradition, sacred text, rituals, and practices, and or institutions entailed by being black in the way that "Judaism" is internally related to Jewry and Jewishness. I'm not sure of all the implications arising from this difference, but it probably affects the ways that each group deals with the vicissitudes of assimilation and separatism. While the existence of Judaism makes it possible to speak of "non-Jewish Jews," that is, Jews (members of the group) who are still recognizably Jewish (possessing group qualities associated with Jews), but no longer religiously observant (a believer in Judaism), nothing like this exists for black diasporic people. The absence of such a shared tradition or "narrative" may explain why race and color remain so important as a source of identity among black people. Of course, there are "Uncle Toms" and "Oreos," but they are not accused of having abandoned a specific ideology/theology or certain sacred rituals or observances. Afrocentrism and black cultural nationalism have been two related forms of identity questing in the post-1960s world. Both seek to discover (or invent) a history and anthropology, even a quasi-religion, to provide a fixed point of origin. That is, "blackness" may have become so important just because there are no institutions, texts, and theology to maintain it.

This suggests that it *might* make sense to consider racism and anti-Semitism (along with sexism and homophobia) as species of "essentialism."

By essentialism, I mean the reification of group characteristics in terms of a single factor such as race, culture, religion, or gender and then a demonization or deification of that group. For instance, biological racism is a relatively short-lived historical phenomenon. Slavery, mass murder, genocide, along with systematic discrimination and intolerance, predate and antedate scientific racism. There have been historical periods such as premodern Europe when difference was "essentialized" in terms of religion and it has often been essentialized in terms of gender. (Yet the argument that biologically grounded prejudice is uniquely dangerous seems plausible, since, unlike religion or culture, the natural is understood to be unchanging and unchangeable.[10]) One implication of Arendt's yoking together of Nazism and Stalinist Communism as "totalitarianism" was that class, as much as race, could provide the warrant for genocide (or "classicide"). The uniqueness of the Holocaust rests neither on the racialization of anti-Semitism nor on the absolute number of people who were exterminated. Rather, it has to do with the fact the Final Solution was planned and carried out according to a coherent ideology proposed by an organized nation-state.[11] But I am aware that to substitute "essentialism" for specific terms such as "racism" or "anti-Semitism" is to risk falling back into the assumption that a single/singular term can encompass all forms of prejudice.

Constructivism and Beyond

The obvious conceptual "other" of essentialism is social constructivism, the idea that individual and group identity are historical products rather than permanent essences, created rather than discovered. Though constructivism has come to be identified with something called "postmodernism," it is merely the contemporary form of environmentalist thinking whose modernist beginnings can be traced back, for instance, to John Locke's idea of the mind/self as a "tabula rasa" and more generally to the Enlightenment's rejection of the Christian idea of original sin. But constructivism need not entail a naïve notion of human innocence and a human incapacity for evil. "All" it suggests is that ideas of innocence and guilt are themselves social products rather than predating organized society. Constructivism has also been central to the modern attack on racism and other forms of essentialism; it was central to Myrdal's claim that race is a social rather than biological concept and lay behind Sartre's influential idea that the Jew (the colonized) was created by the anti-Semite (colonizer). Indeed, it is hard to see how individual or group identity could be anything other than constructed, once religious and racial factors have been excluded from consideration, as they have been generally since the 1930s.

However, constructivism presents its own problems. Rejecting all forms of essentialism, constructivism is not only compatible with, but seems to entail, cultural particularism, that is, cultural relativism. Historically and strategically, cultural relativism was enormously influential in discrediting biological racism and all forms of essentialism. The genuine hero here was the founder of modern antiracism, Franz Boas.[12] But since his time, at least three problems suggest not so much the uselessness as the limitations of cultural relativism.[13]

First, as already mentioned, historical materialism, Marxism's version of social and historical constructivism, has been used to justify systematic oppression and mass murder by regimes such as Stalin's or Mao's in their rage to reconstruct human society along revolutionary lines. As conservative theorists such as Michael Oakeshott and Eric Voegelin have insisted, rational dreams of utopian society and "gnostic" visions of historically immanent social transformation have sanctioned mass murder in the name of human good.[14] In the name of human malleability, constructivism can justify brainwashing, and the murder of recalcitrant human beings was made easier, claim conservatives, once the notion of the individual soul had been discarded. In fact, Arendt also identified a perverted constructivist strain at work in Nazi ideology in the form of a radical attempt to change human nature. Behaviorism, which was once so influential, claimed to go "beyond freedom and dignity" (B. F. Skinner) and is thoroughly chilling in its view of humans as socially interchangeable and infinitely malleable beings.

A second problem with cultural relativism arises from the paradox of particularism. As I mentioned in the introduction, "strong" particularism cannot formulate a coherent theory of moral or cognitive judgment that will carry across, as opposed to applying within, group boundaries. Particularism pushed to its logical conclusion leads to social and moral atomism. Of course, cultural relativists do make judgments that are meant to apply across cultural boundaries all the time, but these judgments are self-contradictory in their own terms. Nor is it to deny that there are real differences among cultures or ethnically/racially self-defined groups. But if there are, strong particularism makes it hard to understand how we can communicate with people in other cultures, much less make judgments about their way of life, values, and institutions; or vice versa.

The third—and fundamental—problem with cultural relativism in its pure form is that it lacks a philosophical anthropology, a notion of what it means to be human and, by implication, what humans need in order to live a decent life. All worries about intergroup judgments aside, it is difficult for social constructivism in its particularist form to formulate a notion of humanity or human being, that is, of the species that we call human. Ultimately, this is a serious failure, since without some notion of what it means to be human in general and what it takes to live a human life specifically, it is difficult to pinpoint what is so wrong about dividing human beings into biological races with allegedly different capacities or even to deny human status to some groups altogether. Nor is it possible, I think, without some tacit sense of what being human means, to go very far with the idea that, surprisingly, has flourished since the 1960s even under postmodern conditions—the idea of human rights. As Michael Ignatieff has recently observed, we can only develop a "thin" notion of human rights without transforming this category of rights into what its critics charge it with being—a thinly disguised form of Western moral and legal imperialism. According to Ignatieff, human rights are not "trumps" or moral overrides of any and all suspicious practices, but "a common framework, a common set of references."[15] William James's pragmatic notion that "truth happens to an idea" may be the best way to view human rights—as something we must make true, rather than discover as true. Finally, at this point in history, the idea that human rights are invalid because they are of "Western" origin no longer really follows for two reasons. First, after a half-century or more of the international discussion of rights—natural, civil, legal, and human—and considered in the context of globalization, it no longer makes sense to assume that there are sharply defined political and legal cultures that are somehow sealed off from one another. Second, after the disastrous effect that the rejection of rights and liberties as "bourgeois" had on Marxism, we should not now repeat that mistake by disqualifying the idea of rights and liberties as "Western."

With similar modesty, we should perhaps concentrate on trying to think through what human beings need. In the process of working on this book, I came to realize that several of the thinkers involved were either trying to develop a philosophical anthropology or were using race and/or culture to define what it means to be human. This was explicitly the case with Arendt, who spoke of a basic human "right to have rights," and with Sartre, who defined humanism in terms of subjectivity and freedom rather than positing a fixed human essence. Both figures were part of the early post-1945 debate among Western thinkers about the viability of humanism, with Martin Heidegger's response to Sartre's "Existentialism Is a

Humanism" initiating the broader debate, and Adorno and Horkheimer's critique of the Enlightenment as another important moment in that debate.[16] The humanism debate in the 1960s and 1970s saw the rejection of Sartre's influence, with structuralism and then poststructuralism providing a critique of subjectivity and a coherent, centered self. But the French debate was, as Robert Young has told us, also influenced by the assertions of Third World intellectuals that humanism was not a universal set of principles but a specifically Western worldview and set of values. "Man," in Michel Foucault's conception, was a historical construct and therefore historically evanescent. But the question of humanism was not an exclusive concern of European thinkers. Certainly one of the central goals of the negritude movement and of black consciousness intellectuals in the United States in the 1960s was also to go beyond traditional Western notions of humanism and develop a position that would not define Africans or people of African descent as human or as possessing a true culture in the terms established by the West.

These are only a few examples. But they suggest that one way to combat racism, that is, essentialism, is not to embrace constructivism "all the way down," but to develop a notion of "human" that will trump biological racism rather than reinforce it. It does not follow, for instance, that because one believes in a fixed human nature or a shared human condition that racism is thereby also entailed and justified, even though both imply the existence of transhistorical characteristics. Nor is reviving the notion of human nature a covert way of resurrecting a belief in innate human depravity. To be plausible, any notion of human nature must include both positive and negative human traits. Finally, in reference to race, we can be constructivists, but in reference to the question of the human, the task is to work out some sort of "empirical universalism," by which we can figure out what, as Martha Nussbaum has suggested, seem to be the minimal conditions for human survival and maximal conditions for human flourishing across cultures.[17]

Whether we call this endeavor "humanism" is unimportant and it may be that the term, like racism, carries too much historical baggage to be of any further use. Indeed, given the attacks on secular humanism by both fundamentalist Christians and poststructuralists and postmodernists, it may be time to jettison the term altogether. Human beings can be the focus of our concern without resorting to their deification or denigration. The task is rather to rethink what it means to be human and what role race and culture should play in that process.

Notes

Introduction

1. Two ideas from the Greeks come close to race in their destructive effects: Plato's notion of the philosopher-king and Aristotle's idea of a slave-by-nature. More recently, the "end of history" has become a conservative echo of one of Marx's and utopian thought's more dubious concepts.

2. In this respect, my approach owes something to Eric Voegelin's discussion of race in these two general senses, particularly in his *Race and State*, translated by Ruth Hein and edited by Klaus Vondung (1933; Baton Rouge: Louisiana State University Press, 1997). For an attack on the idea of race as a social construction and that appeals to cultural constructivism can escape racial essentialism, see Walter Benn Michaels, "Race into Culture: A Critical Genealogy of Cultural Identity," *Critical Inquiry* 18 (summer 1992): 655–85 and "Autobiography of an Ex-White Man," *Transition* 73 (spring 1997): 1–14. But I would generally associate myself with the first of two ways of understanding race that Glenn Loury suggests. The first is the "social-cognitive approach," which understands race to refer to a group of people linked by gross physical characteristics, especially skin color, while the second adopts a "biological taxonomy" in which "genetic endowments" are assumed to have explanatory power. See Glenn Loury, "Reply to J. L. A. Garcia and John McWhorter," *First Things* (May 2002): 15.

3. George Fredrickson, *Racism: A Short History* (Princeton, N.J.: Princeton University Press, 2002), 5–6. See also Elisabeth Young-Bruehl, *The Anatomy of Prejudice* (Cambridge, Mass.: Harvard University Press, 1996) for a distinction between "ethnocentrism," a "group-perpetuating" impulse that is more or less permanent, and modern "ideologies of desire" that are "group creating" (pp. 27–28, 166).

4. George Fredrickson, *The Black Image in the White Mind* (New York: Harper Torchbook, 1974); Stephen J. Gould, *The Mismeasure of Man* (New York: W. W. Norton and Co., 1981); Robert Young, *Colonial Desire: Hybridity in Theory, Culture and Race* (London and New York: Routledge, 1995); and Ivan Hannaford, *Race: The History of an Idea in the West* (Washington, D.C., and Baltimore, Md.: Woodrow Wilson Center Press and Johns Hopkins University Press, 1996).

5. See Elazar Barkin, *The Retreat of Scientific Racism: Changing Concepts of Race in Britain and the United States between the World Wars* (Cambridge: Cambridge University Press, 1992); James McKee, *Sociology and the Race Problem: The Failure*

of a Perspective (Urbana and Chicago: University of Illinois Press, 1993); William H. Tucker, *The Science and Politics of Racial Research* (Urbana and Chicago: University of Illinois Press, 1994); Stefan Kuehl, *The Nazi Connection: Eugenics, American Racism and German National Socialism* (New York: Oxford University Press, 1994).

6. Although he is neither the first nor the only person to apply the universalist/particularist dichotomy that I adopt here, David Hollinger in his *Postethnic America: Beyond Multiculturalism* (New York: Basic Books, 1995), uses it in a typically insightful and illuminating way, albeit without explaining or spelling out the shift in any great detail. Indeed, the binary opposition, or derivatives of it, permeates much of the discussion of race and racism. For instance, in *Race, Culture and Evolution: Essays in the History of Anthropology* (New York: Free Press, 1968), George Stocking notes that the idea of cultural evolution implies a normative universal culture as the destination of various particular cultures at different stages of advancement. More recently, Terry Eagleton, in *The Idea of Culture* (Oxford: Blackwell, 2000) discusses the shift in thinking from the idea of a single human culture (or Culture) to the focus on various particular cultures along with the association between universalism and individualism as opposed to particularism (pp. 38, 54–55).

7. See Ashley Montagu, *Statement on Race* (New York: Henry Schuman, 1951), 11. Montagu's book is an elaboration on the UNESCO Statement of 1950.

8. Hannah Arendt, *Eichmann in Jerusalem: A Report on the Banality of Evil*, rev. and exp. ed. (New York: Viking Press, 1965), 257, 268.

9. Quoted in Eric Sandeen, *Picturing an Exhibition: The Family of Man and 1950s America* (Albuquerque, N.M.: University of New Mexico Press, 1995), 3. See also Edward Steichen, *The Family of Man* (New York: Simon and Schuster, 1955).

10. Sandeen, *Picturing an Exhibition*, 4

11. Quoted in Stephen J. Whitfield, *In Search of American Jewish Culture* (Hanover, N.H.: University Press of New England, 1999), 77. See also Cynthia Ozick, *Quarrels and Quandary* (New York: Alfred A. Knopf, 2000).

12. Harold Cruse, *The Crisis of the Negro Intellectual* (New York: William Morrow and Co., 1967), 280.

13. Kenneth Stampp, *The Peculiar Institution* (New York: Vintage, 1956), vii.

14. Mark Silk, *Spiritual Politics* (New York: Simon and Schuster, 1988); Will Herberg, *Protestant-Catholic-Jew*, rev. ed. (Garden City, N.Y.: Doubleday Anchor, 1960); Gunnar Myrdal, *An American Dilemma* (New York: Harper and Row, 1944); Robert Bellah, *Beyond Belief: Essays on Religion in a Post-Traditional World* (New York: Harper and Row, 1970); and Daniel Bell, *The End of Ideology: On the Exhaustion of Political Ideas in the Fifties* (Glencoe, Ill.: Free Press, 1960).

15. Martin Luther King, "I Have a Dream," March on Washington, August 28, 1963, in *Why We Can't Wait* (New York: Signet, 1964), chapter 5 ("Letter from Birmingham Jail"). In fact, the Supreme Court seemed to ground its decision both in the universalist "equal protection of the laws" and in the fact of damage to the "hearts and minds" of black children. The latter allowed particularist readings of the *Brown* decision to be entertained.

16. Tom Segev, *The Seventh Million: The Israelis and the Holocaust*, trans. Haim Watzman (1991; New York: Hill and Wang, 1993), 347–48.

17. See Saul Friedlaender, *The Years of Persecution, 1933–1939*, vol. 1, *Nazi Germany and the Jews* (1997; New York: Harper Perennial, 1998), chapter 3

("Redemptive Anti-Semitism") for a description of the types of anti-Semitism that fed into Nazi ideology.

18. See Peter Novick, *The Holocaust in American Life* (Boston: Houghton Mifflin, 1999); Thomas Nagel, as cited in Lawrence Weschler, *A Miracle, A Universe* (New York: Pantheon, 1990), 4, distinguishes between *knowledge* of a fact or event and *acknowledgment* of its importance and implications, and this may be one way of describing the temporal and emotional gap the needed to be bridged before the full impact of the Holocaust could be understood.

19. One of the central points of Elizabeth Young-Bruehl, *The Anatomy of Prejudice,* is that not all forms of prejudice are alike. Although I very much agree with Young-Bruehl, Nazi anti-Semitism tended to be racialized, and hence calling it a species of racism does not do too great an injustice to the historical record.

20. Myrdal, *An American Dilemma* (New York: McGraw-Hill, 1964), 1:lxxv–lxxvi.

21. Matthew Frye Jacobson, *Whiteness of a Different Color: European Immigrants and the Alchemy of Race* (Cambridge, Mass.: Harvard University Press, 1998), 265. See also Matthew Pratt Guterl, *The Color of Race in America, 1900–1940* (Cambridge, Mass., and London: Harvard University Press, 2001).

22. Jacobson, *Whiteness of a Different Color,* chapter 3 ("Becoming Caucasian, 1924–1965"), 91–135.

23. Joel Williamson, *New People: Miscegenation and Mulattos in the United States* (New York: Free Press, 1980).

24. See Nikhil Pal Singh, "Culture/Wars: Recoding Empire in an Age of Democracy," *American Quarterly* 50, no. 3 (1998): 471–522, for a fascinating but sometimes opaque discussion of the Cold War as a prefiguration of the later cultural wars of the 1980s and 1990s. For a more straightforward analysis, see Mary L. Dudziak, *Cold War Civil Rights: Race and the Image of American Democracy* (Princeton, N.J., and London: Princeton University Press, 2000).

25. Singh, "Culture/Wars," 475.

26. Theodor Adorno and Max Horkheimer, *The Dialectic of Enlightenment* (1947; New York: Herder and Herder, 1972), 207.

27. This is one of the central themes in Arendt's *The Origins of Totalitarianism,* 2nd ed. (Cleveland: Meridian Books, 1958).

28. Arendt, *Eichmann in Jerusalem,* 269. See also Alice Kaplan, "War on Trial," *Civilization* (October/November 1997): 60–65; and Segev, *The Seventh Million,* 323–84. Chapter 7 will deal at much greater length with the Eichmann trial.

29. For a discussion of this point, see Novick, *The Holocaust in American Life*.

30. See Michael Novak, *The Rise of the Unmeltable Ethnics* (New York: Macmillan, 1972), and also Nathan Glazer and Daniel Moynihan, *Beyond the Melting Pot,* 2nd ed. (Cambridge, Mass.: M.I.T. Press, 1970).

31. Nathan Glazer, "Negroes and Jews: The Challenge to Pluralism," *Commentary* 12 (December 1964): 34.

32. See Richard Wright, *The Color Curtain: A Report on the Bandung Conference* (Cleveland and New York: World Publishing Co., 1956).

33. Aimé Césaire, *Discourse on Colonialism* (1955; New York and London: Monthly Review Press, 1972), 14–15, 72–73.

34. Frantz Fanon, *The Wretched of the Earth* (1961; New York: Grove Press, 1963), 311.

35. Paul Gilroy, *The Black Atlantic: Modernity and Double Consciousness* (London: Verso Books, 1993).

36. Martin Bernal, *Black Athena: The Afroasiatic Roots of Classical Civilization* (London: Free Association Press, 1987); Robert J. C. Young, *White Mythologies: Writing History and the West* (New York and London: Routledge, 1990); Edward Said, *Culture and Imperialism* (New York: Alfred A. Knopf, 1993); and Daryl Michael Scott, *Contempt and Pity: Social Policy and the Image of the Damaged Black Psyche, 1880–1996* (Chapel Hill: University of North Carolina Press, 1997). The scope of Hannaford's *Race was* also of importance as a model.

Chapter 1—Race, Caste, and Class: Myrdal, Cox, and Du Bois

1. Gunnar Myrdal, "Liberalism and the Negro," *Commentary* 37 (1964): 30. Participants in this symposium were Sidney Hook, Nathan Glazer, James Baldwin, and Myrdal.

2. See most recently, Mary L. Dudziak, *Cold War Civil Rights: Race and the Image of American Democracy* (Princeton, N.J.: Princeton University Press, 2000); Azza Salama Layton, *International Politics and Civil Rights Policies in the United States, 1941–1960* (Cambridge: Cambridge University Press, 2000); and Brenda Gayle Plumer, ed., *Window on Freedom: Race, Civil Rights and Foreign Affairs, 1945–1988* (Chapel Hill: University of North Carolina Press, 2003).

3. Walter Jackson, *Gunnar Myrdal and America's Conscience* (Chapel Hill: University of North Carolina Press, 1990), 55. See also David Southern, *Gunnar Myrdal and Black–White Relations* (Baton Rouge: Louisiana State University Press, 1987), and John P. Jackson, *Social Scientists for Social Justice: Making the Case Against Segregation* (New York and London: New York University Press, 1997), 54–58. My analysis of Myrdal is really an elaboration on Walter Jackson's excellent analysis.

4. Timothy Tilton, "Gunnar Myrdal and the Swedish," in *Gunnar Myrdal and His Works*, edited by Gilles Dostaler et al. (Montreal: Harvest House, 1992), 21. Tilton and other contributors to the volume underline Myrdal's strong commitment to the Enlightenment heritage and contrast his "compatibilist" liberalism with Isaiah Berlin's tragic liberalism, in which equality and freedom, for instance, are not compatible in all situations.

5. James O. Eastland, "An Alien Ideology Is NOT the Law of Our Republic," *The American Mercury* 86 (1958): 28.

6. For the charge about Myrdal and the status quo, see Stephen Steinberg, *Turning Back: The Retreat from Racial Justice in American Thought and Policy* (Boston: Beacon Press, 1995), 37.

7. Numan B. Bartley, *The New South* (Baton Rouge: Louisiana State University Press, 1996). Clearly, Bartley's analysis captures some but not all the ingredients in postwar Southern liberalism.

8. For the shift from the focus on race to a concentration on prejudice, see Franz Samuelson, "From Race Psychology to Studies in Prejudice," *Journal of the History of the Behavioral Sciences* 14 (1978): 265–78. Standard works on the shift in social science thinking about race in the interwar years are Dorothy Ross, *The Origins of American Social Science* (Cambridge: Cambridge University Press, 1991); Elazar

Barkin, *The Retreat of Scientific Racism: Changing Concepts of Race in Britain and the United States between the World Wars* (Cambridge: Cambridge University Press, 1992); James McKee, *Sociology and the Race Problem: The Failure of a Perspective* (Urbana and Chicago: University of Illinois Press, 1993); William H. Tucker, *The Science and Politics of Racial Research* (Urbana and Chicago: University of Illinois Press, 1994); and Stefan Kühl, *The Nazi Connection: Eugenics, American Racism, and German National Socialism* (New York: Oxford University Press, 1994).

9. Gary Gerstle, "The Protean Character of American Liberalism," *American Historical Review* 39 (1994): 1045. Gerstle's important *American Crucible: Race and Nation in the Twentieth Century* (Princeton, N.J., and London: Princeton University Press, 2001) is a Myrdalian work insofar as he posits an opposition within twentieth-century American political culture between racial and civic nationalism, that is, the American Creed. Yet Gerstle, much more than Myrdal, sees racial nationalism as a co-herent—and national—ideology rather than as an irrational, largely Southern set of prejudices that Myrdal presents as the rival to the American Creed. See also Tony Kushner, *The Holocaust and the Liberal Imagination* (Oxford: Basil Blackwell, 1994), for an analysis of the shift in racial and ethnic consciousness during and after World War II in both the United States and Great Britain.

10. Walter Jackson makes this point clearly, while Robert Westbrook's *John Dewey and American Democracy* (Ithaca, N.Y.: Cornell University Press, 1991) makes a convincing case for Dewey's democratic, as opposed to technocratic, credentials. Christopher Lasch's polemical analysis of Myrdal's project as emphasizing teamwork, aiming at foundation and government elites (and as "unremittingly dull"), captures this social engineering side of Myrdal's thought and practice. See Christopher Lasch, *The True and Only Heaven: Progress and Its Critics* (New York and London: W. W. Norton and Company, 1991), 439–43.

11. Gunnar Myrdal, *An American Dilemma: The Negro in a White Nation*, vol. 1 (New York: McGraw-Hill, 1964). Chapters 5 and 6 contain the core of his position. Page references to this volume will be included in the main text.

12. McKee, *Sociology and the Race Problem*, 6.

13. Myrdal noted that the Creed was "no American monopoly" but derived from "our common Western civilization" (p. 25).

14. See Gerstle, *American Crucible*, 235–36.

15. For a good account of the wartime mood of social hope, see Ellen Hermann, *The Romance of American Psychology: Political Culture in the Age of Experts* (Berkeley: University of California Press, 1995). See also Gerstle, *American Crucible*, chapter 5 ("Good War, Race War"), 187–237.

16. It is a common misconception to claim that Myrdal felt, in Alexander Saxon's words, that "the exposure of the falsity of racial doctrine would automatically explain the differential treatment of non-whites as the result of misunderstanding and igno-rance" (pp. 4–5). Saxon also seems to hold the common view that the nature of the cause(s) of and the nature of the cure for racism must be the same. See Alexander Saxon, *The Rise and Fall of the White Republic: Class Politics and Mass Culture in Nineteenth-Century America* (London and New York: Verso, 1990), 1–20.

17. See Rogers M. Smith, "Beyond Tocqueville, Myrdal and Hartz: The Multiple Traditions in America," *American Political Science Review* 87 (1993): 533.

18. E. Franklin Frazier, "Review of *An American Dilemma*," *American Journal of Sociology*, 50, no. 6 (May 1945): 556. Frazier was one of the two readers of Myrdal's

completed manuscript. One of Myrdal's other close advisors, Ralph Bunche, also had his doubts about the existence among whites of a moral dilemma about race, although Bunche also pushed a white working class/black alliance in the 1930s, presumably based on shared economic interests rather than moral sensitivities. See Ben Keppel, *The Work of Democracy: Ralph Bunche, Kenneth B. Clark, Lorraine Hansberry and the Cultural Politics of Race* (Cambridge, Mass.: Harvard University Press, 1995), 55–56.

19. Leo Crespi, "Is Gunnar Myrdal on the Right Track?" *Public Opinion Quarterly*, 59, no. 2 (summer 1945); Ralph Ellison, "An American Dilemma: A Review" (unpublished, 1944), in *Shadow and Act* (New York: Signet Books, 1963), 297.

20. Myrdal, "The War on Poverty," *The New Republic*, February 6, 1964, p. 15. In the *Commentary* symposium of March that same year, Myrdal repeated this objection to what became affirmative action.

21. Ibid.

22. A very quick perusal of the table of contents of the *American Sociological Review* between 1945 and 1955 reveals very few articles or book reviews about caste except for Oliver Cox's *Caste, Class and Race*. At the same time, books and articles with race, color, and class in their titles abound.

23. Herbert Aptheker, "A Liberal Dilemma," *New Masses*, May 14, 1946, p. 3. Aptheker also published a critique of Myrdal in *The Negro People in America: A Critique of Gunnar Myrdal's* An American Dilemma (New York: International Publishers, 1946). In recent years, Aptheker has repeated the substance of his charges against Myrdal, without the vicious polemics. See Robin D. G. Kelley, "Interview of Herbert Aptheker," *Journal of American History* 87, no. 1 (June 2000): 158.

24. Aptheker, "A Liberal Dilemma," 4.

25. Aptheker, *The Negro People in America*, 62. Aptheker's attack was effectively answered by Horace Cayton, "Whose Dilemma?" *New Masses*, July 23, 1946, pp. 8–10. Cayton charged Aptheker with "intemperate petulism" (petulance) and with oversimplifying the position of all involved. Specifically, he noted that everyone, including Aptheker, made moral choices at an individual level, and that Aptheker's attacks on Cayton, Drake, and Wright were retaliation against their attacks on the Communist Party late in the war for advocating "caution" and "patience" rather than speaking out against U.S. racism. Two years later, Ernest Kaiser's "Racial Dialectics: The Aptheker-Myrdal School Controversy," *Phylon* 9, no. 4 (1948): 295–302, sought to mediate between the economic emphasis of the Aptheker approach and the moral-psychological tack of Myrdal, Cayton, Drake, and Wright by calling for each camp to take greater account of the other.

26. Biographical information on Cox can be found in Herbert M. Hunter and Sameer Y. Abrahams, "The Life and Career of Oliver C. Cox," in *Race, Class, and World System: The Sociology of Oliver C. Cox* (New York: Monthly Review Press, 1987), xvii–xlx. See also "The Tradition of Sociology Teaching in Black Colleges: The Unheralded Professionals," in *Black Sociologists: Historical and Contemporary Perspectives*, edited by James E. Blackwell and Morris Janowitz (Chicago and London: University of Chicago Press, 1974), where it is said of Cox that he was "the only one of the group with broad-based theoretical concerns." (p. 156). Though not the subject of extended treatment in Cedric Robinson, *Black Marxism: The Making of a Black Radical Tradition* (1983; Chapel Hill and London: University of North Carolina Press, 2000), Cox's important role in the development of a Marxist-oriented black radicalism

is acknowledged there, as is his crucial role in the racial thought associated with the Popular Front/Cultural Front intellectual formation in Michael Denning, *The Cultural Front: The Laboring of American Culture in the Twentieth Century* (London and New York: Verso, 1997), 452–54. See also Adolph Reed, "Race and Class in the Work of Oliver Cromwell Cox," *Monthly Review* (February 2001): 23–31.

27. Oliver C. Cox, *Caste, Class and Race* (New York: Monthly Reader Paperback, 1970), xxxi, 322. Future page references to this work will be included in the main text.

28. Myrdal, *An American Dilemma*, vol. 2, 669.

29. Ibid., xxxii.

30. Everyone who writes about Du Bois is even more in David Levering Lewis's debt, since the second volume of his biography of Du Bois has now appeared: *W. E. B. Du Bois: The Fight for Equality and the American Century, 1919–1963* (New York: Henry Holt and Company, 2000). Lewis's strong suit is Du Bois as a thinker; and he illuminates crucial junctures in Du Bois's political and intellectual development with particular acuity.

31. Ross Posnock, *Color and Culture: Black Writers and the Making of the Modern Intellectual* (Cambridge, Mass.: Harvard University Press, 1998). While Posnock is right to stress the way that Du Bois was torn between being a "race champion and intellectual" (p. 5), Du Bois never really escaped the view that race, however defined, was absolutely central to his own life and the life of his people, and this despite his (rightful) claim that he could commune with the greats of the Western tradition of thought and imagination as well as any white person could.

32. See Adolph Reed, *W. E. B. Du Bois and American Political Thought: Fabianism and the Color Line* (New York: Oxford University Press, 1997), chapter 2 ("Corporate Industrialization, Collectivism, and the New Intellectuals").

33. For Du Bois's German experience and its crucial impact on his intellectual development, see Joel Williamson, *The Crucible of Race* (New York: Oxford University Press, 1984); David L. Lewis, *W. E. B. Du Bois: Biography of a Race, 1868–1919* (New York: Henry Holt and Company, 1994), along with Shamoon Zamir, *Dark Voices: W. E. B. Du Bois and American Thought, 1888–1903* (Chicago and London: University of Chicago Press, 1995); Axel R. Schäfer, "W. E. B. Du Bois, German Social Thought, and the Racial Divide in American Progressivism, 1892–1909," *Journal of American History* 88, no. 3 (December 2001): 925–49; Sieglinde Lemke, "Berlin and Boundaries: *sollen* versus *geschehen*," *boundary 2* (Sociology Hesitant: Thinking with W. E. B. Du Bois), edited by Ronald T. Judy, 27, no. 3 (fall 2000): 45–78; and Kenneth D. Barken, "'Berlin Days,' 1892–94: W. E. B. Du Bois and the German Political Economy," *boundary 2*, no. 3 (fall 2000): 79–101.

34. See Lewis, "Atlanta: The Politics of Knowledge," *W. E. B. Du Bois: The Fight for Equality*, 422–53; and Du Bois, "Memorandums on the Proposed Encyclopedia of the Negro (1937 and 1939)," in *Against Racism: Unpublished Essays, Papers, Addresses, 1887–1961*, edited by Herbert Aptheker (Amherst: University of Massachusetts Press, 1985), 160–72.

35. Lewis, *W. E. B. Du Bois: The Fight for Equality*, 449.

36. Du Bois, "Review of *An American Dilemma*," *Phylon* 5, no. 2 (1944): 118–24.

37. Du Bois, *Dusk of Dawn: An Essay Toward an Autobiography of a Race Concept* (1940; New York: Schocken Books, 1968), viii.

38. Du Bois, "Miscegenation" (1935), in *Against Racism*, 91–92.

39. Du Bois, *Black Folk: Then and Now*, new introduction by Herbert Aptheker (1939; Millwood, N.Y.: Kraus-Thomson Organization Ltd., 1975), 119.

40. Du Bois, "The Conservation of Races" (1897), in *W. E. B. Du Bois: A Reader*, edited by David L. Lewis (New York: Henry Holt and Company, 1995), 21.

41. Tommy Lott, "Du Bois and Locke on the Scientific Study of the Negro," *boundary* 2, 27, no. 3 (fall 2000): 138–40. Lott notes that this apparent inconsistency arose from Du Bois's conviction that science could be pressed into the service of its own self-correction, since racial science obviously traveled under the banner of science.

42. Du Bois, "Conservation," 21.

43. Contemporary arguments now revolve around the question of whether race is a phenotypical or genotypical concept, that is, whether race is a marker for, or an explanation of, group difference. Or if it is both, what is the relative importance of the genotypical factor? Philosopher Kwame Anthony Appiah claims that the concept of race has multiple meanings for Du Bois, and that it is time to jettison the idea of race, since it explains nothing that culture does not do better. See *In My Father's House: Africa in the Philosophy of Culture* (New York: Oxford University Press, 1992). Appiah's rejection of race has been challenged by Lucius Outlaw's "'Conserve' Race? In Defense of W. E. B. Du Bois," in *W. E. B. DuBois on Race and Culture: Philosophy, Politics and Poetics*, edited by B. Bell, E. Groshalz, and J. B. Stewart (New York and London: Routledge, 1996), 15–34. Outlaw's goal is "The formulation of a cogent and viable concept of race that will be of service to the non-invidious conservation of racial and ethnic groups . . ." (p. 22). Outlaw rejects the idea that race is a "natural kind," yet does not want to jettison the biological dimension entirely, preferring, with Du Bois, to see race as a "cluster concept" (p. 28). For an argument for the reality of socially constructed concepts such as race, see Ron Sundstrom, "Accounting for Races as a Human Category," *Philosophy and Social Criticism* 28, no. 1 (2002): 91–115. See also Eric Voegelin's work of the early 1930s, *The Collected Works of Eric Voegelin*, vols. 2 (Race and State) and 3 (The History of the Race Idea from Ray to Carus) (Baton Rouge and London: Louisiana State University Press, 1997 and 1998). There Voegelin draws a distinction between race as a theory (biological or anthropological) and race as an idea that groups hold about themselves. In a sense Du Bois's and Outlaw's use of race as a "cluster" concept is close to Voegelin's race as an idea.

44. Du Bois, "Conservation," 21.

45. Ibid., 23.

46. Ibid., 26.

47. The classic text defining the black Marxist tradition is Cedric J. Robinson, *Black Marxism: The Making of the Black Radical Tradition*. Robinson names Du Bois, along with C. L. R. James and Richard Wright, as the three "founders" of the black Marxist tradition.

48. Du Bois, *Black Reconstruction in America, 1860–1880* (1935; New York: Atheneum, 1969), chapter 1.

49. Du Bois, *The World and Africa: Enlarged, with New Writings on Africa, 1955–1961* (1947, 1965; New York: International Publishers, 1992), 60.

50. Du Bois, "Socialism and the Negro Problem" (1913) in *W. E. B. Du Bois: A Reader*, edited by David L. Lewis, 578; "Marxism and the Negro Problem" (1933), in *W. E. B. Du Bois: A Reader*, 542–43.

51. Du Bois, *Dusk of Dawn*, 215. Page references for the following quotations will be placed in the text.

52. See Gerald Horne, *Black and Red: W. E. B. Du Bois and the Afro-American Response to the Cold War* (Albany, N.Y.: State University of New York Press, 1986), and Penny M. von Eschen, *Race Against Europe: Black Americans and Anticolonialism, 1937–1957* (Ithaca, N.Y.: Cornell University Press, 1997).

53. Du Bois, *The Autobiography of W. E. B. Du Bois* (New York: International Publishers, 1968), 35.

54. Ibid., 24, 26, 34.

55. Lewis, *W. E. B. Du Bois: The Fight for Equality*, chapter 11. As Lewis observes, Du Bois was even accused of being a "propagandist in the pay of Japan" (p. 414).

56. Du Bois, *The World and Africa*, 297.

57. Lewis, *W. E. B. Du Bois: The Fight for Equality*, 421.

58. Ibid., 467.

59. Harold Brackman, "'A Calamity Almost beyond Comprehension': Nazi Anti-Semitism and the Holocaust in the Thought of W. E. B. Du Bois," *American Jewish History* 88, no. 1 (March 2000): 83.

60. Cited in Brackman, "'A Calamity Almost beyond Comprehension,'" 89, and taken from Horne, *Black and Red*, 283–84.

61. Brackman, "'A Calamity Almost beyond Comprehension,'" 86–87.

62. Du Bois, *Autobiography*, 392.

63. Despite being the father of the study of African American folk culture, the formulator of a sophisticated theory of black double consciousness drawn at least in part from Hegel and a pioneer of the cultural history (and achievements) of Africa over the ages, Du Bois seemed to have little interest in *negritude* or in the actual colonized culture(s) of modern Africa as such. Nor did he ever really offer a close analysis of the psychology of colonization or de-colonization in the manner of Frantz Fanon or Albert Memmi, although both drew on the same dialectic of interpersonal and intergroup relationships that had produced Du Bois's idea of double consciousness. See Zamir, *Dark Voices: W. E. B. Du Bois and American Thought*.

64. Du Bois, *The World and Africa*, 18–19.

65. Ibid., 19, 43.

66. Ibid., 23.

Chapter 2—Jean-Paul Sartre and the Creation of the Jew

1. The page references for all citations from Jean-Paul Sartre, *Anti-Semite and Jew*, trans. George J. Becker (New York: Schocken Books, 1976), will be included in the text. An invaluable source for understanding the context of the emergence of Sartre's small book is *October 87* (Winter 1999), an issue entirely devoted to the discussion of *Anti-Semite and Jew*. Steven S. Schwarzschild, "J.-P. Sartre as Jew," *Modern Judaism* 3, no. 1 (February 1983): 39–73, is also a provocative treatment of Sartre's text on anti-Semitism as it relates to his entire *oeuvre* and claims that Sartre came to identify his mature vision with Jewish messianic ethics. For biographical background and Sartre's intellectual milieu, I have consulted Annie Cohen-Solal, *Sartre: A Life* (London: Minerva Books, 1991); H. Stuart Hughes, *The Obstructed Path: French Social Thought*

in the Years of Desperation, 1930–1960 (New York and Evanston, Ill.: Harper and Row, 1968), chapter 5 ("The Marriage of Phenomenology and Marxism"); Mark Poster, *Existential Marxism in Postwar France: From Sartre to Althusser* (Princeton, N.J.: Princeton University Press, 1975); and Tony Judt, *Past Imperfect: French Intellectuals, 1914–1956* (Berkeley: University of California Press, 1993).

2. For the point about gratitude, see Robert Misrahi, "Sartre and the Jews: A Felicitous Misunderstanding," *October 87*, 63–72. In *The Holocaust in American Life* (Boston: Houghton Mifflin, 1999), Peter Novick locates the emergence of the Holocaust as a central fact in modern Jewish consciousness in the mid- to late 1960s.

3. Enzo Traverso, "The Blindness of the Intellectuals: Historicizing Sartre's *Anti-Semite and Jew*," *October 87*, 73. Traverso also notes the considerable difficulty that Primo Levi had in getting his first book *If This Is a Man* published in 1947. It was only much later that Levi's work received the attention it deserved.

4. Naomi Schor, "Anti-Semitism, Jews and the Universal," *October 87*, 107.

5. Hannah Arendt, *The Origins of Totalitarianism*, 2nd ed. (Cleveland: Meridian Books, 1958), 110. See also Albert S. Lindemann, *The Jew Accused: Three Anti-Semitic Affairs: Dreyfus, Beilis, Frank, 1894–1915* (Cambridge: Cambridge University Press, 1991), Chapters 4 and 5 on the Dreyfus case in France.

6. Pierre Vidal-Naquet, "Remembrance of a 1946 Reader," *October 87*, 10.

7. Jean-Paul Sartre, *Notebooks for an Ethics*, trans. and introduction by David Pellauer (Chicago: University of Chicago Press, 1992). Pellauer's very useful introduction provides an analysis of Sartre's uncompleted ethics. For a collection of essays on Sartre's political, social, and ethical topics, see William L. McBride, ed., *Sartre and Existentialism: Philosophy, Ethics, the Psyche, Literature, and the Aesthetic*, 8 vols. (New York and London: Garland Publishing, Inc., 1997).

8. Joseph Catalano has suggested that "good" faith and "bad" faith are part of a descriptive ontology and thus do not have moral or normative connotations, while "authenticity" and "inauthenticity" do. See "Good and Bad Faith: Weak and Strong Notions," in *Sartre and Existentialism*, edited by McBride, 5:89–90, n. 4.

9. Jean-Paul Sartre, *Existentialism Is a Humanism* in *Existentialism*, edited by William V. Spanos (New York: Thomas Y. Crowell, 1966), 277. Mark Poster claims that "existentialism is a humanism" was a response to a Communist Party attack on Sartre and represented Sartre's attempt to develop the concept of "revolutionary subjectivity" (pp. 125–26).

10. Ibid., 279, 291.

11. Ibid., 296. As Pellauer notes, in the introduction to *Notebooks for an Ethics*, there is "an unacknowledged Kantian element in "Existentialism is a Humanism" (p. xi).

12. In my discussion of *Anti-Semite and Jew*, I will follow Sartre's use of the masculine pronoun for the anti-Semite and Jew. This makes it much easier to deal with material cited from the text but should not be taken to suggest that Sartre (or I) see anti-Semitism as essentially or primarily masculine.

13. Theodor Adorno et al., *The Authoritarian Personality* (New York: Harper and Brothers, 1950), n. 1, 971. As Adorno concludes: "That his [Sartre's] phenomenological 'portrait' should resemble so closely, both in general structure and in numerous details, the syndrome which slowly emerged from our empirical observations and quantitative analysis, seems to us remarkable."

14. For this comparison, see Vidal-Naquet, "Remembrance of a 1946 Reader," 22–23, and also Richard Bernstein, *Hannah Arendt and the Jewish Question* (Cambridge and Oxford: Polity Press, 1996), 195–97. For Arendt's more extended discussions of the parvenu and pariah, see Ron H. Feldman, ed., *The Jew as Pariah* (New York: Grove Press, 1978); *Rachel Varnhagen: The Life of a Jewess*, ed. by Liliane Weissberg (Baltimore and London: Johns Hopkins University Press, 1997); and Part I ("Anti-Semitism") in *The Origins of Totalitarianism*.

15. Harold Rosenberg, "Does the Jew Exist? Sartre's Morality Play about Anti-Semitism," *Commentary* 7, no. 1 (January–June 1949): 12. Rosenberg's analysis is perhaps the best critique of Sartre's book in English.

16. Ferenc Feher, "István Bibó and the Jewish Question in Hungary: Notes on the Margin of a Classical Essay," *New German Critique* 21, special issue 3 (autumn 1980): 30. Bibó was an important Hungarian political and social theorist in the postwar years. For a copy of Bibó's essay of 1948, see Karoly Nagy, ed., *Democracy, Revolution, Self-Determination* (Boulder, Colo.: Social Sciences Monographs, 1991), 155–322. One striking thing about Bibó's piece is the way it begins with a very clear statement about the murder of around half a million Hungarian Jews at the end of the war, rather than avoiding the actual facts of murder and extermination as many, even most, did.

17. Robert Bernasconi, "Sartre's Gaze Returned: The Transformation of the Phenomenology of Racism," in *Sartre and Existentialism*, edited by McBride, 5:362. Schwarzschild, "J.-P. Sartre as Jew," 46–48, claims that Sartre admitted this fundamental neglect of Jewish history and tradition late in his life.

18. Hannah Arendt, "What Remains? The Language Remains: A Conversation with Guenter Gaus," in *Essays in Understanding, 1930–1954*, edited by Jerome Kohn (New York: Harcourt Brace and Co., 1994), 12.

19. Arendt, "Preface to Part One: Antisemitism" (1968), in *Origins of Totalitarianism*, xv.

20. Schwarzschild notes that Sartre also suggested late in his life that the creation of the Jewish self by the anti-Semite was consistent with the construction of the self by the "other" as developed in *Being and Nothingness*. The subject in his ontology was "deprived of all the individual characteristics that would have come from the interior." (p. 47).

21. Rosenberg, "Does the Jew Exist?" 18.

22. Feher, "István Bibó and the Jewish Question in Hungary," 19–20.

23. In *Esau's Tears: Modern Anti-Semitism and the Rise of the Jews* (Cambridge: Cambridge University Press, 1997), Albert Lindemann identifies any number of talented people who were anti-Semites. A more defensible point might be the claim that anti-Semitism can make smart people stupid on the particular issue of the nature of Jews.

24. On this issue, Daniel Jonah Goldhagen's *Hitler's Willing Executioners: Ordinary Germans and the Holocaust* (New York: Alfred Knopf, 1996) stands almost alone in stressing the exterminatory dimension of German anti-Semitism, but even he does not extend that claim to other national cultures in Europe.

25. See Albert Memmi, *Portrait of a Jew* (New York: Orion Press, 1962), for the view that it is neither possible nor desirable to expunge differences (pp. 143,172). A Tunisian Jew, Memmi offered a riposte to Sartre's *Anti-Semite and Jew* in this work.

26. Sartre's resort to a kind of existential Kantianism in the "Humanism" essay is thus a throwback to bourgeois subjectivity as the guarantor of basic humanity.

27. Whatever its literary and dramatic merits, Sartre's play *The Respectful Prostitute*, which is set in a Deep South town, sheds little light on the difference between anti-Semitism and antiblack racism. Julien Murphy's "Sartre on American Racism," in J. K. Ward and Tommy Lott, eds., *Philosophers on Race: Critical Essays* (Cambridge, Mass.: Blackwell, 2002), 222–40, reveals little more about Sartre's position that racisms are products of "bad faith" and the desire to deny freedom to the "other." Considered historically, they are products of capitalism. In general, the same will be true of the colonizer's creation of the colonizer in Sartre's thought.

28. Rosenberg, "Does the Jew Exist?" 271.

29. Sidney Hook, "Reflections on the Jewish Question," *Partisan Review* 16, no. 5 (May 1949): 463.

30. Irving Howe, *A Mirror of Hope* (New York: Harcourt Brace Jovanovich, 1982), 254–58.

31. Rosenberg, "Does the Jew Exist?" 11.

32. See Irving Howe with Kenneth Libo, *World of Our Fathers* (New York: Harcourt Brace Jovanovich, 1976).

33. Anatole Broyard, "Portrait of the Inauthentic Negro," *Commentary* 10 (July 1950): 56–64. See also Henry Louis Gates Jr.'s biographical essay, "The Passing of Anatole Broyard," in *Thirteen Ways of Looking at Black Men* (Random House: New York, 1997), 180–214, which is reprinted as "White Like Me" in *Life Stories*, ed. David Remnick (New York: Random House, 2000). Broyard's previous piece on the hipster is "A Portrait of a Hipster," *Partisan Review* 15 (January–June 1948): 721–26. One year after the "Inauthentic Negro" piece, he published "Keep Cool, Man," *Commentary* 11, no. 4 (April 1951): 359–62. Broyard was a regular book reviewer for the *New York Times* for many years, but never quite made it into the top echelon of New York intellectuals or American fiction writers. His unfinished memoir, *When Kafka Was the Rage* (New York: Carol Southern Books, 1993), is a short and often charming book about Broyard's early postwar years in Greenwich Village.

34. Broyard, "A Portrait of a Hipster," 725.

35. Ibid.

36. Broyard, "Keep Cool, Man," 359–62.

37. Sartre's ultimate emphasis falls on choice. Thus, one can, as was the case with the writer-criminal, Jean Genet, choose to be the transgressive figure that society insisted he was: "he utilizes his freedom as a pure universal subject to lower his status to that of an object." Jean-Paul Sartre, *Saint Genet: Actor or Martyr* (New York: George Braziller, 1963), 70.

38. Lewis R. Gordon, "Sartrean Bad Faith and Antiblack Racism," in *Sartre and Existentialism*, ed. William L. McBride, 5:120.

39. Gates rightly sees this knowledge/acknowledgment issue as central to Broyard's life—and the story of his life.

40. Broyard, *When Kafka Was the Rage*, ix.

Chapter 3—The Europeanization of American Prejudice: Adorno and Horkheimer

1. Max Horkheimer and Theodor W. Adorno, *Dialectic of Enlightenment* (New York: Herder and Herder, 1972), 207. See also "Research Project on Anti-Semitism:

Idea of the Project," in *The Stars Come Down to Earth and Other Essays on the Irrational in Culture*, ed. Stephen Crook (London and New York: Routledge, 1994), and Theodor Adorno, "Anti-Semitism and Fascist Propaganda" (1946), *Schriften 8* (Soziologische Schriften I) (Frankfurt: Suhrkamp Verlag, 1972), 397–406.

2. Martin Jay, "Anti-Semitism and the Weimar Left," *Permanent Exiles: Essays on the Intellectual Migration from Germany to America* (New York: Columbia University Press, 1985), 79. Most members of the Frankfurt School and others such as Hannah Arendt were inclined toward this view. See also Jay, "The Jews and the Frankfurt School: Critical Theory's Analysis of Anti-Semitism" (1979), in *Permanent Exiles*.

Generally, Jay's *The Dialectical Imagination: A History of the Frankfurt School and the Institute of Social Research, 1923–1950* (Boston: Little, Brown & Co., 1973) is indispensable on this topic, as is Rolf Wiggershaus's more recent *The Frankfurt School: Its History, Theories and Political Significance*, trans. Michael Robertson (Cambridge: Polity Press, 1994). There is also a massive amount of critical commentary on the Frankfurt School.

3. Peter Gay, *Freud, Jews and Other Germans: Masters and Victims in Modernist Culture* (New York: Oxford University Press, 1978), 165–68. Gay's concern in this part of his book is to counter the notion that all Jews in Germany were resolute modernists and alienated from mainstream German society; Walter Zwi Bacharach, "Jews in Confrontation with Racist Antisemitism, 1879–1933," *Leo Baeck Institute Yearbook*, vol. 25 (London: Secker and Warburg, 1980), 216. See also Marjorie Lamberti, "Liberals, Socialists and the Defense against Antisemitism in the Wilhelminian Period," *Leo Baeck Institute Yearbook*, vol. 25, 147–62.

4. See Martin Bernal, *The Fabrication of Ancient Greece, 1785–1985*, vol. 1 of *Black Athena: The Afroasiatic Roots of Classical Civilization* (London: Vintage, 1991), for an account of anti-Semitism in the German university system; Albert S. Lindemann, *Esau's Tears: Modern Anti-Semitism and the Rise of the Jews* (Cambridge: Cambridge University Press, 1997), 342. See also Fritz Ringer, *The Decline of the German Mandarins: The German Academic Community, 1890–1933* (Cambridge, Mass.: Harvard University Press, 1969); Leon Poliakov, *The Aryan Myth: A History of Racist and Nationalist Ideas in Europe*, trans. E. Howard (London: Sussex University Press and Heinemann Educational Books, 1974); and Ismar Schorsch, "German Antisemitism in the Light of Post-War Historiography," *Leo Baeck Institute Yearbook*, 19 (1974): 257–71.

5. Jay, *Dialectical Imagination*, 34. Adorno apparently had never been close to his father anyway. So uninterested was he in Jewish matters that he once referred, slightingly, to Erich Fromm as a "professional Jew" (*Berufsjuden*). See Hartmut Scheible, *Theodor W. Adorno* (Hamburg: Rowohlt Taschenbuch Verlag, 1989), 17.

6. Wiggershaus, *Frankfurt School*, 104.

7. Lamberti, "Liberals, Socialists," 158.

8. Max Horkheimer, "The Jews in Europe" (1939), in *Critical Theory and Society*, ed. Stephen E. Bronner and Douglas M. Kellner (New York: Routledge, 1989), 77.

9. Ibid., 78. This Hegelian locution—"x" is the truth of "y"—implies that x has been a constant potential and has emerged inevitably from y; that is, x and y partake of the same essence. Wiggershaus notes that the context for Horkheimer's extreme statement was what he saw as the growing conservatism of German émigrés in America, specifically their increasing tendency to link the Soviet Union and Nazi Germany as sharing totalitarian characteristics (p. 257).

10. It is important to note here that what Europeans meant by liberalism resembled the old-style Manchester liberalism more than it did the emerging New Deal liberalism in the 1930s.

11. See Anson Rabinbach, *In the Shadow of Catastrophe: German Intellectuals Between Apocalypse and Enlightenment* (Berkeley: University of California Press, 1997), 187.

12. Jay, *Dialectical Imagination*, 152. H. Stuart Hughes suggests that there are generally three ways to understand the relationship of capitalism to fascism: (1) big business essentially "ran the show"; (2) fascism "worked for the benefit of big business"; and (3) big business generally supported fascism after some hesitation. H. Stuart Hughes, *The Sea Change: The Migration of Social Thought, 1930–1955* (New York: Harper and Row, 1970), 118–19. In general, Hughes's analysis of the Frankfurt School is useful and lucid, though at times uncritical.

13. Herbert Marcuse, *Reason and Revolution* (Boston: Beacon Press, 1960), 412–13; Horkheimer, "The Jews in Europe," 92.

14. Erich Fromm, *Escape from Freedom* (New York and Toronto: Rinehart and Co., Inc., 1941), 221, 225, 228–29.

15. Franz Neumann, *Behemoth: The Structure and Practice of National Socialism* (1942; New York: Oxford University Press, 1944), 39, 159, 297, 299–300, 379.

16. Ibid., 86, 105, 95.

17. Ibid., 107–8. Hughes notes that although Neumann considered "intellectual rationalizations of National Socialism as pure eye-wash," he was "obliged to rehearse them at tedious length" (*The Sea Change*, p. 113). Even more surprisingly, Rabinbach quotes Neumann as saying: "One can represent National Socialism without attributing to the Jewish problem a central role" (p. 184). Whatever Neumann's real feelings, his analysis in *Behemoth* does not read so dismissively, either of Nazi ideology or of the relevance of the "Jewish problem."

18. Adorno, quoted in Wiggershaus, *The Frankfurt School*, 275.

19. See Wiggershaus, *The Frankfurt School*, 350–80, for an account of these institutional, financial, and intellectual issues. Rabinbach also presents a clear account of the origins and development of the project, in particular the textual division of labor—and philosophical tensions—involved in the dual authorship of *The Dialectic of Enlightenment* (pp. 166–73). He also suggests that the original title, *Philosophical Fragments*, might well have been retained since it is hard to maintain that the book has a unifying theme or thesis. Two recent studies have also contributed significantly to an understanding of the institutional context for the Studies in Prejudice project: Stuart Svonkin, *Jews Against Prejudice: American Jews and the Fight for Civil Liberties* (New York: Columbia University Press, 1997), 31–40; and John P. Jackson, *Social Scientists for Social Justice: Making the Case Against Segregation* (New York and London: New York University Press, 2001), 51–54.

20. See Christopher Lasch, "The Discovery of the Authoritarian Personality," in *The True and Only Heaven: Progress and Its Critics* (New York: W. W. Norton, 1991), 445–50, for this point. Lasch clearly prefers *The Dialectic of Enlightenment* to *The Authoritarian Personality*; yet it is the former more than the latter that considers anti-Semitism as all but co-extensive with the history of Western culture, something for which Lasch severely criticizes Horkheimer and Adorno.

21. Jay, "Anti-Semitism and the Weimar Left," 96. Adorno was also writing *Minima Moralia* (1951) at the same time, a book that Wiggershaus characterizes as "a

kind of aphoristic continuation of *The Dialectic of Enlightenment*" (*The Frankfurt School*, 394). Besides Adorno's "Research Project" and "Anti-Semitism and Fascist Propaganda," see also his "Freudian Theory and the Pattern of Fascist Propaganda," in *Gesammelte Schriften*, vol. 8 (Frankfurt: Suhrkamp Verlag, 1972), 408–33, for a clear explication of the psychoanalytic sources of *The Authoritarian Personality* in Freud's *Group Psychology and the Analysis of the Ego*.

22. For an example of how *The Authoritarian Personality* was relatively smoothly incorporated into postwar studies of prejudice, see Gordon W. Allport, *The Nature of Prejudice*, abridged (Garden City, N.Y., Doubleday Anchor, 1958). A more recent general account can be found in Gordon Richards, '*Race,' Racism and Psychology: Towards a Reflective History* (London and New York: Routledge, 1997), chapter 8 ("Racism at Bay: Psychology and 'Race,' 1945–69"), 224–60.

23. See Hannah Arendt, *The Origins of Totalitarianism*, 2nd ed. (Cleveland: Meridian, 1958), 5–7. There she distinguishes between anti-Semitism as scapegoating/projection and as a response to certain "real" Jewish traits or at least to Jews as a perennial "other."

24. Page references for Horkheimer and Adorno, *The Dialectic of Enlightenment*, will be included in the text.

25. See Wiggershaus, *The Frankfurt School*, 332–33, for a summation of the difficulties Adorno and Horkheimer had with the concept of rationality.

26. In 1940, Adorno sent Horkheimer a memo suggesting that, "The abandonment of nomadism was apparently one of the most difficult sacrifices demanded in human history." Because the Jews had never quite given up their wandering, uprooted existence, they were deeply resented by those who had settled, that is, undergone the repression required for the work of civilization. Quoted in Wiggershaus, *The Frankfurt School*, 276–77.

27. Rabinbach, *In the Shadows*, 178, 179. George Steiner has particularly stressed the role of Jews in the creation of Western conscience as crucial in the development of anti-Semitism. Such a line of analysis dovetails with the psychoanalytically oriented emphasis on the relationship between Judaism and Christianity as an Oedipal one. For other discussions of anti-Semitism in the *Dialectic of Enlightenment*, see Paul Connerton, *The Tragedy of Enlightenment* (Cambridge: Cambridge University Press, 1980), chapter 4, which hardly mentions the term "mimesis"; and David Seymour, "Adorno and Horkheimer: Enlightenment and Anti-Semitism," *Journal of Jewish Studies* 51, no. 2 (autumn 2000): 297–312. Seymour in particular raises the issue of whether their analysis of anti-Semitism is of the "eternal anti-Semitism" or of the "scapegoating" sort.

28. Zygmunt Bauman, *Modernity and the Holocaust* (Ithaca, N.Y.: Cornell University Press, 1989), 62–64.

29. Marie Jahoda, Introduction to *Studies in the Scope and Method of "The Authoritarian Personality,"* ed. Richard Christie and Marie Jahoda (Glencoe, Ill.: The Free Press, 1954), 11. See, in addition, the general discussion of *The Authoritarian Personality* in Jay, *The Dialectical Imagination*, chapter 8, and in Wiggershaus, *The Frankfurt School*, 412–30.

30. See Christopher Lasch's mordant but trenchant comments on the new genre in his *The True and Only Heaven*, 440–41. For more judicious (and blander) but useful treatments, see Ellen C. Lagemann, *The Politics of Knowledge: The Carnegie Corporation, Philanthropy and Public Policy* (Middletown, Conn.: Wesleyan

University Press, 1989), and Ellen Herman, *The Romance of American Psychology: Political Culture in the Age of Experts* (Berkeley: University of California Press, 1995). For two insightful analyses at the time, see Nathan Glazer, "The Authoritarian Personality in Profile: Report on a Major Study of Race Hatred," *Commentary* 9 (January–June 1950): 573–83, and Paul Kecskemetti, "Prejudice in the Catastrophic Perspective: Liberalism, Conservatism and Anti-Semitism," *Commentary* 11 (January–June 1951): 286–92.

31. Jay, *Dialectical Imagination*, 242. Gordon Richards notes that some San Quentin prisoners participated in the study, along with some male psychiatric patients.

32. Theodor Adorno, Else Frenkel-Brunswik, Daniel J. Levinson, and R. Nevitt Sanford, *The Authoritarian Personality* (New York: Harper and Row, 1950), 727. All page references from *The Authoritarian Personality* will be included in the text.

33. Richard Christie, "Authoritarianism Re-Examined," in *Studies in the Scope and Method of "The Authoritarian Personality,"* ed. Richard Christie and Marie Jahoda (Glencoe, Ill.: The Free Press, 1954), 169–70. The issue of class differences was of particular interest since it was assumed that there are class-related differences in modes of child rearing.

34. See John Higham, "Anti-Semitism and American Culture," in *Send These to Me: Jews and Other Immigrants in Urban America* (New York: Athenaeum, 1975), 175.

35. Christie, "Authoritarianism Revisited," 127. See Wiggershaus, *The Frankfurt School*, 411, for information about the title.

36. Adorno, "Scientific Experiences of an American Scholar in America," in *The Intellectual Migration: Europe and America, 1930–1960*, vol. 2 of *Perspectives in American History* (Cambridge, Mass.: Charles Warren Center, 1968), 359–60.

37. Ibid., 357.

38. Glazer, "The Authoritarian Personality in Profile," 580. It is not clear in *The Authoritarian Personality* or elsewhere whether the priority of the objective is a theoretical presupposition of Adorno's work or whether it is a contingent historical explanation of the origins and development of the self under the conditions of modernity. I strongly suspect that it is the former.

39. The term "psychodynamic process" is used by Herbert Hyman and Paul Sheatsley in "A Methodological Critique," in Christie and Jahoda, eds., *Studies in the Scope and Method of "The Authoritarian Personality,"* 120–21.

40. Ibid., 95, 104–5.

41. Edward Shils, "Authoritarianism: 'Right' and 'Left,'" in Christie and Jahoda, eds., *Studies in the Scope and Method of "The Authoritarian Personality,"* 44. See also Bauman, *Modernity and the Holocaust*, 152–53, along with Christopher Browning, *Ordinary Men: Reserve Police Battalion 101 and the Final Solution* (New York: HarperCollins, 1992), a case study in the obedience not so much to formal authority as to role expectations.

42. Else Frenkel-Brunswik, "Further Explorations by a Contributor to 'The Authoritarian Personality,'" in Christie and Jahoda, eds., *Studies in the Scope and Method of "The Authoritarian Personality,"* 267.

43. Adorno, "Scientific Experiments," 358.

44. For a discussion of this point, see Jay, *Dialectical Imagination*, 98–103; see also Hughes, "The Advent of Ego Psychology," in *The Sea Change*, 189–239.

45. At this point (p. 759), Adorno did mention Fromm's idea of the "sado-

masochistic" personality as a major contribution to the formulation of underpinnings of the authoritarian personality.

46. Lacan's critique is directed at the "ego" as an "imaginary" entity. It is fundamentally a paranaoic, defensive construct, both too strong and too weak, too rigid and too compliant. The imaginary self (*le moi*) fits the description of the ego of high scorers on the F-Scale quite closely. This suggests that the ego psychologists were far from the fools that Lacan suggested they were. Jacques Lacan, "The Mirror Stage," in *Ecrits* (New York: W. W. Norton, 1977). See also Herbert Marcuse, *Eros and Civilization* (New York: Vintage Books, 1955).

47. I know of no mention of Myrdal's study in any of Adorno's writings. In his essay of 1946, "Anti-Semitism and Fascist Propaganda," Adorno also notes the importance of "democratic ideology" in blunting the effects of American fascist propaganda.

48. Wiggershaus, *The Frankfurt School*, 416.

49. As it was, critics scored *The Authoritarian Personality* for failing to define fascism in ideological rather than characterological terms. See, in particular, Christie, "Authoritarianism Revisited," and Shils, "Authoritarianism: 'Right' and 'Left,'" for these points.

50. The reference to Sartre is on p. 971 of *The Authoritarian Personality*.

51. While recognizing that typologies resemble stereotypes, he contends that they provide a way of linking the subjective and the objective in that they "translate . . . our basic psychological concepts into sociological ones." Thus, for instance, "adulation of the primitive father" becomes translated into a "belief in authority for authority's sake" (p. 750).

52. For a complex psychoanalytic treatment of Himmler, see Peter Loewenberg, "The Unsuccessful Adolescence of Heinrich Himmler," in *Decoding the Past: The Psychoanalytic Approach* (New York: Alfred A. Knopf, 1983), 209–39.

53. Yet the Frankfurt critique was (and is) more sophisticated than the older Romantic tradition. The former did not locate the antidote to modern rationality in a higher form of irrationality or reappearance of transcendence or Being, but in the promise of concrete sensual happiness, avant-garde art, and critical reason. From this perspective, the Institute theorists can be seen not as traitors to the Enlightenment but as its fellow travelers, from the Romantic side. See Charles Taylor, *Sources of the Self: The Making of Modern Identities* (Cambridge: Cambridge University Press, 1989), chapter 21.

54. Axel Honneth, "Integrity and Disrespect: Principles of a Conception of Morality Based on the Theory of Recognition," *Political Theory* 20, no. 2 (May 1992): 187–201.

55. Christie, "Authoritarianism Re-Examined," 195. In *'Race', Racism and Psychology*, Richards notes that something like sixty-four projects had been initiated based on the theory and method of *The Authoritarian Personality* (p. 232). For a recent assessment of these issues, see John T. Jost, Arie Kruglanski, Jack Glaser, and Frank Sulloway, "Political Conservatism as Motivated Social Cognition," *Psychological Bulletin* 129, no. 3 (2003): 339–75.

56. Riesman is cited in Hughes, *The Sea Change*, 152.

57. See Kenneth Clark, "The Effects of Prejudice and Discrimination," in *Personality in the Making: The Fact-Finding Report of the Mid-Century White House Conference on Children and Youth*, edited by Helen Leland Witmer and Ruth Kotinsky

(New York: Harper and Brothers, 1952), 136; Jackson, *Social Scientists for Social Justice*, 54, 111–13.

58. Bruno Bettelheim and Morris Janowitz, *Dynamics of Prejudice: A Psychological and Sociological Study of Veterans* (New York: Harper and Brothers, 1950), 41–42. This study was part of the Studies in Prejudice project that funded Adorno et al.

59. See Pierre van den Berghe, *Race and Racism: A Comparative Perspective* (New York: John Wiley and Sons, 1967), and Joel Kovel, *White Racism* (New York: Vintage, 1971). Interestingly, although Kovel is a psychoanalyst, he did not even mention *The Authoritarian Personality* in his book.

60. Stanley Milgram, *Obedience to Authority* (New York: Harper and Row, 1974), 204–5.

61. Richard Hofstadter, "The Pseudo-Conservative Revolt," in *The New American Right*, edited by Daniel Bell (New York: Anchor Books, 1955); and Fritz Stern, *The Politics of Cultural Despair: A Study in the Rise of the Germanic Ideology* (Garden City, N.Y.: Anchor Books, 1965), 13. The 1960s and early 1970s also saw the emergence of intellectual histories of racism and National Socialism. The two most important intellectual histories of race (in America) were Winthrop Jordan, *White Over Black* (Chapel Hill: University of North Carolina Press, 1968); and George M. Fredrickson, *The Black Image in the White Mind* (New York: Harper Torchbooks, 1974). In addition, Stern's study and George Mosse's *The Crisis of German Ideology: Intellectual Origins of the Third Reich* (New York: Grosset and Dunlap, 1974) exemplified the turn to intellectual history over social psychology.

Chapter 4—Hannah Arendt:
Race, History, and Humanism

1. Two general assessments of the uses of totalitarianism as a concept are Les K. Adler and Thomas G. Patterson, "Red Fascism: The Merger of Nazi Germany and Soviet Russia in the American Image of Totalitarianism, 1930s–1950s," *American Historical Review* 75, no. 4 (April 1970): 1046–64; and Robert Burrowes, "Totalitarianism: The Revision Standard Version," *World Politics* 21 (1968–1969): 280. In his *Totalitarianism: The Inner History of the Cold War* (New York: Oxford University Press, 1995), Abbott Gleason claims that totalitarianism was the central concept of Cold War political thought and culture.

2. Elizabeth Young-Bruehl, *Hannah Arendt: For Love of the World* (New Haven and London: Yale University Press, 1982), 203. For the claim about the relationship between fascism and imperialism, see Robert Young, *White Mythologies: Writing History and the West* (London and New York: Routledge, 1990), 8, 125. Arendt's analysis of totalitarianism did not apply to the fascist regime in Italy.

3. Edward Said, *Culture and Imperialism* (London: Vintage, 1994).

4. Here I should acknowledge Daniel Stone's "Ontology or Bureaucracy? Hannah Arendt's Early Interpretations of the Holocaust," *European Judaism* 32, no. 2 (autumn 1999): 11–25. Although there are differences in emphasis between us—what he calls ontology I call philosophical anthropology—our readings of *Origins* are remarkably similar.

5. Young-Bruehl, *Hannah Arendt*, 104.

6. Arendt, *Essays in Understanding, 1930–1954* (New York: Harcourt Brace and Company, 1994), 12.

7. Young-Bruehl, *For Love of the World*, 158–59.

8. Young-Bruehl, *For Love of the World*, 185. For Arendt's writings on Jewish matters, primarily from the 1940s, see Ron H. Feldman, ed., *The Jew as Pariah* (New York: Grove Press, Inc., 1978). For more general reviews, essays, and heretofore unpublished lectures in the period up to the early 1950s, see Arendt, *Essays in Understanding, 1930–1954*.

9. For examples of her journalistic writings on communism and the dangers of anticommunism, see "The Eggs Speak Up," "The Ex-Communists," and "Religion and Politics" in *Essays in Understanding*. I know of no comment by Arendt on Myrdal's "American Creed."

10. Hannah Arendt, *The Origins of Totalitarianism*, 2nd ed. (Cleveland and New York: Meridian, 1958), viii–ix. I will generally be citing from this 1958 edition. The changes between the first and second editions of *Origins* are generally additions at the end of the text (the "Ideology and Terror" chapter and an epilogue on Hungary), but there are also some textual rearrangements. The first edition I have consulted and occasionally cited is *The Burden of Our Time* (London: Secker and Warburg, 1951). I will include page references to both editions in the text, but I have cited the third edition in the Endnotes.

Though I return later in this chapter to the question of the break in the tradition, the theme of the "break" was one Arendt shared with former mentors Heidegger and Jaspers, as well as with Theodor Adorno and Max Horkheimer. See Anson Rabinbach, "Heidegger's *Letter on Humanism* as Text and Event," in *In the Shadow of Catastrophe: German Intellectuals between Apocalypse and Enlightenment* (Berkeley: University of California Press, 1997), 97–128.

11. See, for instance, Paul L. Rose, *Revolutionary Anti-Semitism in Germany from Kant to Wagner* (Princeton, N.J.: Princeton University Press, 1990), xvi; Arendt, *Origins*, 7. In fact, Rose does not deny that there was a shift from a religious to an ethnic-racial basis for anti-Semitism somewhere around the turn of the eighteenth century and therefore is in rough agreement with Arendt on this point. But he does deny that this distinction made much difference in fact, since "'the destruction of Judaism' was the objective" (p. xvii). Thus, emancipation was synonymous with destruction of Judaism, while the goal of revolutionary anti-Semitism was the destruction of the Jews.

12. Walter Benjamin, "Theses on Philosophy of History," in *Illuminations*, ed. Hannah Arendt (New York: Schocken Books, 1969), 262. In this passage, Benjamin is contrasting the historicist with the historical materialist approach, but his emphasis on *die Jetztzeit* implies a rejection of history as a continuum constituted by cause and effect.

13. Tim Youngs, *Travellers in Africa: British Travelogues, 1850–1900* (Manchester and New York: Manchester University Press, 1994), 197. Youngs's use of this term is in reference to Conrad's *The Heart of Darkness*.

It is interesting to compare general accounts of this period on the issue of imperialism and more specifically this "boomerang" or "reverse colonization" effect. In Carlton J. H. Hayes's *A Generation of Materialism, 1871–1900* (New York: Harper Torchbooks, 1963), which was first published in 1941 and used by Arendt in *Origins*, there are two strong chapters on imperialism and nationalism, including discussions of racial ideologies and their relation to imperialism. Chapter seven is even called "Seed-Time of Totalitarian Nationalism." But Hayes focuses almost exclusively on the effects of European expansion on the conquered territories and not vice versa. Two more recent texts, Arno Mayer, *The Persistence of the Old Regime: Europe to the Great War* (Croom Helm: London, 1981), and Eric Hobsbawm, *The Age of Empire, 1875–1914* (London: Weidenfeld and Nicolson, 1987), adopt contradictory approaches. Mayer neglects European expansion altogether (there is no entry for imperialism in the index) in his concern to focus on the "preindustrial and prebourgeois" (p. 4) nature of the Old Order, while Hobsbawm, in keeping with the book's title, devotes ample space to imperialist expansion and suggests, albeit briefly, both positive and negative noneconomic (i.e., political and cultural) effects of imperial domination on European imperial powers in his chapter 3 ("The Age of Empire"). Though both consider themselves Marxists, Hobsbawm's thesis—that this period saw the "triumph and transformation of capitalism in the historically specific form of bourgeois society in its liberal version" (p. 9)—is the mirror image of Mayer's emphasis upon the "persistence" of the old regime.

14. Arendt's review essay "The Nation" (1946), *Essays in Understanding*, 206–11, is revealing here, and the book she reviewed in it, J. T. Delos's *La Nation*, is one possible source for the state/nation distinction. As she wrote there, the "primary rights" are "rights of men and citizens" while "federation" would make "nationality . . . a personal status rather than a territorial one" (p. 210). Both Hayes's *Generation of Materialism* and Hobsbawm's *The Age of Empire* note that the link of nation, race, and ethnicity, and/or language with the state, that is, every people should have a state and every state should tend toward ethnic homogeneity, only emerged with full force in the last quarter of the nineteenth century. This is the general point that Arendt was making.

15. It is important to emphasize that "masses" and "mass" society are *not* euphemisms in Arendt's thought for the uneducated or poor or the working class generally.

16. Hayden White, "The Forms of Wildness: Archaeology of an Idea," *Tropics of Discourse: Essays in Cultural Criticism* (London and Baltimore: Johns Hopkins University Press, 1978), 178. Interestingly, White uses this phrase in reference to Conrad's representation of native peoples of Africa. In her notes for the "Race and Bureaucracy" chapter of *Origins*, Arendt marked several passages from *Heart of Darkness* as particularly worth attention, especially one where Conrad refers to the frisson of "the thought of your remote kinship with this wild and passionate uproar." Arendt Papers, Manuscript Division, Library of Congress, Container 67 ("Excerpts and Notes: Africa"), n.d.

17. Arendt, Arendt Papers, Letter to Mary B. Underwood, Container 76 ("Outlines and Research Memoranda" File), 4.

18. Most recently, Seyla Benhabib suggests that the link Arendt draws between Africa and totalitarianism "makes little theoretical sense" as a "causal hypothesis." See *The Reluctant Modernism of Hannah Arendt* (Thousand Oaks, London, New Delhi: Sage Publications, 1996), 76.

19. For the Congo, see Neal Ascherson, *The King Incorporated: Leopold II in the Age of Trusts* (London: Allen and Unwin, 1963), and Adam Hochschild, *King Leopold's Ghost: A Story of Greed, Terror, and Heroism in Colonial Africa* (Boston: Houghton Mifflin, 1998). See more generally, Sven Lindqvist, *Exterminate All the Brutes* (New York: New Press, 1996), for the African precedents for extermination.

On German policy and precedents in Southwest Africa, see Woodruff D. Smith, *The German Colonial Empire* (Chapel Hill: University of North Carolina Press, 1978); *The Ideological Origins of Nazi Imperialism* (New York: Oxford University Press, 1986); and *Politics and the Sciences of Culture in Germany* (New York: Oxford University Press, 1991). In general, Smith is skeptical of any strong causal claim for an Africa–Nazi connection of the sort he thinks that Arendt makes and also of any strong influence of German anthropology, shaped by the colonial experience or evidence, on the development of German racial science. Both Kurt Jonassohn, "Before the Holocaust Deniers," *Society* 33, no. 2 (January–February 1996): 31–38, and Dan Stone, "White Men with Low Moral Standards? German Anthropology and the Herero Genocide," *Patterns of Prejudice* 35, no. 2 (2001): 33–45, are more convinced of the importance of the African experience in the development of racial science in Germany. For a lucidly developed comparison between German actions in Southwest Africa and U.S. action in the Philippines, see Helmut W. Smith, "The Logic of Colonial Violence: Germany in Southwest Africa (1904–1907)," in *German and American Nationalism: A Comparative Perspective*, ed. H. Lehrmann and H. Wellenreuther (Oxford and New York: Berg, 1999), 205–31.

20. Besides Stone on this point for Germany, see inter alia, Christopher L. Miller, *Black Darkness: Africanist Discourse in French* (Chicago and London: University of Chicago Press, 1985), and *Theories of Africans: Francophone Literature and Anthropology in Africa* (Chicago and London: University of Chicago Press, 1990), along with V. Y. Mudimbe, *The Invention of Africa: Gnosis, Philosophy, and the Order of Knowledge* (Bloomington and Indianapolis: Indiana University Press, 1988).

21. Arendt also wrote about the conflict between the political and social in Jewish history in *Rahel Varnhagen*, which was her *Habilitationschrift* that remained unpublished until the 1950s, and in Feldman, ed., *The Jew as Pariah*. Arendt took the pariah/parvenu distinction from Bernard Lazare and wrote an introduction to his *Job's Dungheap* (New York: Schocken Books, 1948).

22. Martin Jay has referred to Arendt's thought as a "radical form of anti-modernism" in "Women in Dark Times: Agnes Heller and Hannah Arendt," in *Force Fields* (London: Routledge, 1993), 69, but Seyla Benhabib's emphasis on Arendt's radical ambivalence regarding modernity is a more apt characterization.

23. Arendt to Jaspers, March 4, 1951, in Lotte Köhler and Hans Saner, eds., *Hannah Arendt–Karl Jaspers Briefwechsel* (Munich and Zurich: Piper, 1985), 203. All translations from the *Briefwechsel* are mine, unless otherwise indicated.

24. See Dwight Macdonald, "The Responsibility of Peoples" (1945), in *Memoirs of a Revolutionist* (Cleveland, Ohio: Meridian, 1958). Macdonald's views were undoubtedly influenced by Arendt, since they were good friends. For the best-known attempt to draw an analogy between the concentration camps and (North American) slavery, and a characterization of new world slavery as "unopposed capitalism," see Stanley Elkins, *Slavery* (Chicago, Ill.: University of Chicago Press, 1959).

25. Arendt to Jaspers, March 4, 1951, *Briefwechsel*, 202.

26. Ibid.

27. Aristotle, *Politics*, trans. Benjamin Jowett and Thomas Twining (New York: Viking Press, 1957), 10 (Book First).

28. See, for instance, Winthrop Jordan, *White Over Black* (Chapel Hill: University of North Carolina Press, 1967), and David Brion Davis, *The Problem of Slavery in Western Culture* (Ithaca, N.Y.: Cornell University Press, 1966), for classic discussions

of these issues in reference to the modern West and the United States. See also Ivan Hannaford, *Race: The History of an Idea of Race in the West* (Washington, D.C., and Baltimore, Md.: Woodrow Wilson Center Press and Johns Hopkins University Press, 1996).

29. See Arendt, "What Is Existential Philosophy?" (1946, 1948) and "Concern with Politics in Recent European Philosophical Thought," in *Essays in Understanding, 1930–1954* (New York: Harcourt Brace and Company, 1994), 163–87, and 428–47, respectively, for her attitude toward Heidegger and Jaspers in particular. In general, it is the influence of Jaspers rather than Heidegger that showed up most clearly in her post-World War II thinking about dialogue within a community. See Rabinbach, "The German as Pariah: Karl Jasper's *The Question of German Guilt*," in *In the Shadow of Catastrophe: German Intellectuals between Apocalypse and Enlightenment,* ed. Anson Rabinbach (Berkeley: University of California Press, 1997), 129–65. For a view much more critical of Arendt's relationship with Heidegger and his legacy, see Richard Wolin, *Heidegger's Children* (Princeton, N.J.: Princeton University Press, 2001).

30. Margaret Canovan, *Hannah Arendt: A Reinterpretation of Her Political Thought* (Cambridge and New York: Cambridge University Press, 1992), 196–97. There is a basic sense in which rights, contrary to what Arendt asserts, are "good for" preserving plurality. But her larger concern was that rights not be justified because they, for instance, create the possibility for human happiness. Rather, they are good in themselves. Helmut Smith suggests a useful distinction between a humanism of progress and a humanism of rights. The former allows for violence against those who seem more "primitive," while the latter was, and is, a better safeguard against resorting to violence and denial of self-determination in the name of progress. See n. 19.

31. This was precisely the point Habermas was trying to make in the *Historikerstreit*: the basis of German identity could only properly be a "constitutional patriotism," that is, commitment to basic civil liberties and rights and democratic forms of government, rather than a national identity grounded in the continuity of a specifically German history. See his "Historical Consciousness and Post-Traditional Identity: The Federal Republic's Orientation to the West" (1987), in *The New Conservatism* (Cambridge, Mass: MIT Press, 1989), 249–67, which reads like a more positive rewriting of chapter 9 of *Origins* and a liberal reworking of Heidegger's rectoral address.

32. Chinua Achebe, *Hopes and Impediments: Selected Essays, 1965–1987* (London: Heinemann, 1988), 11; Said, *Culture and Imperialism*, xix. For Hegel on Africa, see Sandor Gilman, *On Blackness without Blacks: Essays on the Image of the Black in Germany* (Boston: G. K. Hall and Co., 1982), and E. Eze, ed., *Race and the Enlightenment: A Reader* (Cambridge, Mass., and Oxford: Blackwell, 1997), chapter 10 ("Race, History and Imperialism").

33. The phrase "ethnocentric strain" is Shiraz Dossa's. Her article "Human Status and Politics: Hannah Arendt on the Holocaust," *The Canadian Journal of Political Science* 13, no. 2 (June 1980): 309–23, was one of the first treatments of Arendt to confront this aspect of *Origins*. See also the essays by Joan Cocks and Anne Norton in Bonnie Honig, ed., *Feminist Interpretations of Hannah Arendt* (University Park: Pennsylvania State University Press, 1995), for further (and less convincing) thinking about this aspect of Arendt's thought.

34. Jürgen Habermas, "Work and *Weltanschauung*: The Heidegger Controversy from a German Perspective," *The New Conservatism*, 140–72. Even with Heidegger, making this distinction distorts the historical and intellectual influences on his thought.

Another problem with such a distinction is the lack of independent criteria for making the distinction. Where the line between philosophy and ideology is drawn will shift over time.

35. Agnes Heller in Jay, "Women in Dark Times," 68.

36. There are actually two issues of evaluation involved here. One is Arendt's specific judgment about African culture. In its undifferentiated form, it is surely wrong. The abstract issue is whether there are criteria to make evaluations across cultures or at least to make evaluations of specific practices in other cultures.

37. Interestingly, in a passage in the second edition of *Origins*, Arendt moves swiftly and almost imperceptibly from speaking of "savages" (of Africa) to speaking of "rightless peoples" of Europe (p. 300).

38. Orlando Patterson, *Slavery and Social Death* (Cambridge, Mass.: Harvard University Press, 1983).

39. David Beresford, *The Guardian*, 22 September 1994, p. 17.

Chapter 5—African American Culture and the Price of Modernization

1. James B. McKee, *Sociology and the Race Problem: The Failure of a Perspective* (Urbana and Chicago, Ill.: University of Illinois Press, 1993), 8. Throughout this chapter I will use Stanley Elkins's terminology to describe two contrasting views of slave culture and, by extension, postslavery black culture—the "damage" view and the "creativity and resistance" view. See "The Two Arguments on Slavery" (1975), in *Slavery*, 3rd ed. (Chicago, Ill.: University of Chicago Press, 1976), 267–302. I am very much indebted to Daryl Scott's *Contempt and Pity* (Chicago, Ill.: University of Chicago Press, 1997) for an invaluable intellectual history of the image of black culture and black personality in the first two-thirds of the twentieth century.

2. For the formulation of the "class formation" and the "ghettoization" model, see James R. Grossman, *Land of Hope: Chicago, Black Southerners and the Great Migration* (Chicago and London: University of Chicago Press, 1989), n. 8, 279. For the classic sociological account of the development of the black community in Chicago, see, of course, St. Clair Drake and Horace R. Cayton, *Black Metropolis: A Study of Negro Life a Northern City*, rev. and enl. ed., 2 vols. (New York: Harcourt, Brace and World, Inc., 1970). Drake and Cayton note the differences between the African American and the white ethnic experience: "In many ways, the position of Negroes in northern urban communities has been similar to that of foreign-born immigrants. . . . In the case of Negroes, however, the process stops short of complete assimilation" (p. 757). As became apparent by the end of the 1960s, it stopped short for white ethnics too, but for different reasons.

3. For the classic statement about the nature of "folk" culture, see Robert Redfield, "The Folk Society," *American Journal of Sociology* 52, no. 4 (January 1947): 293–308, and *Tepozltan: A Mexican Village: A Study of Folk Life* (1930; Chicago and London: University of Chicago, 1974). In the latter, Redfield claims that "The southern Negro is our principal folk" (p. 4). For a more recent discussion, which raises all sorts of questions about the concept of folk culture, see the exchanges among Lawrence Levine, Robin D. G. Kelley, Natalie Zemon Davis, and R. Jackson Lears in *The American Historical Review* 97 (December 1992): 1369–1430.

4. In the case of Germany, modernization theory had to postulate a *Sonderweg* or "exceptionalist" model of modernization to account for the triumph of National Socialism rather than the emergence of a liberal democratic Germany. For an overview of these matters in relation to Germany, see Ian Kershaw, *The Nazi Dictatorship: Problems and Perspectives of Interpretation* (London: Arnold, 1993), 18–19. For an older but very influential view, see Barrington Moore, Jr., *Social Origins of Dictatorship and Democracy* (Boston: Beacon Press, 1966).

5. Gunnar Myrdal, *An American Dilemma* (New York: McGraw-Hill, 1964), 2:927, 1:208. Hereinafter, page references will appear in the text.

6. See Ben Keppel, "Ralph Bunche and American Racial Discourse," in *The Work of Democracy: Ralph Bunche, K. B. Clark, Lorraine Hansberry and the Cultural Politics of Race* (Cambridge, Mass.: Harvard University Press, 1995), 46–47, and Brian Urquhart, *Ralph Bunche: An American Life* (New York and London: W. W. Norton and Co., 1993).

7. For Frazier on Du Bois, see Anthony M. Platt, *E. Franklin Frazier Reconsidered* (New Brunswick and London: Rutgers University Press, 1991), 187–88. For the comparisons with Nazi racial and cultural doctrines, see Annette Trefzer, "'Let us all be Kissing-Friends?': Zora Neale Hurston and Race Politics in Dixie," *Journal of American Studies* 31, no. 1 (1997): 77.

8. Besides Stanley Elkins's *Slavery* for the moralism charge, see Ivan Hannaford, *Race: The History of an Idea in the West* (Washington, D.C., and Baltimore, Md.: Woodrow Wilson Center Press and Johns Hopkins University Press, 1996), 395–96.

9. See Wright, Introduction to Drake and Cayton, *Black Metropolis*, xxi, xxx. For the Wright–Myrdal friendship, see Michel Fabre, *The Unfinished Ordeal of Richard Wright,* 2nd ed. (Urbana and Chicago: University of Illinois Press, 1993), 349. Wright later dedicated *Pagan Spain* (New York: Harper, 1957) to Gunnar and Alva Myrdal.

10. Indeed, Myrdal and his team might have remembered that the late 1930s saw President Roosevelt identify the South as the nation's number one economic problem while the region was also undergoing a literary and cultural reawakening.

11. Myrdal, *An American Dilemma*, 1:84, 89. See also Hannaford, *Race*; Robert Young, *Colonial Desire: Hybridity in Theory, Culture and Race* (London and New York: Routledge, 1995); George Fredrickson, *The Black Image in the White Mind* (New York: Harper Torchbooks, 1974); and Stephen Jay Gould, *The Mismeasure of Man* (New York: W. W. Norton and Co., 1981). Ironically, Myrdal was himself associated with the eugenics movement in Sweden, although it was not racially inflected.

12. McKee, *Sociology and the Race Problem*, 6. Though he expressed it in a somewhat different way, John Diggins made this essential point about the Enlightenment in "Slavery, Race and Equality: Jefferson and the Pathos of Enlightenment," *American Quarterly* 28, no. 2 (1976): 206–28.

13. Walter Jackson, "Between Socialism and Nationalism: the Young E. Franklin Frazier," *Reconstruction* 1, no. 3 (1991): 133.

14. Ibid., 133; Platt, *E. Franklin Frazier Reconsidered*, 150.

15. Platt, *E. Franklin Frazier Reconsidered*, 74; Jackson, "Between Socialism and Nationalism," 123.

16. Oliver C. Cox, quoted in Charles U. Smith and Lewis Killian, "Black Sociologists and Social Protest," in *Black Sociologists: Historical and Contemporary Perspectives*, ed. James E. Blackwell and Morris Janowitz (Chicago and London: University of Chicago Press, 1974), 202–3.

17. Platt, *E. Franklin Frazier Reconsidered*, 196.

18. E. Franklin Frazier, review of *An American Dilemma*, *American Journal of Sociology* 50, no. 6 (May 1945): 555.

19. Frazier, "Race: An American Dilemma," *Crisis* 51 (1944): 105–6.

20. Frazier to Myrdal, June 24, 1942, and Myrdal to Frazier, June 26, 1942, in Frazier Papers, Moreland-Spingarn Center, Howard University Library, Washington, D.C. (hereafter Frazier Papers), Box 131, Folder 16 (1942). See also Oliver C. Cox, *Caste, Class and Race* (New York: Modern Reader Paperbacks, 1970).

21. Frazier to Myrdal, June 27, 1942, Frazier Papers. The specific person that Frazier had in mind was Willis Weatherford, a southern racial "moderate."

22. Frazier to Arnold Rose, [late 1942], and Frazier to Rose, December 14, 1942, Frazier Papers. The last comment about African culture was incorporated into chapter 35, n. 32 of *An American Dilemma*, 2:1394.

23. E. Franklin Frazier, *The Negro Family in the United States*, rev. and abridged ed. (New York: Dryden Press, 1948), 359, 15; Frazier, "Traditions and Patterns of Negro Life in the United States," in *Race and Culture Contacts*, ed. E. B. Reuter (New York and London: McGraw-Hill Book Co. Inc., 1934), 191–94.

24. E. Franklin Frazier, "The Negro's 'Cultural Past,'" *The Nation* 154 (1942): 195–96. See also Melville Herskovits, "The American Negro Family," *The Nation* 150 (1940): 104. For information on Frazier's attitude toward African liberation movements, see Platt, 198–99, and Penny Von Eschen, *Race and Empire: Black Americans and Anticolonialism, 1937–1957* (Ithaca and London: Cornell University Press, 1997).

25. Frazier, *The Negro Family*, 32.

26. Ibid., 100; see also 85.

27. Ibid., 212.

28. Ibid., 366, 359.

29. Herbert Gutman, "The Black Family in Slavery and Freedom: A Revised Perspective," *Power and Culture: Essays on the American Working Class*, ed. Ira Berlin (New York: Pantheon, 1987), 356, 362.

30. Scott, *Contempt and Pity*, n. 6, 215; McKee, *Sociology and the Race Problem*, 206; Platt, *E. Franklin Frazier*, 120.

31. Frazier, "Theoretical Structure of Sociology and Sociological Research," in *E. Franklin Frazier on Race Relations*, ed. G. Franklin Edwards (Chicago and London: University of Chicago Press, 1968), 5–6.

32. Frazier, "The Failure of the Negro Intellectual" (1962), in Edwards, ed., *E. Franklin Frazier*, 270, 277.

33. E. Franklin Frazier, *The Black Bourgeoisie: The Rise of a New Middle Class in the United States* (New York: Collier Books, 1957, 1962), 10, 176.

34. Frazier, "The Failure of the Negro Intellectual," 278.

35. In his *Heroism and the Black Intellectual: Ralph Ellison, Politics and Afro-American Intellectual Life* (Chapel Hill: University of North Carolina Press, 1994), Jerry G. Watts writes that "Frazier was to black social science what Richard Wright was to black fiction" (p. 59). See also Wright, Introduction to Drake and Cayton, *Black Metropolis*.

36. Richard Wright, "Blueprint for Negro Writing," *The Richard Wright Reader*, ed. Ellen Wright and Michel Fabre (New York: DeCapo, 1997), 42.

37. Wright, *12 Million Black Voices*, in Wright and Fabre, eds., *The Richard Wright Reader*, 147, 151.

38. Quoted in Michel Fabre, *The Unfinished Quest of Richard Wright*, trans. Isabel Barzun (New York: Morrow, 1973), 273.

39. Wright, "How Bigger Was Born," *Native Son* (New York: Harper and Row, 1940), viii; xii.

40. Ibid., xiii.

41. Ibid., xxiv.

42. Ibid., xx.

43. Wright, Introduction to Drake and Cayton, *Black Metropolis*, xxv. It is hard to avoid mentioning here the later phenomenon of the Black Panther Party. Though ideologically on the left, the Panthers were attracted to the aesthetics of power, violence, and domination—in short, something closely akin to the fascist aesthetic.

44. Wright, "Blueprint," 45.

45. Wright, *Native Son* (New York: Signet Books, 1961), 329.

46. Wright, *12 Million Black Voices*, 194. See also Jack B. Moore, "The Voice in *12 Million Black Voices*," *The Mississippi Quarterly* 62, no. 4 (fall 1989): 415–24. Among the literary devices that Wright atypically resorts to are the lapel-gripping, false intimacy of the second person mode of address ("you have seen their faces") and the first-person plural voice of solidarity ("we have suffered . . .").

47. Wright, "Blueprint," 41.

48. Wright, *Black Boy* (New York: Signet, 1964), 42–45. The term "black Southern family romance" is meant to allude to my focus in *A Southern Renaissance* (New York: Oxford University Press, 1980) on the white Southern family romance, at whose center stood an imaginary male figure of great cultural authority, because of whose loss the (usually) young man is in some sort of state of mourning.

49. Richard Wright, "Between Laughter and Tears," *The New Masses* 25, no. 2 (October 5, 1937): 22–25. See also Fabre's account in *The Unfinished Quest*, 278–82, and Wright, "Blueprint," 37. For attempts to mediate the conflict, see Guenter Lenz, "Southern Exposures: The Urban Experience and the Re-Construction of Black Folk Culture and Community in the Works of Richard Wright and Zora Neale Hurston," *New York Folklore* 7, nos. 1–2 (summer 1981): 3–39; and William J. Maxwell, *New Negro, Old Left: African-American Writing and Communism Between the Wars* (New York: Columbia University Press, 1999), chapter 5 ("Black Belt/Black Folk: The End(s) of the Richard Wright–Zora Neale Hurston Debate"). Lawrence P. Jackson, "The Birth of the Critic: The Literary Friendship of Ralph Ellison and Richard Wright," *American Literature* 72, no. 2 (June 2000): 321–55, also contains a brief but useful discussion of both Ellison's and Wright's hostility to Hurston. More recently, Tommy Lott has explored the controversy among several of Hurston's contemporaries over her use of black dialect. The issue is a complicated one, involving questions of accuracy, intention, and context. See "Black Vernacular Representation and Cultural Malpractice," *The Invention of Race: Black Culture and the Politics of Representation* (London: Blackwell, 1999), 84–110.

50. Wright, *12 Million Black Voices*, 161–62.

51. Wright, *Native Son*, 14. In *Black Marxism: The Making of the Black Radical Tradition* (1983; Chapel Hill and London: University of North Carolina Press, 2000), Cedric Robinson refers to "the odyssey of his [Bigger's] development of consciousness" (p. 425). The effects of action on consciousness, particularly in reference to violence, anticipate Frantz Fanon's therapeutics of violence in *The Wretched of the Earth* (New York: Grove Press, 1963).

52. Arendt again is relevant here, since she claimed that Adolf Eichmann did not—or could not—"think what he was doing." For Arendt, this is a prerequisite for, even an integral part of, moral consciousness.

53. Wright, *Native Son*, 334.

54. James Baldwin, "Alas, Poor Richard," (1961), in *James Baldwin: Collected Essays* (New York: Library of America, 1998), 253, 256. Three biographies of Baldwin have different strengths but each is worth reading: W. J. Weatherby, *James Baldwin: Artist on Fire* (London: Michael Joseph, 1989); James Campbell, *Talking at the Gates* (London: Faber and Faber, 1991); David Leeming, *James Baldwin* (London: Michael Joseph, 1994). Henry Louis Gates, Jr., "The Welcome Table," in *Thirteen Ways of Looking at a Black Man* (New York: Random House, 1997), 3–20, is a charming and moving account of Gates's meeting with Baldwin and Josephine Baker at Saint-Paul-de-Vence in southern France in 1973. Recent treatments of Baldwin have been more sympathetic than those of the 1970s and 1980s. He is one of the central figures, even heroes, of Carol Polsgrove, *Divided Minds: Intellectuals and the Civil Rights Movement* (New York: W. W. Norton and Co., 2001), especially chapter 6 ("And Then Came Baldwin"). For perceptive readings of Baldwin and Ellison, see Morris Dickstein, *Gates of Eden: American Culture in the Sixties* (New York: Basic Books, 1977), and *Leopards in the Temple: The Transformation of American Fiction, 1945–1970* (Cambridge and New York: Cambridge University Press, 1999), 180–210.

55. Baldwin, "Everybody's Protest Novel," in *James Baldwin: Collected Essays,* 18.

56. Baldwin, "Many Thousands Gone," in *James Baldwin: Collected Essays*, 26.

57. Ibid., 27.

58. Ibid.

59. Baldwin, "Harlem Ghetto," in *James Baldwin: Collected Essays,* 49–50, 53. "Negroes are Anti-Semitic Because They're Anti-White," is also reprinted in *James Baldwin: Collected Essays*, 739–48. See also Emily Miller Budick, *Blacks and Jews in Literary Conversation* (Cambridge: Cambridge University Press, 1998), for a complex and engrossing discussion of Baldwin in relation to Jewish-American literature and polemics.

60. Baldwin, "Everybody's Protest Novel," 18.

61. Wright, *Black Boy*, 45.

62. Baldwin, "Autobiographical Notes," in *James Baldwin: Collected Essays*, 9.

63. Robert Penn Warren, *Who Speaks for the Negro?* (New York: Random House, 1965), 277, 281.

64. James Baldwin in "Liberalism and the Negro: A Round-Table Discussion," *Commentary* 37, no. 3 (March 1964): 37. Besides Baldwin, participants in this discussion were Norman Podhoretz, Nathan Glazer, and Sidney Hook.

65. James Baldwin in "The Negro in American Culture," Transcript, WBAI-FM (New York, 1961), in *The Black American Writer*, vol. 1, ed. C. W. E. Bigsby (Orlando, Fla.: Everett/Edward, Inc., 1969), 79–108. Besides Baldwin, participants included Langston Hughes and Lorraine Hansberry, Nat Hentoff and Alfred Kazin, and Emile Capouya, a former schoolmate of Baldwin's.

66. Baldwin, "The Devil Finds Work," in *James Baldwin: Collected Essays*, 481.

67. See in particular Eldridge Cleaver's "Notes on a Native Son," *Soul on Ice* (New York: Dell, 1968), 97–111, and also a somewhat more sympathetic piece by Calvin Hernton, "Blood of the Lamb: The Ordeal of James Baldwin," *Amistad I:*

Writings on Black History and Culture, ed. John A. Williams and Charles F. Harris (New York: Vintage Books, 1970), 183–99. Both writers, but particularly Cleaver, were bothered, to say the least, by Baldwin's homosexuality.

68. Baldwin, "Autobiographical Notes," 8, 9.

69. Baldwin, "Many Thousands Gone," 29, 34; "Harlem Ghetto," 53; "Alas, Poor Richard," 266.

70. Baldwin, "Stranger in the Village," in *James Baldwin: Collected Essays*, 129.

71. Budick, *Blacks and Jews in Literary Conversation*, 33, 41.

72. Baldwin, "Alas, Poor Richard," 251.

Chapter 6—Culture, Accommodation, and Resistance I: Rethinking Stanley Elkins's *Slavery*

1. Editions of *Slavery* were published in 1959, 1963 (paperback), 1968, and 1976. The core text of each edition has the same pagination, but appendices were dropped and added in the editions after 1963. (Nathan Glazer also provided an introduction to the 1963 paperback, which was not reprinted thereafter.) Ann J. Lane, ed., *The Debate Over Slavery: Stanley Elkins and His Critics* (Urbana: University of Illinois Press, 1971), is an important collection of critical essays dealing with Elkins's *Slavery*. Another useful critique of Elkins is Kenneth M. Stampp, "Rebels and Sambos: The Search for the Negro's Personality in Slavery," *The Journal of Southern History* (1971): 367–92, while Bertram Wyatt-Brown has refused to discard Elkins entirely and incorporates him in his (Wyatt-Brown's) exploration of the African background to slave deference in "The Mask of Obedience: Male Slave Psychology in the Old South," *American Historical Review* 93 (December 1988): 1228–52, and reprinted as "Masks of Obedience: Honor and Male Slave Identity" in Wyatt-Brown's latest book. Daryl M. Scott's *Contempt and Pity: Social Policy and the Image of the Damaged Black Psyche, 1880–1996* (Chapel Hill: University of North Carolina Press, 1997), 114–18, is one of the few books in recent years to devote sustained critical attention to Elkins's *Slavery*. Another is Emily M. Budick's *Blacks and Jews in Literary Conversation* (Cambridge: Cambridge University Press, 1998), 62–86. Budick examines Elkins almost exclusively through the lens of the African American–Jewish American relationship as it emerged in the 1960s. Finally, Orlando Patterson's work has always been a critique of, and oblique dialogue with, Elkins. See his most recent *Rituals of Blood* (New York: Basic Civitas Books, 1998), 241. Finally, I am indebted to several conversations with my colleague Peter Ling and to his review essay, "The Incomparable Elkins," *Rethinking History* 1, no. 1 (spring 1997): 67–74.

2. Hannah Arendt, *The Origins of Totalitarianism*, 2nd ed. (Cleveland: Meridian Books, 1958), 440–41, 455. For further discussions of fabrication, see J. Stanley, "Is Totalitarianism a New Phenomenon?" in *Hannah Arendt: Critical Essays*, ed. L. P. and S. K. Hinchman (Albany, N.Y.: State University of New York Press, 1994), 11; and Michael Halberstam, "Totalitarianism as a Problem for the Modern Conception of Politics," *Political Theory* 26, no. 4 (August 1998): 459–88.

3. Elkins read Bettelheim's article quite early and filed it away in his memory. It was the key to the whole book. Elkins, interview by author, 29 November 1994, Northampton, Mass. It first appeared in *The Journal of Abnormal Psychology*, 38 (October 1943): 417–52, was reprinted in *Surviving and Other Essays* (New York:

Alfred A. Knopf, 1979), 48–83, and vastly expanded in *The Informed Heart: Autonomy in a Mass Age* (Glencoe, Ill.: Free Press, 1960).

4. Elkins, *Slavery*, 104. Page citations from the book will be included in the main text.

5. Arendt, *The Origins of Totalitarianism*, 437–59. See Wyatt-Brown, "Masks of Obedience," where he notes in passing that Russian prisoners of war offered little or no mass resistance to the Nazi forced labor regime and induced starvation (p. 8).

6. Arendt, *The Origins of Totalitarianism*, 455. It is important to note here that Arendt, certainly no fan of Freud or of psychoanalysis, also drew on Bettelheim for her general picture of the concentration camps.

7. See Chapters 8 through 10 for further discussion of these and related issues.

8. See essays by Richard Hofstadter and others in Daniel Bell, ed., *The Radical Right* (Garden City, N.Y., Doubleday Anchor, 1964), and Hofstadter's *The Paranoid Style of American Politics* (New York: Knopf, 1965). In *Contempt and Pity*, Scott makes this point about the influence of Hofstadter on Elkins.

9. In his brief discussion of Frank Tannenbaum's *Slave and Citizen: The Negro in the Americas* (New York: A. A. Knopf and Random House, 1946). Elkins observed that for Tannenbaum, "Slavery as an evil is simply taken for granted" (*Slavery*, 25). This, I think, is Elkins's view as well.

10. In "Masks of Obedience" Wyatt-Brown argues convincingly that certain forms and styles of slave deference in the South can be understood in terms of patterns persisting from Africa.

11. Kenneth Stampp, *The Peculiar Institution* (New York: Vintage, 1956), vii.

12. Surely, both Karl Popper's *The Open Society and Its Enemies* (London: G. Routledge and Sons, 1945) and the core notions of liberal pluralism shaped Elkins's vocabulary here.

13. Not surprisingly, Sambo was not only generic but also (implicitly) gendered. Thus, even if Sambo had existed in roughly the way and proportion that Elkins postulated, over half the slave population (women and children) would have failed to fit the Sambo personality type.

14. See p. 228 in the first and second editions; p. 308 in the third edition of *Slavery*.

15. Primo Levi, *The Drowned and the Saved* (London: Abacus, 1989), 22–51. Gilroy mentions Levi's concept of the grey zone in *The Black Atlantic,* 215, as well.

16. See also Paula Ballinger, "The Culture of Survivors: Post-Traumatic Stress Disorder and Traumatic Memory," *History and Memory* 10, no. 1 (spring 1998): 99–132, for a discussion of numbing as a reaction to a traumatic situation. See Richard Wright, *12 Million Black Voices*, reprinted in *The Richard Wright Reader*, ed. E. Wright and M. Fabre (New York: De Capo Press, 1997), 161–62.

17. In his *The Highest Stage of White Supremacy* (Cambridge: Cambridge University Press, 1981), John Cell refers to "the Elkins School," but names none of its members. In fact, Elkins very quickly was pretty much alone in defending his work, at least in public.

18. Elkins, *Slavery*, 247.

19. Elkins's claim about the centrality of capitalism to the development of modern slavery is supported by enough historians to give pause to those who, in recent years, have posited an intrinsic link between free markets and a free society.

20. Malcolm X, quoted in William L. Van Deburg, *New Day in Babylon: The Black Power Movement and American Culture, 1965–1975* (Chicago: University of

Chicago Press, 1992), 5, and in Taylor Branch, *Pillar of Fire: America in the King Years, 1963–65* (New York: Simon and Schuster, 1988), 585.

21. Addison Gayle, Jr., "Dreams of a Native Son," *The Liberator* 10, no. 2 (February 1970): 5.

22. See, for examples, Eugene D. Genovese, "Rebelliousness and Docility in the Negro Slave: A Critique of the Elkins Thesis," and Orlando Patterson, "Quashee," in *The Debate Over Slavery: Stanley Elkins and His Critics*, ed. Ann Lane, 43–74, 210–19. See also Patterson, "Toward a Future That Has No Past—Reflections on the Fate of Blacks in the Americas," *The Public Interest*, no. 27 (1972): 25–62. There he also notes that Elkins "unnecessarily undermined his own argument in his demonstrably false claim that the Sambo stereotype was uniquely American" (p. 241). See Wyatt-Brown, "Masks of Obedience," for another claim that something like the Sambo type was practically universal.

23. John Blassingame, "Slave Personality Types," in *The Slave Community*, rev. and enl. ed. (New York: Oxford University Press, 1979), 284–322.

24. I owe this insight and several others about Elkins to my colleague Peter Ling.

25. It is not clear to what extent slave narratives recorded, for instance, in the 1930s were potentially available to Elkins. In *American Crucible* (Princeton, N.J.: Princeton University Press, 2001), Gary Gerstle mentions in passing that the slave narratives were not used until late in the 1960s (p. 406).

26. Genovese, "Rebelliousness and Docility," 44. See also Malcolm Bull, "Slavery and the Multiple Self," *New Left Review* 231 (September–October 1998), 94–130.

27. Bettelheim, "The Individual and Mass Behavior," in *Surviving and Other Essays*, 202.

28. See G. Fredrickson and C. Lasch, "Resistance to Slavery" and R. S. Bryce-LaPorte, "Slaves as Inmates, Slaves as Men: A Sociological Look at Elkins' Thesis," in *The Debate Over Slavery: Stanley Elkins and His Critics*, ed. Ann Lane, 223–44, 269–92. In response to these essays, Elkins acknowledged the cogency of the prison analogy and thought his own approach broadly compatible with it. Elkins, "Slavery and Ideology," in *The Debate Over Slavery*, ed. Lane, 353–56. It is also important to note that Goffman used some of the same sources on the concentration camp experience as Elkins did. Another analogy advanced much later, though not at that time, was the one between domestication of animals and of human beings. As K. Jacoby has observed, "There was no such thing as, say, neotenic humans specially suited to being domestic slaves." See "Slaves by Nature? Domestic Animals and Human Slaves," *Slavery and Abolition* 15, no. 1 (April 1994): 95. Yet this was just what plantation slave owners sought to produce—an infantilized worker. As Jacoby also notes, the idea of the slave as animal long predates racial slavery. For an often-stimulating exploration of the human/nonhuman and the brother/other relationship, see Marc Shell, *Children of the Earth* (New York: Oxford University Press, 1993). Shell's basic position is that a universalist "all men are brothers" position tends to lead to the position that "all men who are not my brothers are not men."

29. Besides several of the contributors to the Lane collection, *The Debate Over Slavery: Stanley Elkins and His Critics* (including Fredrickson, Lasch, and Stuckey), more recently Howard McGary and Bill E. Lawson in *Between Slavery and Freedom: Philosophy and American Slavery* (Bloomington and Indianapolis: Indiana University Press, 1992) note that something like brainwashing or indoctrination could have taken place without implying a full-fledged Sambo personality.

30. Genovese, "Rebelliousness and Docility," 64.

31. Daniel Jonah Goldhagen's typology in *Hitler's Willing Executioners* (New York: Alfred A. Knopf, 1996) is useful here, whatever the considerable problems with his controversial book.

32. Although disagreeing on other matters, two recent, well-known works—Goldhagen, *Hitler's Willing Executioners,* and Saul Friedländer, *Nazi Germany and the Jews*, vol. 1 (New York: Harper Collins, 1997)—agree that Germans had little trouble swallowing German-style apartheid, from the mid-1930s on. See Ian Kershaw, *The Nazi Dictatorship*: *Problems and Perspectives of Interpretation*, 3rd ed. (London: Arnold, 1993), chapter 5, for a lucid discussion of this issue.

33. Seymour Drescher, "The Atlantic Slave Trade and the Holocaust: A Comparative Analysis" (1996), in *From Slavery to Freedom* (New York: New York University Press, 1999), 312–99. Drescher also generally agrees with Arendt that the stigma of superfluity marked the attitude of the Nazis toward those headed for extermination or for labor unto death.

34. The three functions of the camps—domination, fabrication, and extermination—come from a reading of Arendt's *The Origins of Totalitarianism* along with Stanley's excellent "Is Totalitarianism a New Phenomenon?" 11.

35. See Terence Des Pres, *The Survivor: An Anatomy of Life in the Death Camps* (New York: Oxford University Press, 1976), 151–55. See also the less polemical, more meditative work by Tristan Todorov, *Facing the Extreme: Moral Life in the Concentration Camps* (New York: Henry Holt and Company, 1996). For a useful overview of the controversy, see P. Marcus and A. Rosenberg, "Reevaluating Bruno Bettelheim's Work on the Nazi Concentration Camps: The Limits of the Psychoanalytical Approach," *The Psychoanalytic Review* 8, no. 3 (fall 1994): 537–63.

36. E. Genovese, *Roll, Jordan, Roll* (New York: Pantheon, 1974).

37. See Gilroy, *The Black Atlantic,* for a compelling account of the centrality of *Slavery* to the culture of modernity and the process of social, economic, and political modernization.

38. Alfred Wallace quoted in Christopher Irmscher, *The Poetics of Natural History: From John Bertram to William James* (New Brunswick and London: Rutgers University Press, 1999), 286; Louis Agassiz is quoted in Stephen J. Gould, *The Mismeasure of Man* (New York: W. W. Norton: 1981), 46, 48; Samuel George Morton is quoted in Gould, 55. For another account of Agassiz in Brazil, see Louis Menand, *The Metaphysical Club* (New York: Farrar Straus and Giroux, 2001), chapter 6.

39. Edgar Thompson, *Plantation Societies, Race Relations and the South: The Regimentation of Population* (Durham, N.C.: Duke University Press, 1975), 115. Plantations are one of the prime places where "new" races emerge, according to Thompson; and "the idea of race is," according to Thompson, "a situational imperative" (p. 117). I would like to thank John Shelton Reed for this reference to Thompson's work. For a similar claim about New World slavery, see Cedric Robinson, *Black Marxism: The Making of the Black Radical Tradition* (Chapel Hill: University of North Carolina Press, 2000): "The invention of the Negro was proceeding apace with the growth of slave labor" (p. 119). David Brion Davis, "At the Heart of Slavery," *The New York Review of Books*, 43, no. 16 (October 17, 1996): 51–54, is an invaluable analysis, among other things, of the various ways, historically, the slave has been "constructed."

40. Besides the works cited in the previous footnote, George Fredrickson, *The*

Black Image in the White Mind (New York: Harper Torchbooks, 1972), remains the definitive account of the development of scientific racism in the course of the nineteenth century. See also Robert J. C. Young, *Colonial Desire: Hybridity in Theory, Culture and Race* (London: Routledge, 1995), chapter 5.

41. Not only Earl Thorpe in *The Debate over Slavery*, edited by Lane, but Kenneth Stampp, as well as Robert Fogel and Stanley Engerman in *Time on the Cross: The Economics of American Negro Slavery* (Boston: Little, Brown, 1974), maintain that the full potential of slavery as an economic system could not have been realized by a race of dependent human beings of the type Elkins suggested. It needed a diversity of types, some of whom would have to have been imbued with something like a work ethic. For a much more recent essay focusing on such issues, see C. Morris, "The Articulation of Two Worlds: The Master-Slave Relationship Reconsidered," *Journal of American History* 85, no. 3 (December 1998): 982–1007. Morris, much more even than Elkins and others, separates the oppressiveness of slavery from either its rationality or its cruelty.

42. For persistence of ethnicity and the rise in black–Jewish tensions are Nathan Glazer and Daniel P. Moynihan, *Beyond the Melting Pot*, 2nd ed. (Cambridge: MIT Press, 1970), and Gary T. Marx, *Protest and Prejudice: A Study of Belief in the Black Community* (New York: Harper and Row, 1967). Another useful collection is James Baldwin et al., *Black Anti-Semitism and Jewish Racism*, introduction by Nat Hentoff (New York: Schocken Books, 1969). John Murray Cuddihy, *The Ordeal of Civility* (New York: Basic Books, 1974), especially chapter 22, analyzes the victimhood competition between African Americans and Jewish Americans. More recently, Budick's *Blacks and Jews in Literary Conversation* focuses considerable attention on the 1960s. For the modern political history of the conflicting ideologies of civic and racial nationalism, see Gerstle, *American Crucible*.

43. See Peter Novick, *The Holocaust in American Life* (New York: Houghton Mifflin, 1999).

44. For an exploration of these and other issues, see Budick's *Blacks and Jews in Literary Conversation*. Whether Elkins's Jewishness was known to his readers is difficult to say.

45. Pat Watters, *The South and the Nation* (New York: Pantheon, 1969), 352. For a wider discussion of the role of émigré Germans teaching at black colleges in the South in the postwar era, see Gabrielle Simon Edgcomb, *From Swastika to Jim Crow: Refugee Scholars at Black Colleges* (Malabar, Fla.: Krieger Publishing Co., 1993).

46. R. Staples, "Black Ideology and the Search for Community," *The Liberator* 9, no. 6 (June 1969): 11; A. Sivanandan, "Culture and Identity," *The Liberator* 10, no. 6 (June 1970): 11; Addison Gayle, Jr., "Cultural Nationalism: The Black Novel and the City," *The Liberator* 9, no. 7 (July 1969): 16; Gayle, "Dreams of a Native Son," *The Liberator* 10, no. 2 (February 1970): 9. Gayle's observation may have been prompted by Richard Wright's allusion to the potential attractiveness of fascism to the likes of Bigger Thomas in "How Bigger Was Born."

47. Again, Cell, otherwise so insightful, assumes the opposite regarding the role of Jews in *Slavery*. Early in his discussion of Elkins's book, he writes: "Like the Jewish survivors of the concentration camps, Elkins argues, slaves became childish, docile, and imitative." Cell, *The Highest Stage of White Supremacy*, 235. It is also telling that Budick, in *Blacks and Jews in Literary Conversation*, 78, prefaces a passage from Elkins that refers "to people in a complex state of civilization" with the

phrase "the Jews of Europe," when in fact Elkins merely writes "people" in *Slavery*, 89. This illustrates the way that it is now assumed that Elkins was commenting on the effects of the camps on Jews rather than on Europeans generally. By the 1960s, Bettelheim came to focus much more explicitly on the Jewish experience in the concentration and extermination camps. See chapter 7 of this volume for a more detailed discussion of his position.

48. Novick, *The Holocaust in American Life*, 65.

49. Orlando Patterson explicitly intends *Rituals of Blood* (New York: Basic Civitas, 1998), 45–46, to be a rehabilitation of the position associated with Frazier and Moynihan on the negative effects of slavery on the African American family structure and conjugal bonds down to the present.

50. For the Moynihan Report and the accompanying documentation of the controversy, see Lee Rainwater and William L. Yancey, eds., *The Moynihan Report and the Politics of Controversy* (Cambridge, Mass.: MIT Press, 1967).

51. Elkins did use the phrase "the normal residue of pathology" in his 1975 essay, "The Two Arguments on Slavery," which is included in the third edition of *Slavery*. The passage is quoted in Budick, *Blacks and Jews in Literary Conversation*, 82.

52. In his *Domination and the Arts of Resistance: Hidden Transcripts* (New Haven and London: Yale University Press, 1990), James C. Scott notes that there generally seem to be "far fewer lasting consequences" of compliance "than might have been supposed" (p. 110).

53. Elkins, "Slavery and Ideology" (1971), in *The Debate Over Slavery: Stanley Elkins and His Critics*, ed. Ann Lane, 356. For Ellison's comments, see *The Collected Essays of Ralph Ellison* (New York: Modern Library, 1995), 736.

54. See Scott, *Contempt and Pity*, 117, for confirmation of the distance Elkins wished to put between himself and Moynihan.

55. Orlando Patterson, *Slavery and Social Death* (Cambridge, Mass.: Harvard University Press, 1982), 97.

56. Patterson, "Toward a Future That Has No Past," 42.

57. Patterson, *Rituals of Blood*, 241.

58. For a very strong statement of role theory as social and political theory, see Scott's *Domination and the Arts of Resistance*. A chief weakness of theories of internalization, such as psychoanalysis, lies in their inability to explain or take account of role-playing in any interesting way. The work of Jacques Lacan, which itself represented a certain Hegelianizing of Freud, goes a way toward remedying this shortcoming.

59. The role-playing explanation has been most convincingly used by Christopher Browning, *Ordinary Men: Reserve Police Battalion 101 and the Final Solution in Poland* (New York: HarperCollins, 1992), and Zygmunt Bauman, *Modernity and the Holocaust* (Cambridge: Polity Press, 1989). Stanley Milgram's *Obedience to Authority* (New York: Harper and Row, 1974) is also relevant to this debate in showing how situational constraints and expectations, not innate aggression, lead subjects to inflict pain. The most recent challenge to this position comes, of course, from Goldhagen's *Hitler's Willing Executioners*.

60. Patterson, *Rituals of Blood*, 32, 50–51.

61. Strictly speaking, someone *internalizes* values, beliefs, and attitudes, while he or she *identifies with* a person.

62. See Jonathan Spence, "In China's Gulag," *New York Review of Books* 42, no. 13 (August 10 1995): 15–18, for an account of the effects of incarceration in China

during and after the Cultural Revolution. In many respects, it reads like a gloss on Elkins's book.

63. My observations here derive from a discussion held at the Southern Intellectual History Circle in February 2000 at St. Petersburg, Florida. The points about the damage caused by role-playing were made with particular force by James Horton of George Washington University.

64. If we update the Elkins thesis for our time, it might go something like the following: assuming that slaves (or any individual or group at the mercy of something approaching absolute power in something approaching a closed system) are human and, in that sense, equal to those who hold power, to what degree is the humanity of slaves and masters restricted, distorted, diminished—or perhaps even augmented—by their life in such a system? One thing is immediately clear—such a question is not simply a matter for empirical investigation and comparison. To answer the question implies that "we" agree upon what it means to be human and thus what supports or diminishes that humanity. This is a matter that most students of slavery in general fail to address. But until some sort of consideration of the question of human nature is part of their training, the issues that Stanley Elkins raised in *Slavery* will not be resolved, since participants in the debate will not be clear on what it is they are arguing about.

Chapter 7—Culture, Accommodation, and Resistance II: The Eichmann Trial and Jewish Tradition

1. The source for the claim that 87 percent of Americans had heard of the Eichmann trial is Tony Kushner, *The Holocaust and the Liberal Imagination* (Oxford and Cambridge, Mass.: Blackwell, 1994), 247–55. For the most recent overview of the controversy in and around the Eichmann trial, see Peter Novick, *The Holocaust in American Life* (Boston: Houghton Mifflin, 1999), especially 127–45. Jennifer Ring, *The Political Consequences of Thinking: Gender and Judaism in the Work of Hannah Arendt* (Albany, N.Y.: State University of New York Press, 1997) is more theoretically oriented but also places Arendt's controversial book in the context of the New York Jewish intellectuals' postwar rediscovery of their Jewish roots.

For an analysis of post–World War II American Jewish experience, and the importance of the Eichmann trial, including the controversy about Arendt's book (and to a lesser degree over the contribution of Hilberg and Bettelheim), see Nathan Glazer, *American Judaism* (Chicago: University of Chicago Press, 1957); Stephen J. Whitfield, *Voices of Jacob, Hands of Esau: Jews in American Life and Thought* (Hamden, Conn.: Archon Books, 1984); and Edward S. Shapiro, *A Time for Healing: American Jewry since World War II* (Baltimore and London: Johns Hopkins University Press, 1992).

2. See Bruno Bettelheim, "Individual and Mass Behavior in Extreme Situations" (1943), in *Surviving and Other Essays* (New York: Alfred A. Knopf, 1979), 48–83, which is only a slightly modified version of the original essay. Bettelheim's *The Informed Heart: Autonomy in a Mass Age* (Glencoe, Ill.: Free Press, 1960) is an extended elaboration on his original essay. For a critical, yet not entirely unsympathetic, biography of Bettelheim, see Nina Sutton, *Bettelheim: A Life and a Legacy* (Boulder, Colo.: Westview Press, 1997). Arendt cited and was clearly influenced by Bettelheim's 1943 essay in *The Origins of Totalitarianism* (1951) where she emphasizes that the camps were vast experimental laboratories for the transformation of human nature.

3. Ring, *Political Consequences of Thinking*, chapter 5, 111; Dwight Macdonald, *Partisan Review* 31, no. 2 (spring 1964): 268. For more recent and persisting animus against Arendt, see Richard Wolin, *Heidegger's Children: Hannah Arendt, Karl Loewith, Hans Jonas and Herbert Marcuse* (Princeton, N.J.: Princeton University Press, 2001); and Idith Zertal, "Undermining Arendt, Yet Again," *Haaretz*, October 28, 2002 (available at: www.haaretzdaily.com).

4. The most readily accessible English-language version of the Scholem–Arendt exchange can be found in Ron H. Feldman, ed., *The Jew as Pariah: Jewish Identity and Politics in the Modern Age* (New York: Grove Press, 1978), 240–51. Scholem's charge came in his first letter to Arendt of June 23, 1966 (p. 242 in Feldman).

5. Whether Elkins and/or Arendt skewed the debate about resistance and accommodation in ways that foreclosed a fruitful discussion is another matter.

6. Wolin, *Heidegger's Children*, 57.

7. Besides Arendt's *Eichmann in Jerusalem: A Report on the Banality of Evil*, rev. enl. ed. (New York: Viking Press, 1965), and Raul Hilberg, *The Destruction of the European Jews* (Chicago: Quadrangle Books, 1961), see Harold Rosenberg, "The Trial and Eichmann," *Commentary* 32, no. 5 (November 1961): 369–81; Tom Segev, *The Seventh Million: The Israelis and the Holocaust* (New York: Hill and Wang, 1993); Peter Novick, *The Holocaust in American Life* (Boston: Houghton Mifflin, 1999); and Amos Elon, "The Politics of Memory," *A Blood-Dimmed Tide: Dispatches from the Middle East* (New York: Columbia University Press, 1997). All page references from Arendt's *Eichmann in Jerusalem* will be inserted in the main text.

8. I do not agree with Daniel Jonah Goldhagen's thesis that the German people were uniquely anti-Semitic nor that extermination was inevitable. One can say that there was a kind of passive consensus among Germans (and probably among other Europeans) that something like an apartheid society in which Jews were set apart and discriminated against was tolerable. For a general account of the change in the interpretation of Holocaust that took place in the 1960s, see Kushner, *The Holocaust and the Liberal Imagination*, and Novick, *The Holocaust in American Life*.

9. Segev, *The Seventh Million*, 327.

10. See Gabriel Motzkin, "Hannah Arendt: Von ethnischer Minderheit zu universeller Humanitaet," in *Hannah Arendt Revisited: "Eichmann in Jerusalem" und die Folgen*, ed. Gary Smith (Frankfurt: Edition Suhrkamp, 2000). Motzkin's stimulating article makes the point that Arendt's voice was that of the "refugee" and not the "survivor." Her basic political standpoint was shaped in the interwar years and thus never quite accommodated itself to a Jewish state in which Jews were the dominant ethnic group. Maybe so. But the message of *The Origins of Totalitarianism* was precisely that the age of totalitarianism had demonstrated the hollowness of the appeal to general human rights enforced by supranational bodies. This also accounts for much of her deep ambivalence toward Israel and its decision to put Eichmann on trial. I will return to this issue later in the chapter.

11. See Segev, *The Seventh Million*, pp. 11, 349; and Shoshana Felman, "Theaters of Justice: Arendt in Jerusalem, the Eichmann Trial, and the Redefinition of Legal Meaning in the Wake of the Holocaust," *Critical Inquiry* 27 (winter 2001): 212–16.

12. Besides Felman, "Theaters of Justice," see Annette Wieviorka, "Die Entstehung des Zeugen," in *Hannah Arendt Revisited: "Eichmann in Jerusalem" und die Folgen*, 136–59; Mark Osiel, *Mass Atrocity, Collective Memory, and the Law* (New Brunswick, N.J., and London: Transaction, 1997); and Lawrence Douglas, *The Memory of*

Judgement: Making Law and History in the Trials of the Holocaust (New Haven, Conn., and London: Yale University Press, 2001). All these sources note and/or criticize Arendt for her conservative and formal notion of jurisprudence, her view that the trials should be oriented primarily toward the perpetrators not the victims, and her skepticism concerning the pedagogic-nationalistic purposes of, in this instance, the Eichmann trial.

13. As already seen in Chapter 4, Arendt's thesis of a fundamental break in the history of anti-Semitism is not universally accepted. Most recently, James Carroll, *Constantine's Sword: The Church and the Jews—A History* (Boston: Houghton Mifflin, 2001), has questioned not so much the discontinuity thesis as the Arendtian claim that religious anti-Semitism was less murderous than modern racial anti-Semitism. Although Carroll emphasizes the responsibility of the Roman Catholic Church, he does not see this as an inevitable development in Roman Catholic theology or Church doctrine.

14. Raul Hilberg, *The Destruction of the European Jews* (Chicago, Ill.: Quadrangle Books, 1961), 206–8. Page numbers of material cited from this text are in the main body of the chapter.

15. See Oscar Handlin, "Jewish Resistance to the Nazis," *Commentary* 34, no. 5 (November 1962): 398–405; and Norman Podhoretz, "Hannah Arendt on Eichmann: A Study in the Perversity of Brilliance," *Commentary* 36, no. 3 (September 1963): 205. Handlin's piece was published before Arendt's book appeared, but he did attack the "impiety" of Hilberg's account of Jewish resistance.

16. Christopher R. Browning, "The Revised Hilberg," in *Simon Wiesenthal Center Annual*, vol. 3, edited by H. Friedländer and Sybil Milton (White Plains, N.Y.: Kraus International Publications, 1986), 298. See also Raul Hilberg, "German Railroads/ Jewish Souls," *Society* 35, no. 2 (January/February 1998): 162–75, for an analysis of the *Reichsbahn* as the lynchpin of the entire system.

17. Hilberg, *The Politics of Memory: The Journey of a Holocaust Historian* (Chicago, Ill.: Ivan R. Dee, 1996), 124.

18. Browning, "The Revised Hilberg," 296–97.

19. Bettelheim, "Individual and Mass Behavior," 49; Primo Levi, *The Drowned and the Saved* (London: Abacus Books, 1988), 74; and Arendt, *The Origins of Totalitarianism*. However, in commenting on the writing about the concentration camp experience, Levi writes: "Their interpretations, even those of someone like Bruno Bettelheim who went through the trials of the Lager, seem to me approximate and simplified, as it someone wished to apply the theorems of plain geometry to the solution of spheric triangles" (p. 65).

20. Bettelheim, *The Informed Heart*, 19–25.

21. Bettelheim, "The Concentration Camp as a Class State," *Modern Review* 1 (October 1947): 628–37.

22. Bettelheim, "The Victim's Image of the Anti-Semite," *Commentary* 5 (February 1948): 176. Subsequent page references to this article will be placed in the main body of the text.

23. Bettelheim, "Freedom from Ghetto Thinking," *Midstream* 8, no. 2 (spring 1962): 19. Future page references will be placed in the main body of the text.

24. See also Elie Wiesel, "Eichmann's Victims and the Unheard Testimony," *Commentary* 32, no. 6 (December 1961): 510–16. In this article, Wiesel attributes the lack of Jewish resistance to the Jewish culture of guilt.

25. Bettelheim, "Survival of the Jews," *The New Republic* (July 1967): 23–30.

26. Hannah Arendt, Reply to Bruno Bettelheim, *Midstream* 8, no. 3 (September 1962): 85–87. Future page references to this article will be in the main body of the text.

27. Arendt, "Zionism Reconsidered (October 1944)," in Feldman, ed., *The Jew as Pariah,* 150.

28. Arendt, "Peace or Armistice in the Near East (January 1950)," in Feldman, ed., *The Jew as Pariah*, 196.

29. Arendt, "Jewish History, Revised," in Feldman, ed., *The Jew as Pariah*, 96. Subsequent page references will be placed in the main text.

30. Arendt, "The Jewish State: Fifty Years After: Where Have Herzl's Politics Led?" (May 1946) in Feldman, ed., *The Jew as Pariah*, 167.

31. Arendt, *The Origins of Totalitarianism*, 10.

32. See Arendt's articles on Palestine and the question of a bi-national versus a Jewish state in Palestine in Feldman, ed., *The Jew as Pariah.*

33. Moshe Zimmerman, "Hannah Arendt: The Early 'Post Zionist,'" in *Hannah Arendt in Jerusalem*, ed. Steven E. Aschheim (Berkeley: University of California Press, 2001), 192.

34. See Seyla Benhabib, "Taking Ideas Seriously," *Boston Review* (December 2002/January 2003): 10 (Internet version). Benhabib notes that recent work has established close ties between Ben Gurion's ruling Mapai Party and Hungarian Jewish leader Rudolf Kästner, who negotiated with Eichmann for the release of a number of Jews. This would suggest that the Israeli government feared raising the issue of the co-operation of the Jewish councils with Eichmann, since some of its members would thereby be implicated.

35. Hilberg, *The Politics of Memory*, 150.

36. Ibid., 134.

37. See Felman, "Theaters of Justice," 231. Felman actually uses these terms to describe the essential message of Arendt's *Eichmann in Jerusalem*.

38. Bauer, *Rethinking the Holocaust*, 128. Bauer is a judicious and often fair-minded critic. Though he disagrees fundamentally with Hilberg's position, Bauer praises him as a historian. Yet there are any number of issues where Bauer accepts (or repeats) points made first by Arendt but gives her no credit for them.

39. Here I am not concerned with distinguishing conscious from unconscious intentions or motives; nor am I concerned with distinguishing intentions and motives. One might provisionally suggest that intentions are conscious and motives are unconscious or subliminal.

40. Susan Neiman, "Theodicy in Jerusalem," in *Hannah Arendt in Jerusalem*, ed. Steven E. Aschheim (Berkeley: University of California Press, 2001), 65–90; and Neiman, *Evil in Modern Thought: An Alternative History of Philosophy* (Princeton, N.J.: Princeton University Press, 2002), 267–78, 298–304. Neiman reads *Eichmann in Jerusalem* as the twentieth century's most distinguished attempt to formulate a modern, secular theodicy.

41. Scholem to Arendt, in Feldman, ed., *The Jew as Pariah*, 243.

42. Browning, *Simon Wiesenthal Center Annual*, 297; Daniel Bell, "The Alphabet of Justice," *Partisan Review* 30, no. 3 (fall 1963): 423.

43. Hilberg, *The Politics of Memory*, 149.

44. Bettelheim, "Eichmann, The System, The Victims," in *Surviving*, 259–60.

45. Arendt to Scholem, in Feldman, ed., *The Jew as Pariah*, 251. Neiman reads

354 *Notes to Pages 190–99*

this as a relatively optimistic conception of evil, one that allows us to imagine its defeat. Arendt's conception of evil might be contrasted here with the novelist's Aharon Appelfeld's comments to Philip Roth: "We came into contact with archaic mythical forces, a kind of dark subconscious meaning of which we did not know, nor do we know it to this day. . . . I didn't understand, nor do I yet understand, the motives of the murderers." Roth, *Shop Talk* (New York: Vintage Books, 2002), 25.

46. Lionel Abel, "The Aesthetics of Evil: Hannah Arendt on Eichmann and the Jews," *Partisan Review* 30, no. 2 (summer 1963): 219. Interestingly, Abel praises Hilberg's work as a "careful, massive, and valuable study" (p. 212). Abel's review was generally seen by Arendt and her supporters as the most hostile of those that appeared from American intellectuals. Abel's praise for Hilberg and condemnation of Arendt in particular raise the suspicion that more than just the merits of Arendt's case was at issue in Abel's review.

47. Arendt, *Eichmann in Jerusalem*, 287; Arendt, *The Life of the Mind: Thinking* (New York and London: Harcourt Brace Jovanovich, 1978), 4.

48. Dwight Macdonald, Response, *Partisan Review* 31, no. 2 (spring 1964): 262–69. See also Neiman, *Evil in Modern Thought*, 278.

49. Neiman, *Evil in Modern Thought*, 302.

50. Arendt, "Organized Guilt and Universal Responsibility," in Feldman, ed., *The Jew as Pariah*, 231–32; *The Origins of Totalitarianism*, 338.

51. Elizabeth Young-Bruehl, *For Love of the World* (New York: Harcourt Brace Jovanovich, 1982), 370.

52. Yaacov Lozowick, "Malicious Clerks: The Nazi Security Police and the Banality of Evil," in *Hannah Arendt in Jerusalem*, ed. Steven E. Aschheim, 221.

53. Rosenberg, "The Trial and Eichmann," 376.

54. Michael Marrus, "Eichmann in Jerusalem: Justice and History," in *Hannah Arendt in Jerusalem*, ed. Steven E. Aschheim, 209.

55. Bettelheim, "Eichmann, The System, The Victims," *Surviving*, 266.

56. See previously cited works by Mark Osiel, Lawrence Douglas, and, from a somewhat different perspective, Shoshana Felmen. Osiel and Douglas also want to defend the importance of regular legal trials in situations where more recently truth and reconciliation commissions have been established.

57. Arendt, *Eichmann in Jerusalem*, 6.

58. Osiel, *Mass Atrocity, Collective Memory and the Law*, 62.

59. Douglas, *The Memory of Judgment*, 173, 177.

60. Arendt rephrases this distinction slightly on p. 269 of *Eichmann in Jerusalem*. See also Alice Kaplan, "War on Trial," *Civilization* (October/November 1997): 60–65.

61. Arendt, *Eichmann in Jerusalem*, 257, 268–69.

62. Ibid., 269.

63. Douglas, *The Memory of Judgment*, 117–18; n. 51, 289.

Chapter 8—From Roots to Routes: Wright and James

1. The best (and best-known) account of James's upbringing and early formative experiences is his memoir of 1963, *Beyond a Boundary* (London: Serpent's Tail, 1994). There are numerous useful collections of essays about James's work and his life. Kent Worcester, *C. L. R. James: A Political Biography* (Albany: State University

of New York Press, 1996), and Aldon Lynn Nielsen, *C. L. R. James: A Critical Introduction* (Jackson: University Press of Mississippi, 1997), are good single volumes on James's thought, while Anthony Bogues, *Caliban's Freedom: The Early Political Thought of C. L. R. James* (London and Chicago: Pluto Press, 1997), covers very well what its title indicates. Farrukh Dhondy's recent *C. L. R. James: A Life* (New York: Pantheon, 2001) contains some interesting anecdotal material but is closer to a personal essay on James than a full biography.

Alistair Hennessy, ed., *Spectre of the New Class: The Commonwealth Caribbean*, vol. 1 of *Intellectuals in the Twentieth-Century Caribbean* (London: Macmillan, 1992) contains three useful chapters on James and his work. Cedric Robinson's "C. L. R. James and the Black Radical Tradition," in *Black Marxism: The Making of a Black Radical Tradition* (1983; Chapel Hill: University of North Carolina Press, 2000), 241–86, is always strongly argued, but neglects James's literary and cultural work and is critical of James's Eurocentric orientation. V. S. Naipaul, whose early work James very generously supported, has offered what some consider a portrait of James in "On the Run," in *A Way in the World* (London: Minerva, 1995), 103–57. The profile is vintage Naipaul—etched in acid but also fascinated with Lebrun, a revolutionary in search of some revolution. The tension, even contradiction, between Lebrun's Marxist and nationalist commitments captures some of the complexity of James's own political, ideological, and moral concerns, although Naipaul does not get the proportions right. James also appears as one of the central figures in Edward W. Said, *Culture and Imperialism* (London: Vintage, 1994); and more recently Hazel Carby has devoted a chapter to James in her *Race Men* (Cambridge, Mass.: Harvard University Press, 1998), 113–32. Thanks to the late Jim Murray and Ralph Dumain at the C. L. R. James Institute for sharing their vast knowledge of James and the resources of the Institute with me.

2. See "Native Son and Revolution: A Review of *Native Son*" (1940), in *C. L. R. James and Revolutionary Marxism: Selected Writings of C. L. R. James, 1939–1949*, ed. Scott McLemee and Paul LeBlanc (Atlantic Highlands, N.J.: Humanities Press International, 1994), 88–91.

3. C. L. R. James, "Paul Robeson: Black Star" (1970), in *Spheres of Existence* (London: Allison and Busby, 1980), 256; "The Black Jacobins" (1936, 1967), in *The C. L. R. James Reader*, ed. Anna Grimshaw (Oxford and Cambridge, Mass.: Blackwell, 1992), 67–111.

4. C. L. R. James, Letter of 1945 (Undated) to Constance Webb, in *Special Delivery: The Letters of C. L. R. James to Constance Webb, 1939–1948*, edited and introduced by Anna Grimshaw (Oxford and Cambridge, Mass.: Blackwell, 1996), 190.

5. Besides Robinson, *Black Marxism*, see also Anthony Bogues, "James and the Race Question," *Caliban's Freedom*, 76–96.

6. Paul Gilroy, *The Black Atlantic: Modernity and Double Consciousness* (London: Verso Books, 1993).

7. C. L. R. James, *Mariners, Renegades and Castaways: The Story of Herman Melville and the World We Live In*, intro. by Donald E. Pease (Hanover, N.H., and London: University Press of New England, 2001) has only recently been re-issued.

This edition also restores a controversial last chapter to James's book, one devoted to James's own experience at Ellis Island and his dealings with the Stalinists interned there.

8. Gilroy, *The Black Atlantic*, 186. Here I will be using "modernization" and

"Westernization" as rough synonyms for what Wright and his generation referred to as "development" and/or "industrialization" and "urbanization." Although generally assumed to imply capitalism, for Wright, modernization could also imply development along socialist or mixed economy lines.

9. Andrew Ross, "Civilization in One Country? The American James," in *Rethinking C. L. R. James*, edited by Grant Farred (Cambridge and Oxford: Blackwell, 1996), 76.

10. This is not to deny that James was engaged with the black power/black consciousness movement as it emerged in the United States in the late 1960s. But it is too much to say that James was, as Robin Kelley asserts in "The World the Diaspora Made: C. L. R. James and the Politics of History," in *Rethinking C. L. R. James*, ed. Grant Farred (Cambridge and Oxford: Blackwell, 1996), "quite taken with the Black Power movement" (p. 119).

11. Writing to Albert Murray in August 1954, Ralph Ellison commented on *Black Power* in the following way: "[T]hough I'm somewhat annoyed with his self-importance, I think the book is important and I'm trying to work out a comment." See Albert Murray and John F. Callahan, eds., *Trading Twelves: The Selected Letters of Ralph Ellison and Albert Murray* (New York: Modern Library, 2000), 79. In his "A Long Way from Home: Wright in the Gold Coast" (1987), in *Richard Wright*, ed. Harold Bloom (New York and Philadelphia: Chelsea House, 1987), 173–90, Kwame Anthony Appiah, a native of Ghana, suggests that Wright's condescension and paranoia about Africa and Africans arose from his unrequited affection for the place. Jack Moore in his "*Black Power* Revisited: In Search of Richard Wright," *The Mississippi Quarterly* 51, no. 2 (spring 1988): 161–86, reports on his interviews with several people who talked with Wright during his three-month stay in 1953. They were equally divided between thinking that Wright captured something essential about the place and feeling that he was out of his depth. See also Virginian Whatley Smith, ed., *Richard Wright's Travel Writing: New Reflections* (Jackson: University Press of Mississippi, 2001). It contains three useful essays on Wright in West Africa and two on his visit to the Bandung Conference in 1955. In addition, several of the essays address the "genre" question in relation to *Black Power*. And Manthia Diawara's *In Search of Africa* (Cambridge, Mass.: Harvard University Press, 1998) suggests that Wright was "prescient about the unprepared state of Africans to face modernity or globalization" (p. 69), and that he "was right in his assessment of ethnicity, tradition, and religion" (p. 75).

12. Richard Wright, *Black Power: A Record of Reactions in a Land of Pathos* (New York: Harper Perennial, 1954), 6–7. Subsequent page references to *Black Power* will be included in the main text.

13. Appiah, "A Long Way Home," *Richard Wright*, 187.

14. Gerald Horne, *Black and Red: W. E. B. Du Bois and the Afro-American Perspective on the Cold War* (Albany: State University of New York Press, 1986), 260. See also Penny M. Von Eschen, *Race Against Europe: Black Americans and Anticolonialism, 1937–1957* (Ithaca and London: Cornell University Press, 1997) for the history of the split in African American ranks after the war over support for the Soviet Union. There was little love lost between Wright and Du Bois. Du Bois objected to *Black Boy*'s negative depiction of black life, while Wright was deeply suspicious of Du Bois's pro-Soviet orientation. See Hazel Rowley, *Richard Wright: The Life and Times* (New York: Henry Holt and Company, 2001), 311.

15. See Bogues, *Caliban's Freedom*, 46, 80–81, for this point generally and James's acceptance of this position.

16. Richard Wright, *The Color Curtain*: *A Report on the Bandung Conference* (Cleveland and New York: World Publishing Co., 1956), 299. Other references to *The Color Curtain* will be included in the main text.

17. Michel Fabre's work on Wright is essential to the understanding of the topic under consideration here. Fabre's *The Unfinished Quest of Richard Wright* (New York: Morrow, 1973) includes seven pages on the Congress but most authoritative is his "Wright, Negritude and African Writing," *The World of Richard Wright* (Jackson: University Press of Mississippi, 1985), 192–213. See also Addison Gayle, *Richard Wright: Ordeal of a Native Son* (Garden City, N.Y.: Anchor Press/Doubleday, 1980), especially 265–70, and Rowley, *Richard Wright*, 474, for accounts that stress the possibility that Wright was supplying information to the U.S. Embassy concerning the threat of possible communist activity at the Congress. James Campbell, *Paris Interzone: Richard Wright, Lolita, Boris Vian and others on the Left Bank, 1946–60* (London: Secker and Warburg, 1994), chapter 6 is also a readable account of this period, including the events at the Congress. Still, the best-known account of the Congress in English is James Baldwin, "Princes and Powers," *Baldwin: Collected Essays* (New York: Library of America, 1998), 143–69. V. Y. Mudimbe, ed., *The Surreptitious Speech*: Présence Africaine *and the Politics of Otherness, 1947–1987* (Chicago and London: University of Chicago Press, 1992), offers a wide-ranging collection of essays on the history and orientation of the journal since its inception, while Benetta Jules-Rosette, "Antithetical Paris: Conferences and Festivals of *Présence Africaine, 1956–1973*," in *Black Paris: The African Writers Landscape* (Urbana: University of Illinois Press, 1998), 49–78, and Eileen Julien, "*Terrains de Rencontre*: Césaire, Fanon, and Wright on Culture and Decolonization," *YFS 98 (The French Fifties)*, 149–66, are insightful treatments of the issues involved in the first Congress. See also Diawara, *In Search of Africa*, 59–65.

18. Leopold Senghor, "The Spirit of Civilisation or the Laws of African Negro Culture," *Présence Africaine* 18–19, nos. 8–10 (June–November 1956): 64. Subsequent page references to and titles of speeches at the Congress will be included in the main text.

19. Bennetta Jules-Rosette, "Conjugating Cultural Realities: *Présence Africaine*," in *The Surreptitious Speech*, ed. V. Y. Mudimbe (Chicago and London: University of Chicago Press, 1992), 14–44, is particularly valuable in offering an account of the central issues raised at the Congress.

20. This was clearly a veiled reference to the Communist Party position in the early 1930s, which advocated the establishment of a black nation in the Deep South, that is, in the Black Belt.

21. That none of the American delegation raised the possibility of combining political inclusion with cultural nationalism demonstrates Harold Cruse's central thesis in *The Crisis of the Negro Intellectual* (New York: William Morrow and Co./Apollo Editions, 1968).

22. Richard Wright, "The Neuroses of Conquest," *The Nation* (October 20, 1956): 328. See also O. Mannoni, *Prospero and Caliban: The Psychology of Colonization*, trans. P. Powerland, foreword by Philip Mason (London: Methuen and Co. Ltd., 1956), 85. Mannoni's work also belongs with the work of Erich Fromm, Wilhelm Reich, and the Frankfurt School in trying to understand the sources of mass obedience to authoritarian/totalitarian regimes and their leaders.

23. The Wright–Senghor debate anticipates both the debate over Stanley Elkins's "Sambo" thesis in *Slavery* (1959) and the controversy that Hannah Arendt's *Eichmann in Jerusalem* (1963) created.

24. Michel Fabre, "Margaret Walker's Richard Wright: A Wrong Righted or a Wright Wronged?" *The Mississippi Quarterly* 52, no. 4 (fall 1989): 436.

25. It is highly unlikely that Wright had read Mannoni's book before he went to the Gold Coast in 1953, since it had not as yet been translated.

26. See Edward Margolies, "Richard Wright's Opposing Freedoms," *The Mississippi Quarterly*, 52, no. 4 (fall 1989): 409–14.

27. V. S. Naipaul, *Finding the Center* (Harmondsworth, U.K.: Penguin, 1985), 160.

28. In 1956, Ellison asked Murray in a letter: "But who the hell wants to live in Africa?" See Murray and Callahan, *Trading Twelves*, 151.

29. C. L. R. James, *A History of Pan-African Revolt* (Washington, D.C.: Drum and Spear Books, 1969), chapter 3. The first six chapters of this text are the original *A History of Negro Revolt* published in 1938. It also contains a highly condensed account of the Haitian revolt. See also W. E. B. Du Bois, *Black Reconstruction in America, 1860–1880* (New York: Atheneum, 1969), and E. P. Thompson, *The Making of the English Working Class* (New York: Pantheon, 1963).

30. C. L. R. James, "Stalinism and Negro History" (1949), in *C. L. R. James and Revolutionary Marxism: Selected Writings of C. L. R. James, 1939–1949*, edited by Scott McLemee and Paul LeBlanc (Atlantic Highlands, N.J.: Humanities Press International, Inc., 1994), 202. See also Anthony Bogues, *Caliban's Freedom*, 6, 71, for claims about the theme of action as central to James's work.

31. C. L. R. James, *The Black Jacobins: Toussaint L'Ouverture and the San Domingo Revolution*, 2nd ed., rev. (New York: Vintage, 1989), 47–55. In 1971, James gave three lectures in which he revisited and reassessed *The Black Jacobins*. They have recently been published in *Small Axe: A Journal of Criticism* (The Demands of History) 8 (September 2000): 61–117. James also anticipated the work of his former student, Eric Williams, in *The Black Jacobins*. See also Eric Williams, *Capitalism and Slavery* (Chapel Hill: University of North Carolina Press, 1944). For two recent reassessments of Williams's pioneering work, see Seymour Drescher, "Eric Williams: British Capitalism and British Slavery" (1987), and "*Capitalism and Slavery* after Fifty Years" (1997), in *From Slavery to Freedom: Comparative Studies in the Rise and Fall of Atlantic Slavery* (New York: New York University Press, 1999), 355–78, 379–95, respectively.

The revolutionary tradition delineated by Edmund Wilson in *To the Finland Station* (Garden City, N.Y.: Doubleday and Company, Inc., 1940) is made up of figures such as Michelet, Marx, and Trotsky who both made *and* wrote history. James, the activist, as well as the historian and novelist, clearly belongs in that tradition. James gave Wilson's book mixed notices when it appeared. See James, "To and From the Finland Station: A Review of *To the Finland Station*," in *C. L. R. James and Revolutionary Marxism: Selected Writings of C. L. R. James, 1939–1949*, ed. Scott McLemee and Paul LeBlanc, 88–91.

32. Besides Hegel's famous analysis of the master–slave relationship in his *The Phenomenology of Spirit*, see David Brion Davis, "Toussaint L'Ouverture and the Phenomenology of Mind," *The Problem of Slavery in the Age of Revolution, 1770–1823* (Ithaca and London: Cornell University Press, 1975), 557–64, and Susan Buck Morss's exemplary "Hegel and Haiti," *Critical Inquiry* 26 (summer 2000): 821–65.

For the dichotomy between "history as rhetoric" and "history as scholarship," see Drescher, "*Capitalism and Slavery* after Fifty Years," 391. Although it may be itself rhetorically useful, such a binary opposition is ultimately untenable. All first-rate historiography is both.

33. James, *The Black Jacobins*, 117. See also John D. Garrigus, "White Jacobins/Black Jacobins: Bringing the Haitian and French Revolutions Together in the Classroom," *French Historical Studies* 23, no. 2 (2000): 259–75.

34. James, "How I Wrote *The Black Jacobins*," in *Small Axe: A Journal of Criticism*, 72–73.

35. James, *The Black Jacobins*, 51. Hereafter, page numbers of all citations from *The Black Jacobins* will be incorporated into the text.

36. Karl Marx, excerpts from *The German Ideology*, in *Marx and Engels: Basic Writings on Politics and Philosophy*, ed. Lewis Feuer (Garden City, N.Y.: Anchor Books, 1959), 246; and excerpts from *The Eighteenth Brumaire of Louis Napoleon*, 320.

37. See, for instance, Donald L. Robinson, *Slavery in the Structure of American Politics, 1765–1820* (New York: Harcourt Brace Jovanovich, 1971), 361–76. Robinson traces the uneven, zigzagging commercial and diplomatic policy of the United States vis-à-vis Haiti between 1791 and 1805.

38. James later acknowledged how his interest swung between a focus on the masses and a fascination with Toussaint himself. See James, "*The Black Jacobins* and *Black Reconstruction*: A Comparative Analysis," in *Small Axe: A Journal of Criticism*, 84–86.

39. Later research has revealed that many male slaves had been soldiers in Africa and thus already trained as disciplined fighters. See, for instance, John K. Thornton, "African Soldiers in the Haitian Revolution," and Carolyn E. Fick, "The Saint Domingue Slave Insurrection of 1791: A Socio-Political and Cultural Analysis," in *Caribbean Slavery in the Atlantic World*, ed. Verene A. Shepherd and Hilary McD. Beckles (Kingston: Ian Randle Publishers, 2000), 933–45, 961–82, respectively.

40. Eugene D. Genovese, *From Rebellion to Revolution: Afro-American Slave Revolts in the Making of the Modern World* (Baton Rouge: Louisiana State University Press, 1979), 92.

41. James, "How I Wrote *The Black Jacobins*," 79.

42. James, "Black Sansculottes" (1964), in *At the Rendezvous of Victory* (London: Allison and Busby, 1984), 160; Genovese, *From Rebellion to Revolution*, 89–90.

43. Anna Grimshaw and Keith Hart, eds., Introduction to *American Civilization*, by C. L. R. James (Cambridge, Mass. and Oxford: Blackwell, 1993), 11.

44. Dwight Macdonald's "Politics Past," in *Memoirs of a Revolutionist* (Cleveland: Meridian Books, 1963), 3–53, is an often-hilarious account of the sectarianism of the independent, particularly the Trotskyist left in the 1930s and early 1940s. Delmore Schwartz remembers meeting James at Dwight Macdonald's house in 1939 (McLemee and LeBlanc, eds., *C. L. R. James and Revolutionary Marxism*, 215), while James refers several times in passing to Macdonald and Irving Howe in *Special Delivery*. Both Macdonald and, after the war, Howe, had run-ins with James. Many of the debates concerning the nature of the Soviet Union were carried in the pages of *Partisan Review* and Macdonald's magazine, *Politics,* during and after the war. See Alan Wald, *The New York Intellectuals: The Rise and Decline of the Anti-Stalinist Left from the 1930s to the 1980s* (Chapel Hill: University of North Carolina Press, 1987), for a brief

discussion of James's activities among the New York intellectuals, several of whom were or had been Trotskyists. See LeBlanc, "C. L. R. James and Revolutionary Marxism," in McLemee and LeBlanc, eds., *C. L. R. James and Revolutionary Marxism*, for a thorough discussion of James's ideological and organizational peregrinations from the late 1930s to the early 1950s.

45. In "In England, 1932–1938," in *C. L. R. James: His Life and Work*, ed. Paul Buhle (London and New York: Allison and Busby, 1986), Robert A. Hill notes that most Trotskyists saw Trotsky as someone who could "offer a possibility of sustaining the revolutionary political principles of Lenin" (p. 71); James, "New Society, New People" (1958), *At the Rendezvous with Victory* (London: Allison and Busby, 1984), 82.

46. James, "New Society, New People," in *At the Rendezvous of Victory*, 82. In "Lenin and the Vanguard Party" (1963), in Grimshaw, ed., *The C. L. R. James Reader*, 327–30, James tried to explain (away) Lenin's advocacy of the vanguard party by noting the small and beleaguered size of the Bolshevists after the revolution. In light of that fact, the idea of the vanguard party made a certain amount of sense.

47. C. L. R. James, *American Civilization* (Oxford and Cambridge, Mass.: Blackwell, 1995), 229–30.

48. See, for instance, Paul Berman, "Facing Reality," in Buhle, ed., *C. L. R. James,* 206–11. Berman suggests that James was much closer to an anarchist position than he would admit. James does refer to Arendt's *The Origins of Totalitarianism* in a letter of 1957 and later alludes indirectly to her "Epilogue: Reflections on the Hungarian Revolution," which was added to the second edition of *Origins* in 1958. Since her *The Human Condition* did not appear until 1958, James could not have known about the central role that the Greek polis also played in Arendt's thought. It was in *Facing Reality* (1958) and *Modern Politics* (1960), but particularly the former, that James discussed the workers councils at any great length. He also devoted the last ten pages of the latter both praising Arendt's work on Hungary and challenging her contention that the emergence of the workers councils came out of the blue, as it were. Robert Wicke in "C. L. R. James's Modern Politics," *Radical America* 3, no. 5 (September 1969): 61–71, notes the similarities and differences between James and Arendt. Otherwise, the links between the two thinkers have not been noted in print.

49. James, Letter of 25 March, 1957, in *The C. L. R. James Reader*, 275.

50. James, Letter of 18 November, 1956, in *The C. L. R. James Reader*, 264.

51. James, Letter of 20 March, 1957, in *The C. L. R. James Reader*, 269.

52. James, "Notes on the Life of George Padmore" (1959–1960), in *The C. L. R. James Reader*, 293–94. In a 1967 speech on black power, James gave a fuller account of Lenin's position, which James followed faithfully into the 1950s. See "Black Power" (1967), *The C. L. R. James Reader*, 372–74.

53. The focus of *Mariners, Renegades and Castaways* falls on the political implications of the strong and charismatic Captain Ahab, whom James sees as exemplifying "the totalitarian readiness to destroy the whole world in revenge." He is "the totalitarian leader himself who has molded his crew of hard-working sailors and an assortment of ship's officers to obey his mad purposes." C. L. R. James, *Mariners, Renegades and Castaways* (New York: C. L. R. James, 1953), 6, 90.

54. James, *American Civilization*, 201–2. James's fellow Trotskyist, Dwight Macdonald, made a similar point in his "Responsibility of Peoples" (1945), in *Memoirs of a Revolutionist*.

55. James, *American Civilization*, 204–5, 207.

56. Ibid., 85, 91.

57. Ibid., 211.

58. I will be drawing mainly on Scott McLemee's introduction to James's writings on race in the 1940s as well as on those writings themselves in *C. L. R. James on the "Negro Question,"* ed. McLemee (Jackson: University Press of Mississippi, 1996). See also Anthony Bogues, "James and the Race Question," in *Caliban's Freedom*, 76–96.

59. Reading through James's letters to Constance Webb in *Special Delivery* is one way to get a sense of how much James was engaged in the issue of race in America through the 1940s. His growing friendship with Richard Wright was also part of this process, as was Webb's decision to write a pamphlet on Wright's work.

60. James, "The Historical Development of the Negroes in American Society" (1943), in *C. L. R. James on the "Negro Question,"* 64; James, "Preliminary Notes on the Negro Question" (1939), in *C. L. R. James on the "Negro Question,"* 10–11; James, "The Historical Development of the Negroes," 86.

61. James, "The Historical Development of the Negroes," 87, 4, 145, 73, 75.

62. James, "Marcus Garvey" (1940) in McLemee, ed., *C. L. R. James on the "Negro Question,"* 114–15; James, "Preliminary Notes," 16.

63. James, "The Historical Development of the Negroes," 83.

64. James, *American Civilization*, 201.

65. This sentence was quoted from an anonymous correspondent by Daniel Guerin, a French analyst of American culture. According to Robert A. Hill, James's literary executor, it is clear that the unnamed correspondent is James, who had translated Guerin's book from the French. See "Literary Executor's Afterword," in *American Civilization*, 344.

66. James, "Three Black Women Writers: Toni Morrison, Alice Walker, Ntozake Shange," in *The C. L. R. James Reader*, 415.

67. James, "The Old World and the New" (1971), in *At the Rendezvous of Victory*, 207.

68. Constance Webb, "C. L. R. James, the Speaker and his Charisma," in *C. L. R. James: His Life and Work*, 174.

69. James, *Special Delivery*, 356.

70. Ibid., 32.

71. James, "The Case for West Indian Self-Government" (1932), in *The Future in the Present*, 25.

72. James, *Beyond a Boundary*, 64–65.

73. James, "The Mighty Sparrow" (1962), in *The Future in the Present*, 199.

74. James, "The Old World and the New" (1971), in *At the Rendezvous of Victory*, 202.

75. James, "A National Purpose for Caribbean Peoples" (1964), in *At the Rendezvous of Victory*, 143–58.

76. Ibid., 199.

77. James, "From Toussaint L'Ouverture to Fidel Castro" (1963), in *The Black Jacobins*, 399.

78. Ibid., 394

79. Ibid., 402.

80. James, "The West Indian Middle Classes" (1961), in *Spheres of Existence*, 131–40.

81. James, "Black Studies and the Contemporary Student" (1969), in Grimshaw, ed., *The C. L. R. James Reader*, 404.

82. Ibid., 397.

83. James, *Nkrumah and the Ghana Revolution* (London: Allison and Busby, 1977).

84. Ibid., 46, 49, 62, 82, 84, 108.

85. James praised Du Bois's *Black Reconstruction* just for this quality of attending to the voices of the people, while admitting that he had failed to do this in *The Black Jacobins*. See "*The Black Jacobins* and *Black Reconstruction*: A Comparative Analysis," in *Small Axe: A Journal of Criticism*, 83–98.

86. Ibid., 184, 185, 87, 188. James was also taken with the ideas and experiments in Julius Nyerere's Tanzania.

Chapter 9—Negritude, Colonialism, and Beyond

1. In the first couple of decades, contributions were heavily Francophone and concerned with Africa, while American and Anglophone contributions lagged behind. For the history, development, and critique of *Présence Africaine* and inevitably of negritude, see the contributions to V. Y. Mudimbe, ed., *The Surreptitious Speech: Présence Africaine and the Politics of Otherness, 1947–1987* (Chicago and London: University of Chicago Press, 1992). For a statistical breakdown of the contributions according to language, geographical origins, and focus, see Catherine Coquery-Vidrovitch, "*Présence Africaine*: History and Historians of Africa," in *The Surreptitious Speech*, ed. V. Y. Mudimbe, 59–94. There was very little on South Africa, Spanish- or Portuguese-speaking Latin America, or the Caribbean in *Présence Africaine*. For another historical overview of the journal, see Bennetta Jules-Rosette, *Black Paris: The African Writers' Landscape* (Urbana and Chicago: University of Illinois, 1998). Emmanuel Chukwide Eze, *Achieving Our Humanity: The Idea of the Postracial Future* (New York and London: Routledge, 2001), includes two chapters (chapter 4, "Negritude," and chapter 5, "Negritude and Modern Africana Philosophy") that are invaluable in understanding where the contemporary debate about negritude stands, while Stephen Howe, *Afrocentrism: Mythical Pasts and Imagined Homes* (London and New York: Verso, 1998), 23–27, offers a brief but extremely critical overview of negritude.

2. As James Arnold sums it up: "The Negritude Movement was conceived in 1934, was born in 1939 after a long gestation, and experienced its youthful triumphs in the forties" (p. 280), in *Modernism and Negritude: The Poetry and Poetics of Aimé Césaire* (Cambridge, Mass. and London: Harvard University Press, 1981). See also Janet G. Vaillant, *Black, French and African: A Life of Leopold Sedar Senghor* (Cambridge, Mass.: Harvard University Press, 1990), chapter 4 ("The Milieu of Negritude"); and Mercer Cook, "Some Literary Contacts: African, West Indian, Afro-American" in *The Black Writer in Africa and the Americas*, ed. Lloyd W. Brown (Los Angeles, Calif.: Hennessey and Ingalls, Inc., 1973), 119–40.

3. For a very useful introduction to Césaire's poem and the context of its conception, composition, and publication, see Mireille Rosello, "Introduction," *Notebook of a Return to My Native Land* (*Cahiers d'un retour au pays natal*), trans. by Mireille Rosello with Annie Pritchard (Newcastle upon Tyne: Bloodaxe Books, 1995), 9–68. See also David Macey, *Frantz Fanon* (New York: Picador, 2000), 179–84.

4. See Jock McCulloch, *Black Soul, White Artifact: Fanon's Clinical Psychology and Social Theory* (Cambridge: Cambridge University Press, 1983), 5. Historically, nineteenth- and early twentieth-century black diasporic intellectuals such as E. W. Blyden and Marcus Garvey formulated what Mia Bay in *The White Image in the Black Mind* (New York: Oxford University Press, 2002) has called the tradition of "black ethnology," which became politicized as black nationalism in the twentieth century. But this was fairly far removed from the more literary and cultural orientation of negritude, the case for which was made by contributions of Africans such as Senghor and Cheik Anta Diop.

5. Cheikh Anta Diop, "The Cultural Contributions and Prospects of Africa," *Présence Africaine*, nos. 8–10 (June–November 1956), 347, 350. For a critical overview of Diop's work, see Mamadou Diouf and Mohamad Mboodj, "The Shadow of Cheikh Anta Diop," in *The Surreptitious Speech*, ed. V. Y. Mudimbe, 118–35. An even more critical assessment of Diop can be found in Howe, *Afrocentrism*, 163–92. Maghan Keita, *Race and the Writing of History: Riddling the Sphinx* (New York: Oxford University Press, 2000), focuses on African American historians—W. E. B. Du Bois, Frank Snowden, William Leo Hansberry—who pioneered the Afrocentric approach in anticipation of Martin Bernal's (and of Diop's) work, and of the American Afrocentrists from the 1980s on. Keita treats Diop much more gently (pp. 171–79) than does Howe. For further critical treatment of the thesis concerning the Egyptian origins of Greek thought, see Mary Lefkowitz, *Not Out of Africa: How Afrocentrism Became an Excuse to Teach Myth as History* (New York: Basic Books, 1996), which was a response to Martin Bernal's *Black Athena: The Afroasiatic Roots of Classical Civilization* (New Brunswick, N.J.: Rutgers University Press, 1987).

6. Cheikh Anta Diop, *The African Origin of Civilization: Myth or Reality*, ed. and trans. by Mercer Cook (Chicago: Lawrence Hill Books, 1974), 22–24; "Cultural Contributions," 348. Diop's *African Origin* includes selections taken from two of his early texts, one from 1955 and the other from 1967.

7. Diop, "African Cultural Unity," *Présence Africaine*, nos. 24–25 (February–May 1959): 70.

8. Diop, *African Origin*, 67; Howe, *Afrocentrism*, 167.

9. Diop, "Cultural Contributions," 350–53.

10. Howe, *Afrocentrism*, 170.

11. Cited in Tsenay Serequeberhan, "Fanon and the Contemporary Discourse of African Philosophy," in *Fanon: A Critical Reader*, ed. Lewis Gordon et al. (Oxford and Cambridge, Mass.: Blackwell, 1996), 247.

12. Leopold Senghor, "The Spirit of Civilization or the Laws of African Negro Culture," *Présence Africaine*, nos. 8–10 (June–November 1956): 52.

13. Paulin J. Hountondji, "An Alienated Literature," *African Philosophy: Myth and Reality*, 2nd ed. (1976; trans. 1983; Bloomington and Indianapolis: Indiana University Press, 1996), 37.

14. Lilyan Kesteloot, *Black Writers in French: A Literary History of Negritude*, trans. by Ellen Conroy Kennedy (1963; Philadelphia, Penn.: Temple University Press, 1974), xxi.

15. Kesteloot, *Black Writers*, 103; Aimé Césaire, "Interview" (1967), *Radical America* 5, no. 3 (May–June 1971): 37.

16. See Vaillant, *Black, French, and African*, and Cook, "Some Literary Contacts."

17. Vaillant, *Black, French, and African*, 244.

18. Césaire, "Interview," 35.

19. Macey, *Frantz Fanon*, 184.

20. Cited in ibid., 181.

21. In *Modernism and Negritude*, 37–41, Arnold identifies points in Césaire's work where he seems to be referring to blood as a biological substance.

22. Césaire, *Notebook*, 125; and quoted in Kesteloot, *Black Writers*, 320.

23. Césaire, *Notebook*, 105.

24. Ibid, 127.

25. In terms of African American writing, Césaire might be seen as the poet LeRoi Jones/Amiri Baraka could have become, but did not.

26. Vaillant, *Black, French, and African*, 265–66.

27. Leopold Sedar Senghor, Discussion Session, 20 September 1956, *Présence Africaine*, nos. 8–10 (June–November 1956): 219.

28. Robert J. C. Young in particular stresses the pervasive commitment, at least rhetorically, to the idea of African socialism in decolonizing Africa. See *Postcolonialism: An Historical Introduction* (Oxford: Blackwell, 2001). See also McCulloch, *Black Soul, White Artifact*.

29. LeRoi Jones/Amiri Baraka, "Aimé Césaire," in *The Baraka Reader*, ed. William J. Harris in collaboration with Amiri Baraka (New York: Thunder's Mouth Press, 1991), 327. In the French literary context, surrealism has historically been associated more closely with political radicalism than has been the case in Anglophone modernism.

30. Aimé Césaire, *Discourse on Colonialism* (1955; New York: Monthly Review Press, 1972), 20, 26. Césaire's judgment here was questionable considering that Europe had been the site of the systematic massacre of millions of people during World War II and in the years leading up to it, a record that the United States could not come close to matching.

31. Ibid, p. 57.

32. Césaire, *Letter to Maurice Thorez* (Paris: Editions Présence Africaine, 1957), 3–5.

33. Ibid., 6, 13, 12.

34. Ibid., 15.

35. Ibid.

36. Alioune Diop, Opening Address, September 19, *Présence Africaine*, nos. 8–10 (June–November 1956), 9; Leopold Sedar Senghor, "The Spirit of Civilization, or the Laws of African Negro Culture," September 19, *Présence Africaine*, 51.

37. Senghor, "The Spirit of Civilization," 51.

38. Ibid., 52–53.

39. Ibid., 57, 59, 62.

40. Ibid., 63.

41. Ibid., 64.

42. Ibid.

43. J. S. Alexis, Discussion, September 19, *Présence Africaine*, nos. 8–10 (June–November 1956), 68–70.

44. Césaire, Discussion, September 19, *Présence Africaine*, nos. 8–10, 73.

45. Senghor, Discussion, September 19, *Présence Africaine*, nos. 8–10, 74.

46. Césaire, "Culture and Colonization," 193, and Discussion, September 20, 225, in *Présence Africaine*, nos. 8–10.

47. Césaire, "Culture and Colonization," 202.

48. Indeed, one might say that this is true by definition, since any coherent culture involves subjective appropriation of materials, however objectively disparate its component parts are. Ibid., 204.

49. Ibid., 196.

50. Mercer Cook, Discussion, September 20, *Présence Africaine*, nos. 8–10, 216.

51. Macey, *Frantz Fanon*, 184.

52. Jean-Paul Sartre, "Black Orpheus" (1948), *Poetry and Drama*, vol. 2 of *The Black American Writer*, ed. C. W. E. Bigsby (Deland, Fla.: Everett/Edwards, Inc., 1969), 5–40. Page references to material cited from this essay will be included in the text.

53. Jean-Paul Sartre, *What Is Literature?* (1947; New York: Harper and Row, 1965), 57, 59. One obvious exception is the work of Celine, unless Sartre is speaking specifically of a novel that takes as its central theme the praise of anti-Semitism. Certainly good novels can manifest anti-Semitic tendencies.

54. Ibid., 74.

55. David Macey's observation that both negritude and its critics such as Sartre were part of a decidedly "masculinist discourse" should be noted here, though it was not entirely true in the West Indies. See Macey, *Frantz Fanon*, 179–80.

56. See Eze, *Achieving Our Humanity*, 159–63; and V. Y. Mudimbe, *The Invention of Africa: Gnosis, Philosophy, and the Order of Knowledge* (Bloomington and Indianapolis: Indiana University Press, 1988), 83–87, for critiques of Sartre's "Black Orpheus."

57. Eze, *Achieving Our Humanity*, 158–59.

58. Sartre, "Colonialism Is a System" (1956), in *Colonialism and Neocolonialism*, trans. by H. Hadden, S. Bower, and T. McWilliams (London and New York: Routledge, 2001), 31.

59. Ibid., 41.

60. Ibid., 44–45.

61. Sartre, Preface to *The Wretched of the Earth* (1961), 144–45.

62. Sartre, *Critique of Dialectical Reason*, vol. 1 (1960; London: New Left Books, 1976), 720.

63. Albert Memmi, *The Colonizer and the Colonized* (New York: Orion Press, 1965), 28–30. See also "The Colonial Problem and the Left" (1958) in *Dominated Man: Notes Toward a Portrait* (Boston, Mass.: Beacon Press, 1968), 52–71.

64. Memmi, *Colonizer and Colonized*, 74, 68.

65. Ibid., 120, 127.

66. Ibid., 131.

67. Ibid., 131, 138.

68. Ibid., 152.

69. Memmi, "Negritude and Jewishness" (1968), in *Dominated Man: Notes toward a Portrait*, 28–31. Memmi's analysis is very close to Arendt's in *The Origins of Totalitarianism*, but there is no indication that he is drawing on her work.

70. Ibid., 34. It is important to note that Judaism is not, in the first instance, a critique of Christianity and thus the analogy breaks down on this particular point.

71. Ibid., 37; Memmi, "Racism and Oppression," in *Dominated Man: Notes Toward a Portrait*, 204–5.

72. Memmi, *Dominated Man: Notes Toward a Portrait*, 204. I assume that the word "luckily" should have been translated as "happily."

73. Three important reassessments of Fanon in the context of the newly emerging colonial and postcolonial discourse appeared in the mid- to late 1980s and early 1990s: Homi Bhabha, "Of Mimicry and Man: The Ambivalence of Colonial Discourse," *October 28* (spring 1984): 125–33; Edward Said, "Representing the Colonized: Anthropology's Interlocutors," *Critical Inquiry* 15, no. 2 (winter 1989): 205–25; and Henry Louis Gates, Jr., "Critical Fanonism," *Critical Inquiry* 17, no. 3 (spring 1991): 457–70. For two recent collections of essays on Fanon, see Lewis Gordon et al., eds., *Fanon: A Critical Reader* (Oxford and Cambridge, Mass.: Blackwell, 1996), and Alan Read, ed., *The Fact of Blackness: Frantz Fanon and Visual Representation* (London: ICA Press, 1996). My own previous reading of Fanon stresses the differences between his early and late thought, but retains the emphasis on violence in his thought while examining him in the context of the American civil rights movement; see Richard H. King, *Civil Rights and the Idea of Freedom* (New York: Oxford University Press, 1992), chapter 7 ("Violence and Self-respect: Fanon and Black Radicalism"), 172–200.

74. Frantz, Fanon, "The So-Called Dependency Complex of Colonized Peoples," *Black Skin, White Masks* (1952; New York: Grove Press, 1967), 85. Note that in his use of "inferiority complex," Fanon actually misunderstands Mannoni's use of the term. Mannoni applies it to the Europeans who have a need to prove themselves and come to the colonies to forge a new life of mastery. See also McCulloch, *Black Soul, White Artifact*, appendix 1, 213–22, for a somewhat sympathetic view of Mannoni in this controversy.

75. Fanon, "The So-Called Dependency Complex," 93.

76. Robert J. C. Young, *Postcolonialism: An Historical Introduction* (Oxford and Cambridge, Mass.: Blackwell, 2001), 274–83.

77. Sartre, "A Victory" (1958), in *Colonialism and Neocolonialism*, trans. by H. Hadden, S. Bower, and T. McWilliams (London and New York: Routledge, 2001), 65–77.

78. Arendt's claim in *The Origins of Totalitarianism* (1958) that totalitarian ideologies develop a kind of blind inexorability that may lead to the extermination of ideological enemies is very much to the point here. But for Arendt, neither Marxism nor Darwinism was inherently totalitarian. Rather, becoming totalitarian is something that happens to a system of thought.

79. Frantz Fanon, *The Wretched of the Earth* (1961; New York: Grove Press, 1963), 94.

80. Christopher Miller, *Theories of Africans: Francophone Literature and Anthropology in Africa* (Chicago and London: University of Chicago Press, 1990). 50.

81. Frantz Fanon, "The Reciprocal Basis of National Cultures and the Struggles for Liberation," *Présence Africaine* (February–May 1959): 89–97.

82. Macey, *Frantz Fanon*, 389.

83. Fanon, *Black Skin, White Masks*, 123, 124, 130. In *Black Skin, White Artifact*, McCulloch argues that Fanon became more rather than less sympathetic to negritude over time. On my reading, Fanon, at least in print, is always quite critical of negritude. Though in *The Wretched of the Earth*, Fanon grants that something like negritude can be a kind of psychological refuge, he is clearly committed to the national rather than the racial basis of culture.

84. Fanon, *Black Skin, White Masks*, 135, 138.

85. Ibid., 197.

86. Ibid., 230.

87. Ibid., 231.

88. Fanon, "Racism and Culture," *Présence Africaine* (September 19, 1956): 123, 124.

89. Ibid., 127–29. See also Fanon, "The So-Called Dependency Complex of Colonial Peoples," for an earlier version of the claims about the unity and identity of racisms.

90. See Mudimbe, ed., *The Surreptitious Speech*, for the claim that Fanon's speech was controversial in part because he warned against "plac[ing] too much faith in purely literary and artistic endeavor" (p. 35). See also Bennetta Jules-Rosette, *Black Paris*, 59.

91. Fanon, *The Wretched of the Earth*, 212.

92. Ibid., 214.

93. Ibid., 233.

94. Robert Bernasconi, "Casting the Slough: Fanon's New Humanism for a New Humanity," in *Fanon: A Critical Reader*, ed. L. R. Gordon, 115 (quoted from R. Young), and 116.

95. Fanon, "Racism and Culture," 131.

96. Fanon, *White Skin, Black Masks*, 85, 86.

97. Ibid, 89.

98. Ibid., 122, 163.

99. Ibid, 165, 180. There is, of course, a distinct sense in which the Nazis did see Jews as a distinct biological danger, as like vermin needing eradication in body as well as mind and soul.

100. Elisabeth Mudimbe-Boyi, "Harlem Renaissance and Africa: An Ambiguous Adventure," in *The Surreptitious Speech*, ed. V. Y. Mudimbe, 178. I am aware that the author is speaking here of the attitude toward Africa expressed in the Harlem Renaissance, but I think it applies to much of the rhetoric of negritude as well.

101. Abiola Irele, "In Praise of Alienation," in Mudimbe, ed., *The Surreptitious Speech*, 215.

Chapter 10—The Cultural Turn: Rediscovering African American Culture in the 1960s

1. Mark Naison, *Communists in Harlem During the Depression* (Urbana: University of Illinois Press, 1983), and Michael Denning, *The Cultural Front: The Laboring of American Culture in the Twentieth Century* (London and New York: Verso Press, 1997), are invaluable in tracking black cultural production and self-consciousness in the 1930s. For histories of the rich tradition of African American painting and the plastic arts, including the 1930s, see Richard Powell, *Black Art and Culture in the Twentieth Century* (London: Thames and Hudson, 1997), and Sharon F. Patton, *African-American Art* (New York and London: Oxford University Press, 1998).

2. James C. Hall, *Mercy, Mercy Me: African American Culture and the American Sixties* (New York: Oxford University Press, 2001), viii. Hall also stresses the religious, depth psychological, and internationalist orientation of this antimodernist movement of the 1960s. In this respect, Hall's work belongs with Paul Gilroy's *The Black Atlantic: Modernity and Double Consciousness* (Cambridge, Mass.: Harvard Uni-

versity Press, 1993), and is strongly influenced by it. The figures Hall takes up—Robert Hayden, Paule Marshall, and William Demby, John Coltrane, Romare Bearden, and Du Bois—are scarcely mentioned in the two big texts of the black arts/black aesthetics movement.

3. Richard Gilman, "White Standards and Black Writing," *The Confusion of Realms* (New York: Random House, 1969), 3, 19. Gilman was speaking, for instance, of Eldridge Cleaver's *Soul on Ice* and Malcolm X's *Autobiography*.

4. Besides information scattered throughout works by Cruse, including *The Crisis of the Negro Intellectual* (New York: Morrow, 1967), *Rebellion or Revolution* (New York: William Morrow, 1968), "Revolutionary Nationalism and the Afro-American" (1962), in *Black Fire: An Anthology of Afro-American Writing*, ed. LeRoi Jones and Larry Neal (New York: Morrow, 1968), 39–63, "My Jewish Problem and Theirs," *Black Anti-Semitism and Jewish Racism*, intro. by Nat Hentoff (New York: Schocken Books, 1970), 143–88, two interviews with Cruse are invaluable: C. W. E. Bigsby, ed., "Harold Cruse: An Interview," *The Black American Writer*, vol. 2 (Deland, Fla.: Everett/Edwards, 1969), and Van Gosse, "Locating the Black Intellectual: An Interview with Harold Cruse," *Radical History Review* 71 (spring 1998): 96–120. The latter interview is included in a useful anthology of Cruse's writings, some of which were previously unpublished: *The Essential Harold Cruse: A Reader*, edited by William Jelani Cobb (New York: Palgrave, 2002).

5. Cruse, *Rebellion or Revolution*, 214, 272–73.

6. Cruse, *The Crisis of the Negro Intellectual*, 183, 364.

7. C. Wright Mills, "The New Left," *Politics, Power and People* (New York: Oxford Galaxy, 1967), 254–56. See Gosse, "Locating the Black Intellectual," 115.

8. Cruse, *The Crisis of the Negro Intellectual*, 310; 564. As Gerald Horne notes, Du Bois changed his position again by the time he joined the CPUSA in 1961. His position by then was that black Americans were a "national minority struggling for equality" and not a separate nation as posited in the "black belt" thesis. Gerald Horne, *Black and Red: W. E. B. Du Bois and the Afro-American Response to the Cold War* (Albany, N.Y.: State University of New York Press, 1986), 307.

9. In his *Plural but Equal: A Critical Study of Blacks and Minorities and America's Plural Society* (New York: Morrow, 1987), Cruse tries to do for the political-legal and the economic spheres what *Crisis* did for the cultural sphere—explore the possibility of autonomous black politics (such as a separate black political party) and of alternative forms of economic communalism.

10. Cruse, "The Integrationist Ethic as a Basis for Scholarly Endeavors" (1969) in *The Essential Harold Cruse*, 117; *The Crisis of the Negro Intellectual*, 6, 317; "James Baldwin, The Theater and His Critics," in *The Essential Harold Cruse: A Reader*, ed. William Jelani Cobb (New York: Palgrave, 2002), 33.

11. Cruse, *The Crisis of the Negro Intellectual*, 85.

12. Cruse, "Rebellion or Revolution?—I" and "Behind the Black Power Slogan," in *Rebellion or Revolution*, 110–25, 245–46.

13. Cruse, *The Crisis of the Negro Intellectual*, 282; *Rebellion or Revolution*, 124.

14. Cruse, "Revolutionary Nationalism," 42, 40.

15. Cruse, *The Crisis of the Negro Intellectual*, 317.

16. Ibid., 3, 395.

17. Ibid., 148–49.

18. Ibid., 168.

19. See Winston James, "Harold Cruse and the West Indians: Critical Remarks on *The Crisis of the Negro Intellectuals*," in *Holding Aloft the Banner of Ethiopia: Caribbean Radicalism in Early Twentieth-Century America* (London and New York: Verso, 1998), 262–91, for a strong rebuttal of Cruse's claims about the alleged conservative influence of West Indian intellectuals in the United States. James's point is not to deny that there were tensions between African Americans and those who came to the United States from the Caribbean. Rather, it was that the influence of the Afro-Caribbeans was, if anything, politically radical rather than conservative.

20. Ibid., 482–83.

21. See Cobb, ed., *The Essential Harold Cruse*, 156–57, for a brief discussion of Senghor.

22. Ibid., 364–65.

23. Ibid., 236.

24. Ibid., 288.

25. *The Journal of Ethnic Studies* 5, no. 2 (summer 1977) includes three critiques of Cruse from a Marxist perspective. Though often acute, they tend to criticize Cruse for not (still) being a Marxist. One of their main criticisms is Cruse's failure to develop the specifics of his position or to develop his major concepts to any significant degree. More recently, Emily Miller Budick, *Blacks and Jews in Literary Conversation* (New York: Cambridge University Press, 1998), contains some perceptive analysis of Cruse's position on Jews and Blacks.

26. William Eric Perkins, "Harold Cruse: On the Problem of Culture and Revolution," *Journal of Ethnic Studies* 5, no. 2 (1977): 116.

27. While Cruse rejected blanket exclusion of whites from dealing with black topics or criticizing black writers, he did note that "the white critic has a tendency to encourage the black writer not to be a black writer at all." Bigsby, "Harold Cruse: An Interview," 227.

28. By 1987, Cruse had given up this particular argument. As he wrote in *Plural But Equal*, "[W]hen blacks, whites, and other nonwhites in America *believe* in the concept of race, then race, myth or not, *is* a reality and a social fact and must be dealt with as such" (p. 29).

29. In his analysis of Cruse's work, Eugene Genovese suggested that the problem really was "a class question with a deep racial dimension." Genovese, "Black Nationalism and American Socialism: A Comment on Harold Cruse's *Crisis of the Negro Intellectual*" (1968), in *In Red and Black: Marxian Explorations in Southern and Afro-American History* (Knoxville: University of Tennessee, 1984), 190.

30. Ibid., 392.

31. I have found the following useful in trying to understand the ins and outs of CPUSA policy on the Negro question: Theodore Draper, *American Communism and the Soviet Union* (1960; New York: Vintage, 1986); Naison, *Communists in Harlem*, particularly the appendix "Black-Jewish Relations in the Harlem Communist Party," 321–28; Joseph Starobin, *American Communism in Crisis, 1943–1957* (Cambridge, Mass.: Harvard University Press, 1972); and Cedric Robinson, *Black Marxism: The Making of a Black Radical Position* (1983; Chapel Hill and London: University of North Carolina Press, 2000), 221–28, 387.

32. See Draper, *American Communism*, 315–56; also Penny Von Eschen, *Race Against Empire: Black Americans and Anticolonialism, 1937–1957* (Ithaca and London: Cornell University Press, 1997).

33. Starobin, *American Communism in Crisis*, 201; Cruse's "Marxism and the Negro," in *Rebellion or Revolution*, 143–51, confirms his agreement with the position outlined by Starobin.

34. C. L. R. James, "Black Studies and the Contemporary Student" (1969), in *The C. L. R. James Reader*, ed. Anna Grimshaw (Oxford and Cambridge, Mass.: Blackwell, 1992), 400; Naison, *Communists in Harlem*, xviii, 323, 116, respectively.

35. Ibid., 187, 203–13.

36. Budick, *Blacks and Jews*, 89, 98.

37. Genovese, "Black Nationalism," 196–99. Genovese also noted that Cruse needed a class analysis to stave off the "nihilist and terrorist wing of black nationalism" (p. 193).

38. Ernest Allen, "The Cultural Methodology of Harold Cruse," *The Journal of Ethnic Studies* 5, no. 2 (1997): 37.

39. Stephen E. Henderson, "'Survival Motion': A Study of the Black Writer and the Black Revolution in America," in *The Militant Black Writer in Africa and the United States*, ed. Mercer Cook and Stephen B. Henderson (Madison: University of Wisconsin Press, 1969), 124; Mercer Cook, "African Voices of Protest," in *The Militant Black Writer*, 11; and William L. VanDeburg, *New Day in Babylon: The Black Power Movement and American Culture, 1965–1975* (Chicago: University of Chicago Press, 1992), 195.

40. St. Clair Drake, "The Negro's Stake in Africa: The Meaning of 'Negritude,'" *Negro Digest* 13, no. 8 (June 1964): 33–34; and John O. Killens, "Brotherhood of Blackness," *Negro Digest* 15, no. 7 (May 1966): 4–6.

41. Houston Baker, Jr., *Afro-American Poetics: Revisions of Harlem and the Black Aesthetic* (Madison: University of Wisconsin Press, 1988), 175.

42. Addison Gayle, Jr., "The Function of Black Literature at the Present Time," in *The Black Aesthetic*, compiled by Addison Gayle (Garden City, N.Y.: Doubleday, 1971), 418; Larry Neal, "And Shine Swam On," in *Black Fire: An Anthology of Afro-American Writing*, ed. LeRoi Jones and Larry Neal (New York: Morrow, 1968), 647; 654. Interestingly, Cruse was also dubious about the general concept and experience of double consciousness among black people.

43. Don L. Lee as quoted in Neal, "The Black Arts Movement," in Gayle, comp., *The Black Aesthetic*, 273.

44. John O. Killens, "The Black Writer vis-à-vis His Country," in Gayle, comp., *The Black Aesthetic*, 381; Hoyt Fuller, "Towards a Black Aesthetic," in Gayle, comp., *The Black Aesthetic*, 5.

45. Fuller, "Towards a Black Aesthetic," 11. For the next generation's analysis of the black aesthetics/black arts movement, see Henry Louis Gates, Jr., "Literary Theory and the Black Tradition," in *Figures in Black: Words, Signs and the "Racial" Self* (New York: Oxford University Press, 1987), 3–58; and Houston Baker, Jr., "Discovering America: Generational Shifts, Afro-American Literary Criticism, and the Study of Expressive Culture," in *Blues, Ideology, and Afro-American Literature: A Vernacular Theory* (Chicago and London: University of Chicago Press, 1984), 64–112. Recently, Adolph Reed, Jr., has grouped Gates and Baker with the more radical black aesthetics group as racial essentialists. According to Reed, they neglect class divisions among black Americans and assume instead that there is a common mentality or set of characteristics that inheres in all African American expression. See *W. E. B. Du Bois and American Political Thought: Fabianism and the Color Line* (New York: Oxford University Press, 1997).

46. John Henrik Clarke, "Reclaiming the Lost African Heritage," in Jones and Neal, eds., *Black Fire*, 11.

47. Amiri Baraka, "The Changing Same (Rhythm and Blues and New Black Music)," in Gayle, comp., *The Black Aesthetic*, 120. See also Baraka, *Blues People: The Negro Experience in White America and the Music that Developed From It* (New York: Morrow, 1963). Jerry G. Watts, *Amiri Baraka: The Politics and Art of the Black Intellectual* (New York and London: New York University Press, 2001), is a long and uneven but often very acute (and critical) examination of Jones/Baraka's career.

48. John O'Neal, "Black Arts: Notebook," in Gayle, comp., *The Black Aesthetic*, 56, 58; Baraka/Jones, "The Legacy of Malcolm X and the Coming of the Black Nation," in Baraka, *Home: Social Essays* (New York: Morrow, 1966), 246.

49. Baraka, "The Changing Same," 122–23; *Blues People*, 155.

50. Ron Karenga, "Black Cultural Nationalism," in Gayle, comp., *The Black Aesthetic*, 35; Neal, "The Black Arts Movement," 273; Baraka/Jones, "Brief Reflections on Two Hotshots," in *Home*, 117. James later changed his opinion and public rhetoric about Baldwin.

51. Karenga, "Black Cultural Nationalism," 33.

52. Killens, "Brotherhood of Blackness," 391.

53. Neal, "And Shine Swam On," 639; Gayle, "Dream of a Native Son," *Liberator* 10, no. 2 (February 1970): 7; Carolyn Gerald in *Negro Digest* 19, no. 1 (November 1969): 28. Ever refusing to fit into neat categories, Ishmael Reed, in an interview in *The Journal of Black Poetry* 1, no. 12 (summer–fall 1969): 73, spoke of Malcolm X as a "universalist, a humanist, and a global man" and claimed that "this tribalism is for the birds."

54. Baraka/Jones, "American Sexual Reference: Black Male," in Baraka, *Home*, 224; Cleaver, *Soul on Ice* (New York: Delta Books, 1967); Norman Mailer, "The White Negro" (1957), in *Advertisements for Myself* (New York: Signet Books, 1957), 302–22.

55. Neal, "And Shine Swam On," 653; Ron Wellburn, "The Black Aesthetic Imperative," in Gayle, comp., *The Black Aesthetic*, 133.

56. Peter Labrie, "The New Breed," in Jones and Neal, eds., *Black Fire*, 66–67; Calvin Hernton, "Dynamite Growing Out of Their Skulls," in Jones and Neal, eds., *Black Fire*, 78, 101, 104.

57. Ron Karenga, "Black Cultural Nationalism," in Gayle, comp., *The Black Aesthetic*, 38; Don L. Lee, "Don't Cry . . . Scream!!" *Nommo* 1, no. 1 (1969): 17–19.

58. LeRoi Jones, "The Dutchman," in *The Amiri Baraka/LeRoi Jones Reader*, 113.

59. Larry Neal, *Black Theater* 4 (April 1970): 14–15. See also Houston Baker, "Critical Change and Blues Community: An Essay on the Criticism of Larry Neal," in *Afro-American Poetics* for a characterization of Neal's view of the blues as "the consummate expressive spiritual form to be emulated" (pp. 158–59).

60. Jones/Baraka, "The Changing Same," 128, 126, respectively. It is this emphasis on the spiritual that James C. Hall identifies as one of the salient traits of black antimodernist expression in the 1960s.

61. Ortiz M. Walton, "A Comparative Analysis of the African and the Western Aesthetics," in Gayle, comp., *The Black Aesthetic*, 164, 161, 166, respectively.

62. Jimmy Stewart, "Introduction to Black Aesthetics in Music," in *The Black Aesthetic*, 82; 84

63. Darwin Turner, "Afro-American Literary Critics: An Introduction," in *The Black Aesthetic*, 59–77; Wellburn, "The Black Aesthetic Imperative," 140.

64. Walter Lowenfels, "The White Literary Syndicate," *The Liberator* 10, no. 3 (March 1970): 9; James A. Emanuel, "Blackness Can: A Quest for Aesthetics," in *The Black Aesthetic*, 198–202.

65. Addison Gayle, Jr., "Cultural Strangulation: Black Literature and the White Aesthetic," in *The Black Aesthetic*, 46.

66. Gayle, "The Function of Black Literature at the Present Time," in *The Black Aesthetic*, 409.

67. LeRoi Jones, "How You Sound?" (1959), in Harris, ed., *The Amiri Baraka/LeRoi Jones Reader*, 17.

68. Baraka/Jones, *Blues People*, 200.

69. See Paul Gilroy, *The Black Atlantic* (London: Verso Books, 1993), for historical and cultural links between modernity and double consciousness.

70. Baraka, "It's Nation Time," in Harris, ed., *The Amiri Baraka/LeRoi Jones Reader*, 219–20.

71. I should note that I wrote the term "vulgarity" here several years before reading Watts's discussion of Jones/Baraka in *Amiri Baraka*, and finding that he used the same term (p. 148). Watts's confrontation of this issue is admirably unequivocal in its condemnation of Baraka on these matters.

72. Hannah Arendt claimed that Bertolt Brecht's poetry deteriorated markedly when he began to write in direct praise of Stalin. It may be an illusion to think so, but I can't help notice a similar decline in Baraka's prose and poetry as he became more ideologically rigid and adopted the rhetoric of racial and political abuse. See Arendt, "Bertolt Brecht, 1898–1956," in *Men in Dark Times* (New York: Harvest Books, 1968), 207–49.

73. Baraka, "Confessions of a Former Anti-Semite," *The Village Voice* 25, no. 50 (December 17–23, 1980): 18–22.

74. James Emanuel, "Blackness Can," 209, 211, 218–22.

75. Baraka/Jones, "The Myth of a 'Negro' Literature," in *Home*, 108; Gayle, "The Function of Black Literature at the Present Time," 407–19. Watts claims that Baraka was not raised in a "black literary tradition," but rather in the tradition of Afro-American music. Watts, *Amiri Baraka*, 113.

76. Larry Neal, quoting a 1943 statement of Ellison's in "Ellison's Zoot Suit," in *Ralph Ellison*, edited by John Hersey (Englewood Cliffs, N.J.: Prentice-Hall, 1974), 67. Houston Baker's contribution to the development (and surpassing) of the black aesthetic since the 1970s has been his focus on the folkloric origins of the African American literary and cultural tradition.

77. For a biographical sketch of Ellison, see David Remnick, "Visible Man," in *The Devil Problem and Other True Stories* (New York: Random House, 1996), 238–49; for Murray, see Henry Louis Gates, Jr., "King of Cats," in *Thirteen Ways of Looking at a Black Man* (New York: Random House, 1997), 21–46. See also Jerry G. Watts, *Heroism and the Black Intellectual: Ralph Ellison, Politics and African American Intellectual Life* (Chapel Hill: University of North Carolina Press, 1994).

78. Ralph Ellison, "Recent Negro Fiction," *New Masses* 40, no. 6 (August 5, 1941), 11; Albert Murray, *Conversations with Albert Murray*, ed. Roberta S. Maguire (Jackson: University Press of Mississippi, 1997), 147, 132, respectively. See also

Murray, *From the Briarpatch File: On Context, Procedure, and American Identity* (New York: Pantheon, 2001), 158–59, for the same characterization of the Harlem Renaissance, and Albert Murray and John F. Callahan, eds., *Trading Twelves: The Selected Letters of Ralph Ellison and Albert Murray* (New York: Modern Library, 2000).

79. Ellison, "Recent Negro Fiction," 22–26 (collected). See Henry Louis Gates, Jr., "Dis and Dat: Dialect and the Descent," in *Figures in Black: Words, Signs and the "Racial" Self* (New York: Oxford University Press, 1987), 167–95, for a fascinating exploration of the uses and abuses of dialect in black American poetry; and Tommy Lott, "Black Vernacular Representation and Cultural Malpractice," in *The Invention of Race: Black Culture and the Politics of Misrepresentation* (Oxford: Blackwell, 1999), 88–94, for a discussion of the controversy surrounding Hurston's use of dialect in her writing. Kenneth Jackson, "The Birth of the Critic: The Literary Friendship of Ralph Ellison and Richard Wright," *American Literature* 72, no. 2 (June 2000): 321–55, contains a brief discussion of both men's relationship with Hurston.

80. Zora Neale Hurston, *Dust Tracks in the Road* (1942; New York: Harper Perennial, 1995), 291. Particularly useful for the comparisons with Ellison and Murray is Gates's "Zora Neale Hurston: 'A Negro Way of Saying,'" the Afterword to *Dust Tracks on a Road*. Many of the stories and tales incorporated in *Dust Tracks* are found in her major collection of folklore, *Mules and Men* (Bloomington: Indiana University Press, 1978), which was first published in 1935. For a discussion of Sterling Brown's significance, see "Songs of a Racial Self: On Sterling Brown," in *Figures in Black*, 225–34. The contrast that Gates draws between "simplicity" and "simple-mindedness" is a valuable one.

81. Ellison, "*An American Dilemma*: A Review," in *Collected Essays*, preface by Saul Bellow, edited with an introduction by John F. Callahan (New York: Modern Library, 1995), 339. Just why Ellison's review was not published is not clear, even after examining his papers. When he submitted it to Paul Bixler, chair of the editorial board of the *Antioch Review*, Ellison spoke disparagingly of the review and offered to make any requested cuts or modifications. (Ellison to Bixler, November 30, 1944, Essays and Essay Collections—*Shadow and Act*, 1964—Drafts, Ralph Ellison Papers, Library of Congress, Washington, D.C.) Bixler's response was far from hostile. He noted that several members of the board had read Ellison's review "for the most part favorably." He added that the spring issue, for which Ellison's review of Myrdal was scheduled, was overcrowded and for that reason, along with the fact that several board members had still not read the review, he had decided to delay its publication. (Letter of Bixler to Ellison, December 13, 1944.)

In an unpublished, five-page essay written probably in 1964 while *Shadow and Act* was in preparation, Ellison noted that his review essay of Myrdal had been "promptly rejected." On the evidence referred to in the previous paragraph, this does not seem quite right. Indeed, on the second page of the short essay, Ellison modified his first comment by saying that he thought that the editors "were willing to allow me to spell things out a bit" [but] "the war was still raging and there simply wasn't time." (Unpublished, Ellison, 1964, Drafts, Ralph Ellison Papers, Library of Congress, Washington, D.C.)

82. Albert Murray, *The Omni-Americans* (New York: Avon, 1971), 3, 73, 16, respectively. Murray also drew heavily on Constance Rourke's classic *American Humor: A Study of American National Character* (Garden City, N.Y.: Anchor Books,

1953), in which she postulated an American popular culture shaped by these three cultural components.

83. Ellison, "Some Questions and Some Answers" (1958), in *Collected Essays*, 292.

84. Ellison, "Society, Morality and the Novel" (1957), in *Collected Essays*, 702. Morris Dickstein has observed that "[c]ultural appropriation is the great theme of Ellison's essays," and his position falls somewhere between "cultural pluralism" and "melting pot" models. See "Native Sons: James Baldwin and Ralph Ellison," in Dickstein, *Leopards in the Temple* (Cambridge, Mass.: Harvard University Press, 1998), 198.

85. Murray, *Conversations*, 59.

86. Remnick, "Visible Man," 249.

87. Murray, *The Omni-Americans*, 56–58; *Conversations*, 146; *From the Briarpatch File*, 39.

88. Murray, *The Omni-Americans*, 54.

89. Albert Murray, *The Hero and the Blues* (1973; New York: Vintage 1995), 83. For Murray's views on realism and naturalism, see *Conversations*, 16.

90. Murray, *Conversations*, 16; *Omni-Americans*, 4.

91. Murray, *Omni-Americans*, 136–41.

92. Murray, *The Hero*, 92.

93. Ellison, "The World and the Jug" (1963–1964), in *Collected Essays*, 158, 183. For Howe's original statement, see "Black Boys and Native Sons" (1963), in *Selected Writings, 1950–1990* (New York: Harcourt Brace Jovanovich, 1990), 119–39; Ellison, "Brave Words for a Startling Occasion" (1953), in *Collected Essays*, 151.

94. Ellison, *Collected Essays*, 482.

95. Murray, *Omni-Americans*, 38, 2, respectively.

96. Murray, *The Hero*, 93–96.

97. Wright, "How Bigger Was Born," *Native Son* (New York: Harper and Row, 1940), viii.

98. This kind of argument creates a dangerous precedent. One might also judge Ellison's protagonist in *Invisible Man* to be hardly representative of the black community or that Faulkner should not have made Thomas Sutpen the protagonist of *Absalom, Absalom!* since Sutpen is, if anything, less morally self-aware than Bigger Thomas is.

99. Ellison, "The World and the Jug," 185, 164, respectively. Ellison was the best man in Wright's first wedding. See Michel Fabre, *The Unfinished Quest of Richard Wright*, 2nd ed. (Urbana and Chicago: University of Illinois Press, 1993), 200.

100. Ralph Ellison, "Richard Wright's Blues" (1945), in *Collected Essays*, 139, 136–37, 139, 134–35, respectively.

101. See Bruno Bettelheim, "Individual and Mass Behavior in Extreme Situations," *Journal of Abnormal and Social Psychology* 28 (October 1943). In the unpublished 1964 essay explaining the significance of the unpublished Myrdal review, Ellison made the connection explicit between Myrdal's pathology thesis and Elkins's Sambo thesis and characterized them both as gross mischaracterizations of the African American experience (Unpublished essay, Essays and Essay Collections—*Shadow and Act*, 1964—Draft, Ellison Collection, Library of Congress).

102. Ellison, "Richard Wright's Blues," 139.

103. Ibid., 143.

104. Ibid., 133.

105. Ibid., 144; Ellison, "Harlem Is Nowhere," in *Collected Essays,* 326. Harlem's Lafargue Clinic was founded in 1946 as a place where residents of Harlem could receive free psychiatric care. Frederic Wertham was one of the guiding spirits behind the project, and he received considerable help from Richard Wright and journalist Earl Brown in raising money.

106. Ellison, "That Same Pain," in *Collected Essays*, 74.

107. Ellison, "The World and the Jug," 162.

108. Ibid., 160.

109. Ibid., 166.

110. Ellison, "Remembering Richard Wright" (1971), in *Collected Essays*, 670; Howe, "Black Boys and Native Sons," in *Selected Writings*, 121.

111. Ellison, "Remembering," 670, 667.

112. Although I would not go as far as Houston Baker, Jr., when he writes that "neither Ralph Ellison . . . nor James Baldwin possessed a fraction of Wright's intelligence with respect to the dynamics of an unfolding world of post colonial colored people," I do think that Wright's vision of the black world captured its own share of truth, and that share is largely missing from either Ellison's or Murray's vision. See Houston A. Baker, Jr., *Critical Memory: Public Spheres, African American Writing, and Black Fathers and Sons in America* (Athens: University of Georgia Press, 2001), 9. In fact, this was, I suspect, what Irving Howe was getting at in his critique of Baldwin and Ellison.

113. Ellison, "The World and the Jug," 165.

114. Murray, *The Hero*, 68.

115. Watts, *Heroism and the Black Intellectual*, 99.

116. Ibid., 104.

117. Albert Murray, *South to a Very Old Place* (New York: McGraw-Hill, 1971), 178. This entire book was devoted to the rediscovery of the shared "southernness" of white and black Southerners.

118. Thanks to Steve Whitfield for helping me develop this point.

Conclusion

1. David Hollinger, *Postethnic America: Beyond Multiculturalism* (New York: Basic Books, 1995).

2. Gunnar Myrdal, *An American Dilemma*, vol. 1 (New York: McGraw-Hill, 1965), 53.

3. George Fredrickson, *Racism: A Short History* (Princeton, N.J.: Princeton University Press, 2003), 26.

4. See Kenneth R. Stow, *Alienated Minority: The Jews of Medieval Latin Europe* (Cambridge, Mass., and London: Harvard University Press, 1992), for a more complex view of this topic.

5. Jean-Paul Sartre, "Black Orpheus" (1948), in *Poetry and Drama*, ed. C. W. Bigsby, vol. 2 of *The Black American Writer* (Deland, Fla.: Everett/Edwards, Inc., 1969).

6. See Elisabeth Young-Bruehl, *The Anatomy of Prejudices* (Cambridge, Mass.: Harvard University Press, 1996), 4–5.

7. Ibid., 23–39. Another way to draw the difference between anti-Semitism and racism, at least in America, is to say that the anti-Semite fears castration, of being denied potency, while the color-coded racist fears uncontrolled desire, which suggests a preemptive castration of the black male.

8. Fredrickson, *Racism*, 95.

9. Laurence Thomas, *Vessels of Evil: American Slavery and the Holocaust* (Philadelphia: Temple University Press, 1993), 197–201.

10. Contrary to Walter Benn Michaels in his "Race into Culture: A Critical Genealogy of Cultural Identity," *Critical Inquiry* 18 (summer 1992), not all generalizations about shared group characteristics are functionally racist: "The modern concept of culture is not, in other words, a critique of racism; it is a form of racism" (p. 683).

11. Steve T. Katz, *The Holocaust in Historical Context* (New York: Oxford University Press, 1994).

12. George Stocking, *Race, Culture and Evolution: Essays in the History of Anthropology* (New York: Free Press, 1968).

13. Though I will suggest three problems with cultural relativism, I want to distance myself from the easy and, I think, demagogic attacks from conservatives on cultural relativism as the equivalent of moral nihilism.

14. Michael Oakeshott, *Rationalism in Politics* (New York: Basic Books, 1962), and Eric Voegelin, *The New Science of Politics* (Chicago: University of Chicago Press, 1952).

15. Michael Ignatieff, *Human Rights as Politics and as Idolatry*, edited and introduction by Amy Gutman (Princeton, N.J.: Princeton University Press, 2001), 20.

16. Martin Heidegger, "Letter on Humanism," in *Basic Writings*, ed. David F. Krell (New York: Harper and Row, 1977).

17. Martha Nussbaum, "Human Functioning and Social Justice: In Defense of Aristotelian Essentialism," *Political Theory* 20, no. 2 (May 1992): 202–46.

Index

Abel, Lionel, 190, 240
abolitionism, 228
Absalom, Absalom! (Faulkner), 375*n*98
Achebe, Chinua, 116–17
acquiescence of slaves and Jews, 161,
    179, 306. *See also* resistance; victims
Adorno, Theodor W., 70–95; on
    American mass society, 8; and ego
    structure, 181; and Jewishness, 49,
    71; on psychological impulse and
    racism, 305; purpose of study of, 22;
    questioning claims of, 111; on
    Sartre's analysis of anti-Semite, 58.
    See also *The Authoritarian
    Personality; The Dialectic of
    Enlightenment;* Frankfurt School and
    Institute of Social Research
Africa: Arendt on, 100, 105–7, 115–19;
    and behavior patterns in slavery, 155;
    and complicity of societies in own de-
    struction, 213–14; Du Bois's attitude
    toward, 47–48; and European culture
    compared, 240–41; extermination and
    enslavement of Africans by
    Europeans, 100, 157; Frazier on, 134;
    genocide in, 107; and independence,
    10; interest in colonized, 325*n*63;
    religion of, 220; West Africa culture,
    240–41; Wright on, 139, 141, 154–55,
    202–8, 211, 212. *See also* negritude
African American culture, 121–72,
    266–303; and African cultural

survivals, 126, 155, 205; on African
    roots of black American culture, 132,
    266, 267; and black aesthetic
    movement, 277–90; Ellison-Murray
    on, 290–303; and expressive culture,
    125–26; judging "performance " of,
    306–7; and pathology of black
    culture, 33, 34, 43, 66–67, 125–31,
    167–69, 306; and political resistance,
    126; and price of modernization,
    123–50; rediscovering in 1960s,
    165–69, 266–303; sociologist view of,
    26. *See also* black church; culture;
    individual authors
African Americans: alienation of, 203,
    206, 252, 264, 287; and anti-
    Semitism, 165; "black is beautiful,"
    10; Broyard on, 65–68; and Census
    data, 7; and college admission, 7;
    comparison with Jews, 166, 256–57,
    312; conflict with Jewish intellectuals,
    275–76; as consumers, 44; as ethnic
    group, 66, 273–74; and family
    structure, 134–35, 136, 167–69; full
    humanity of, 29–30; "Great
    Migration" of, 124, 168; historical re-
    sistance to slavery, 32; illegitimacy
    rates of, 168; meaning of "black,"
    25–26; model of ghetto formation of,
    124; political discontent of, 127; post-
    emancipation life of, 168; and psychic
    injuries of race, 147; self-awareness

377